MAGILL'S
LITERARY ANNUAL
2016

Essay-Reviews of 150 Outstanding Books
Published in the United States During 2015

With an Annotated List of Titles

Volume Two
L-Z

Edited by
Matthew Akre
Kendal Spires
Gabriela Toth

SALEM PRESS
A Division of EBSCO Information Services, Inc.
Ipswich, Massachusetts

GREY HOUSE PUBLISHING

Cover photo: Photograph of Ta-Nehisi Coates. John D. & Catherine T. MacArthur Foundation/CC BY 4.0/Wikimedia Commons

Magill's Literary Annual, 2016, published by Grey House Publishing, Inc., Amenia, NY, under exclusive license from EBSCO Information Services, Inc.

∞ The paper used in these volumes conforms to the American National Standard for Permanence of Paper for Printed Library Materials, Z39.48-1992 (R2009).

Publisher's Cataloging-In-Publication Data
(Prepared by The Donohue Group, Inc.)

Names: Magill, Frank N. (Frank Northen), 1907-1997, editor. | Wilson, John D., editor. | Kellman, Steven G., 1947- editor. | Goodhue, Emily, editor. | Poranski, Colin D., editor. | Akre, Matthew, editor. | Spires, Kendal, editor. | Toth, Gabriela, editor.
Title: Magill's literary annual.
Description: <1977->: [Pasadena, Calif.] : Salem Press | <2015->: Ipswich, Massachusetts : Salem Press, a division of EBSCO Information Services, Inc. ; Amenia, NY : Grey House Publishing | Essay-reviews of ... outstanding books published in the United States during the previous year. | "With an annotated list of titles." | Editor: 1977- , F.N. Magill; <2010-2014>, John D. Wilson and Steven G. Kellman; <2015>, Emily Goodhue and Colin D. Poranski; <2016->, Matthew Akre, Kendal Spires, and Gabriela Toth. | Includes bibliographical references and index.
Identifiers: ISBN 978-1-61925-880-8 (2016 edition : set) |
    ISBN 978-1-61925-882-2 (2016 edition : vol. 1) | ISBN 978-1-61925-883-9 (2016 edition : vol. 2) | ISSN: 0163-3058
Subjects: LCSH: Books--Reviews--Periodicals. | United States--Imprints--Book reviews--Periodicals. | Literature, Modern--21st century--History and criticism--Periodicals. | Literature, Modern--20th century--History and criticism--Periodicals.
Classification: LCC PN44 .M333 | DDC 028.1--dc23

FIRST PRINTING
PRINTED IN THE UNITED STATES OF AMERICA

CONTENTS

CONTENTS

COMPLETE ANNOTATED LIST OF TITLES

VOLUME 1

The story of a woman who grows up among a large family in rural Ireland but spends most of her life isolated in the most populous city of the United States, Academy Street *packs more than fifty years of heartbreak, disappointment, disillusion, and indecision into a small volume.*

In his first novel, Ben Metcalf writes about childhood life in rural Goochland County, Virginia, in a deliberately disjointed and nonlinear fashion, portraying country life in a hostile light.

Olen Steinhauer adds a new twist to the spy genre with this intelligent and intriguing tale about two former lovers and CIA colleagues who reunite for dinner six years after experiencing a horrific terrorist incident together in Vienna, Austria.

Among the Ten Thousand Things, *Julia Pierpont's debut novel, is a nuanced exploration of the effect of infidelity on a family. Pierpont's narrative traces the emotional ebb and flow of the various members as they grapple with what has happened and its aftermath.*

Ancillary Mercy *is the final book in the Imperial Radch space opera trilogy by American author Ann Leckie.*

A graphic memoir written by cartoonist and filmmaker Riad Sattouf, The Arab of the Future *chronicles the author's varied childhood experiences growing up in Libya, Syria, and France.*

Aurora *is the story of a generational starship and the people aboard. The novel explores the practicality of space expeditions and colonization, as well as who bears the responsibilities and consequences of the success or failure of such a voyage.*

John Irving returns to form with Avenue of Mysteries, *a complex, multifaceted novel about a Mexican American writer who, after falling into a drug-induced dream state during a trip to the Philippines, accesses his most beloved childhood memories in 1970s Mexico.*

A collection of ten short stories about millennial characters who are struggling with life, sex, and family issues.

In Barbarian Days, *journalist William Finnegan recalls how surfing has shaped his life. From his formative years in Hawaii in the 1960s and his youthful search for the perfect wave to his journalistic travels and his present home in New York City, the surfing life has beckoned Finnegan from every corner of the globe.*

The Beauty *is the latest collection of verse by acclaimed poet Jane Hirshfield. It deals in simple, accessible, but often very subtle phrasing and forms and addresses a wide variety of topics, showing the poet's familiarity with both everyday life and scientific facts.*

Beauty Is a Wound *is a sprawling novel that explores Indonesian society, culture, traditions, customs, and beliefs through the exploits and relationships of several generations. One family endures the turbulence of the country's social and political upheavals during the twentieth century, through Dutch colonization, Japanese occupation, and independence.*

Narrated by a middle-aged autistic man, Best Boy *vividly illustrates many of the difficulties of diagnosing, managing, and treating mental conditions in general and developmental disorders in particular.*

Inspired by James Baldwin's classic 1963 book The Fire Next Time, *journalist Ta-Nehisi Coates began a letter to his teenage son that became a book-length essay and memoir about his intellectual coming-of-age.*

Binary Star, *a short novel told from the perspective of a young woman struggling with eating disorders, is an exploration of codependence and self-destruction.*

Laura Ruby's new novel Bone Gap *combines ancient myth, fairy tale, and mid-western realism to produce a story about friendship, betrayal, and learning to love someone for who they are.* Bone Gap *was a finalist for the National Book Award for Young People's Literature in 2015.*

Bonita Avenue *is a generation's spanning novel about the Sigerius family and son-in-law Aaron Bever. Told from the perspectives of four characters, the novel explores the dark side and frailties of human nature in a digital age. The story is told in a fast-paced style that finds each chapter jumping between time periods in the narrative.*

The Book of Aron *explores the Holocaust and one of its heroes, Polish doctor and writer Janusz Korczak, from the perspective of an ordinary child. Aron, a young boy growing up in Warsaw's Jewish ghetto, learns to survive in desperate times by stealing, smuggling, and even becoming an informer for local police. When Aron loses everything, he is taken in by Korczak, who runs an orphanage and offers hope and kindness to children trapped in the bleakest of circumstances.*

Book of Numbers *is an exploration of the modern age of technology. This novel engages the reader in an examination of what it means to be truly transparent on both sides of any interaction in the Internet age.*

Carly Simon shares personal stories about her family, her music, and her relationships ranging from her childhood through the end of her marriage to James Taylor.

Bright Dead Things *is the latest collection of verse by the prize-winning poet Ada Limón, author of three earlier volumes of poetry. Her latest poems are often set in Kentucky and deal with such topics as love, death, and familial relationships.*

In his seventh novel—his first in ten years—Kazuo Ishiguro takes readers on an allegorical journey through medieval England during the dark period after both the Romans and King Arthur had departed.

Don Winslow describes in graphic detail the workings of the Mexican drug trade and the savagery associated with the struggle for dominance among the country's drug cartels, and he dramatizes the personal tragedies of innocent victims caught up in the violence.

Challenger Deep *describes a boy's struggles after he begins to experience symptoms of schizophrenia. Shusterman wrote the novel to help open a dialogue about mental illness and reduce its stigma. The illustrations are by his son, Brendan, who was diagnosed with schizoaffective disorder as a teenager.*

Ann Packer's The Children's Crusade *offers a stirring examination of family reality and dysfunction in a California home where four children grow to adulthood in the shadow of their benevolent father and distant mother.*

The sequel to the best-selling Crazy Rich Asians *(2013) and the second entry in a planned trilogy,* China Rich Girlfriend *continues the chronicle of relationships, activities, and aspirations of a group of fabulously and ostentatiously wealthy Asians as they maneuver to compete in status and influence.*

This historical novel reimagines the early life of Beryl Markham, who was raised in Africa. It closes with her famous flight west across the Atlantic Ocean; Markham was the first person to make this flight successfully.

City on Fire *is a sprawling tale of New York City in the 1970s. Told from multiple points of view, this novel paints a gripping picture of a troubled time, intertwining a mystery in the process.*

In Counternarratives, *a collection of thirteen short stories and novellas, John Keene reimagines black history through revised accounts of colonization, slavery, war, and black resistance from the seventeenth century to the present. Both employing and subverting forms and genres including historical documents, textbooks, slave narratives, diaries, and gothic fiction, Keene suggests that black resistance to white supremacy has long pulsed just below the surface of the historical register.*

In his latest collection, author Thomas McGuane presents seventeen new, mostly comic stories about the misadventures of Montana men.

A Cure for Suicide *is Jesse Ball's fifth novel. In this dystopian work, Ball explores the nature of identity, memory, the ability to re-create oneself, and the consequences of well-intentioned actions.*

Dead Wake: The Last Crossing of the Lusitania *details the final days of the luxurious British ocean liner, one of the world's largest ships, prior to its sinking on May 6, 1915, off the coast of Ireland after being hit by a torpedo fired from a German U-boat. Among the drowned passengers were a significant number of Americans, and the incident helped propel the previously neutral United States into participation in World War I.*

Death and Mr. Pickwick *follows the investigative work of two literary sleuths as they uncover information supporting their claim that Charles Dickens stole credit for creating* The Pickwick Papers *from the book's original illustrator, Robert Seymour.*

James Hannaham's second novel, Delicious Foods, *takes its title from a fictitious farm that exploits down-on-their-luck workers. The story focuses on Eddie and his crack-addicted mother, Darlene, who work for the farm and try desperately to escape their plantation-like surroundings.*

June Reid lives a quiet life in Litchfield, Connecticut, with her boyfriend, Luke. But on the morning of her daughter's wedding day, a gas explosion kills June's entire family and changes her life forever. Did You Ever Have a Family *follows June in the months after her family tragedy as she seeks answers, grieves, and begins to imagine how she might move on.*

The debut novel of author Sarai Walker, Dietland *explores the effects of the beauty industry and gender inequality on American women.*

Ottessa Moshfegh burnishes her reputation as one of the literary world's brightest new voices with Eileen, *an unsettling coming-of-age noir about a lonely young Massachusetts woman whose life is forever changed when she becomes drawn into a bizarre crime.*

In The Empty Form Goes All the Way to Heaven, *Brian Teare chronicles his experience living with a debilitating chronic disease. To cope, he turns to visual art, meditation practice, and alternative medicine in order to gain insight into the nature of suffering and the limitations of the body.*

Lauren Groff's third novel, Fates and Furies *views a marriage through a mythic lens.*

The Fifth Season *is the first novel in N. K. Jemisin's forthcoming Broken Earth series. It takes place in an apocalyptic world in which people called orogenes are able to control the plates of the earth by the strength of their will.*

A haunting exploration of the power of literature, Finders Keepers *focuses on two bibliophiles who are profoundly affected by the works of a famous reclusive author. Stephen King combines elements of horror, suspense, and drama in this sequel that sees the return of retired detective Bill Hodges and his fellow investigators, Holly Gibney and Jerome Robinson.*

The First Bad Man *is the first novel by artist and filmmaker Miranda July. It follows a middle-aged woman named Cheryl Glickman as she battles a bullying houseguest and finds love in an unexpected place.*

The Fishermen, *the debut novel from Nigerian author Chigozie Obioma, is about the disintegration of one family in Akure but is also a parable about Nigeria's turbulent past.*

The Folded Clock *is a record of two years of Heidi Julavits's life. Each chapter captures a day or memory and is structured as a diary entry. Told in a nonlinear order, the book tells the story of the life of a woman through travels abroad, her life at home in New York City and Maine, and the lives of her family members.*

Pulitzer Prize–winning novelist Adam Johnson presents six long stories in a collection that won the 2015 National Book Award for Fiction.

Events in Diane Seuss's life inspired these highly mythologized and inventive poems centering on loss, beauty, and desire and peopled with four-legged girls and ghosts in porkpie hats. This collection represents an imaginative exploration of femininity and what it means to be a strong woman.

Funny Girl follows a young starlet named Sophie Straw in 1960s London. Straw, a working-class girl from Northern England, miraculously lands a once-in-a-lifetime role as the star of a sitcom. The novel is about women in comedy, the trappings of fame, and making art that lasts.

Lawson shares her personal ups and downs as she learns to live with a variety of mental-health issues while trying to function as a wife, mother, and successful author.

Kelly Link's third collection of short stories, Get in Trouble, *explores the sex lives of superheroes, the trouble with Ghost Boyfriends, and the nature of reality.*

Ghettoside *is a brilliantly written exploration of the epidemic of unsolved murders plaguing many urban minority neighborhoods. Jill Leovy dissects the forces underlying these murders while chronicling the efforts of a Los Angeles police detective to track the killers of a fellow officer's son.*

The Girl in the Spider's Web *is the fourth novel in the Millennium series and the first to be written by Lagercrantz. It tells the story of the aftermath of a successful hacking of the databases at the NSA.*

A psychological mystery, The Girl on the Train *is about the disappearance of a young woman and the commuter who tries to help the investigation by telling what she witnessed from aboard a passing train. When the book came out in January 2015, it quickly became one of the best-selling adult mysteries in publishing history.*

Girl Waits with Gun *is historical fiction based on real incidents in the life of Constance Kopp, one of the first women to serve as a deputy sheriff in the United States. Constance Kopp and her two sisters face harassment from a wealthy textile-factory owner, and they are drawn into a battle involving threats, intimidation, and shootouts. Along the way, Constance helps find a missing child and discovers her unexpected strengths as an independent woman of the twentieth century.*

Inspired by real-life events, this darkly absorbing novel centers on three pro-tagonists who are forced to confront the consequences wrought by their violent and rebellious actions.

Anna Benz lives an ideal life as the wife of a successful banker and mother in a small town near Zurich, Switzerland. But when Anna starts having illicit affairs with other men, her life spirals out of control, and she must learn some of the most dif-ficult lessons of all.

Phillips's poems are eclectic and sophisticated, often dealing with the topic of poetry itself and featuring allusions to various other texts in a style full of rich sound effects.

A History of Loneliness *chronicles societal changes since the 1960s and their ef-fects on Ireland—especially the evolving attitudes toward the dominance, power, and reputation of the Irish Catholic Church—as observed and experienced by a disillu-sioned priest who has remained isolated and uninvolved throughout his professional career.*

Hold Still *offers thoughtful reflections on the photographer's art, exploring Sally Mann's work from her earliest photographs through her current oeuvre. At the same time, the book excavates the history of Mann's family across several generations by tracing the complex confluence of personalities that flow into a single individual.*

Honeydew *collects twenty of author Edith Pearlman's short stories, which tend to focus on small-town life but often veer into the realm of fable and fairy tale.*

How to Be Drawn, *a finalist for the National Book Award, is the latest collection of verse by the Pushcart Prize–winning poet Terrance Hayes, author of three earlier volumes of poetry.*

Written by best-selling novelist Lisa Lutz, How to Start a Fire *chronicles the lives and friendships of three women over the course of twenty years.*

Hunger Makes Me a Modern Girl *chronicles the youth, musical development, and personal evolution of rock star and actor Carrie Brownstein, both onstage and off.*

Author Reif Larsen's second novel consists of several, almost freestanding, narratives that are gradually woven into the central narrative focusing on the life of the protagonist, Radar Radmanovic. The author eventually peels back the layers of the past to tie together the disparate elements into a main thread, and in so doing, explores the psychology behind being "the other" who deviates from the conventional.

Mia Alvar shares nine stories of the Filipino diaspora. The characters, who range in class status, live and work in the Philippines, Bahrain, and the United States.

In the Unlikely Event, *based on events during her own eighth-grade year, is Blume's fourth novel for adult readers.*

Susan Barker's sprawling historical novel The Incarnations *recounts the past lives of a Beijing cab driver and his mystery soul mate.*

The Invention of Nature *is a sweeping biography that narrates and champions the life of Prussian scientist and explorer Alexander von Humboldt. The book follows Humboldt on his travels while also introducing the reader to his intellectual journeys and his spheres of acquaintance and influence.*

Isabel Allende's Japanese Lover, *like much of her earlier fiction, bridges cultures and generations in a multi-stranded narrative of love and war. The novel was one of* Publishers Weekly's *top ten works of literary fiction for 2015.*

Killing and Dying *is the latest collection of Adrian Tomine's enigmatic comics, featuring men and women searching for love, security, and meaning in their lives in a stark suburban landscape.*

J. Ryan Stradal's debut novel, Kitchens of the Great Midwest, *chronicles Eva Thorvald's growth from a misfit child to a sought-after but elusive celebrity chef.*

COMPLETE LIST OF ANNOTATED TITLES

VOLUME 2

In her very accessible account of the later years of the American Revolution, Sarah Vowell examines the role that the Marquis de Lafayette, a French aristocrat and army officer, played in the war and the phenomenon of his continued popularity in the United States long after the war with Britain was over.

Through the vehicle of a coming-of-age novel, an odyssey, and a picaresque hero, Last Bus to Wisdom *chronicles the journey of an eleven-year-old orphan during the summer of 1951, recalling an era when children traveled in a more innocent atmosphere. Ivan Doig uses a series of vignettes and portraits to weave the tale, with the last stop symbolizing the lessons the boy learns through his adventures.*

A Little Life *is the story of the lifelong friendship between four men who meet in college. The second novel by Hanya Yanagihara,* A Little Life *was a 2015 National Book Award finalist, short-listed for the 2015 Man Booker Prize, and a finalist for the 2015 Kirkus Prize for fiction.*

Part journal, part travelogue, part rumination on the process of writing, M Train *is a memoir by poet and rock singer Patti Smith that evades easy categorization. Critics have lauded Smith's book for its lyricism and treatment of memory and loss.*

The debut novel of Jennine Capó Crucet, Make Your Home among Strangers *is a coming-of-age story for first-generation Americans.*

A Manual for Cleaning Women *is a posthumous collection of Lucia Berlin's previously published stories about the varied lives of strong-minded women.*

A moving visual and verbal account, March: Book Two *continues the story of the American civil rights movement of the 1960s from the perspective of a key participant: activist, nonviolence advocate, demonstration organizer, and eventual congressman John Lewis.*

The Mare *tells the story of an affluent, insecure white woman and the deep, unexpected bond she forms with a Latina girl from the Fresh Air Fund. Their connection is emboldened by the talented young girl's introduction to the world of horses and equestrian competition.*

   Mrs. Engels, *the first novel from the Irish writer Gavin McCrea, brings to vivid life Lizzie Burns, the illiterate, working-class companion of Friedrich Engels, co-author—with Karl Marx—of* The Communist Manifesto. *From Lizzie's perspective, readers experience Marx and Engels wrestling with domestic complications while they strive to inspire a revolution.*

   Longtime feminist activist and author Gloria Steinem writes about how her unusual upbringing and years of travel have shaped her world view in her memoir My Life on the Road.

   Part autobiography, part confession, part fiction, My Struggle: Book 4 *is the fourth installment of an epic six-volume, 3,500-page work to be translated from Norwegian into English. In this entry, recent high school graduate and protagonist Karl Ove Knausgaard is hired to teach at a school in the far north of Norway.*

   A man who grew up in Baton Rouge, Louisiana, delivers a confessional narrative of his teenage years to come to grips with the guilt he feels for exposing information about the rape of a young girl on whom he had a crush some twenty years earlier.

   The novel Mycroft Holmes *presents a suspenseful Victorian-era transatlantic adventure, featuring the titular hero, the elder brother of Sherlock Holmes, in a mysterious case that seems to have supernatural overtones.*

   Armand Gamache becomes involved in a murder investigation that turns out to have national significance and connections to a previous case.

   Pulitzer Prize–winning critic Margo Jefferson recalls her childhood among the African American elite in her memoir Negroland. *The title, a word of her own devising, refers to the rarified world of black privilege in 1950s Chicago.*

   The Nightingale *is a story of war and family. It follows a pair of sisters through the tragedies, violence, and heroism of life in France during World War II. Amid such significant events, it calls readers to focus on the meaning of family bonds.*

The Story of My Teeth *is an experimental novel about Gustavo "Highway" Sánchez, a legendary auctioneer who excels at storytelling. Told in six parts, with a seventh part added for the English edition, the narrative uses unconventional methods, like assigning allegories to teeth on an auction block, to tell the story.*

The Story of the Lost Child *is the fourth and final installment of the Neapolitan novels, an internationally successful series published by Elena Ferrante. The final book continues the story of lifelong friends Elena Greco and Raffaella Cerullo.*

The ninth novel by Nobel Prize–winning author Orhan Pamuk, A Strangeness in My Mind *is a love story that unfolds over the course of decades. As in Pamuk's other works, this novel centers on life in Istanbul.*

A Stranger's Mirror *offers twenty-five new poems by the distinguished poet Marilyn Hacker, plus a generous selection of previous works. It illustrates Hacker's command of varied subjects, styles, and forms.*

A dystopian satire of the future of France, Submission *is the sixth novel by the controversial French author Michel Houellebecq.*

Surrounded by Friends *is the newest book of poems by Matthew Rohrer, author of numerous previous volumes. This book is understated in tone and phrasing, modest in ambition and topics, and appealing in its accessibility, its lightheartedness, and its emphasis on connections with others, including various poets of the past.*

The Sympathizer *is an ingenious and powerful spy novel that focuses on a Communist sleeper agent who has been ordered to spy on South Vietnamese émigrés in Southern California who are working to spark a counterrevolution in their homeland.*

The Thing about Jellyfish *is Ali Benjamin's critically acclaimed first novel. A New York Times best seller and a 2015 finalist for the National Book Award in young people's literature, it tells the story of a young girl's difficult adjustment to the death of her best friend.*

War of the Foxes *is the second collection of poetry by Richard Siken, whose previous volume,* Crush, *won the Yale Series of Younger Poets prize. The book returns repeatedly to issues of artistic representation in general and painting in particular, giving the book a kind of developing coherence rare in volumes of collected lyric poems.*

In her debut novel, Natasha Pulley blends historical fiction, science fiction, and fantasy to tell the story of a young man in an alternate Victorian Britain whose life is changed through his acquaintance with a mysterious watchmaker.

The Water Knife *is a hard-boiled thriller set in a dystopian near future where catastrophic climate change has forced states in the arid American Southwest to compete, sometimes violently, for rapidly diminishing water resources.*

Welcome to Braggsville *is a satirical novel about the state of race relations in the United States. Four college students set out to draw attention to racial injustice in a small Georgia town, in the process bringing both small-town southern life and American academia under the author's microscope.*

Award-winning novelist Richard Price, publishing under the name Harry Brandt, writes about justice and revenge in his new crime novel The Whites.

Michael Cunningham's short-story collection A Wild Swan *pairs contemporary concerns with the timeless motifs of fairy tales to create fresh interpretations for twenty-first-century adults.*

World Gone By *is a novel by Dennis Lehane set in the criminal underworld of 1940s Florida that follows retired gangster Joe Coughlin as he confronts the wrongdoings of his past.*

Two-time Pulitzer Prize–winning author David McCullough presents a meticulously researched chronicle of Wilbur and Orville Wright's pioneering efforts to build and fly the first airplane—an invention that would ultimately lead to modern commercial air and space travel.

X chronicles the formative years of Malcolm Little, the young boy who grew up to become civil rights leader Malcolm X. The story is presented as historical fiction, and it traces his life story from the age of five to his imprisonment at age twenty and concludes with his conversion and acceptance of Islam during his incarceration.

Lafayette in the Somewhat United States

Author: Sarah Vowell (b. 1969)
Publisher: Riverhead Books (New York).
  274 pp.
Type of work: Biography, history
Time: 1777–81, 1824
Locales: France, the United States

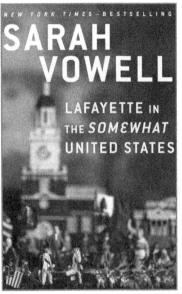

(Courtesy of Riverhead Books)

In her very accessible account of the later years of the American Revolution, Sarah Vowell examines the role that the Marquis de Lafayette, a French aristocrat and army officer, played in the war and the phenomenon of his continued popularity in the United States long after the war with Britain was over.

Principal personages:

MARQUIS DE LAFAYETTE, French nobleman and military officer who fought for the United States during the American Revolution

GEORGE WASHINGTON, commander in chief of the American Continental Army, first president of the United States

BENJAMIN FRANKLIN, American intellectual and statesman

THOMAS JEFFERSON, governor of Virginia during part of the American Revolution, ambassador to France, and third president of the United States

SILAS DEANE, American diplomat to France

LOUIS XVI OF FRANCE, king of France from 1774–93

CHARLES GRAVIER, Comte de Vergennes, French foreign minister under King Louis XIV

BARON FRIEDRICH WILHELM VON STEUBEN, Prussian army officer, inspector general of the Continental Army

GENERAL CHARLES CORNWALLIS, British general and commander of British forces during the American Revolution

Sarah Vowell's books have been described as popular history combined with social commentary. Her history, while generally accurate, is written in a lively, entertaining manner and appeals to a wide range of tastes. Readers often remark that Vowell's writing is the antithesis of drier, more technical works of academic historians. While the pages of her books are not peppered with footnotes and scholarly references, she does include a bibliography that lists several respected historical works. Vowell interlaces her history with social commentary on American politics and society that is sometimes laugh-out-loud funny and sometimes bitingly critical.

Lafayette in the Somewhat United States is not only a biography of the Marquis de Lafayette. It also examines his role in the American Revolution and the place accorded him in the hearts and minds of the American people. Some background on his family and his early life is provided, as is detailed coverage of the trip he made throughout the United States beginning in 1824, when over the course of thirteen months, he toured all twenty-four of the existing states and was given a hero's welcome everywhere he went.

Lafayette, as Vowell contends, came to the United States as a nineteen-year-old orphan for three reasons. First, he admired the republican ideals for which the Americans were fighting. Also, as a French noble from a military family, he felt great animosity toward Great Britain. Finally, he longed for personal glory, which was most likely to be attained on the battlefield. France was at the time, however, in the midst of a rare stretch of sustained peace. Lafayette arrived in America in June 1777 and served throughout the duration of the war except for a brief trip back to France. He was present at General Charles Cornwallis's surrender at the Siege of Yorktown in Virginia in October 1781, and he returned to France shortly afterward.

(Bennett Miller)

Lafayette in the Somewhat United States *is Sarah Vowell's sixth nonfiction book on US history. She has also been a contributing editor to* NPR's This American Life, *a columnist for major newspapers, and a voice-over actor for Pixar's 2004 animated film* The Incredibles.

Besides describing Lafayette's convoluted route to getting to America, which involved first seeking permission from the French crown and then departing secretly when permission was denied, Vowell also chronicles the complicated process that eventually brought France into an open alliance with the United States. Patriot leaders knew that a foreign ally would be essential in the war against Great Britain, and France, with its long-standing hatred toward the British, seemed to be the most likely nation to help. The French were reluctant to openly commit to the Americans until they saw some proof that the United States had a chance of winning. The defeat of General John Burgoyne at Saratoga in upstate New York is usually cited by historians as the event that convinced the French, and Vowell covers it in some detail. She also notes that George Washington's attack on Germantown in October 1774 influenced the French decision. Even though the attack failed, the French were impressed by the audacity that Washington exhibited in risking the assault.

After a brief description of Lafayette's family background and youth, most of the book focuses on the years he spent with the Continental Army from his arrival in June 1777 until the surrender of Cornwallis at Yorktown in October 1781. No one really knew it at the time, but Cornwallis's surrender was in many ways the end of the war.

Skirmishes would go on between Patriot and Loyalist militia until a preliminary peace treaty was signed in November 1782, but Yorktown was the last major battle between the Continental Army and British regular forces.

Washington developed a strong attachment to Lafayette. During most of his service in America, Lafayette, who had been given a commission as a major general in the Continental Army, was a member of Washington's staff and served close by his side. For a brief time, he was given an independent command because of his desire to have the experience of leading troops in battle. Vowell suggests that perhaps Lafayette looked upon Washington as a father figure since he had lost his own father, who died fighting the British in the Seven Years' War, at a young age. For his part, Washington on several occasions said that he considered Lafayette to be one of his own family. When Lafayette was slightly wounded by a musket ball at the Battle of Brandywine Creek in September 1777, Washington told the surgeon attending him to "Take care of him as if he were my own son."

Vowell puts Lafayette's service to the Continental Army into context by discussing some of the other European military figures who also came to aid the American cause, including Baron Friedrich Wilhelm von Steuben, a veteran of the Prussian army during the Seven Years' War. George Washington appointed him inspector general of the Continental Army, and Von Steuben's regimen of training is widely credited with turning Washington's ragtag army into an effective fighting force. In contrast to older, experienced men like Von Steuben, Lafayette, who had served in the French army but never fought in combat, was important as a symbol of French sympathy with the revolutionaries and because of his close ties to powerful aristocrats at the court of Louis XVI.

Vowell also gives thorough coverage to the role of the French navy and French troops at the Battle of Yorktown. The arrival of a French fleet commanded by Admiral Comte de Grasse off the coast of Virginia dashed Cornwallis's hopes of being rescued by the British navy and completed the entrapment that led to his surrender. In addition, more than nine thousand French infantry troops were involved in the Siege of Yorktown, under the command of the Comte de Rochambeau—a force roughly equal to the number of American troops there at the time. Thus, in the last significant engagement of the war, the full impact of the French alliance was clearly exhibited.

The phrase in Vowell's title about the "Somewhat United States," besides being witty and reflecting her strong sense of irony, derives from Vowell's contention that the United States has never truly been united. Even in the midst of fighting a war against one of the greatest military powers of the time, the thirteen nascent states and their representatives in Congress could not agree on basic matters such as the need to provide sufficient money and supplies for the Continental Army to function effectively. Washington found, just as Confederate general Robert E. Lee would almost a century later during the US Civil War, that it is hard to fight a war in a nation committed to limited government.

Americans generally like to dwell on the heroic sufferings of General Washington's army in its winter quarters at Valley Forge. While some of that suffering was no doubt inevitable, a good bit of it was caused by the failure of Congress to provide the proper uniforms, equipment, and rations the army needed for its survival. Vowell draws connections from this to more recent events, such as a shut-down of nonessential government offices during a congressional budget impasse, which had an impact her own access to historic sites she visited while researching this book, and the scandals involving the Veteran's Administration inability to give timely medical treatment to America's military veterans.

Vowell makes it clear that she finds it remarkable that Lafayette was greeted with virtually universal appreciation both during the war and when he visited the United States again in 1824 as an old man and the last surviving general of the Continental Army. Lafayette was one of the few things upon which the divided people of the United States could agree. Vowell suggests that perhaps it was because Lafayette was an outsider and Americans could freely embrace him. "As a Frenchman who represented neither North nor South, East nor West, left nor right, Yankees nor Red Sox, Lafayette has always belonged to us all."

Vowell's unorthodox writing style is a strength, but it is also one that can lead a writer into problems. Her frequent forays into social commentary connected to twenty-first-century America gives her book a sense of relevance, but some readers may feel these digressions disrupt the flow of the narrative, and at times her interpretations are a bit too simplistic. Occasionally, she refuses to allow a pesky fact to preclude a snarky remark. However, these few problems do not outweigh the value of Vowell's book. Her irreverence and humor draw people into reading history they might otherwise neglect, and that is something of great value. Many readers will discover that history can be read just for fun, and a book like this would be a good place for them to start.

Mark S. Joy

Review Sources

Dwyer, Colin. "'Somewhat United' Brings Lafayette Down from His Pedestal." Rev. of *Lafayette in the Somewhat United States*, by Sarah Vowell. *NPR Books.* NPR, 21 Oct. 2015. Web. 9 Feb. 2016.

Gilsdorf, Ethan. Rev. of *Lafayette in the Somewhat United States*, by Sarah Vowell. *Boston Globe.* Boston Globe Media Partners, 28 Oct. 2015. Web. 9 Feb. 2016.

Green, Jaime. "Founding Father Fails: Sarah Vowell on Embracing the Inconsistencies and Shortcomings of Great Men." Rev. of *Lafayette in the Somewhat United States*, by Sarah Vowell. *Slate.* Slate Group, 2 Nov. 2015. Web. 9 Feb. 2016.

Rev. of *Lafayette in the Somewhat United States*, by Sarah Vowell. *Kirkus Reviews.* Kirkus Media, 6 May 2015. Web. 9 Feb. 2016.

Pierce, Charles P. "Sarah Vowell's 'Lafayette in the Somewhat United States.'" Rev. of *Lafayette in the Somewhat United States*, by Sarah Vowell. *New York Times.* New York Times, 17 Nov. 2015. Web. 9 Feb. 2016.

Last Bus to Wisdom

Author: Ivan Doig (1939–2015)
Publisher: Riverhead Books (New York). 464 pp.
Type of work: Novel
Time: 1951
Locales: Montana, Wisconsin

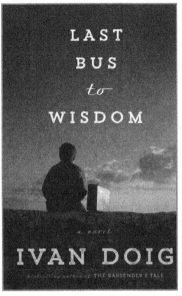

(Courtesy of Riverhead Books)

Through the vehicle of a coming-of-age novel, an odyssey, and a picaresque hero, Last Bus to Wisdom *chronicles the journey of an eleven-year-old orphan during the summer of 1951, recalling an era when children traveled in a more innocent atmosphere. Ivan Doig uses a series of vignettes and portraits to weave the tale, with the last stop symbolizing the lessons the boy learns through his adventures.*

Principal characters:
DONAL "DONNY" CAMERON, a.k.a. Red Chief, eleven-year-old protagonist
GRAM, his grandmother
AUNT KITTY, his great-aunt
HERMAN, his great-uncle, a postwar German immigrant
WENDELL WILLIAMSON, owner of the Double W Ranch
RAGS RASMUSSEN, rodeo star
LETTY, waitress Donny meets on the bus
HARV, Letty's boyfriend

Critics largely agree that *Last Bus to Wisdom*, which marked the end of Ivan Doig's long writing career after he died from multiple myeloma in early 2015, is a memorable final addition to his oeuvre that remains true to his reputable storytelling ability and his devotion to depicting the landscape and culture of the western United States. While this book's narrative crosses state lines, the majority of his works focused on his native Montana. As the semiautobiographical book was inspired by Doig's own experiences as a young boy, it is an especially fitting story to have served as his last in a total of sixteen.

The story begins when the ailing grandmother of eleven-year-old orphan Donny Cameron sends the boy on the "dog bus" (a.k.a. Greyhound) with a wicker suitcase to stay with a great-aunt in Wisconsin. Departing Minnesota armed with his autograph book, Donny meets sundry travelers and soon learns through both the friendliness of some and the indifference of others that he is riding among "an entire busload of all kinds, here for the taking with a Kwik-Klik [pen]." Subsisting on a diet of Mounds bars and conversation, Donny travels eastward through escapades and mishaps, past characters of all sorts before arriving at the depot in Manitowoc, Wisconsin, where he is met by his Aunt Kitty, whom he had naively believed to be the "treasured vocalist" Kate Smith.

After callously smoothing out the case of mistaken identity, the overbearing Aunt Kitty finds Donny's high-spirited presence incompatible with her lifestyle and her need to be the mistress of all she surveys. She puts him back on a bus to Montana without concern for his welfare. Donny fears that he will be sent to an orphanage—or worse, the poor farm, a locale one does not speak of in polite company.

On the second leg of his odyssey, Donny finds he is accompanied by his great-uncle Herman, a German war veteran and the other casualty of Aunt Kitty's ire, with whom Donny has bonded during the short weeks under the same roof. The two mismatched refugees' travels send them up against a

(Carol Doig)

Ivan Doig was born in Montana in 1939 and grew up on the edge of the Rocky Mountains, where most of his novels are set. Through the publication of sixteen books, he became a chief spokesman for the American West of the nineteenth and twentieth centuries. Doig passed away in 2015. Last Bus to Wisdom *is his final book.*

slick, fast-talking preacher, writer Jack Kerouac, the Crow Fair festival, bronco busters, and a posse of coarse but kindly hoboes who welcome the pair into their midst as Donny edges himself into the haying business to make enough money to continue their journey. Considering such a varied cast of characters as Letty the waitress; the three soldiers destined for Korea; the rodeo hero Rags Rasmussen; the hoboes Highpockets, Shakespeare, and Skeeter; and Herman the war refugee, *Kirkus Reviews* called *Last Bus to Wisdom* "a marvelous picaresque showing off the late Doig's ready empathy for all kinds of people and his perennial gift for spinning a great yarn."

Without mentioning specific people or events, except for passing references to the Korean War and Senator Joe McCarthy, Doig manages to re-create the setting of the early 1950s, when Greyhound buses moved folks from state to state, and from church to summer camp; children could travel unaccompanied because they were watched over benevolently by other adults; and words, colorful turns of phrase, jaunty rhymes, and limericks were aplenty to fill in such pages as Donny's autograph book. The historical lens of the novel often focuses on cultural features of the time period, allowing the reader to better understand the environment in which Donny is navigating. References that help to set the scene include the Crow Fair, the attraction of the rodeo, the crowds at Old Faithful, the hoboes in search of work, and even items such as Orange Crush and Mounds bars. In this backdrop, reminiscences abound. Thumbnail sketches of a variety of believable personalities complement the reality of the post–World War II world that provides a backdrop to the novel.

Last Bus to Wisdom fulfills the requirements of a picaresque novel in that it employs a first-person narrative hero—with a character and story that is even reminiscent of Mark Twain's Huckleberry Finn—who gets by on his wits. Since there is no real plot other than the string of adventures that lead Donny from seat to seat or bus to bus, the episodic nature of events satisfies that facet of the genre. The novel combines a series of big and small stories, snapshots of people met, and a few scenarios that help to weave together the fabric of a thready plot. At the same time, Doig does create a rich, resourceful, and well-fleshed character in Donny, who relates his tale with a plainness of language and thought realistically evocative of young people. Since Donny's actions in some instances fall just short of the criminal, his rascality places him in a heroic position. Elizabeth Toohey, in a review for the *Christian Science Monitor*, noted that in addition to this honest characteristic of children, Donny also exhibits a tendency toward imaginative storytelling, describing him as "a bit of a rogue who specializes in inventing wish-fulfillment stories about his life and family." While the tale emerges picaresque to be sure, the story also contains echoes of Homer's classic the *Odyssey* (ca. 700 BC), including the long voyage from home, the sorceress Circe (Aunt Kitty), the Cyclops (alluded to more overtly through the one-eyed Herman), the Sirens of the rodeo, and the many calamities of Scylla and Charybdis on the dog bus.

In addition, as in most picaresque stories, Doig's narrative does depend somewhat heavily on a succession of coincidences to continue moving the adventure forward. However, as was the case with classics such as Twain's *Adventures of Huckleberry Finn* (1885), the perceived existence of these coincidences is largely negated by the power of Doig's storytelling and the captivating dimensions of his colorful characters.

Last Bus to Wisdom is also a coming-of-age novel reminiscent of Doig's previous work, *The Bartender's Tale* (2012). The two novels share a similar narrator's voice of innocence and wonderment. Children follow their dreams while adults guide the way. This concept is no less true here. There are myriad interesting adults who line the path of the bus's route, many of them maternal. Donny's voice evokes an emerging masculine perspective, which is evident in his use of the new vocabulary he learns, his wanting to use cuss words, his description of his first kiss with Letty, and his colorful depictions of the waitress herself—including observations regarding her cleavage. The primary female characters are seen through the eyes of the preadolescent: Gram and Aunt Kitty as the unambiguously good and bad and Letty as the attraction, the Calypso of Donny's odyssey. The questions of sexuality in an emerging adolescent occur in juxtaposition to the sense of filial obligation to and evocative memory of his grandmother.

The narrative voice of *Last Bus to Wisdom* holds much introspection from an eleven-year-old boy thinking through the incidents of his odyssey and thinking ahead to the denouement of each adventure. With the eager, wide-eyed wonderment and excitement of a child on his first away-from-home solo adventure, the story's hero learns that "life is what it throws at you." A repertoire of expressions of the day fuels Donny's narration as he comments on phrases he has learned from many sources, including sayings he recalls from his late parents, the down-home quips of Gram, and other snippets either heard in the multitude of conversations on the bus or those peppered into his autograph book. This new lexicon, mixed with the perspicacity of an eleven-year-old orphan who has had to deal with adults using a new voice, endears the young hero to the reader. In the opinion of reviewer Bruce Barcott for the *New York Times*, Doig "kicks subtlety to the curb and adopts the sort of exaggerated patter that the Coen brothers put to use in *O Brother, Where Art Thou?*" Other critics lauded Doig's ability to portray his young narrator so authentically, as Malcolm Forbes wrote in his review for SFGate, "His novel is that rare thing: a mature, career-end work that captures the buoyancy of youth."

As the novel approaches its conclusion near the town of Wisdom, however, less is heard about the autograph book and Donny makes fewer observations about the linguistic buffet of his acquaintances. In fact, both he and Herman begin to take on a variety of pseudonyms out of necessity, and it is more Scotty (Donny) who leads Franz (Herman) through the morass of situations. Perhaps in this way, as the odyssey closes and the book's picaresque hero begins to come of age, the reader understands that childhood pursuits are put aside in favor of more pertinent matters. For, in the end, having arrived at his destination, as Donny would say, he "got it knocked."

Richard Ladd

Review Sources

Barcott, Bruce. Rev. of *Last Bus to Wisdom*, by Ivan Doig. *New York Times*. New York Times, 10 Aug. 2015. Web. 8 Dec. 2015.

Forbes, Malcolm. Rev. of *Last Bus to Wisdom*, by Ivan Doig. *SFGate*. Hearst, 19 Aug. 2015. Web. 8 Dec. 2015.

Rev. of *Last Bus to Wisdom*, by Ivan Doig. *Kirkus Reviews*. Kirkus Media, 17 May 2015. Web. 8 Dec. 2015.

Miner, Valerie. Rev. of *Last Bus to Wisdom*, by Ivan Doig. *Chicago Tribune*. Tribune, 13 Aug. 2015. Web. 8 Dec. 2015.

Toohey, Elizabeth. "*The Last Bus to Wisdom* Is Ivan Doig's Final Tribute to the American West." Rev. of *Last Bus to Wisdom*, by Ivan Doig. *Christian Science Monitor*. Christian Science Monitor, 19 Aug. 2015. Web. 8 Dec. 2015.

A Little Life

Author: Hanya Yanagihara (b. 1975)
Publisher: Doubleday (New York). 736 pp.
Type of work: Novel
Time: Modern day
Locales: New York, Boston

(Courtesy of Penguin Random House)

A Little Life *is the story of the lifelong friendship between four men who meet in college. The second novel by Hanya Yanagihara,* A Little Life *was a 2015 National Book Award finalist, short-listed for the 2015 Man Booker Prize, and a finalist for the 2015 Kirkus Prize for fiction.*

Principal characters:

JUDE, a lawyer who has suffered significant physical and emotional abuse that he struggles to overcome

WILLEM, his best friend who achieves fame and recognition as an actor

JB, their friend who works for years to achieve recognition as a gifted artist

MALCOLM, their friend who becomes an award-winning architect

ANDY, a medical student who treats Jude when he is young and continues to care for his medical needs into adulthood

HAROLD, a professor and mentor of Jude who, along with his wife, adopts Jude when he is an adult

A Little Life is the second novel by Hanya Yanagihara. In his review for the *Wall Street Journal*, critic Sam Sacks wrote that *A Little Life* "announces her [Yanagihara], as decisively as a second work can, as a major American novelist." Sexuality, sexual identity, and their expression are major themes in this work, which reviewer Garth Greenwell described for the *Atlantic* as "the most ambitious chronicle of the social and emotional lives of gay men to have emerged for many years." *A Little Life* also explores just how normal a life is possible for someone who has suffered horrific abuse and betrayal during childhood and adolescence, or, as *New York Times* reviewer Carol Anshaw writes, "How does someone go from years of suffering and shame to live out the rest of a life?"

Yet while *A Little Life* delves into sexual exploration and survival from abuse, it also transcends those themes and strays from the narratives typically found in gay literature. As critic Jon Michaud describes it in the *New Yorker*, "*A Little Life* is a surprisingly subversive novel—one that uses the middle-class trappings of naturalistic fiction to deliver an unsettling meditation on sexual abuse, suffering, and the difficulties of recovering." The eloquence with which the book handles that meditation speaks to what multiple reviews refer to as the brilliance of Yanagihara's work.

At its simplest, *A Little Life* traces the lives of four men—Jude, Willem, JB, and Malcolm—from the formation of their friendship in college, on through to middle age. Each of the men is fully drawn, with a distinct personality and interests that are examined over the course of the novel. Each has areas in his life that are less than perfect, but it is Jude who has a past so troubled that it interferes significantly with his ability to function on a daily basis. As the book continues, Jude becomes the central character. Over time it becomes clear to all of them that Jude is not just quiet about his past; it is so traumatic that he dares not speak of it. They all observe the ways in which that trauma plays out beneath the surface, but only Willem ultimately knows the entire truth. Each does his best to step up for Jude, leaving the reader to explore the question of just how much one person can do for another, even as the reader grapples with the question of just how much one person can bear in a lifetime.

After years of friendship, Jude and Willem become a couple. By this time, each of the four main characters has worked his way to success. Willem is a very successful actor. JB is an artist recognized for his talent, a talent that has best been expressed through his work depicting his three best friends. Malcolm's architectural designs have won him awards. Jude is known as a viciously effective litigator.

As each of them has worked toward his individual success, each must resolve issues with his family and his past. He must also answer the question as to what precisely defines the perfect partner for him and how that partnership fits within his larger aspirations. For Willem, the question of what to do with his friendship with Jude takes years to resolve. Ultimately he realizes that, while he might not classify himself strictly as a gay man, he does identify as a person in love with Jude, who is a man. This realization leads Willem more deeply into Jude's past, as well as his present struggles with the injuries and physical pain from that past. As Willem discovers that he cannot fix Jude or guide him to finding redemption, Jude comes to the realization that even a "little life" may be more than he can sustain. He must push himself past his self-imposed, protective boundaries if he is to have the sort of relationships he envies in others.

One way that Jude attempts to cope with the shame and the physical and emotional pain he carries with him is by cutting himself. Yanagihara writes about Jude's cutting in graphic detail. She begins with the emotional damage that leads to his need, then walks the reader through each event. Andy, Jude's doctor, is the character that is most familiar with Jude's self-harming behavior. It is through Andy's eyes that the reader sees the extent of the damage Jude inflicts upon himself. Yanagihara also describes Jude's attempts to conceal his scars and his early injuries from those closest to him. In addition to the cutting, Jude also suffers from lasting injuries from his youth: he walks with a pronounced limp and has spinal cord damage that leaves him in chronic pain.

One of the most unsettling aspects of *A Little Life* lies in Jude's inability to identify who is good for him and who is not. As he retraces his youth, Jude dwells on each of those who betrayed his trust. Even as he does this, he finds that some of those people from his past were better to him than others. This leaves him doubting his ability to identify a healthy relationship in his present life. At one point of despair, Jude arranges for his body to be discovered after he commits suicide. Because of a misunderstanding about the time, he is found in time to be saved. From that moment in the novel, the overarching question is whether or not he will be able to carry on and resist the out from his little life that only suicide can provide. With the stakes raised, Jude continues to refuse to share the details of his past, or the extent of his current struggles, with anyone—even those who have proven to be behind him for decades.

And yet, Jude does arrive at the decision that Willem is the person he most wants to be with. He cannot commit to being in a sexual relationship with Willem and must ultimately share enough details of his past for Willem to understand and accept this. Abandoned as a baby, Jude was taken in at a monastery, where he was regularly subjected to sexual and physical abuse. He escaped with someone who promised that he and Jude would live as father and son, but just abused Jude further. Willem values Jude

Hanya Yanagihara's first novel was The People in the Trees. A Little Life *is her second novel. A former editor at large at* Condé Nast Traveler, *Yanagihara works as deputy editor at* T: The New York Times Style Magazine.

because Jude is the only person in his life who knows who Willem really is and has been there since before his fame. Jude helps him to be centered and to deal with his fame. Jude does not recognize the value that holds for Willem. He simply considers himself to be beyond lucky that Willem cares for him so deeply. Similarly, Jude cannot see why Harold—his former professor and adoptive father—cares for him as a son. He worries that once Harold learns the truth about him, he will be rejected. Harold skirts these issues with Jude, understandably not wanting to push Jude to far while also leaving all entrees to a better understanding of Jude unexplored.

Against all odds, Jude does arrive at a moment when he has everything he has ever dared to hope for. He is in a committed relationship. He has parents who love him. He has friends who care for him. At first, even with all of this, he continues to harm himself as a means of relieving the constant raging turmoil he carries within. Ultimately, he uses every bit of resolve to move past this and into a place of relative peace. He is cautiously hopeful for his future, even going so far as to introduce the people he works with to Willem. He is content to share himself with Willem and to maintain the relationships with his friends and adoptive family. He has reached a point where he can reflect on his past in bits and pieces, without his past overwhelming him. When events occur to shatter that peace, the reader is drawn along with Jude as he plummets.

Yanagihara does not let up for a moment. Several reviews cite the improbability of any one person suffering all of the abuse and misery she gives to Jude. It is that very level of violence and incredulity that renders Jude such a powerful character. *Washington Post* reviewer Nicole Lee writes, "Hanya Yanagihara's new novel, *A Little Life*, is a witness to human suffering pushed to its limits, drawn in extraordinary detail by incantatory prose." *A Little Life* is a heartbreaking novel that explores the meaning of male friendship, of romance, the possibility of building a life after extraordinary trauma.

Gina Hagler

Review Sources

Anshaw, Carol. "Their Secret History." Rev. of *A Little Life*, by Hanya Yanagihara. *New York Times* 5 Apr. 2015: BR9. Print.

Greenwell, Garth. "*A Little Life*: The Great Gay Novel Might Be Here." *Atlantic.* Atlantic Monthly Group, 31 May 2015. Web. 19 Dec. 2015.

Lee, Nicole. "Book Review: *A Little Life*, by Hanya Yanagihara, Inspires and Devastates." Rev. of *A Little Life*, by Hanya Yanagihara. *Washington Post.* Washington Post, 10 Apr. 2015. Web. 8 Dec. 2015.

Michaud, Jon. "The Subversive Brilliance of *A Little Life*." Rev. of *A Little Life*, by Hanya Yanagihara. *New Yorker.* Condé Nast, 28 Apr. 2015. Web. 12 Dec. 2015.

Sacks, Sam. "Fiction Chronicle: Jude the Obscure." Rev. of *A Little Life*, by Hanya Yanagihara. *Wall Street Journal.* Dow Jones, 5 Mar. 2015. Web. 10 Dec. 2015.

Smith, Claiborne. "Best Books of 2015: Hanya Yanagihara." Rev. of *A Little Life*, by Hanya Yanagihara. *Kirkus Reviews.* Kirkus Media, 16 Nov. 2015. Web. 4 Dec. 2015.

M Train

Author: Patti Smith (b. 1946)
Publisher: Alfred A. Knopf (New York). 272 pp.
Type of work: Memoir
Time: 1950s–2010s
Locales: New York, Morocco, Suriname, Germany, Iceland, Mexico, France, and Japan

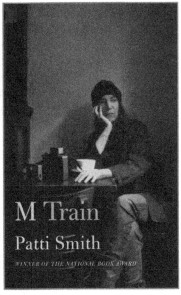

(Courtesy of Knopf)

Part journal, part travelogue, part rumination on the process of writing, M Train *is a memoir by poet and rock singer Patti Smith that evades easy categorization. Critics have lauded Smith's book for its lyricism and treatment of memory and loss.*

Principal personages:

PATTI SMITH, a singer, poet, artist, and memoirist

FRED "SONIC" SMITH, her husband, the father of her son and daughter, a guitarist

LENNY KAYE, her friend, a guitarist and member of the Patti Smith Group

ROBERT MAPPLETHORPE, an early lover and friend of hers, a controversial photographer

SAM WAGSTAFF, Mapplethorpe's lover and supporter, a financial backer of hers

SAM SHEPARD, another early friend and supporter of hers; a playwright, actor, and director

PAUL BOWLES, an American expatriate writer, long a resident of Tangier

ZAK, a barista at the Café 'Ino in Greenwich Village

Like many young people, Patti Smith moved to New York City before she had come of age. Like many, she set off with little more than bus fare, a friend's address, and the dreams and energy of youth. Unlike some, she had no ruling passion; she wrote poetry and had performed in college plays but mainly wanted to inhabit the bohemian world of the French poets, painters, and performers of earlier decades. And unlike all but a few, she had the good fortune to meet a young man—a boy, as she thought of him—who quickly came to love her and to share his passion for the visual arts as well as a strong belief in her talents. Theirs was not an easy relationship, for he soon began to wonder about his sexual orientation, though, as a former altar boy from a conservative Catholic family, he dared not talk about it. But he had a major talent. His name was Robert Mapplethorpe, and he became one of the most celebrated photographers of his time, though he died an early death during the AIDS epidemic.

Before he died, Mapplethorpe made Smith promise to tell their story. She had never written anything like a memoir and spent the next two decades wondering how she would keep the promise. She made her fame as a performance artist, reading her poetry as a warm-up act for the New York Dolls and other bands. She then became a singer for a rock-and-roll band, a sort of protorapper. Through rock she found an audience for her published poems. She also wrote *Woolgathering* (1992), a small book of vignettes from her childhood as well as other observations. But not until she was in her sixties did she turn her memories, including the family stories that she had long been telling, into the promised book. Her 2010 memoir, *Just Kids*, told of her childhood and her days with Mapplethorpe. The book's title came from an overheard conversation of tourists who saw the young couple in Washington Square. The perceptive wife told her husband to photograph them because they must be artists. He declined, saying, "They're just kids."

Patti Smith made her reputation as a poet who performed her lyrics to rock music. She was inducted into the Rock and Roll Hall of Fame in 2007. Her previous memoir, Just Kids, *won the National Book Award for Nonfiction in 2010. A still earlier memoir,* Woolgathering *(1992), was reprinted with a new introduction in 2011.*

M Train picks up where the earlier memoir left off, with Smith's marriage to the rock guitarist Fred Smith and her single life in Manhattan after he has died; their children have left home, and she is responsible only for three cats. The drama is reduced considerably. The big question is no longer where she will find her next meal, but whether she will get her regular table at the neighborhood café. Meanwhile, the narrative goes inward. When readers last saw the young Patti, she was sitting on the floor of the loft she shared with Mapplethorpe, surrounded by sheets with poems on them; her story now goes into the poems themselves and the dreams of which the poems are made.

Midway through the memoir, when travels have taken Smith far from New York, she has a dream about the M train, a line of the New York subway system that connects the boroughs of Manhattan, Brooklyn, and Queens. After returning to Greenwich Village, she decides to take the train to Queens and visit the boardwalk beside the Atlantic Ocean at Far Rockaway. This turns out to be the first of many visits. Although Smith learns that the A train is the better choice, she could hardly give her book that title because readers would likely first think about the other end of the train's route, in Harlem, and of Billy Strayhorn's song "Take the A Train," as played by the Duke Ellington Orchestra. More importantly, though, the M train is the train of thoughts and memories that she rides daily, wherever she is—a train that stops at what the ancient orators called "memory stations," along a trajectory of time. In interviews, Smith has called *M Train* "a roadmap to my life."

The book also takes readers on travels far beyond New York. It takes one to Suriname, where Smith goes to honor a dream of the French novelist Jean Genet; to Germany, where she attends a meeting of the tiny and exclusive Continental Drift Club, commemorating the legacy of the early-twentieth-century geologist Alfred Wegener; to Mexico, where she writes about coffee and visits the home of the painters Frida Kahlo and Diego Rivera; to Japan, where she visits the graves of famous writers and film directors; to France, to write about the Symbolist poet Arthur Rimbaud, an early influence; and to Morocco, to attend a conference on Beat poets and visit the grave of Jean Genet. Some travels are recalled from years past, but most of them from the last half-decade. There are also concerts and book deals that keep Smith moving about the planet. Wherever she goes, she writes and takes photos with her Polaroid camera.

M Train is very much concerned with writing and the writing process. Smith starts without a subject, unless it is the challenge of writing about nothing in particular. She has the discipline of writing every day, both on paper and in her mind. But she writes to see where the writing will go. She therefore goes from writing about her everyday existence, her small rituals, and moves on to extended memories of people, places, and things that come to mind. The book also says much about Smith's reading preferences and procedures. Her tastes are eclectic, but she tends toward the romantic strain in poetry, while resisting loose ends in fiction. She confesses that she sometimes wants to write to ask the author about a mysterious place in a novel like *The Wind-Up Bird Chronicle*, by Haruki Murakami.

In many ways, the memoir is also the journal of a year in the author's life, really a year and a half, running from late 2011 through 2012 and the devastations of Hurricane Sandy into the spring of 2013. She too was affected by the hurricane, which struck only weeks after she bought a house just yards from the Atlantic Ocean. The house was damaged and is being renovated in the final chapters.

The book holds together well on its own but will have more meaning for those who have read *Just Kids*. For example, the Ethiopian cross that Patti takes on every trip was a gift from Mapplethorpe's lover Sam Wagstaff. The one-hundred-line poem she works on is one she started some forty years earlier, while living in the Chelsea Hotel. Passing references to her siblings develop on stories from *Just Kids*. Even the dedication, "for Sam," makes better sense in light of her account of her old friend Sam Shepard. Before Smith knew who he was, the playwright introduced himself to her as a displaced cowboy drummer named Slim. Later they wrote a short play called *Cowboy Mouth*. In *M Train*, there are recurrent dreams of a "philosophic cowpoke" who comes up with such lines as the book's first: "It's not so easy writing about nothing." The cowboy is also Fred, who had a prized cowboy figure among his toy soldiers, but it has a dramatic role in the new book.

Meanwhile, there are parallels and symmetries within *M Train* that show it to be more carefully crafted than it seems in a first reading. For example, Smith undertakes the first and last major trips recounted in the book to visit sites associated with Genet, the French poet, playwright, and novelist. Even more obviously, the narrative starts with a visit to the Café 'Ino in Greenwich Village; it follows her favorite barista, Zak, to his new café on the boardwalk at Rockaway Beach, later destroyed in the hurricane; and it ends with a last visit to the Greenwich Village café, where Zak serves a last cup of coffee before it closes and a passing friend takes the photo of Smith that appears on the book's cover. In the first visit to Café 'Ino, Smith recalls reading *The Beach Café* by the Moroccan storyteller Mohammad Mrabet and wanting to open her own café. On the last major trip, she is taken to the site where the real café stood, and she recalls her interview with the elderly Paul Bowles, who had translated Mrabet's stories decades earlier.

Small black-and-white photographs are sprinkled throughout the book, some with captions, others with identities to be inferred from the surrounding text. There are almost five dozen of them, all but a few taken with one of Smith's Polaroids and most of the others by her friends.

Reviewers of *M Train* have been hard pressed to classify it. Some are reluctant to call it a memoir, noting, as does David Ulin, the reviewer for the *Los Angeles Times*, that it lacks a "sustained narrative"; Jane Henderson, reviewer for the *St. Louis Post-Dispatch*, notes that it has less appeal than the earlier memoir because it consists of "a series of associative leaps" interrupting the ordinary routines of daily life. In Blakean terms, the smaller stories, which come as digressions within the larger narrative, are "songs of experience," often quite sad and reflective compared to the "songs of innocence" in *Just Kids*. Another critic, Michiko Kakutani, in the *New York Times*, calls *M Train* "achingly beautiful": beautiful because it recounts meaningful moments in often luminous prose, but achingly so because many of these moments involve people Smith has long outlived. *Toronto Star* critic Ben Rayner calls it "a free-form meditation on how the past and the present continually coexist."

It may seem odd to call *M Train* a sentimental journey, for there is nothing saccharine or schmaltzy about Smith's writing. However, she has her passions and is true to them. From her longtime base in Greenwich Village, she travels to the graves of her personal heroes, including Ryūnosuke Akutagawa, Arthur Rimbaud, and Sylvia Plath, as well as Genet. She photographs such iconic objects as Roberto Bolaño's chair, Hermann Hesse's typewriter, Friedrich Schiller's writing table, Virginia Woolf's walking stick, and Frida Kahlo's crutches and dress. She has feelings for them all, feelings that come out in her prose as well as her poetry, and that surely is sentiment.

Thomas Willard

Review Sources

Damsker, Matt. "Hitch a Ride on Patti Smith's 'M Train.'" Rev. of *M Train*, by Patti Smith. *USA Today*. Gannett, 3 Nov. 2015. Web. 8 Dec. 2015.

Henderson, Jane. "Patti Smith, Older, Wiser, Duller in 'M Train.'" Rev. of *M Train*, by Patti Smith. *St. Louis Post-Dispatch* 18 Oct. 2015: D7. Print.

Kakutani, Michiko. "Rock's Star Poet Has Miles to Go." Rev. of *M Train*, by Patti Smith. *New York Times* 2 Oct. 2015: C23. Print.

Rayner, Ben. "Patti Smith's M Train Delves into Mind and Memory." Rev. of *M Train*, by Patti Smith. *TheStar.com*. Toronto Star Newspapers, 13 Oct. 2015. Web. 8 Dec. 2015.

Ulin, David L. "Looking across the Days: Patti Smith on Life and Death in 'M Train.'" Rev. of *M Train*, by Patti Smith. *Los Angeles Times* 4 Oct. 2015: F8. Print

Make Your Home among Strangers

Author: Jennine Capó Crucet
Publisher: St. Martin's Press (New York).
400 pp.
Type of work: Novel
Time: 1999–2000
Locales: New York and Florida

(Courtesy of St Martin's Press)

The debut novel of Jennine Capó Crucet, Make Your Home among Strangers *is a coming-of-age story for first-generation Americans.*

Principal characters:
LIZET RAMIREZ, the narrator, an eighteen-year-old student at Rawlings College in New York
LEIDY, her older sister, who lives in Hialeah
LOURDES, her mother, who becomes an immigration activist
OMAR, her boyfriend, who lives in Hialeah
ETHAN, a resident assistant at Rawlings College

Despite the fact that immigration is an integral part of American culture, the experiences of migrant families and first-generation citizens are not widely explored in contemporary literature. As a result, there are few references for the children of immigrant parents to utilize when attempting to both navigate adulthood and forge their own identities. Unlike their peers with families who immigrated decades or centuries earlier, many first-generation Americans feel caught between two cultures. In *Make Your Home among Strangers* (2015), protagonist Lizet Ramirez likens this fragmented feeling to having a kind of "double vision." A Cuban American from the predominantly Latino city of Hialeah, Florida, Lizet struggles to balance her family's vision for her future with her own. Chronicling the pivotal events of Lizet's life during her first year at college, author Jennine Capó Crucet illustrates how, for many first-generation Americans, dreaming of a better life can often put them at odds with their families.

Make Your Home among Strangers begins the week of Thanksgiving in 1999. When Crucet first introduces Lizet, she is a freshman flunking out of Rawlings College, a prestigious, fictional, liberal arts school set in upstate New York. Lizet narrates the story in first-person past tense, often making statements that suggest she is in the present reflecting back on the time in her life when her identity was in a state of conflict. Crucet emphasizes this conflict in a series of character dichotomies; for example, Lizet secretly believes that she is not good enough for Rawlings College but too good for a working-class life in her hometown of Hialeah, Florida. At home, Lizet goes by the nickname of El; at school, she is known by her white peers as Liz. Ultimately, Lizet feels as though she does not quite belong in either world. The theme of being caught between two worlds is furthered by the novel's ancillary story line of Ariel Hernandez. Just as Lizet begins her journey home to Hialeah for Thanksgiving, news breaks that a five-year-old named Ariel Hernandez has been rescued from a raft outside the coast of Florida. As his mother died during the journey from Cuba, where Ariel "belongs," soon erupts into a national issue. Despite Ariel having family in Miami and being initially taken in by the American government as a political refugee, his father in Cuba demands his return. Ariel Hernandez is a fictional representation of Elián González, a young Cuban refugee who became the focus of an international custody battle between the United States and Cuba in 1999. In interviews, Crucet has stated that she was a college student during the height of the Elián González story and was often asked by her white classmates for her opinion on the matter as a Cuban American. However, Crucet and her family were unlike many of their Hialeah neighbors in that they did not take a stand on the Elián González issue. According to Crucet, *Make Your Home among Strangers* is in part a speculative look at what could have happened to Crucet's family had they become involved in the Elián González's controversy.

No character has become more invested in the fate of Ariel Hernandez than Lizet's mother, Lourdes. Throughout the novel, Lourdes is depicted as a woman who is slowly unraveling. This is largely due to the fact that after twenty years of marriage, her husband has left her and sold the family house. Lourdes views her ex-husband's decision to leave, despite his unhappiness, as an unforgivable act of betrayal. She holds a similar opinion about Lizet's decision to go away to college. Rather than tell Lizet that she is proud of her and her academic achievements, she punishes her daughter by being emotionally distant. Beyond her tendency to exacerbate Lizet's fragmented sense of identity, the character of Lourdes serves as the direct connection to the Ariel Hernandez story line. To her daughters' chagrin, Lourdes finds a new sense of purpose by becoming a frontline activist against Ariel's deportation. In this way, Crucet ensures Lourdes's character is ripe with irony; despite becoming a symbol of Cuban motherhood in the media, Lourdes neglects the emotional well-being of her own daughters.

Although Lizet is unsure of who she is, she has a clear understanding of who she does not want to become. Of the novel's many nuanced characters, two are representative of identities that Lizet is eager to defy: her sister, Leidy, and another Rawlings student named Jacquelin. Leidy, who is two years older than Lizet, became pregnant in an effort to get her boyfriend to marry her. When her boyfriend refused, Leidy was forced to live at home with their mother and raise the child on her own. While Leidy loves Lizet, she feels abandoned by her and often accuses her being stuck-up. By staying in Hialeah and not having any future career ambitions, Leidy ultimately represents the life that Lizet most directly rejects. Jacquelin, another Latina student at Rawlings, is similar to Lizet in that they both are minorities far from home who are trying to make better lives for themselves. Jacquelin willingly embraces her minority status and asks for remedial tutoring assistance, something Lizet looks down upon. As Lizet does not want to be viewed as different socially or economically from her white classmates, she avoids building a meaningful friendship with Jacquelin.

While Crucet balances a number of different social and political identity issues throughout the narrative of *Make Your Home among Strangers*, race and culture are arguably at the forefront. Lizet sees herself as an amalgam of cultures, but she is perceived by her white peers as exclusively Cuban. Meanwhile, Crucet encapsulates the foreignness and seeming elitism of the Northeast's white culture in the character of Jillian, Lizet's roommate. Jillian often speaks insensitively to Lizet about Cuban culture, making uninformed statements regarding what it means to be Latino in America. The only white friend that Lizet makes during her freshman year at Rawlings is Ethan, a resident assistant from Seattle who also comes from a poor family. Lizet develops confused feelings for Ethan. She has affection for him, but it is not clear whether her feelings are the

Jennine Capó Crucet is a Cuban American writer from Miami, Florida. Her collection of short stories, How to Leave Hialeah *(2009) won the Iowa Short Fiction Award and the John Gardner Book Prize. She is a professor at the University of Nebraska-Lincoln.*

result of her loneliness at Rawlings or out of a desire to date him. The latter is impossible, however, as Lizet is still involved with her boyfriend, Omar, from Florida. Crucet poses Omar and their relationship as another conflict that Lizet must endure throughout her freshman year. Omar is kind, handsome, and patient, and the only person who truly understands Lizet's fragmented identity. He also represents her old life in Hialeah. Consequently, Lizet feels as though she must push him away.

Despite the fact that the novel takes place in the short time span from Thanksgiving to Easter vacation, Crucet infuses the plot with a matrix of issues and story lines. Beyond improving her academic performance at Rawlings, fixing her love life, and forming an opinion on the Ariel Hernandez controversy, Lizet must make peace with her estranged father and decide what kind of relationship she wants with her mother. The central conflict of defining her own identity comes to a head when one of Lizet's professors offers her the opportunity to work in a biology lab in California over the summer. To accept this opportunity would mean Lizet was choosing herself over her family, who need her help at home. Furthermore, they would never forgive her for leaving. As Lizet grapples with this decision, her priorities become increasingly nebulous. By designating the stakes here as the loss of her family and former self, Crucet demonstrates just how complex and delicate the process of working toward a better life can be for first-generation Americans.

Reviews of *Make Your Home among Strangers* have been predominantly positive. In her *Miami Herald* review, Connie Ogle commends Crucet's skill in encapsulating the emotional challenges that come with being a child of immigrants, especially when the issue of walking in two worlds. Ogle writes that Crucet is successful in "examining the detritus of growing up and away from your family confronting an identity you have always taken for granted." It is Crucet's nuanced and powerful storytelling skills that ultimately ensure that the issue of identity remains compelling throughout the narrative. Consequently, *Kirkus Reviews* describes Lizet's journey as exciting and "deeply fulfilling" and concludes that *Make Your Home among Strangers* marks the birth of "a talented novelist to watch."

The dialogue and secondary characters of *Make Your Home among Strangers* have also been praised, with some critics stating that it is the strength of these literary elements that keep the story moving forward when the plot becomes repetitive. Arguably the novel's weakest point is the way in which Crucet draws out the familial conflicts for longer than necessary. Kathryn Ma writes in the *New York Times* that the novel's "action sags midway" and that Lizet's cyclical bouts of guilt dilute the plot. Although the issue of repetition does briefly slow the narrative's momentum, this is a minor flaw that is easily eclipsed by the novel's many other strengths. What ensures *Make Your Home among Strangers* is affecting is the way in which Crucet infuses her characters with authentic emotion. This unfiltered quality of the prose ultimately gives the novel an intimate tone. Arguably what makes Lizet's story so genuine and compelling in this regard is the fact that much of it is inspired by Crucet's own experiences. Like her protagonist, Crucet was a first-generation American born and raised in the predominantly Cuban city of Hialeah, Florida. She too left home to go to a prestigious liberal arts school (for her, Cornell University). While Crucet has stated that the character of Lizet is much different than she was at that age, it is undeniable that she has tapped into her own experiences to write her debut novel, just as she did with her collection of short stories, *How to Leave Hialeah* (2009). With dynamic characters, humor, and heart, *Make Your Home among Strangers* is a powerful coming-of-age story for Americans whose voices are too often ignored.

Emily E. Turner

Review Sources

Lee, Stephan. Rev. of *Make Your Home among Strangers,* by Jennine Capó Crucet. *Entertainment Weekly.* Time, 6 Aug. 2015. Web. 8 Feb. 2016.

Ma, Kathryn. Rev. of *Make Your Home among Strangers*, by Jennine Capó Crucet. *New York Times.* New York Times, 14 Aug. 2015. Web. 8 Feb. 2016.

Rev. of *Make Your Home among Strangers*, by Jennine Capó Crucet. *Kirkus Reviews.* Kirkus Media, 13 May 2015. Web. 8 Feb. 2016.

Partington, Heather Scott. "Jennine Capó Crucet's *Make Your Home among Strangers* Illuminates." *Los Angeles Times.* Tribune, 27 Aug. 2015. Web. 8 Feb. 2016.

Ogle, Connie. Rev. of *Make Your Home among Strangers*, by Jennine Capó Crucet. *Miami Herald.* Miami Herald, 31 July 2015. Web. 8 Feb. 2016.

A Manual for Cleaning Women

Author: Lucia Berlin (1936–2004)
Publisher: Farrar, Straus and Giroux (New York). 403 pp.
Type of work: Short fiction

(Courtesy of Farrar Straus & Giroux)

A Manual for Cleaning Women is a posthumous collection of Lucia Berlin's previously published stories about the varied lives of strong-minded women.

Although some reviewers have said that Lucia Berlin's stories often read more like stream-of-consciousness memories than like fiction, the prize-winning short-story writer Lydia Davis, in her foreword to this generous collection of forty-three stories by a writer not well known during her lifetime, refuses to yield to the easy assumption that Berlin's work is merely casual memoir writing. However, Davis admits that Berlin's stories fit into what French critics have called "autofiction," a form of fiction that is based on "the narration of one's own life, lifted almost unchanged from the reality, selected and judiciously, artfully told."

Instead of examining Berlin's life in her foreword, Davis focuses on the rhythm of her purposeful prose, which ranges from the rambling and easy to the staccato and speedy. As one of Berlin's narrators says, she sometimes gets fiction and reality mixed up, a description that could be applied to Berlin herself. Nevertheless, Davis emphasizes what other critics familiar with Berlin's work have noted—that her stories are always "deeply felt" and "emotionally important," regardless of their inspiration.

For all this insistence on the priority of the prose, to navigate this collection, it is helpful to have a brief biography of Berlin, for the stories in this collection draw heavily on Berlin's lived experiences. When her father went to war in 1941, her mother took her and her younger sister to El Paso, where her grandfather was a dentist. Berlin developed scoliosis as a child and often had to wear a steel brace. After the war, the family moved to Santiago, Chile, where Berlin lived a life of parties and privilege. She went to school at the University of New Mexico, married, and had two sons.

After her first husband left, she met Race Newton, a jazz musician, whom she married in 1958. By this time she was writing and had moved to New York. In 1960, she abruptly left Newton and went off to Mexico with their friend Buddy Berlin, who became addicted to drugs. With him she had two more sons, but they divorced in 1968. Between 1971 and 1994, she lived in Berkeley and Oakland, California, and worked at various jobs as a teacher, switchboard operator, hospital ward clerk, cleaner, and emergency room nurse. In 1991 and 1992, she lived in Mexico City, where she tended to her sister, who was dying of cancer. Between 1994 and 2000, she taught at the University of Colorado Boulder, retiring in 2000 to move to Los Angeles. She died in 2004 of cancer. The stories in this book touch on all these stages of her life.

The semiautobiographical stories are arranged roughly in chronological order, although, since many are filled with memories of earlier times, her persona, often with different names, may appear at various ages at various times. The title story is a first-person account of a young cleaning woman in California whose husband has died. Although the primary focus is on details of the women she works for and, as the title suggests, advice for other cleaning women, embedded throughout are references to her loneliness and despair. She collects sleeping pills from different houses for that time when the despair may become too much for her. The story is an important example of Berlin's ability to transcend the mere recording of details of daily life to create a story with universal significance. By contrast, the piece indicatively entitled "Emergency Room Notebook, 1977" does not engage the narrator in a personal conflict and thus seems less like a story than a journal.

Among the memorable characters in the collection are an alcoholic dentist modeled after the author's grandfather. In the story "Dr. H. A. Moynihan," the dentist asks his granddaughter to pull out all his teeth so he can put in a new set of dentures that he made for himself, of which he is very proud. When she has trouble getting them all out, he takes the pliers and begins pulling them out himself—"the sound was the sound of roots being ripped out, like trees being torn from winter ground." She screams with horror because his face looks like a skull, a scary monster, a teapot come alive, for he has told her to stuff tea bags in his mouth to stop the bleeding. Although the event in the story may have actually occurred, Berlin transforms it into a grotesque surrealistic nightmare that is both horrifying and comic at once.

The story "My Jockey" is a very short piece about an emergency room nurse, a job that Berlin herself held. The nurse likes her job, she says, because you meet real men there. She attends to a jockey who comes into the emergency room, cradling him in her arms like a baby while the doctor examines him, as he sleeps like an "enchanted prince." She carries him down the hall like King Kong in her arms, quiets him as he blows and snorts softly like a "splendid young colt," thinking how marvelous he is. It is an effective, lyrical, poetic, impressionistic piece that, like the title story, becomes a meaningful, unified story rather than merely a memory.

Lucia Berlin's short stories have been collected in nine volumes. Her story "My Jockey" won the Jack London Short Prize in 1985, and her collection Homesick (1990) won the American Book Award in 1991. A Manual for Cleaning Women was a finalist for the 2015 Kirkus Prize.

The one story in which Berlin talks about writing, entitled "Point of View," opens with her observation that Anton Chekhov's story "Grief" (sometimes translated "Lament" or "Misery") would have not been so effective had it been written in the first person rather than in Chekhov's impartial third-person voice, which conveys the author's compassion for the old cab driver and gives him the dignity he has in the story.

Then she illustrates her analysis by beginning her own story in the first person to show how weak that approach would have been, before starting again in third person. She says by using "intricate detail" and a third-person narration, she hopes to make the woman in the story so believable that the reader cannot help but feel sorry for her. As usual, in some ways the woman is Berlin, who has scoliosis, or what she calls a "hunchback."

In "Phantom Pain," Berlin recalls when she was five years old and living in Montana when her father worked at a mine. At the time of the story, she must put her father in a nursing home for his worsening dementia. The title refers specifically to a man's pain in his missing legs, which his nurse calls "phantom pain"; when the narrator asks her if the pain the man feels is real, the nurse wisely answers, "All pain is real." It is a judgment that could apply to many of the stories in this collection. The central character is caught in a difficult position of knowing her father no longer has a life but being unable to facilitate his release. On a Memorial Day picnic, she pushes him to the top of a hill in his wheelchair, and when he releases the brakes and begins to roll downhill, she hesitates a moment before catching the chair just as it is picking up speed.

Several stories seem to be inspired by Berlin's sister, who lived in Mexico and died of cancer. For example, "Fool to Cry" emphasizes how two sisters, after many years, have finally become friends in midlife. When a man asks the narrator, in this story named Carlotta, how she will ever pick up the pieces of her life, she says she does not want any of those old pieces. However, as the stories in this collection amply testify, this is not true, for throughout her writing career Berlin drew on all the old pieces of her life. The story "Panteón de Dolores" also seems to be about her sister, recalling how crazy and cruel their mother was to them. The narrator says her mother saw ugliness and evil everywhere and that she is terrified she is becoming like her, losing all sense of what is precious and true. There is so much family history in this piece that one wonders why Berlin did not use these experiences to write a novel about her life rather than all these stories, for this is less a story than it is fragments of her family past.

In "Melina," the central character lives in Albuquerque, New Mexico, with her sculptor husband Rex and her baby, Ben. She becomes friends with a young saxophone player named Beau, who gets involved with a young married woman named Melina, a tough mysterious beauty whom the narrator wants to be like. Later she is married to a jazz piano player named David. She says both are quiet men, prompting her to observe that she does not know why she married such quiet guys because the thing she likes best in the world is to talk—an observation that seems obvious from her stories, which sound much like talk. She later meets a young woman named Melina and realizes it is the same woman with whom Beau had fallen in love. When she tells Melina her life story from what Beau has told her, the woman thinks the narrator is a witch. It is a complex magical realistic story about a young mother and the magical Melina, who was loved by two men in her life, making the reader believe what seems unbelievable.

Berlin is also adept at creating comic episodes. "Sex Appeal" is a story about Bella Lynn, a woman in El Paso who flies to Hollywood wearing a brassiere that could blow up like two balloons to make her breasts look larger. When the plane reaches a certain altitude, the bra explodes. The narrator says Bella never told her about this for twenty years but slyly adds she does not think that is the reason Bella never became a starlet in Hollywood. "502" is a comic story of a woman who is drunk in her apartment when her car rolls down the street and hits another car; she is almost arrested for reckless driving until her wino acquaintances come to her rescue.

"Let Me See You Smile" begins with the point of view of a male lawyer, Mr. Cohen, whom a young man named Jesse urges to defend his roommate, who has been arrested for assaulting a police officer. The story shifts to the point of view of the woman Carlotta, who tells about an encounter at the airport when two police officers begin beating Jesse and she grabs a flashlight and hits the cop on the head. When she licks the blood off Jesse's eyes she is accused of committing sexual acts on a minor. The point of view shifts back and forth between Carlotta and the lawyer, who says he has fallen in love with all of them. It is one of the longest stories in the collection and ends with the case against Carlotta being dismissed.

A Manual for Cleaning Women received nearly universal praise. While Lucia Berlin's stories did not attract much notice during her lifetime, *A Manual for Cleaning Women*, which was published eleven years after the author's death, struck chords with several critics who reviewed the collection for the *New York Times*. Among them were John Williams, who compared her to celebrated fiction writers Lorrie Moore and George Saunders, and Dwight Garner, who argued that the "downward trajectories" of Berlin's work evoke Raymond Carver—all of which suggest that Berlin was truly a master of the short-story form.

Charles E. May

Review Sources

Franklin, Ruth. "Marginal Gaze." Rev. of *A Manual for Cleaning Women*, by Ruth Berlin. *New York Times* 16 Aug. 2015: BR15. Print.

Garner, Dwight. "Everyday Struggles, Leavened by Wit." Rev. of *A Manual for Cleaning Women*, by Ruth Berlin. *New York Times* 19 Aug. 2015: C1. Print.

Rev. of *A Manual for Cleaning Women*, by Lucia Berlin. *Kirkus*. Kirkus Media, 3 June 2015. Web. 30 Nov. 2015.

Seaman, Donna. Rev. of *A Manual for Cleaning Women*, by Lucia Berlin. *Booklist Online*. Booklist, Aug. 2015. Web. 30 Nov. 2015.

Williams, John. "Darkly Wry Stories Reflecting a Roving, Rowdy Life." Rev. of *A Manual for Cleaning Women*, by Lucia Berlin. *New York Times* 17 Aug. 2015: C1. Print.

March
Book Two

Authors: John Lewis (b. 1940) and Andrew Aydin (b. 1983)
With artwork by: Nate Powell
Publisher: Top Shelf (Marietta, GA). Illustrated. 192 pp.
Type of work: Graphic novel, history, memoir
Time: 1960–2009
Locales: Nashville, Tennessee; Birmingham and Montgomery, Alabama; Jackson, Mississippi; Atlanta and Albany, Georgia; Cairo, Illinois; New York City; Washington, DC

(Courtesy of Top Shelf Productions)

A moving visual and verbal account, March: Book Two *continues the story of the American civil rights movement of the 1960s from the perspective of a key participant:* activist, nonviolence advocate, demonstration organizer, and eventual congressman John Lewis.

Principal personages:

JOHN ROBERT LEWIS, a civil rights leader, later a member of the US House of Representatives

MARTIN LUTHER KING JR., an African American Baptist minister and preeminent civil rights leader

JAMES FARMER, a civil rights activist and cofounder of the Committee (later Congress) of Racial Equality (CORE)

STOKELY CARMICHAEL, a Trinidadian American civil rights activist

EUGENE "BULL" CONNOR, commissioner of public safety for Birmingham, Alabama, 1957–63

FLOYD MANN, public safety director for Alabama, 1959–63

GEORGE WALLACE, governor of Alabama, 1963–67

In 2013, coauthors John Lewis and Andrew Aydin and artist Nate Powell collaborated on the Robert F. Kennedy Award–winning *March: Book One*, the first entry in an intended trilogy of graphic novels about the American civil rights movement. The focus of the trilogy is on Lewis's growing awareness of and involvement in the struggle for African American equality in education, politics, and society, particularly in the Deep South. *Book One* opens at a dramatic historical event: on March 7, 1965, demonstrators marching from Selma to Montgomery, Alabama, for voting rights were violently attacked by phalanxes of state and local law-men while attempting to cross the Edmund Pettus Bridge. One participant, John Lewis, now a US congressman for Georgia, re-flects on that long-ago event as he prepares to attend the 2009 inauguration of Barack Obama. Flashbacks illustrate defining mo-ments of Lewis's youth relative to the ad-vance or retreat of civil rights. Lewis reads of the outlawing of segregation in schools and about Rosa Parks's refusal to sit at the back of a bus. He hears Martin Luther King Jr. speak on the radio and learns about the murder of Emmett Till. He joins the Nash-ville Student Movement, studies nonviolent techniques, and helps put theory into prac-tice at lunch counter sit-ins, enduring insults, beatings, and imprisonment.

(John Lewis, courtesy Eric Etheridge)

Civil rights leader and March coauthor John Lewis was chairman of the Student Nonviolent Coordinating Committee (SNCC) from 1963 to 1966. He has rep-resented Georgia's Fifth Congressional District in the US House of Represen-tatives since 1987. He has received the Profile in Courage Award, the Spingarn Medal, and the Presidential Medal of Freedom, among many other honors.

March: Book Two continues the saga. The same low-key, fact-based narration that graced the best-selling first work is re-peated with effect in the sequel. As before, the imminent first inauguration of President Obama—in this volume, he is sworn in—serves as the catalyst for a journey into the past to show the events that helped pave the way for the election of the United States' first black president.

Book Two begins in 1960, following the election of John F. Kennedy as presi-dent. In Nashville, Tennessee, following the successful integration of downtown lunch counters after extended sit-ins, volunteers with the Student Nonviolent Coordinating Committee (SNCC) attempt to expand on their victory by ending segregation at other restaurants via the same techniques. As before, their peaceful efforts are met with hostility and violence. Undeterred, the group's members step up their campaign early in 1961 by beginning "stand-ins," attempting to gain entrance to segregated movie theaters. These likewise result in onlookers hurling objects and racial epithets and police officers responding with unwarranted brutality when summoned to the venues. Despite the escalation of opposition to their strategy, Lewis, who helps lead the SNCC while studying at American Baptist Theological Seminary, is determined to continue demonstrating. He leads the next theater stand-in and is arrested, along with twenty-five others.

Later in 1961, Lewis volunteers for a Congress of Racial Equality (CORE) test of the US Supreme Court decision *Boynton v. Virginia* (1960), which outlawed racial discrimination on buses and in bus terminals. In Washington, DC, Lewis meets with CORE cofounder James Farmer and a dozen other volunteers, both black and white, who will later be known as Freedom Riders. After signing wills and sending letters announcing their intentions to the Federal Bureau of Investigation (FBI), US attorney general Robert F. Kennedy, and others, they split into two groups, buy one-way tickets, and board buses bound for New Orleans, Louisiana. Traveling south and west, individual Freedom Riders are arrested, insulted, or beaten for attempting to exercise their rights in segregated bus terminals; they do not resist the assaults and do not press charges against their assailants. John Lewis, punched, kicked, and bloodied in South Carolina, receives a telegram inviting him to Philadelphia for an interview to lead a volunteer nonviolent program in India. He leaves the Freedom Riders, intending to rejoin the bus campaign after the interview.

Lewis's India sojourn never transpires, because he learns that the bus he was on was attacked by a mob and burned in Anniston, Alabama. The second bus is stopped in Birmingham, Alabama, where the Freedom Riders are arrested and briefly jailed before being transported in police vehicles back to the Alabama-Tennessee state line.

The Freedom Riders return and stubbornly resume their journey in Birmingham, this time with a police escort. Upon arriving in Montgomery, Alabama, the bus is met by an angry mob of club-wielding whites, who swarm the riders, beating them mercilessly until the attackers are stopped by a warning shot fired by pistol-toting state official Floyd Mann. The following day, Dr. Martin Luther King Jr. flies to Montgomery to rally the demonstrators at the First Baptist Church, while a crowd of angry white people gather outside. A phone call to Attorney General Kennedy summons US marshals to help protect the church before the Alabama National Guard arrives to take over.

(Andrew Aydin, courtesy Bob Adelman)

March coauthor Andrew Aydin has been an aide to John Lewis since the late 2000s, serving variously as communications director, press secretary, and digital director and policy advisor to the congressman.

(Nate Powell, courtesy Rett Peek)

Artist Nate Powell created the artwork for March: Book Two.

The riders, their numbers swelled by additional volunteers, continue their trip, heading for Jackson, Mississippi. There, twenty-seven activists, including Lewis, are arrested and fined. Refusing to pay the fines, they are jailed and eventually sent to Mississippi State Penitentiary, where they practice civil disobedience until their eventual release.

By 1962, the civil rights movement is beginning to split into two factions: those like Lewis, who stand for nonviolence, and those like Stokely Carmichael, who advocate taking action when met with violence. Through that year and the next, tensions ratchet upward. James Meredith becomes the first African American to enroll at the University of Mississippi. Segregationist George Wallace is elected governor of Alabama. Birmingham police chief Eugene "Bull" Connor steps up harassment of demonstrators with fire hoses and police dogs. Civil rights activist Medgar Evers is murdered outside his own home in Jackson, Mississippi.

In 1963, Lewis is elected chairman of SNCC and invited to the White House to meet with other civil rights leaders to discuss President Kennedy's proposed civil rights bill and a planned march on Washington. Later that year, Lewis is one of the "Big Six"—along with King, Farmer, A. Philip Randolph, Roy Wilkins, and Whitney Young—who meet in New York City to organize the Washington march. The March on Washington for Jobs and Freedom occurs on August 28, 1963, and attracts about 250,000 people to the national capital. John Lewis, the sixth of fourteen speakers (and the only speaker still alive in 2015), makes an impassioned appeal for government protection of African Americans and civil rights activists in the Deep South. The penultimate speaker, Dr. King, delivers his immortal "I have a dream" oration. *March: Book Two* ends just weeks after the March on Washington with an incident that shocked the nation and galvanized the civil rights movement: the dynamiting of the African American 16th Street Baptist Church in Birmingham, which killed four young girls and injured twenty-two other churchgoers.

The dramatic narration of the *March* books is greatly enhanced by the uncluttered, minimalist graphic illustration style of Nate Powell. Details are presented in close-ups, medium views, and long shots in stark black-and-white drawings (though covers are done in muted colors). Rather than draw known figures in photorealistic fashion, Powell instead suggests and slightly exaggerates their key features, striking a realistic balance between portraiture and caricature. Individual drawings, supplemented with appropriate sound effects, vary throughout from full-page scenes to comic-strip-like panels and orderly grids to odd-shaped inserts, effectively matching the tone and pace of the action.

A dynamic, highly charged account of the sacrifices made in the fight for equality, *March: Book Two* depicts a crucial point in the struggle, when black and white volunteers, acting in concert, willingly put themselves in harm's way to end segregation in the South. The third entry in the trilogy will highlight the results of the volunteers' efforts—the passage of the 1964 Civil Rights Act and the 1965 Voting Rights Act, and the counterattacks launched by opponents who attempt to circumvent the law—and continue John Lewis's personal journey, including the beginning of his political career.

Even fifty years after the events portrayed, the story of *March* is highly relevant. The Voting Rights Act, designed to guarantee Fourteenth and Fifteenth Amendment voting rights by prohibiting racially targeted voting requirements such as literacy tests and poll taxes, was largely dismantled by the US Supreme Court decision *Shelby County v. Holder* in 2013. In the wake of that ruling, several southern states immediately enacted laws imposing new rules aimed at disenfranchising minority voters, effectively undoing much of what was won through the shedding of blood, sweat, and tears by such stalwarts as John Lewis.

Jack Ewing

Review Sources

Brown, Hillary. Rev. of *March: Book Two*, by John Lewis and Andrew Aydin, illus. Nate Powell. *Paste Magazine*. Paste Media Group, 19 Jan. 2015. Web. 7 Jan. 2016.

Rev. of *March: Book Two*, by John Lewis and Andrew Aydin, illus. Nate Powell. *Publishers Weekly* 26 Jan. 2015: 157. Print.

Schneider, Dean. Rev. of *March: Book Two*, by John Lewis and Andrew Aydin, illus. Nate Powell. *Horn Book*. Lib. Jours., 20 May 2015. Web. 7 Jan. 2016.

The Mare

Author: Mary Gaitskill (b. 1954)
Publisher: Pantheon Books (New York).
464 pp.
Type of work: Novel
Time: Contemporary
Locales: Crown Heights, Brooklyn, New York; upstate New York

The Mare *tells the story of an affluent, insecure white woman and the deep, unexpected bond she forms with a Latina girl from the Fresh Air Fund. Their connection is emboldened by the talented young girl's introduction to the world of horses and equestrian competition.*

Principal characters:
VELVETEEN VARGAS, a young, impoverished girl from Brooklyn
GINGER ROBERTS, a middle-aged woman who decides to mentor a child
PAUL ROBERTS, Ginger's husband, an academic
SILVIA, Velveteen's uneducated mother
DANTE, Velveteen's younger brother
FUGLY GIRL/FEISTY GIRL, a horse

(Courtesy Pantheon Books)

Mary Gaitskill has earned a reputation among literary critics for not shying away from the seedier side of life. Often her short stories and novels deal directly with behaviors and issues that make many people uncomfortable and anxious. In her prose, she has tackled such issues as self-mutilation, masochism, mental illness, domestic violence, teenage promiscuity, prostitution, and gender inequality. Her writing has been praised for its lack of sentimentality or mawkishness; even when recording the most unusual activity, she does so in a nonjudgmental, clear-eyed way. Gaitskill chronicles real-life incidents that are often hushed up or not discussed in real-life gatherings.

It is because of Gaitskill's standing as an author who gravitates toward peeling back what happens to people behind closed doors that *The Mare* has earned such high but consistently quizzical praise. Reviewers have pointed out time and again, that the plot of *The Mare*, her third novel, is the most accessible of all her endeavors. Some critics have speculated that this book is a likely candidate for book group discussions or a reading selection destined to get a seal of approval from television hosts and magazine publishers.

One of the main reasons that *The Mare* is considered such a radical departure for Gaitskill is that its plot mirrors that of a well-known coming-of-age novel and movie,

National Velvet. Published in 1935 by Enid Bagnold, the book follows a young girl, Velvet Brown, as she fiercely transforms herself and her horse, the Piebald, into Grand National champions. In 1944, the novel was made into an award-winning film costarring Elizabeth Taylor and Mickey Rooney. The story celebrates how any person, regardless of age, size, gender, or economic background, can achieve great things with determination, grit, and confidence.

Gaitskill's take on this theme of empowerment is twofold. In her novel, it is not only the young and financially insolvent Velveteen Vargas who will grow over the space of the book but also her mentor and surrogate mom, Ginger Roberts. Though Velveteen, who goes by the nickname of Velvet, is eleven years old when the book begins, and Ginger is in her late forties, both female characters have personalities that are not yet fully formed. Velvet, who comes from the hardboiled streets of Brooklyn, has not had exposure to the better things that the world can offer; Ginger, who is educated and has pursued a career in the arts, has still not grown into who she wants to be. Over the course of two weeks during the summer, and then through constant contact over the next three years, these two characters from different worlds will inspire and educate one another, each motivating the other to chase her dreams and realize who she really is.

The book is told through different narrators, allowing readers the chance to see exactly how the events are influencing and changing the two protagonists. Additionally, this device allows readers to see the characters' past experiences and how they have reacted to their fortunes and misfortunes. Gaitskill provides glimpses into the minds and emotions of these narrators as they grow and evolve. As the protagonists, Velvet and Ginger are also the primary narrators. They are joined, to a smaller extent, by Paul, Ginger's professorial husband, and Silvia, Velvet's strict mother. The other central character, who is a force of nature and the catalyst for all the change, is a horse named Fugly Girl. The spirited horse does not have the opportunity to share in the narration, but that does not mean she is voiceless. Her presence is the vehicle through which Velvet discovers her innate talents. Riding, a hobby usually reserved for people of a certain class and social standing, is the pastime by which Ginger gives Velvet a chance to excel and to escape the sorrow and limitations of her own life and background. Fugly Girl is the creature that unleashes untapped potential.

The author very shrewdly imbues the horse with her own journey of advancement, strength, repurposing, and salvation. To Velvet, the horse is every inch a Feisty Girl, which is what she names her. Depending on who is talking in the book, the horse is known by either name, the demeaning one or the celebratory one. By the novel's end, it becomes clear that Velvet and Feisty Girl are meant to compete together for a prize and for Velvet's own self-worth. How they gets there, and how Velvet has to overcome in the obstacles of her home life, is every bit as treacherous and enthralling as a steeplechase race.

When Velveteen Vargas first arrives in upstate New York to share the Roberts's home, she becomes part of an experiment. Because Ginger married late in life and never had children, she is beginning to wonder if motherhood is the missing jigsaw piece that would complete her. Before she decides to commit to pursuing an adoption, she convinces her husband, Paul, to take part in the Fresh Air Fund, a program that matches inner-city children with rural hosts. The couple enters into the summer exchange uncertain if it is a wise thing to do and aware of the implications of the program, which Paul sees as catering to white guilt. Ginger convinces herself that at worst it will just be a way to "give a kid a nice summer, anyway." However, when Paul and Ginger meet Vel-

Mary Gaitskill is the author of two previous novels, Two Girls, Fat and Thin *(1991) and the National Book Award nominee* Veronica *(2005), as well as the short-story collections* Bad Behavior *(1988),* Don't Cry *(2009), and the PEN/Faulkner Award nominee* Because They Wanted To *(1997).*

vet, it is an immediate, electric moment for Ginger. Ginger is smitten instantly with the girl: "We came forward. The child turned her eyes fully on us. I had an impulse to cover my stunned heart with my hand, and a stronger impulse to touch the girl's face. . . . She was ours!"

Velvet grew up with a stern mother who often used harsh punishments and scathing words, so she is more cautious and more protective of her feelings. Though she is not instantly drawn to Ginger, Velvet gradually warms to her and accepts her as she sees Ginger's foibles and weaknesses. She responds to her host's imperfections: "The way she looked from behind, like when she was cooking food or something, made it seem like she didn't even know where she was for sure. She blinked a lot. She always forgot things, like even her bank card in the ATM. It made her seem even more nice, I don't know why."

In fact, it is the acceptance of imperfections that is at the heart of this narrative. When Ginger brings Velvet to the nearby stable, a popular place for riding lessons, Velvet only goes out of a sense of compliance; she does not want to be rude to her host family, but the notion of horses is a foreign, remote one to the Brooklyn girl. Seeing all the different horses sparks a reaction in Velvet, however; it is almost as if she can interpret what they mean by their nickering, whinnying, and kicking. The one that speaks most directly to her is Fugly Girl, a horse that the stable staff has decided is not fit to be ridden or liked. With Velvet's own difficult lifestyle and her mother's unmasked preference for her younger brother, Velvet feels an affinity for the horse. She sizes Fugly Girl up and decides the mare is the horse she wants to ride.

As Ginger and Velvet provide the majority of the narration, readers come to know them and see their changes most intimately. Yet Gaitskill does not shy away from giving a backstory to Silvia, Velvet's illiterate, rough, and domineering mother. An immigrant from the Dominican Republic, Silvia has witnessed and survived horrible things that have deadened her on some level, and she fears for her daughter's safety. Silvia never gives permission for Velvet to ride. All of her daughter's growth as a rider and as an independent woman has to be hidden from her mother. When Silvia finally arrives to watch her daughter at an event, she is amazed at the poised and determined girl that she sees. This is a side to her daughter that she does not see at home. Immersion in the world of horses and pursuing her own dreams has transformed Velvet. She has grown into her full potential. Silvia grows as a mother and understands that her daughter is not tied to one strict way of doing things.

It is quite telling that Velvet's formal birth name is Velveteen, and readers eventually learn that her mother watched the movie version of the children's fable *The Velveteen Rabbit* when she was pregnant with her daughter. Silvia did not understand the English dialogue, but she was affected by the notion that a child's toy is made real by love. When Silvia gave birth to her daughter, she was surprised by how dark her baby's skin was. Silvia's aunt Maria took note of the newborn daughter and simply asserted, "Black Velveteen," then shook her head, believing "the child would have hard luck all her life."

While Velvet grows through horse riding, Ginger finds solace in her relationship with Velvet. However, as she explores new ways to find fulfillment, such as community theater, Paul drifts away and cheats on her. Yet despite the difficulties both women face, this ultimately hopeful novel finds meaning in the power of female relationships.

Stephanie Finnegan

Review Sources

Akins, Ellen. Rev. of *The Mare*, by Mary Gaitskill. *Star Tribune*. StarTribune, 31 Oct. 2015. Web. 15 Feb. 2016.

Garner, Dwight. "In *The Mare*, Mary Gaitskill Writes about a Girl Caught in a Domestic Swirl." Rev. of *The Mare*, by Mary Gaitskill. *New York Times*. New York Times, 26 Oct. 2015. Web. 15 Feb. 2016.

Gilman, Priscilla. Rev. of *The Mare*, by Mary Gaitskill. *Boston Globe*. Boston Globe Media Partners, 7 Nov. 2015. Web. 15 Feb. 2016.

Schwartz, Alexandra. "Uneasy Rider: Mary Gaitskill's Fictions of Mastery." Rev. of *The Mare*, by Mary Gaitskill. *New Yorker*. Condé Nast, 9 Nov. 2015. Web. 15 Feb. 2016.

The Mark and the Void

Author: Paul Murray (b. 1975)
Publisher: Farrar, Straus and Giroux (New York). 459 pp.
Type of work: Novel
Time: Early twenty-first century
Locale: Dublin, Ireland

(Courtesy of Farrar Straus & Giroux)

Paul Murray's The Mark and the Void *is a satirical comic novel that takes aim at the international banking crisis while also poking fun at many aspects of modern life, including writers and literature.*

Principal characters:
CLAUDE MARTINGALE, a lonely French banker living in Dublin
ARIADNE, his love interest, a Greek waiter and artist
ISH, his coworker
JURGEN, his coworker
PAUL, an Irish novelist stuck in a creative and financial slump
CLIZIA, Paul's wife, a brilliant and cynical ex-stripper from an impoverished eastern European country
IGOR, Paul's thuggish Russian sidekick
PORTER BLANKLY, head of the Bank of Torabundo

The Mark and the Void is a comic novel about a serious subject: the international banking crisis and the subsequent economic collapse that caused a worldwide recession in the first decade of the twenty-first century. Reviewing the novel for *Library Journal*, John G. Matthews called Paul Murray's satirical look at a mild-mannered banker and a financially challenged novelist looking for a get-rich-quick scheme "morally authoritative and laugh-out-loud funny." With its Russian math whiz hired to calculate improbable formulas to "monetiz[e] failure" and its comparison of derivatives traders to bookies, *The Mark and the Void* spoofs the absurdities and inequities of big banking, but it also takes aim at materialism, the literary scene, and the anonymous, rootless nature of twenty-first-century life. Comparisons to James Joyce's *Ulysses* (1922) underscore the differences between the Dublin of Joyce's hero Leopold Bloom and the Dublin that Murray's characters inhabit, a city of sterile office buildings, hastily built and half-empty luxury apartments, and pseudo-ethnic restaurants serving tasteless food. The financial boom that brought this new Ireland into being was, as the title suggests, built on a void—an industry based on immaterial goods, banks that do business with imaginary money.

Claude Martingale seems an unlikely subject for a novel. A Frenchman living in Dublin and working as a financial analyst for a bank based in a tropical island nation, he spends his days and nights in the service of money, with little excitement, romance, or drama in his existence. Even Claude's coworkers are surprised when novelist Paul tours the office and announces his plan to write a novel about banking with Claude as his everyman hero. The prospect of being immortalized in fiction engages the imagination of the other bank employees, a quirky group that includes Ish, who longs to escape to her native Australia if she can ever pay off her mortgage, and Jurgen, former lead guitarist of German reggae band Gerhardt and the Mergers. After shadowing Claude's office routine for a few days, Paul brings in a Russian colleague, Igor, introducing him as a poet and professor, though Igor's only artistic interest seems to be in pornographic films. Claude eventually realizes that he has been chosen as a "mark," or fall guy, for Paul and Igor's scheme to rob the bank.

When Paul learns that the bank has no vault and no actual money on the premises, his interest in the novel fades quickly, but Claude is unwilling to let his life slip back into its usual routine. While meeting with Claude in a diner, Paul suggested giving the fictional Claude a love interest, choosing their waiter, Ariadne, at random. A few conversations with Ariadne stir Claude's interest, and he decides to hire Paul to script a romance with her, in a nod to Edmond Rostand's play *Cyrano de Bergerac* (1897). Visiting Paul in his home, a once-luxurious apartment built at the height of the "Celtic Tiger" Irish economic boom and now falling apart, Claude gets a glimpse of the writer's less-than-inspiring life. Paul has a young son and an unhappy wife, Clizia, who emigrated from eastern Europe and was working in a strip club when she and Paul met. Paul helped her by buying out her exploitative contract, but now he has not worked in seven years, and Clizia is supporting the family by cleaning houses. A bad review of Paul's previous book so discouraged him that he no longer writes, instead making up bizarre money-making schemes, including a website called "myhotswaitress.com" (essentially a guide for men who want to stalk waiters they like) and the plan to rob Claude's bank. As Paul and Claude hatch various real and fictional plots together, the two men develop an unlikely but genuine friendship. Claude encourages the disillusioned Paul to put his energies back into writing, and he decides to take some chances in his own life so that he can be more than a character whom nothing happens to.

Paul Murray is an Irish writer whose first novel, An Evening of Long Goodbyes *(2003), was short-listed for the Whitbread Prize and nominated for the Kerry Irish Fiction Award. His second novel,* Skippy Dies *(2010), was long-listed for the Man Booker Prize and the Bollinger Everyman Wodehouse Prize for comic fiction.*

This synopsis only skims the surface of Murray's ambitious but sometimes tangential novel, which also includes art fraud, protesters dressed as zombies, a rampaging elephant, a sinking island, a financial philosopher, and a novel about a rapping rat. *New York Times* reviewer Antoine Wilson found some flaws in the novel, including character inconsistencies and a tendency to edge into caricature, but praised Murray's skill in weaving together the many "wild and unruly" elements into a coherent whole. *Kirkus Reviews* compared Murray to Victorian novelist Charles Dickens, both for the loose, rambling structure of his novel and for the way he combines satire with sympathy. Also like Dickens, Murray creates memorable comic characters, such as Paul's criminally inclined sidekick Igor and the golfer-turned-chief-executive Porter Blankly, who seems to ruin marriages and companies with equal aplomb.

Alex Clark, writing for the *Guardian*, called *The Mark and the Void* "messy, profound, and hilarious," noting the complicated story line, multiple subplots, and metafictional twists and turns of this novel about a novelist and praising its use of both high and low humor. Joanne Wilkinson wrote for *Booklist* that the novel succeeds as a satire of the banking crisis while also showing the human cost of the financial industry's irresponsibility. Claude's love interest, Ariadne, emigrated from Greece, a country torn apart by debt, the banking crisis, and harsh austerity measures. The bankers who failed are protected by their money, she explains to Claude, but poor working people are left paying off their debts forever. The "zombies" who demonstrate outside Claude's office building are not merely parodying the popular horror-movie staples; a "zombie," Claude tells Paul, is a name for a bank that continues to trade, even though it is financially insolvent. Even Paul's "hot waitress" venture, absurd as it seems, has a serious underside. In a contemporary society dependent on technology and electronic communication, Paul explains, many men are so disconnected from other people that a daily chat with their waiter is their only real human contact. Claude recognizes his own loneliness and "fully networked isolation" in this; his work is so all-consuming that even his social life revolves around entertaining visiting bankers. Paul Murray uses parody and exaggeration to reveal the moral and political corruption that allows banks and corporations to be bailed out while safety nets for the poor are cut.

Paul Murray's fiction often contrasts a romanticized view of Ireland's past with its grittier present. His debut novel, *An Evening of Long Goodbyes* (2009), stood out for the comic voice of its narrator, nostalgic aristocrat Charles Hythloday, and his head-on collision with the modern-day working world, which he is forced to enter to save his beloved family estate. *Skippy Dies* (2010), a quirky coming-of-age story, is set in a beautiful and historical Irish secondary school with an efficiency-driven headmaster, known as "The Automator," who is eager to tear down the old to make way for the new. The boys in *Skippy Dies* live in a world of cell phones, video games, and anonymous suburbs, with little connection to the past. At one point they visit a World War I monument, created to honor boys little older than themselves who died in the war. Yet when a teacher asks them to name a country that fought in World War I, the boys are clueless, suggesting Uruguay or "the Jews."

In *The Mark and the Void*, Ireland is depicted as a country that enjoyed a brief economic boom as part of a global economy but lost much of its unique cultural identity by doing so. Iconic Irish writer James Joyce is often evoked, but the provincial and distinctive Ireland that Joyce wrote about no longer exists. Significantly, few of the major characters in Murray's novel are actually Irish, and one who is, Paul, is an unsuccessful writer whose novel *For Love of a Clown* was overshadowed by *The Clowns of Sorrow*, a similarly clown-themed novel by an Indian author. In one telling scene, Claude and Ariadne visit a monument to those who died in Ireland's nineteenth-century famine. As Claude views the gaunt, tragic figures of the sculpture, Ariadne points to the names inscribed at its base: not the men, women, and children who starved, but the banks and corporations who sponsored the monument. "Ask yourself," says Ariadne, "who does this artwork want you to remember?"

John G. Matthews praised Murray's "surprising and inventive" writing, deeming *The Mark and the Void* a worthy follow-up to *Skippy Dies*. Most other reviewers agreed, noting the novel's many subplots and rough edges but admiring Murray's ambition and ability to bring together disparate elements. The novel's wide appeal is bolstered by its blend of humor and social commentary; Murray has spoken about his commitment to keeping his work accessible rather than writing books that will only be appreciated by other writers. In *The Mark and the Void*, many reviewers agree, he has succeeded in creating a book that appeals to readers of all kinds.

Kathryn Kulpa

Review Sources

Clark, Alex. "Messy, Profound and Hilarious." Rev. of *The Mark and the Void*, by Paul Murray. *Guardian*. Guardian News and Media, 22 July 2015. Web. 28 Jan. 2016.

Jones, Radhika. "What's So Funny about the Financial Crisis? A Lot." Rev. of *The Mark and the Void*, by Paul Murray. *Time* 2 Nov. 2015: 52. Print.

Rev. of *The Mark and the Void*, by Paul Murray. *Kirkus Reviews* 1 Sept. 2015: 42. Print.

Matthews, John G. Rev. of *The Mark and the Void*, by Paul Murray. *Library Journal* 15 Oct. 2015: 75. Print.

Wilkinson, Joanne. Rev. of *The Mark and the Void*, by Paul Murray. *Booklist* 15 Sept. 2015: 27. Print.

Wilson, Antoine. "'Dublin Bubble." Rev. of *The Mark and the Void*, by Paul Murray. *New York Times Book Review* 13 Dec. 2015: 22. Print.

The Meursault Investigation

Author: Kamel Daoud (b. 1970)
Publisher: Other Press (New York). 143 pp.
First published: *Meursault, contre-enquête,*
    2013, in Algeria
Translated from the French by: John Cul-
    len
Type of work: Novel
Time: 1942–2012
Locale: Algeria

*In his debut novel, Algerian journalist Kamel
Daoud revisits Albert Camus's* The Stranger
*(1942), one of the most famous novels of the
twentieth century, from the local Arab point
of view.*

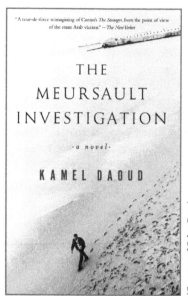

(Courtesy of Other Press)

Principal characters:
MEURSAULT, a thoughtful Frenchman born
    and living in Algiers
MUSA, an Arab in living in a poorer area of Algiers
HARUN, his younger brother, the narrator of the tale
MAMA, their mother
MARIEM, a schoolteacher loved by Harun
JOSEPH LARQUAIS, a Frenchman attached to the family for which Harun once worked

The French writer Albert Camus (1913–60) was born in Algeria, where he studied and
lived for much of his life. He is best known for his first novel, *L'Étranger* (1942; *The
Stranger*, 1946), which, along with his first book of philosophy, *Le mythe de Sisyphe*
(1942; *The Myth of Sisyphus*, 1955), secured his reputation as an exponent of existentialism, which he preferred to call absurdism. He also wrote for newspapers in both
France and Algeria. Camus won the Nobel Prize in Literature in 1957.

   The Stranger is narrated by a man known only as Meursault, which is also the name
of a town in the Burgundy region of France. In his native Algiers, Meursault is tried
and executed for the murder of a nameless Arab who threatened him as he walked on
a beach. Although he pleads that he acted in self-defense, he is too honest to deny that
he buried his mother on the same weekend and did not cry at her funeral. As Camus
once summarized the novel, "Every man who does not weep at his mother's funeral
risks being condemned to death."

   Published a dozen years before the Algerian War of Independence (1954–62), *The
Stranger* portrays Algeria under French colonial rule, when the local Arab population
constituted a lower class of society than their French patrons. Camus, who served in
the Algerian Resistance during World War II, sympathized with the Arab cause and

refused to take sides in the conflict, as does the main character in his well-known short story "The Guest" ("L'Hôte," 1957), which was adapted to film and titled *Far from Men* (*Loin des hommes*, 2014). In *The Stranger*, the Arabs, also known as Moors, are nameless people in the background. Meursault encounters them only as he encounters the sun and the sea, until his neighbor has an affair with the wife of an Arab man and is threatened by the man's relatives. The man begins to carry a pistol, but he asks Meursault to hold it for him when they encounter a relative on the beach. Later that day, Meursault sees the same man and, feeling threatened, uses the pistol. As the novel progresses and as he awaits execution, he tells of his arrest, incarceration, and trial for an act he still does not understand. He is reconciled to his fate, but the circumstances of the story seem absurd to him.

(Courtesy of D.R.)

Kamel Daoud is editor of Le quotidien d'Oran, *a French-language daily in Algeria's second-largest city. His opinion column is widely read as a "daily dose of subversion" in a country where the state controls the media.* The Meursault Investigation *won the Prix Goncourt du Premier Roman (Goncourt Prize for First Novel) in 2015.*

The circumstances do not seem absurd, however, to the Arabs who suffered under French occupation of their country, and especially to the murdered man's family. For them, the murder victim deserves just as much sympathy as Meursault, if not more. Kamel Daoud has undertaken to tell the nameless man's story in the language of his killer. His narrator is the victim's younger brother, who, over several evenings in a bar, tells the story to a visiting writer who has studied the narrative of Meursault and wants to learn all he can about his "hero" and the trial. In Daoud's telling, the story becomes one of a septuagenarian Arab and a younger writer who are engaged in a largely one-sided conversation that continues nightly over wine at a small bar in the Algerian city of Oran.

The narrator, who calls himself Harun, starts out as an angry old man. He is angry that Meursault did not name the murder victim, his brother Musa, and that he seemed to blame the murder on the hot and blinding sun, or on a god that did not exist. Harun's life has been ruined by the loss of his older brother, which occurred a few years after their father disappeared. He is forced to literally and symbolically wear his brother's shoes as he spends the next two decades in his shadow, while their mother tries obsessively to learn the details about what happened to Musa's body, which they have been unable to bury. They are forced to move from Algiers to the smaller city of Oran, where Harun's mother finds work and shelter on the estate of French farmers. She does not let him take part in the struggle for independence from France because one of her sons has already been "martyred." However, she all but forces him to take revenge on at least one of the "Meursaults" before they all flee the country.

As Harun's narrative continues, it becomes clear that he does not see independence as a solution. Buildings have been left to run down, and streets are full of litter. The Islamic faith, once a rallying point for the oppressed, is now an excuse for both laziness and hypocrisy, especially on the Sabbath. Drinking wine, as Harun does nightly, is no longer a cause for punishment, but it gives people a reason to look down on him. For his part, Harun regards religion as a form of "public transportation" that he does not use.

It becomes increasingly clear that Harun has become an Arab counterpart of Meursault. He has lived the story of murder on the beach so frequently that he has played all the parts in his mind and has wondered whether he did not invent all of them. He has been Meursault as well as Musa, Cain as well as Abel. He, too, has been interrogated about a man's death, and part of him wishes to be sentenced for it. He, too, has grown attached to a woman, whose name is Meriem—the Arabic counterpart of Meurseult's Marie—but he is unable to say whether he loves her. He, too, has grown apart from his mother and feels no great sadness about her inevitable death. He, too, doubts the existence of God. In his last speech, he describes his life as "absurd." Meursault is a "stranger" in Algeria, as are all French colonists; however, Harun becomes known to his fellow Arabs for his "strangeness." At first he suggests that Meursault is a made-up name, the equivalent of the French *meurt seul* (dies alone). In the end, he sees it as a version of the Arabic *merssoul* (envoy, messenger). Truth or untruth, his story is almost an allegory of mankind in the postcolonial world.

At the same time, Harun can be viewed as a literary double. Remarking that Musa was killed at two in the afternoon, he repeatedly calls his older brother Zujj, which in Algerian Arabic means "two." Moreover, the names Musa and Harun are the Arabic equivalents of Moses and Aaron, leading several reviewers to see a parallel between them and the biblical brothers, who were a prophet and a priest, respectively. Harun tells the young investigator, who is the stand-in for the reader, that he used to walk on the beach at two o'clock, hoping to be overwhelmed by the afternoon sun, and that he imagined being washed out to sea with the vanished corpse. In the confusion provoked by his advancing age and nearly lifelong trauma, Harun even wonders whether he has created Musa himself and therefore is Musa. Indeed, his long-running efforts to understand his brother's killer make him wonder whether he is not Meursault himself. Just as Meursault was questioned about why he did not cry at his mother's funeral, Harun has been asked why he did not fight in the War of Liberation.

Daoud is not the first to ponder Camus's strange silence about the condition of the majority population in Algiers. In *Orientalism* (1978), literary critic Edward Said wrote that the setting of *The Stranger* shows Camus's anxiety about French rule in Algeria; the Irish writer Cruise Conner O'Brian complained that the trial of Meursault is an unbelievable fiction because no colonial court would have passed the death sentence on a Frenchman who killed an Arab. In an interview with the *New Yorker*'s fiction editor, Daoud stated that when he delved deeply into *The Stranger*'s brilliant prose, he was trying to understand Camus and simply wanted to "pay tribute" to a novel that still provokes discussion in Algeria: "I'm not responding to Camus—I'm finding my own path through Camus." He added that the intense relationship between the narrator and his mother is also an allegory of the troubled relationship that a writer has with his mother country. Meanwhile, in interviews on Algerian television, Daoud has maintained that *The Meursault Investigation* is a work of fiction and that any negative comments about Algeria or Islam are those of a fictional character. Although his writing has earned him a fatwa from a little-known Algerian Salafist group calling for his execution, he has been determined not to go into exile, insisting that he too is Muslim and Algerian, though not an Islamist. He has also implied that the fatwa shows how intolerance has damaged Algerian society.

John Cullen's English translation is fluent and generally faithful not only to the letter of Daoud's French but to the spirit. Camus's famous opening, "*Aujourd'hui, maman est morte*," was translated first as "Mother died today" and more recently "Maman died today," keeping the colloquial French word for "mommy." Cullen has rendered Daoud's variation, "*Aujourd'hui, M'ma est encore vivante*," as "Mama is still alive today," a natural cadence for what is purportedly a spoken line. Elsewhere, when Daoud employs a term of French existentialism such as *mauvaise foi*, Cullen is careful to preserve the English equivalent (bad faith), even though Daoud does not apply it to any one character but rather to the perceived hypocrisy of religious fundamentalists. The translation necessarily follows the stylistic shifts in Harun's narrative as Daoud creates it.

The Meursault Investigation has received favorable responses from both French and English readers. The reviews in the Paris newspapers *Le Figaro* and *Le Monde* emphasized what the first called the *jeu de mirrors*, or "game of mirrors," between Camus and Daoud. North American reviewers also compared Daoud's writing to that of Camus; writing for the *Toronto Star*, Piali Roy praised Daoud for not attempting to imitate the impeccable style of Camus and settling instead for a more discursive tone, while David L. Ulin, the reviewer for the *Los Angeles Times*, lauded Daoud's "audacity" in writing as though *The Stranger* were the written memoir of Meursault rather than an absurdist novel by Camus. In her review for the *New York Times*, Laila Lalami, a published novelist from Morocco, admired Daoud's determination to write in a country that does not appreciate his truthfulness, and *Sydney Morning Herald* reviewer Owen Richardson compared the novel's "anti-religious" sentiments to those of the satirical magazine *Charlie Hebdo*.

Tom Willard

Review Sources

Lalami, Laila. Rev. of *The Meursault Investigation*, by Kamel Daoud. *New York Times*. New York Times, 8 June 2015. Web. 31 Dec. 2015.

Richardson, Owen. "*The Meursault Investigation*: Kamel Daoud's Reworking of Camus' *The Outsider*." Rev. of *The Meursault Investigation*, by Kamel Daoud. *Sydney Morning Herald*. Fairfax Media, 3 Oct. 2015. Web. 31 Dec. 2015.

Roy, Piali. Rev. of *The Meursault Investigation*, by Kamel Daoud. *Toronto Star*. Toronto Star Newspapers, 13 June 2015. Web. 31 Dec. 2015.

Ulin, David L. "*The Mersault Investigation* Re-imagines Camus' *Stranger*." Rev. of *The Meursault Investigation*, by Kamel Daoud. *Los Angeles Times*. Tribune, 28 May 2015. Web. 31 Dec. 2015.

Mislaid

Author: Nell Zink (b. 1964)
Publisher: Ecco (New York). 256 pp.
Type of work: Novel
Time: 1960s–1980s
Locale: Virginia

Mislaid, the second novel by author Nell Zink, deconstructs the nature of identity in the United States by satirizing issues of race, sexual orientation, and social class.

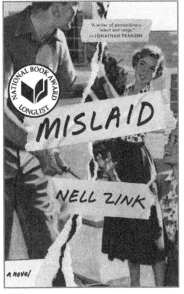

(Courtesy of HarperCollins)

Principal characters:
PEGGY VAILLAINCOURT, a.k.a. Meg, an aspiring lesbian playwright
LEE FLEMING, her professor and later husband, a gay poet and heir to a southern aristocratic family
MIREILLE FLEMING, a.k.a. Karen, their daughter
BYRDIE FLEMING, their son
TEMPLE MOODY, Karen's boyfriend

A person's place in American society is often the result of the identity groups to which he or she belongs. For centuries, race, gender, sexual orientation, and class have dictated how different American citizens are perceived, treated, and subsequently able to live. In *Mislaid*, author Nell Zink attempts to challenge this societal reality through a comedic narrative, an intention evident even in the novel's title. To be "mislaid" is to be temporarily put in the wrong place, an experience that Zink's characters repeatedly endure. Central to the novel's plot is the story of an openly gay man and a lesbian woman falling into a heteronormative lifestyle and marriage. Later, two white, wealthy female characters live inconspicuously as poor African Americans. By ironically putting her protagonists in the "wrong" societal places, Zink illustrates the arbitrariness of labels and social expectations.

Mislaid begins in the 1960s in Virginia, a time and place largely defined by prejudice and strict social order. In her introduction to protagonist Peggy Vaillaincourt, Zink employs several identity stereotypes as comedic fodder. Peggy, who was born into a wealthy, conservative family, realizes that she is gay by spending time with her female gym teacher. She intends to run away to the army after high school but ends up attending the all-female Stillwater College, which Zink cheekily describes as a "mecca for lesbians." Despite being surrounded by other openly gay women at Stillwater, however, Peggy soon becomes romantically involved with Lee Fleming. Lee is a professor, Stillwater's most famous faculty member, a poet and the heir to a wealthy southern family. He is also a gay man.

By employing an anonymous, omniscient narrator, Zink is able to explain both the significance of the narrative's events as well as the impetus for her characters' actions. The moment that readers begin to question the likelihood of Peggy and Lee starting a passionate, physical relationship, the narrator quickly explains that the characters themselves are mystified. According to the narrator, it may have been Peggy's androgynous physique that attracted Lee and facilitated their relationship. Beyond dispelling readers' doubt, the literary device of the narrator provides *Mislaid* with an old-fashioned tone that aligns well with the narrative's timeline and provides a vessel for Zink's sardonic commentary.

Once Peggy gets pregnant, she and Lee marry. Over the course of the next ten years, the two have a son, whom they call Byrdie, and a daughter named Mireille. As her life becomes increasingly focused on being a mother and a wife, Peggy's unhappiness intensifies. Not only has she lost her identity to Lee, but her dreams of becoming a famous playwright are further out of reach. When she discovers that Lee is being unfaithful to her, Peggy's frustration comes to a head. She decides to enact her revenge on Lee by driving his beloved Volkswagen Thing into Stillwater Lake, an event she later describes to a policeman as "a theater of cruelty."

Peggy's reference is both highly specific and meticulously placed by Zink. A twentieth-century French avant-garde theater movement, the Theater of Cruelty required actors to shock their audiences' senses in an effort to release subconscious emotions. According to the movement's founder, Antonin Artaud, the intention of the Theater of Cruelty was to wake people up. Peggy drives Lee's car into the manmade Stillwater Lake, a symbol of artifice and stagnancy, to wake him up to the fact that their relationship is failing. Throughout *Mislaid*, Zink is arguably attempting to do the same. By ensuring that her characters' actions are outrageous, often bordering on offensive, Zink aims to shock her readers out of their complacency on the issue of identity in America.

Nell Zink is an American novelist and the author of The Wallcreeper *(2014). Her second novel,* Mislaid*, was long-listed for the National Book Award. She lives outside of Berlin, Germany.*

Upon Lee's threat to check her into a mental institution, Peggy runs away with Mireille to a poor, backwoods town in Virginia, where the two adopt African American identities. Although both are blond, fair, and have blue eyes, no one doubts their claim thanks to the "one-drop rule" of the South, which infers that anyone with an African ancestor, no matter how distant, is black. To provide their new identities with some credibility, Peggy steals the birth certificates of a deceased African American family. Consequently, Peggy becomes Meg, and Mireille becomes Karen. Karen grows up poor and believing that she is black. Her closest friend is her classmate Temple Moody, a gifted African American boy.

In Stillwater, Lee and Byrdie continue to live a life of privilege. Despite Lee's modest income from the college, Byrdie grows up beloved by his wealthy, aristocratic grandparents. Furthermore, being male, white, and upper-class gives Byrdie the benefit of respect wherever he goes. At private school, he becomes popular among his classmates for both his confidence and his innate sense of how to spend money. Zink portrays Byrdie as calm, with an effortless air about him; things come easily to Byrdie, and this is ingrained in his personality. While Byrdie knows how to play tennis and order oysters on the half shell, one of the most exciting moments of Karen's adolescent life is going to her first restaurant, a Pizza Hut.

Byrdie and Karen attend the University of Virginia simultaneously. Unaware that they are siblings, the two meet at a Halloween party thrown by Byrdie's fraternity. Zink uses their encounter as an opportunity to explore the lifelong effects of social constructs such as race and class. This is particularly evident in her efforts to compare and contrast Byrdie with Temple, who accompanies Karen to the party. In many ways, the boys are the same; both are gifted academically and have a penchant for literature. However, Byrdie has an inherent sense of pride that Temple does not. Without an inner foundation of dignity, Temple is prone to humiliating himself.

The Halloween party, arguably the most significant plot device implemented by Zink, turns out to be an entrapment sting operation. In an effort to quiet claims that the police were only arresting African American drug users, local law enforcement targets Byrdie's white fraternity. After an undercover police officer charges the fraternity members for possession of LSD, Byrdie and Karen are both roped into a lawsuit. The subsequent trial ultimately forces Peggy and Lee to face the consequences of their actions over the years.

The tongue-in-cheek tone of *Mislaid* is essential to its madcap plot and the delivery of its message. Consequently, Zink's comedic voice saturates every part of the novel. The title, which insinuates the theme of temporary misplacement, also winks at the unlikely sexual relationship between Peggy and Lee. Meanwhile, the plot resembles a Shakespearean comedy in its use of mistaken identities, the separation and reunification of characters, and the escape from near tragedies. True to this dramatic style, Zink forces her characters to suffer humiliation and emotional hardship but keeps them from bodily harm. When a gas deliveryman discovers Peggy hiding out as Meg, for example, it initially appears that she has been caught and may be sent to the authorities for kidnapping her daughter. However, the narrator quickly reveals that two hours after Peggy's encounter, the deliveryman is dead. Similarly, Zink creates a scene where Karen is found unconscious at the Halloween party and could easily have been sexually assaulted but is not. It is Zink's relatively gentle treatment of her characters that maintains the narrative's capacity for comedy.

As a satire on race, *Mislaid* is comparable to Mark Twain's *Pudd'nhead Wilson* (1894), in which an enslaved woman named Roxy, who is one-sixteenth black, attempts to give her infant son a better quality of life by switching him with her owner's white son. The boys grow up as different races, unbeknownst to themselves and the world around them. Like *Pudd'nhead Wilson*, *Mislaid* aims to demonstrate how much race is a social construct rather than a reality. This intention is particularly evident in Zink's portrayal of Karen. When Temple declares that anyone can tell the fair, blond Karen is African American, Zink is suggesting that people see what they want to see, and therefore identity groups such as race are often arbitrary in their designation. Yet these social labels are immensely powerful in their ability to determine the quality of one's life and to narrow one's opportunities.

The unique perspective from which Zink examines the issue of identity in America is the result of her time as both a southerner and an expatriate. Raised in the same rural Virginia that constitutes the setting of *Mislaid*, Zink brings a feeling of authenticity to her depiction of postwar southern life. This is particularly evident in her ability to capture the absurdity of everyday southern racism. When the plausibility of Peggy's plan to live as an African American woman comes into question, the narrator poses that maybe readers have to be from the South in order to get their head around the idea of blond African Americans. In this instance, Zink refers to her own southern childhood as a reliable witness to how far the concept of race can be stretched. Equally important to the critical eye that Zink employs when scrutinizing the demographic pigeonholes of American society are the nearly two decades she spent living as an expatriate in Germany, which provided her the opportunity to examine American social constructs from a distance in an international context.

As a writer, Zink has been called a compelling new voice in literature. Her overwhelmingly positive reception by the critical community is a result of both her talent as a storyteller and her unusual personal history. After a lifetime of odd jobs, including bricklaying, Zink broke into the literary scene at the age of fifty-one when she was discovered by acclaimed novelist Jonathan Franzen. To prove to Franzen that she could write fiction, Zink produced the first draft of her debut novel, *The Wallcreeper* (2014), over the course of four days. *Mislaid* has been lauded by reviewers who have praised Zink's use of humor to explore the heavy themes of identity. The novel's absurdist plot has caused critics to label *Mislaid* as a "screwball comedy." Walter Kirn wrote for the *New York Times* that *Mislaid* "harks back to Elizabethan comedy, and Zink exploits its potential with zany verve."

Despite the nearly universal acclaim for its originality and subversive humor, *Mislaid*'s pacing and conclusion have received less favorable reviews. Many critics have argued that Zink loses the story's thread in the second half of the novel and that ultimately her comic sense is better than her narrative sense. In a review for the *Washington Post*, Ron Charles wrote that *Mislaid* becomes tedious toward the end and is subsequently better read in excerpts than as a whole novel. Similarly, Dwight Garner, also reviewing the book for the *New York Times*, noted that the book's "serious resonances are cashed for small coin." While to some readers the plot development of *Mislaid* may outweigh its payoff, the novel's conclusion is in fact true to a Shakespearean comedy. Thanks to Zink's funny, inexorable voice, *Mislaid* is one of the most entertaining pieces of American literature published in 2015.

Review Sources

Charles, Ron. "*Mislaid*: Nell Zink's Subversive Novel Takes On Racism and Sexuality." Rev. of *Mislaid*, by Nell Zink. *Washington Post*. Washington Post, 12 May 2015. Web. 31 Dec. 2015.

Gardner, Dwight. "In Nell Zink's *Mislaid*, Sex, Race, Marriage and Other Cosmic Jokes." Rev. of *Mislaid*, by Nell Zink. *New York Times*. New York Times, 19 May 2015. Web. 31 Dec. 2015.

Kirn, Walter. Rev. of *Mislaid*, by Nell Zink. *New York Times*. New York Times, 4 June 2015. Web. 31 Dec. 2015.

Lorentzen, Christian. "Nell Zink's Brilliant *Mislaid* Is a Parody of a Satire of Race." Rev. of *Mislaid*, by Nell Zink. *Vulture*. New York Media, 20 May 2015. Web. 31 Dec. 2015.

Walls, Seth Colter. "A Novel of Thrillingly Complicated Sympathies." Rev. of *Mislaid*, by Nell Zink. *Guardian*. Guardian News and Media, 19 May 2015. Web. 31 Dec. 2015.

Mistaking Each Other for Ghosts

Author: Lawrence Raab (b. 1946)
Publisher: Tupelo Press (North Adams, MA). 84 pp.
Type of work: Poetry
Time: 1940s–2010s

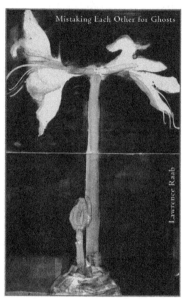

(Courtesy of Tupelo Press)

Mistaking Each Other for Ghosts is the tenth collection of verse by the prize-winning poet Lawrence Raab, whose latest poems are accessible, conversational, meditative, and often flecked with humor.

Lawrence Raab's poems are colloquial in the fullest, truest senses of that term. They not only use language that sounds hauntingly familiar, but also often engage in figurative conversations. Sometimes the speaker talks to himself; sometimes he directly addresses another person. Often he directly addresses the reader. The effect is one of immediacy and engagement. The words "I," "you," and "we" recur frequently from poem to poem, as in the brief text titled "Riddle" (*"from the Anglo Saxon"*) that serves as an epigraph to the present book:

> All that I adorns me keeps me
> silent as I step among the grasses
> or trouble the water. Sometimes
> I'm lifted by the high winds far above
> your houses, and when the sweep
> of clouds carries me away you may think
> you can hear my song—how clear
> and strange it is—the voice of a being
> traveling alone and far from sleep—
> a spirit, a ghost, no one like yourself.

Here are many of the standard features of a "typical" poem by Raab: simple diction, clear syntax, disarmingly commonplace imagery of nature, frequent use of enjambment, absence of both rhyme and obvious meter, and the seeming artlessness but also the hint of deeper implications, of meanings above and beyond the obvious. That last line in particular—"a spirit, a ghost, no one like yourself"—is especially tantalizing, partly because it may (or may not) be ironic. Raab's poems often give readers much to ponder despite their surface clarity; they are poems that invite rereading, and some of them are almost unforgettable. It is hard, for instance, to put poems such as "Last Day on Earth" or "When Time Slows Down" out of one's mind after one reads them, nor does one really want to. The first deals with death, the second with sickness. Like many of Raab's poems, they meditate on the kinds of archetypal topics that matter to most people. Rarely, if ever, does a Raab poem seem contrived or self-consciously clever. Almost always he seems to be speaking seriously (if sometimes whimsically) about serious things. The typical "voice" of the poems sounds authentic—not invented for mere dazzle or display.

(Jane Howland)

Lawrence Raab, who teaches at Williams College, is the author of numerous previous collections of poems. These include Visible Signs: New and Selected Poems *(2003),* The History of Forgetting *(2009), and* A Cup of Water Turns Into a Rose *(2012).*

To say all this, however, is to miss calling attention to the appealing humor that often provokes smiles or even laughter when one is reading Rabb. Raab is not afraid to be funny, and indeed the light touch that often appears in his poems helps highlight their real and frequent depths. Barbara Hoffert, in her review for *Library Journal*, likens his voice here to "a slightly snarky uncle full of blackly witty advice." Most readers will be hard put to think of a more amusing (but by no means, *merely* amusing) contemporary poet. One poem, for instance, begins with these lines: "Let's say you feel someone is better off / dead, but you don't do anything about it." Another imagines that the narrator of "The Fall of the House of Usher" has come back to revisit the story and explain his questionable behavior. A poem titled "Ophelia at Home" starts this way:

> I didn't drown. All those eloquent
> reports were a misunderstanding,
> and that jumping into the grave
> was added later, the way things often are
> to make a scene more exciting.
> Horatio got it to work as a play,
> though I never thought it made such sense.

This is one of the more overtly and insistently comical poems in the book, but Raab often uses humor glancingly or unexpectedly, to provide the kind of twist that happens in spontaneous speech. Frequently, in fact, Raab's poems create a sense of spontaneity and surprise: just when a reader might think she knows where a poem is headed, the poem veers off in some unexpected direction. Part of the pleasure of reading the poems derives from their frequent quirkiness, their refusal to develop as they might have been predicted to do. Raab's poems are often witty in ways that seem rare these days, but the wit is often linked with a sense of real wisdom, too.

The most haunting poems, however, are the most serious. In "I Was about to Go to Sleep," for instance, the speaker is talking to a reporter about a neighbor from across the way—a veteran unable to forget the war or readjust to civilian life, unable to do anything, eventually, except sit in his yard and stare and then (apparently) kill himself. This could easily have been a maudlin, preachy poem; it could easily have been an overt indictment of war and the suffering it causes. But Raab feels no need to insist on such obvious points, and in fact, Raab rarely insists on anything. His tones are typically quiet, and they are all the more effective for that reason. As David Orr for the *New York Times* says, "his eminently approachable, low-key lines are never quite as affable as they seem, and the book is all the better for that." The poem about the veteran, for example, ends this way:

> I can hear myself speaking to him now.
> "Is it like you're a ghost?" I ask, and he
> replies, "Yes, sir, that's what it's like."
> Leave that out, please, when you write your story.
> Just say I saw him and was afraid.

That last line sticks in the mind. The speaker saw the vet's pain but could do nothing about it. He spoke to the vet but had no answers to offer. The speaker was "afraid," perhaps, that the vet might really harm himself, or perhaps he was afraid that the vet's feeling of being a ghost said something about human life in general. In any case, the poem ends with a subtle sense of guilt, all the more powerful for never being explicitly stated. The fear mentioned in the final word lingers, not only in the speaker's mind but in that of readers'.

"When Time Slows Down," another especially haunting poem, imagines the speaker lying "in a narrow hospital bed, / waiting for my tests to come back" and watching the minutes pass, the clock reminding him of "the clocks in the schoolrooms / of childhood, where the big hand *clicked* / loudly as another minute was forced into place." He recalls being sent to the principal's office for some long-ago offense he cannot remember:

> Whatever I did is gone, but not
>
> the certainty of time slowing down,
> or the desire to rise from my chair
> —or now this bed—and float
> outside, unfettered
> and careless, beyond judgment or change.

Who (at least of a certain age) has not been in both of these positions and felt exactly these same feelings? Who has not wished to escape confinement, time, judgment, and especially mortality? Who has not desired to be free? The questions are important because Raab's poems often speak both to and for other people. Rather than seeming self-involved or self-indulgent, either in their thoughts or in their phrasing, the speakers in Raab's poems often seem to state what anyone might think, feel, or say. One senses that many of his poems will still seem relevant a decade or even a century from now in ways that are less true of the writings of more experimental poets. Raab writes in an idiom likely to retain its clarity, and he writes about subjects likely to retain their enduring relevance. Nowhere is this truer, perhaps, than in a poem titled "Last Day on Earth," which begins:

> If it's the title of a movie, you expect
> everything to become important—a kiss,
> a shrug, a glass of wine, a walk with the dog.

> But if the day is real, life is only
> as significant as yesterday—the kiss
> hurried, the shrug forgotten . . . . .

This poem is one of Raab's most satisfying, not only because it explores an archetypal situation—one's last day alive—but also because of the way it is designed and develops. Nearly all of Raab's trademark techniques appear here, including the use of "you" to refer both to speaker and reader; the long, flowing lines with the smooth enjambments; the intimate, conversational tone; and the specific and realistic setting. The listing in lines 2–3 is effective, but even more effective is the way the listing is revisited and complicated later, as well as the way the speaker creates a strong sense of the present moment even when seeming to describe, eventually, the recent past. Sound effects are subtle but present, as in the alliteration and assonance in such phrases as "sky darkening beyond the pines" or "cold towers of clouds." The poem brilliantly evokes a vivid moment just before the realization that the moment is gone. The tone is simultaneously celebratory and elegiac, joyous and melancholy, appreciative and sad, but never sentimental. The poem could have made the speaker seem a mere victim of fate, but instead it ends by emphasizing choice:

> And I was happy, you hear yourself saying,

> because it felt as if I'd been allowed
> to choose my last day on earth,
> and this was the one I chose.

It could have been a simple lamentation, but instead it seems strangely affirmative. Much like Wallace Stevens's "Sunday Morning," this is a poem that makes readers appreciate life by reminding them of death—a poem that faces up to loss in a way that makes existence seem all the more precious and worthy of praise.

Robert C. Evans

Review Sources

Eleveld, Mark. Rev. of *Mistaking Each Other for Ghosts*, by Lawrence Raab. *Booklist Online*. Booklist Publications, 31 Aug. 2015. Web. 1 Jan. 2016.

Hoffert, Barbara. "Top Fall Indie Poetry: Fourteen Great Poets to Discover or Rediscover." Rev. of *Mistaking Each Other for Ghosts*, by Lawrence Raab. *Library Journal* 15 Nov. 2015: 91. Print.

Orr, David. "The Best Poetry Books of 2015." Rev. of *Mistaking Each Other for Ghosts*, by Lawrence Raab. *New York Times Sunday Book Review*. New York Times, 23 Dec. 2015. Web. 1 Jan. 2014.

Rev. of *Mistaking Each Other for Ghosts*, by Lawrence Raab. *Publishers Weekly*. PWxyz, Sept. 2015. Web. 1 Jan. 2016.

Monograph

Author: Simeon Berry (b. 1973)
Publisher: University of Georgia Press (Athens). 96 pp.
Type of work: Poetry

Monograph *is the second award-winning volume by Simeon Berry, a poet and poetry editor. It is a satirical send-up of the shallow, sex-obsessed lives of avant-garde "artist types" linking (but never loving) in a metropolitan area.*

(Courtesy of University of Georgia Press)

Simeon Berry's newest book of poems, *Monograph*, can be read as a brilliant satirical send-up of the inbred world of contemporary avant-garde verse—a world in which there are almost as many magazines as there are poets and almost as many writers' conferences and MFA programs as there are college positions for authors to safely occupy. The reviews that contemporary poets offer of each other's works tend to be mostly glowing, and the foundations and grant-offering agencies that help support publications of poets' verse also help ensure that lots of verse gets written and published. Whether much of it is widely read, especially when it often seems remote from the concerns of ordinary people, is an open question. In any case, the backers of *Monograph* are to be applauded for supporting a book so entertaining in the ways it spoofs the current scene.

The fun begins with the verse form Berry adopts, which consists of tiny paragraphs of unadorned prose printed in small type, so that each page of the book is mostly blank except for the appearance of perhaps five or six brief sentences. The contrast between the small rectangular blocks of black type and the outsized white spaces surrounding them corresponds to the theme of isolation so prevalent in the book. That theme is emphasized repeatedly because the speaker, although engaged in numerous interactions with many people (lovers, friends, family, coworkers), seems really intimate with no one. The connections the book depicts rarely seem caring or loving; each person is more or less on his own, and the speaker, rather than trying to forge any genuine or deep bonds with others, seems content to treat others as superficially as they treat him. Berry is mocking the hip, shallow, narcissistic culture in which his self-pitying speaker finds himself. Reading the book is like visiting a small corner of hipster hell, in which everyone spends so much time trying to be clever and sophisticated that no one seems to have any real time or true consideration for others. Berry's satire of this self-centered universe, with its self-consciously witty denizens, is brilliant. Why anyone would really want to live in such a place, with such people, is a question the book cleverly insinuates almost from the beginning.

The first poem does briefly suggest the possibility that the book will genuinely explore loneliness in poignant ways.

> Thought back to that first
> October after moving to the city.
> Both of us temping. Broke and
> in debt. Barely able to afford the
> rent on a basement efficiency
> next to the elevator. Our sole
> extravagance a bonsai tree stiff-
> ening on the window.

> Fairly certain we were
> doomed as a couple. Repeating
> this to myself every night as I
> walked home in darkness through
> the close, suburban streets, the
> smell of the sea infiltrating the
> fog. Utterly ecstatic with rage.

There is much to admire in the phrasing here. The use of fragments (e.g., "Both of us temping. Broke and / in debt," lines 2-3) may suggest the fragmentary nature of the speaker's experiences and of his broken relationship with his unidentified partner. The October setting is appropriate to a mood of gloom, impending darkness, and cold. The city setting suggests distance from the consolations and beauty of nature. The fact that the speaker and his partner are "temping" seems symbolic as well as literal: nothing seems permanent in their lives together. They are broke both financially and emotionally, living in a cramped apartment next to an elevator (yet another symbol of impermanence), and their only contact with nature is a tiny tree apparently dying in a basement window. The sudden shift from the doomed tree to the doomed couple is expertly handled. The speaker walks home alone in darkness on apparently deserted streets, and the final brief sentence brilliantly twists the tone of the work from frustrated ennui to deep anger. Not even the smell of the sea (a common symbol of vitality) can revivify this speaker's dark mood or the grim mood of the poem as a whole.

In phrasing such as this, and in such sharp vignettes, Berry cleverly sets up his readers for all the forthcoming humor. Reading the aforementioned poem, one might assume that the entire book will sensitively explore the speaker's melancholy isolation, one to which readers can genuinely relate. This serious mood continues into the book's second poem and occasionally reappears throughout, but it is not long before Berry begins shifting his focus to satire of the modern "hookup" lifestyle, especially

when the speaker begins describing his relationship with his partner, a woman identified only as "N." Their "links" with each
other frequently involve handcuffs, kinky
sex, and mutual emotional sadism, although
the speaker seems to be on the receiving end
of more than his fair share of psychological
abuse. "N" and her clever friends and oaf-
ish family seem to delight in belittling him,
making him feel mocked and ridiculed. Some
readers may eventually ask themselves why
he puts up with it. Surely Berry is having fun
by detailing this sort of over-the-top emotional masochism. Few people in their right
minds would stay in the sort of relationship
the speaker has with N. Nor would many
sane people continue to inhabit this sort of
hollow social environment or think that shallow wit, superficial cleverness, and faux intellectual sophistication could even begin to
compensate for the superficial, loveless lives

(Fritz Ward)

Simeon Berry, an editor of Ploughshares
*magazine, is the author of one previous
collection of poems,* Ampersand Revisited. *Both that book and* Monograph *won
National Poetry Series awards.*

depicted here. Hence the brilliance of Berry's satire: he suggests what is missing by
implicitly reminding readers of all the possible alternatives most people would actually choose rather than be satisfied with such emptiness.

The characters in *Monograph* fit so many avant-garde stereotypes that they may
strike some readers as a bit hard to believe. N. blatantly cheats on the speaker with
another woman, having sex with her right in front of him before the three of them head
off later that night to a "grad school poetry reading, when / N. sits between us in the
front / row and holds both our hands." As if to up the ante of "shock the bourgeoisie"
sophistication, the speaker mentions that the poem to which the hand-holders are listening consists of "couplets about wisteria / and sperm." Months later, the speaker is
back to sleeping with N. after she asks him "to tie her to a / cold radiator," while her
former lesbian lover can only sit nearby and "write poems entitled The Loss to / the
Heterosexual Dream." However, N. is annoyed when she learns that the speaker is
considering "writing an essay comparing / performance art to pornography." Such are
the limited, narrow concerns of most of the characters in this book, who are usually
interested mostly in various ways of having sex (rarely, if ever, in making or express-
ing love). They seem to have few of the concerns most people deal with daily or the
normal sources of happiness and satisfaction. Most of the persons who populate this
book seem to be living in an alternate bohemian universe, a kind of Greenwich Village
Twilight Zone populated by childish egotists. Part of the devastating effectiveness of
Berry's satire is that he manages to mock these people without ever obviously con-
demning them. The sarcasm and irony are merely implied, and half the fun of Berry's

own wit is the way he silently skewers people who pride themselves of being so witty, especially his navel-gazing speaker.

There are times in Berry's book, especially toward the end, when he does begin to call attention to the joke, just in case anyone may have missed it. At one point, for instance, the speaker says of the work of a fellow writer, "there are no people in his / poems, just a sensibility." Readers who are "in the know" will immediately realize this self-reflexive wit: Berry's speaker is alluding to the very kinds of poems in which he himself continually appears. Likewise, at one point the speaker fantasizes about his potential death and his desire not to be resuscitated if his case looks hopeless. This, too, is a bit of satirical cleverness about a speaker who rarely seems truly alive to begin with and who never faces any really serious challenges. Later, in an especially devastating example of implied satire, the speaker mentions the way Thomas Mann, on the day Hiroshima was destroyed by an atomic bomb, filled a whole diary entry by describing "how satisfied / and happy he was about the very nice / pair of shoes he had just bought." The speaker then continues:

> I think of this whenever someone
> tries to argue that writers are more
> sensitive—that they *feel* more than
> other people.

This is the key to the whole book, cleverly planted right there for anyone who had not already figured out what Berry has really been up to. A self-involved poet figure who ignores anything truly important: that is what this book is really all about.

Few contemporary poets could have pulled off a book as subtle but also as daring as this. Why risk offending one's peers by satirizing them so mercilessly? Not everyone would have been willing to tackle so comically the pretenses of modern urban academic culture, with its shallow values, superficial relationships, and trivial playing at life. Only a writer as shrewd as Berry could have made such an effort and succeeded so well.

Robert C. Evans

Review Sources

Cavalieri, Grace. "2015 Exemplars: Poetry Reviews by Grace Cavalieri." Rev. of *Monograph*, by Simeon Berry. *Washington Independent Review of Books*. Washington Independent, 20 Nov. 2015. Web. 4 Feb. 2016.

Delaney, Nora. "Kintsugi: On Two New Collections by Simeon Berry." Rev. of *Monograph*, by Simeon Berry. *Critical Flame: A Journal of Literature and Culture*. Critical Flame, 8 Nov. 2015. Web. 4 Feb. 2016.

Spuckler, Joseph. Rev. of *Monograph*, by Simeon Berry. *Evil Cyclist's Blog*. Spuck-
　　ler, 2 Aug. 2015. Web. 2 Feb. 2016.

More Happy Than Not

Author: Adam Silvera (b. 1990)
Publisher: Soho Press (New York). 304 pp.
Type of work: Novel
Time: Near future
Locale: Bronx, New York City

(Courtesy of Soho Teen)

More Happy Than Not is a young-adult novel by American author Adam Silvera that examines the role memory plays in people's lives as well as the meaning of happiness.

Principal characters:
AARON SOTO, the sixteen-year-old narrator
THOMAS, his new best friend
GENEVIEVE, his girlfriend
BRENDAN, his previous best friend, who has been growing distant
COLLIN, a friend from his past

Memories are often considered the building blocks of selfhood. A person's identity is an accumulation of the events, environment, and individuals that make up his or her formative years. Aligned to this belief is the idea that people whose pasts are fraught with trauma and hardship have little chance for normal, happy lives. In *More Happy Than Not*, author Adam Silvera explores this theory by examining the role of memory and identity in people's lives and posing the question of whether erasing a person's past can make for a better future.

Silvera has described his debut novel as semiautobiographical. While he originally drafted it as a memoir, he ultimately decided to rework *More Happy Than Not* as contemporary young-adult fiction with a science-fiction twist. Unfettered by the strict laws of realism, Silvera's narrative is able to explore the significance of identity and memory on a greater theoretical scale. To navigate these themes while staying true to his own adolescent experiences, Silvera employs Aaron Soto as the novel's protagonist and narrator. Aaron shares many characteristics with Silvera, in that he is Puerto Rican, struggles with depression, and lives in the Bronx projects. Unlike Silvera, however, Aaron does not realize that he is gay. Furthermore, he lives in the near future, where the technology exists for people to have unwanted memories erased.

The futurism of *More Happy Than Not* is contained exclusively to the plot device of the Leteo Institute, a fictitious organization that provides a memory-erasing service to residents of the Bronx. Silvera introduces the Leteo Institute and the concept of its procedure to readers on the novel's first page. This not only establishes a sense of the world that Aaron exists in but also aims to immediately dispel any disbelief readers may have about the Leteo procedure. In his narration, Aaron admits that he was initially skeptical of the procedure, but upon learning that his friend Kyle has successfully erased the memory of being responsible for the tragic death of his twin brother, Kenneth, he is convinced of its effectiveness.

Beyond facilitating readers' acceptance of *More Happy Than Not*'s futuristic elements, Silvera's decision to introduce the Leteo procedure at the beginning of the narrative also serves to establish it as a very real and very possible choice, a viable alternative for people who want to forget the emotionally challenging aspects of their lives. Aaron's life, it is soon revealed, involves a significant amount of personal hardship. Living with his mother and brother in a one-bedroom apartment in the Bronx, money is often hard for Aaron to come by, despite all three family members having jobs. Additionally, Aaron is still recovering from both his father's suicide and his own subsequent suicide attempt.

(Margot Wood)

Adam Silvera was born and raised in the Bronx. Before becoming a novelist, he worked as a bookseller and a marketing assistant. More Happy Than Not *(2015) is his first novel.*

More Happy Than Not is written in the first-person present tense, a literary style that infuses Aaron's narration with a confessional quality, lending it an honest, vulnerable tone that is particularly effective in young-adult fiction. Aaron's story begins two months after he tried to take his own life. In an effort to be happier, he has decided to focus on his relationship with his girlfriend, Genevieve. Aaron feels indebted to Genevieve; not only is she "a catch," but she has also continued to love him unconditionally despite his struggle with depression. To convey that Aaron and Genevieve are ostensibly the perfect couple, Silvera ensures that the two characters share analogous qualities: both are artists, love fantasy, and live in single-parent households in the Bronx projects.

While Aaron cares deeply for Genevieve and recognizes that she is objectively attractive, his inner dialogue suggests that there may be something missing in their relationship. He repeatedly notes that significant romantic moments between he and Genevieve are not as they should be. In what he considers to be embarrassing incidents of gender-role reversal, it is Genevieve who both asks Aaron to be her boyfriend and later facilitates the opportunity for them to have sex. When he is walking to her apartment, where the two plan to have sex for the first time, Aaron wonders why he is not running in excitement. By ensuring that Aaron's inner dialogue alludes to something being off but not providing any clues as to what, Silvera fashions Aaron as an unreliable narrator. Aaron's unreliability, although unwitting on his part, is what ultimately fosters the narrative's feeling of suspense and later allows for effective plot twists.

The problem in his relationship with Genevieve becomes clear once Aaron meets Thomas. Silvera employs the character of Thomas as the foil to Aaron's quest for normalcy, which he equates with happiness. When Aaron meets Thomas, he is in need of a good friend, and Brendan, whom he describes as his "sort of" best friend, has become increasingly emotionally unavailable. Once Genevieve goes away to art camp for the summer, Aaron and Thomas begin spending more time together. Thomas, unlike most of Aaron's peers, is sensitive, open-minded, and easy to talk to. Soon, Aaron begins speculating that there might be something more to their friendship.

When Aaron confesses that he is gay, Thomas compassionately accepts him for who he is but does not reciprocate his romantic feelings. Instead, he tells Aaron that he is certain of his own heterosexual orientation. Learning that he and Thomas can never be together, Aaron undergoes an identity crisis. He becomes determined to "reboot" himself by undergoing the Leteo procedure, believing that he will finally be able to find happiness if he can forget being gay. This decision, of whether or not to erase both his identity and the memories of the people he once cared about in order to make his life easier, becomes the central conflict in the novel's final act. To ensure that Aaron's decision is not easy, Silvera carefully portrays the potential downsides to each of the two options that he is considering. His purpose is to demonstrate that while being gay comes with challenges, not being gay does not automatically make life become better. For many people, happiness will always be hard to come by.

In interviews, Silvera has said that sexual orientation is commonly mistaken as an issue of nature versus nurture, when in fact people cannot choose whom they fall in love with. Consequently, he wanted to explore a fictional world where sexuality was actually a choice. To elevate the sense that Aaron is living in a world where he could choose this life or that, Silvera implements several symbolic dualities within the story. The twins Kyle and Kenneth are one such example; when Kyle erases the memory of Kenneth, Aaron witnesses firsthand how deeming someone forgettable invalidates his or her significance as a human being. In addition, Silvera presents Genevieve and Thomas as two opposing forces, pathways to different lifestyles. Aaron feels consistently torn between the two, a fact that manifests in the graphic novel that he is working on, in which the hero, Sun Warden, must decide between saving his girlfriend or his best friend.

As a young-adult novel, *More Happy Than Not* goes against many of the genre's standard literary norms. Although Silvera weaves common adolescent themes of alienation and self-hatred into the narrative, *More Happy Than Not* is unusual in the fact that its protagonist is gay and Latino. Silvera also veers away from catering to mainstream audiences by using authentic, often profane adolescent language and depicting scenes of sex and substance use without serious consequences. Perhaps even more revolutionary is the setting of *More Happy Than Not*. By having Aaron's story exist solely in a poor neighborhood in the Bronx, Silvera defies the unspoken, commonly held notion that the stories of poor and working-class characters are only worth exploring peripherally. Moreover, Silvera's portrayal of poverty is notable for its multidimensionality; while being poor presents Aaron with challenges, it does not define his life or his relationships.

Silvera ensures that the central theme of happiness is everywhere throughout the narrative, from Aaron's internal dialogue to the smiley faces printed within the novel's chapter titles. Yet happiness continually eludes Aaron himself. Silvera's decision to focus on happiness stems from his own struggles with depression. Through Aaron's story, Silvera is able to examine the fickle nature of happiness and its relationship to hardship. Through the character of Thomas, Silvera expresses that hardship is necessary, as it enables people to recognize happiness. Consequently, erasing one's self, no matter how bad one's memories may be, eradicates a person's ability to appreciate what it means to be happy.

More Happy Than Not has been met with widespread acclaim by critics, who praised Silvera for his deft ability to balance and explore the complex social issues of sexual identity, class politics, and traumatic memory. His genuine depiction of adolescence outside of the white, middle-class, heterosexual experience is notable not just for its authenticity but for its representation of an otherwise severely underrepresented demographic. Ginia Bellafante noted in a review for the *New York Times* that *More Happy Than Not* is powerful because it truly captures the challenges of coming out in an environment that lacks a progressive perspective on sexuality. While Ebony Elizabeth Thomas of the *Los Angeles Times* also described *More Happy Than Not* as revolutionary, her commendation focused more on the fact that it is a piece of science fiction led by young, diverse characters.

Silvera's highly engaging narrative can be attributed to his skillful employment of a variety of literary tools, including an authentic unreliable narrator, plot twists, and flashbacks. Silvera also succeeds in captivating readers' attention and driving the story forward by infusing the novel with personal meaning. By mining his own experiences and struggles as a gay teenager in the Bronx, Silvera has been able to craft a clear, genuine message about the ubiquitous human struggle for self-acceptance. Ultimately, this message acts as the guiding force to which Silvera aligns his plot.

More Happy Than Not has been compared to the film *Eternal Sunshine of the Spotless Mind* (2004). While this comparison could be interpreted as a criticism of Silvera's lack of originality, it is important to note that Silvera has stated in interviews that he had never heard of the film when he originally conceived the idea for the novel. Despite the plot device of a memory-erasing service having been used before, *More Happy Than Not* leverages it in a new, original way. By focusing on the roles that traumatic memory and sexual identity play in people's lives, Silvera is ultimately able to create a wholly unique and unpredictable narrative. A poignant coming-of-age story, *More Happy Than Not* is an important book for the next generation.

Emily E. Turner

Review Sources

Bellafante, Ginia. Rev. of *More Happy Than Not*, by Adam Silvera. *New York Times*. New York Times, 19 June 2015. Web. 23 Dec. 2015.

Rev. of *More Happy Than Not*, by Adam Silvera. *Kirkus Reviews* 15 Apr. 2015: 65. Print.

Quiroa, Ruth. Rev. of *More Happy Than Not*, by Adam Silvera. *School Library Journal* May 2015: 124. Print.

Thomas, Ebony Elizabeth. "YA Science Fiction Delights: *Shadowshaper* and *More Happy Than Not*." Rev. of *Shadowshaper*, by Daniel José Older, and *More Happy Than Not*, by Adam Silvera. *Los Angeles Times*. Tribune, 18 June 2015. Web. 23 Dec. 2015.

Most Dangerous
Daniel Ellsberg and the Secret History of the Vietnam War

Author: Steve Sheinkin (b. 1968)
Publisher: Roaring Brook Press (New York). 370 pp.
Type of work: Literary history
Time: 1960s and 1970s
Locales: United States, Vietnam

Steve Sheinkin writes a lucid and suspenseful account of the United States' involvement in the Vietnam War for a younger audience, focusing on Daniel Ellsberg, the military analyst turned whistle-blower who leaked the Pentagon Papers. The publication of the top-secret government documents played a significant role in ending the war and engendered the Watergate scandal, which led to the resignation of President Richard Nixon in 1974.

Principal personages:
DANIEL ELLSBERG, military analyst turned antiwar activist and government whistle-blower
PATRICIA (MARX) ELLSBERG, his wife, a journalist
RICHARD NIXON, president of the United States from 1969 to 1974
HENRY KISSINGER, secretary of state from 1973 to 1977 and Nixon's close advisor, an architect of the war in Vietnam
ROBERT MCNAMARA, secretary of defense from 1961 to 1968

For most American adults, the words Pentagon Papers, Watergate, the Cold War, and Vietnam have a real and visceral meaning, if not a direct relationship with lived experience. But for a generation of young people, however well informed, these words can be an abstraction, a template upon which modern-day events can be contextually placed. The Vietnam War—and its corresponding domestic fallout—is often presented as a kind of historical quagmire, impossible to fully comprehend beyond its dangerous miscalculations and dated political rhetoric.

However, Steve Sheinkin, an award-winning author of young-adult literature and a former textbook writer, does not share this view of the period. His new book *Most Dangerous: Daniel Ellsberg and the Secret History of the Vietnam War* is a fast-paced, lucid account of the adult life of Daniel Ellsberg, the former military analyst who leaked an incriminating report about the war known as the Pentagon Papers, and a history of US involvement in Vietnam going back to World War II. Sheinkin's book educates without condescending to its younger audience and reads like a political thriller. From the absurd comedy of the Plumbers, the clumsy task force that broke into the office of Ellsberg's psychiatrist in Los Angeles and the office of the Democratic National Committee (DNC) at the Watergate apartment complex in Washington, DC, to the grotesque method of scorekeeping on the ground in Vietnam known as the "kill ratio," Sheinkin unspools his story with humor, verve, and humanity. *Most Dangerous* is aimed at teenage readers, but adults would do well to read it, too. The book does not merely explain the debts a current generation of young people owes their elders; it implores people of all ages to see their own place in history differently.

Before the publication of *Most Dangerous*, which was a finalist for the National Book Award for young people's literature in 2015, Sheinkin was best known for a 2010 book about Benedict Arnold, the infamous traitor of the American Revolutionary War, and *Bomb: The Race to Build—and Steal—the World's Most Dangerous Weapon* in 2012. *Bomb* was also a finalist for the National Book Award. Sheinkin is attracted to stories that are exciting to tell, but also ones that raise moral and ethical questions about how people and governments should behave. In *Bomb*, Sheinkin invites readers to think about the consequences of building the atomic bomb and then using it in Japan to end World War II. In *Most Dangerous*, he encourages a healthy skepticism of government leaders and policies enacted in the name of national security. Sheinkin takes the reader through Ellsberg's agonized decision to leak the Pentagon Papers, and then, the Supreme Court's careful decision upholding his right (or rather, the right of the *New York Times*) to share them with the public. Even Sheinkin's title begs a question: Was Ellsberg, as then secretary of state Henry Kissinger famously said, "the most dangerous man in America?" Or was he the exact opposite?

After a brief prologue foreshadowing the events leading to Watergate, *Most Dangerous* begins in 1964. Ellsberg, a brilliant economist, is hired by the US Department of Defense. On his first day, August 2, there is a mysterious disturbance in the Gulf of Tonkin, half a world away. Though it is not immediately clear what caused the disturbance, the White House chooses to believe that the USS *Maddox* was attacked by Communist forces and responds by bombing North Vietnam. (The reports were soon proven inaccurate—the crew of USS *Maddox* thought they were under attack but were not.) The bombing is the first decisive action in the Vietnam War.

At the time, Ellsberg was a self-described "Cold Warrior"; he supported the United States' policy of "containment," which dictated that Communism must not spread past the borders in which it already existed. North Vietnam was Communist, but South Vietnam—however problematic its government—was not. For North Vietnam to overtake South Vietnam would be a foreign-policy failure. Ellsberg played a significant part in escalating the war early on. Following an order from Secretary of Defense Robert McNamara, he compiled lists of atrocities perpetrated by North Vietnamese soldiers, or the Viet Cong, in an effort to convince President Lyndon Johnson to approve a sustained bombing campaign in North Vietnam. By the war's end, the United States dropped twice as many bombs on Vietnam, Laos, and Cambodia than it had in Europe and Asia during World War II.

Steve Sheinkin is an award-winning author and a former textbook author and teacher. His books for young adults include The Notorious Benedict Arnold: A True Story of Adventure, Heroism and Treachery *(2010) and* Bomb: The Race to Build—and Steal—the World's Most Dangerous Weapon *(2012), which was a finalist for the National Book Award.*

In 1965, as an employee of the State Department, Ellsberg traveled to Vietnam. He was tasked with winning the "hearts and minds" of South Vietnamese citizens, convincing them that the Americans were their allies—not Ho Chi Minh, the leader of the North Vietnamese. Ellsberg traveled from village to village learning about land mines and frightened local militias. He learned that most Vietnamese were ambivalent about the war—they did not care who won, they just wanted it to be over. Later, he followed an American platoon slogging through North Vietnam, enduring constant attacks from Viet Cong hidden in the dense forests. He saw the frustration of the soldiers as they hacked through rice paddies on their never-ending march, observing, "It was hard to believe we were accomplishing anything at all." Ellsberg's experiences in Vietnam (he returned to the United States in 1967) contributed to his changing views about the war and his growing anger at the White House for perpetuating it. His change of heart coincided with public opinion, which turned strongly against the war in 1968, the same year that Nixon was elected president.

Ellsberg first read the seven thousand–page report now known as the Pentagon Papers in 1968. The report was commissioned by McNamara and was meant to educate future administrations about the government's failures in Vietnam. What it amounted to, however, was a well-documented story of deception that began in the Truman administration. If US policy was failing in Vietnam, Ellsberg had wondered, why stay? Why continue to wage a costly, unwinnable war? With the reports as evidence, the answer was as painfully simple as it was inhumane: no president wanted to claim responsibility for a lost war. Yet there was no way to win the war, so each president sent just enough troops to Vietnam (never as many as generals on the ground asked for) to perpetuate the conflict until the next election.

Still, it took Ellsberg a year to decide to leak the Pentagon Papers to the public, and another two years to copy the document and get it into the hands of the press. (Ellsberg spent months lugging the papers around, painstakingly copying them on Xerox machines; Sheinkin wryly notes in the epilogue that the entire report would, today, be copied instantly and take up only a fraction of space on a ten-dollar flash drive.) The *New York Times* began to publish the papers on June 13, 1971—though Ellsberg's role did not end there. After a judge forced the newspaper to stop printing the Pentagon Papers, Ellsberg and his small coterie of allies distributed the remaining documents at newspapers around the United States. The Pentagon Papers tarnished the government's reputation, but they did little to affect how the public saw President Nixon, specifically. The papers, after all, mostly focused on previous administrations—but Nixon went after Ellsberg as a matter of principle. He directed his aides to dig up dirt on Ellsberg in order to publicly smear him. However, after the scheme was discovered, it worked in Ellsberg's favor. The legal case against him—in which it looked likely that he would be sentenced to life in prison—was thrown out, and in 1974, two years after his landslide reelection, Nixon resigned the presidency in disgrace.

Critics praised *Most Dangerous* for being well written, well researched, and timely; indeed, in the book's epilogue, Sheinkin briefly relates the tale of Edward Snowden, who, in 2013, leaked thousands of documents that revealed a domestic spying program overseen by the National Security Agency (NSA). Sheinkin draws a comparison between the two men, noting that Snowden is still wanted on the same charges that Ellsberg serendipitously avoided over forty years ago. In 2014, Ellsberg wrote an op-ed for the *Guardian* in support of Snowden in which he decried the Espionage Act. (Ellsberg was the first American to ever be charged under the act—Snowden's would be one of many subsequent cases.) But the moral of Sheinkin's book has little to do with legal matters, and all to do with keeping authority in check. He subtly divides the book's numerous characters between those who follow orders blindly and those who stop to think about them. In one passage, he quotes White House aide Egil Krogh, who was put in charge of forming the special tasks unit that became known as the Plumbers. He followed the orders handed down by Nixon's close advisor, he later said, because "I certainly wasn't in the habit of questioning the orders or wisdom of my superiors."

Molly Hagan

Review Sources

Grandin, Greg. Rev. of *Most Dangerous: Daniel Ellsberg and the Secret History of the Vietnam War*, by Steve Sheinkin. *New York Times*. New York Times, 6 Nov. 2015. Web. 20 Jan. 2016.

Kopple, Jody. Rev. of *Most Dangerous: Daniel Ellsberg and the Secret History of the Vietnam War*, by Steve Sheinkin. *School Library Journal*. SLJ, 3 Sept. 2015. Web. 20 Jan. 2016.

Rev. of *Most Dangerous: Daniel Ellsberg and the Secret History of the Vietnam War*, by Steve Sheinkin. *Publishers Weekly*. PWxyz, 1 Sept. 2015. Web. 20 Jan. 2016.

Nolan, Abby McGanney. "*Most Dangerous*: A Fast-Paced Young People's Biography of Daniel Ellsberg." Rev. of *Most Dangerous: Daniel Ellsberg and the Secret History of the Vietnam War*, by Steve Sheinkin. *Washington Post*. Washington Post, 14 Sept. 2015. Web. 20 Jan. 2016.

Parravano, Martha V. Rev. of *Most Dangerous: Daniel Ellsberg and the Secret History of the Vietnam War*, by Steve Sheinkin. *Horn Book Magazine*. Horn Book, 25 Aug. 2015. Web. 20 Jan. 2016.

Mothers, Tell Your Daughters

Author: Bonnie Jo Campbell (b. 1962)
Publisher: W. W. Norton (New York). 272
   pp.
Type of work: Short fiction
Time: Present day
Locale: Michigan

Bonnie Jo Campbell tells the stories of women of all ages in Mothers, Tell Your Daughters, *a set of tales that encourages women to take care of themselves and each other.*

Principal characters:

MARY BETCHER, a woman who cares for her
   dying husband
SHERRY, a woman whose desire to love and
   be loved alienates her family
JANIE, a young woman who comes to terms
   with problems of substance abuse
MARIKA, a generous girl who gives everything away
BUCKEYE, a circus worker in love with an abused man

Mothers, Tell Your Daughters is a collection of short stories that addresses issues affecting women of all ages. Though the focus is on middle-class women, many of the characters have a lower socioeconomic status. The characters and situations vary from teenage girls sneaking make-out sessions to women at or near the end of their lives. Some women struggle to understand the purpose of their experiences, while others struggle with the ups and downs of sexuality.

One notable aspect of the collection is author Bonnie Jo Campbell's talent for intertwining several themes in each story. Themes of marriage, divorce, pregnancy, abortion, parenting, and sexuality work alongside issues of silence, caution, fear, and awakening. The title story, which appears sixth out of sixteen stories, contains many of these ideas. It relates the experiences of an unnamed woman who has had a stroke. While she lies in bed reflecting on her life, she is entrapped by the silencing force of her stroke. Though she wants to share her regrets with her middle-aged daughter, she is unable to do so. As the story progresses, her daughter's bitter relationship with her mother is clarified, as readers learn that the mother allowed her child to be molested by a man that she, the mother, had brought into the home. Both women struggle with the tragic aftermath of that abuse, and the mother realizes that her choice to later return to a relationship with that man created a breach that cannot be mended between herself and her daughter. This story, among others in the book, portrays the potentially tragic effects of silence, the mistakes mothers make, and the judgments that daughters construct.

The second story in the collection, "Playhouse," gives a glimpse into the life of Janie, a young woman in her twenties, who also battles the repercussions of silence. It starts with Janie wondering whether she should have remained silent after an argument with her brother, who is the custodial parent of his three-year-old daughter. The fight, which took place at a party he hosted, led Janie to imbibe more alcohol than she should have, resulting in a blackout. She finds out that she was raped by two of her brother's friends during that lost time and that her brother knew of the rape, but he neither did anything to protect her nor empathized with her afterward. She questions whether keeping silent about her niece drinking all of the leftover alcohol at the party would have saved her from her brother's silence and the memories of the rape that are starting to overwhelm her.

Many of the characters in the tales struggle with issues relating to molestation or sexual assault. In a way that brings Dorothy Allison's short stories from *Trash* (1988) or her novel *Bastard out of Carolina* (1992) to mind, Campbell includes at least four pieces where a young girl is molested by an older man. "Mothers, Tell Your Daughters" shows a mother who chose her lover over her daughter. However, in the story "Tell Yourself," Campbell relates a mother's fears that her daughter will be molested. The main character is so overwhelmed by her own abuse as a young woman that she is almost paralyzed by fear. As a result, she cannot have a healthy relationship with a man, and she worries constantly about her daughter's relationships with the men she comes into contact with throughout her life. In "To You as a Woman," another single mother is so trapped in poverty that she allows a neighbor man to babysit her seven-year-old son and two-year-old daughter despite the red flags the man's behavior sends up. She feels especially hopeless after being gang-raped right outside her apartment. Campbell does something slightly different with the idea in "Somewhere Warm." In this story, Sherry is the middle-aged divorced mother of a sixteen-year-old daughter. The daughter accuses Sherry of causing problems in her marriage because she smothered her husband with her love. To pay her mother back for her father's departure, the girl seduces Sherry's new twenty-five-year-old boyfriend, and the two run off together.

Some readers may find it difficult to handle the collection's overwhelming sense of hopelessness and despair. There are, however, a number of stories that hint at a more hopeful ending for the women and girls involved. In "A Multitude of Sins," for example, Carl Betcher's wife, Mary, has been cowed by her husband her whole life. The story starts with the news that Carl has a brain tumor that is slowly killing him. The elderly Mary, as his primary caregiver, has to put up with constant verbal and physical abuse that is excused by his mental state and medication side effects. The problem is that Carl has been emotionally and physically abusing Mary their whole marriage; this behavior is nothing new. One day when Carl hits her, Mary's reserve breaks, and she strikes back, at last realizing that she has the power to protect herself. Maybe because her husband can no longer comprehend her, she makes strides to become her own woman. In doing this, she begins to tell him what she has thought silently about him for years. She turns the torture he put her and their children through around and begins to control the reigns of her own destiny. Her final empowerment comes after Carl's death with the thought that she should have taken care of her own desires first rather than trying to save them for last and having them be trampled into the ground; she grabs handfuls of life and charges into the new philosophy. Much as the stories about molestation bring comparisons to Allison, Mary's transformation may remind readers of Kate Chopin's 1899 novella *The Awakening*, but with a more positive ending.

"Blood Work, 1999" is another more upbeat tale. In this story, Marika is a phlebotomist, the best and most sought after in the area. She revels in the fact that when the hospital where she works eliminated all phlebotomist positions, they kept only Marika on. Yet Marika spends her whole life, and a small fortune, trying to help others rather than standing up for herself. By the end of the tale, she decides that helping a patient feel alive, despite knowledge that she could lose her job, is vital, and as the story ends, she "felt herself bursting open like flowers in sunlight, overflowing into the new millennium."

A third protagonist who finds her life changing in a positive way is Johanna, a twenty-five-year-old woman who discovers herself and her own desires for the first time while visiting Romania at a time when the country is ruled by a cruel dictator. In "Children of Transylvania," a poor Romanian couple's wedding celebration teaches Johanna that happiness can be found even when soldiers thunder past, threatening the very lives of the celebrants. The awakening of the characters in these three pieces provides some encouragement for a woman's ability to move beyond the realms of abuse, self-destruction, and loss of self.

Campbell also finds a way to introduce some humor into the collection through a number of ironic situations. In "My Dog Roscoe," the narrator, a young pregnant woman, adopts a stray dog who she thinks is the reincarnation of her late fiancé, Oscar. Since Oscar died when he fell out of the hayloft where he was having sex with someone else, it is fitting that he would come back as a dog. As the young woman projects Oscar's traits onto the dog, Roscoe, she is able to work through her lingering feelings about their relationship and move on with the better man whom she has married.

Bonnie Jo Campbell was a 2011 Guggenheim Fellow. She holds an MFA in writing from Western Michigan University and teaches writing for Pacific University. She writes both novels and short stories and has won several awards for her short fiction.

Aside from the thematic range, another notable trait of the collection is Campbell's use of point of view to draw readers into the experiences of her characters. For instance, "Playhouse" is told in first person, creating a connection between Janie, whose experiences are beyond the scope of many readers' lives. The first-person narration enhances the tragic irony in "Mothers, Tell Your Daughters" as the silenced mother talks to her daughter for the first time, while her daughter is unable to hear her mother's outpouring. Campbell switches into second-person pronouns in several stories to engage reader empathy. This is most notable in "Tell Yourself," where the main character cautions mothers to protect their daughters while she remembers her own abuse:

You close your eyes and tell yourself that not all men are like that neighbor who allowed you to skip school at his house and smoke bowl after bowl until you couldn't form a complete sentence. Not all teachers—even those who take a girl's hair in their hands— are like your tall, brown-eyed social-science teacher, whose attentions flattered you so much that you would never have said no.

If the intensity of the first- and second-person pronouns becomes too heavy, Campbell falls back on third person in many stories to provide some distance from the often overwhelming sadness and fear in the collection.

With its combination of tragedy, hope, and dark comedy, this collection of stories is one that can reach all audiences, especially audiences of women who will be able to relate in some way to at least one character in the set. Further, Campbell's masterful use of first-, second-, and third-person point of view draws readers into women's experiences in such a way that even the most despicable choices can be understood.

Theresa L. Stowell

Review Sources

Bettencourt, Donna. Rev. of *Mothers, Tell Your Daughters*, by Bonnie Jo Campbell. *Library Journal* 1
    Aug. 2015: 90. Print.
Flowers, Mark, and Meghan Cirrito. Rev. of *Mothers, Tell Your Daughters*, by Bonnie Jo Campbell.
    School Library Journal Dec. 2015: 38. Print.
Rev. of *Mothers, Tell Your Daughters*, by Bonnie Jo Campbell. *Kirkus Reviews* 1
    Aug. 2015: 9–10. Print.
Rev. of *Mothers, Tell Your Daughters*, by Bonnie Jo Campbell. *Publishers Weekly* 3
    Aug. 2015: 31–32.
Seaman, Donna. Rev. of *Mothers, Tell Your Daughters*, by Bonnie Jo Campbell.
    Booklist 1 Aug. 2015: 29. Print.

Mrs. Engels

Author: Gavin McCrea (b. 1978)
Publisher: Catapult (New York). 389 pp.
Type of work: Novel
Time: 1842–78
Locales: Manchester and London, England

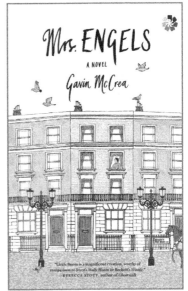

(Courtesy of Catapult)

Mrs. Engels, the first novel from the Irish writer Gavin McCrea, brings to vivid life Lizzie Burns, the illiterate, working-class companion of Friedrich Engels, coauthor—with Karl Marx—of The Communist Manifesto. *From Lizzie's perspective, readers experience Marx and Engels wrestling with domestic complications while they strive to inspire a revolution.*

Principal characters:

LIZZIE BURNS, the longtime companion and eventual wife of Friedrich Engels
MARY BURNS, her sister and Engels's first common-law wife
MOSS O'MALLEY, her first love and an Irish nationalist
FRIEDRICH ENGELS, her lover and husband as well as the leader, with Karl Marx, of the Communist movement
KARL MARX, Engels's friend and leader and chief theoretician of the Communist movement
JENNY MARX, Karl Marx's wife
ELEANOR "TUSSY" MARX, Karl and Jenny Marx's daughter
HELENE "NIM" DEMUTH, Karl and Jenny Marx's housekeeper

Gavin McCrea was inspired to write *Mrs. Engels* when he learned of Lizzie Burns, the illiterate Irish working-class woman who lived with Friedrich Engels for fifteen years before he married her as she lay dying. Little is known of Lizzie Burns; she left no record for posterity. Yet she was a witness to the labors of Engels and his lifelong friend Karl Marx, the men who founded the Communist movement and cowrote *The Communist Manifesto* (1848). In *Mrs. Engels*, McCrea makes Lizzie the first-person narrator of the story. The result is a captivating novel that renders Lizzie far more interesting than the famous people around her.

Mrs. Engels is an imaginative piece of historical fiction that relies on the successful resuscitation of the shadowy character of Lizzie. To accomplish this feat, McCrea did extensive research for the novel, including combing through the voluminous correspondence of Marx and Engels. He is able to convincingly evoke these men in the story. He also offers brilliantly rendered pictures of Manchester and London, giving them the three-dimensional life that can be found in the detailed novels of the great Victorians William Makepeace Thackeray, Charles Dickens, and Anthony Trollope. However, Lizzie propels the novel forward. It is McCrea's ability to limn a vibrant personality on the page, to provide a compelling and plausible voice to Lizzie that lifts the novel from history lesson into art. Lizzie's mordant, pragmatic, yet passionate perspective throws textbook delineations of Marx and Engels off-kilter. McCrea does not portray Marx and Engels as the retrospectively lionized giants of international socialism. Rather, readers are able to see these eminent men humanized through the eyes of a genuine proletarian, for whom their books and speeches are decidedly secondary to their conventional domestic relations. The result is unsettling, illuminating, and often humorous.

(Eugene Langan)

Gavin McCrea received an MA from University College Dublin and a PhD from the University of East Anglia. Mrs. Engels *is his first novel.*

The novel begins in 1870, as Lizzie and Engels prepare to take up residence in London. Although Lizzie and Engels's officially unmarried state shocks the neighboring ladies, there is nothing else unconventional, and certainly nothing proletarian, about their living arrangements. They reside in a comfortable townhouse in a fashionable neighborhood. For the first time in her life, Lizzie finds herself supervising a small team of servants. This situation sets up one of the central paradoxes of the novel: the distance between Marx and Engels's revolutionary principles and their cozily bourgeois lifestyle. Lizzie notes but is untroubled by this disparity between word and action. She grew up in working-class poverty and wants nothing more to do with it.

Much of the book consists of flashbacks to Lizzie's early life. She and her sister, Mary, were born in the industrial slums of Manchester. Penniless and without prospects, they worked in the Ermen and Engels textile mill. There, Mary, who was spirited and pretty, met Engels in 1842. His parents had dispatched him from Germany to learn about the family business. An easygoing womanizer, Engels was entranced by Mary. Already a radical despite his family's wealth, he disregarded Mary's low social standing, and she became his guide to the world of his workers. After returning to mainland Europe in 1844, Engels began his partnership with Karl Marx. Returning to England and his position at the mill in 1849, he also resumed his relationship with Mary. They would live together until her death in 1863.

Meanwhile, early in her life, Lizzie had her own abortive fling with romance. She took up with a young Irishman named Moss O'Malley, living with him for a time. However, the relationship did not work out because of O'Malley's drinking, and she left him to move in with her sister. Over the course of years she became close to

Engels, and when Mary died, their shared grief brought them together; Lizzie took the place of her sister. In the novel, she is always uncomfortably aware that she was the second sister in Engels's affections.

In London, Lizzie must negotiate the complexities of the relationship between Marx and Engels. The Marx family now lives nearby, and as the de facto spouse of Engels, Lizzie must deal with Marx's wife, Jenny. Being the wife of a revolutionary thinker and activist is not an easy task, and Jenny struggles to aid her husband while maintaining a measure of gentility for her daughters and herself. Here, McCrea imaginatively explores the moral implications of the actual historical bond between Marx and Engels. The fundamental problem was that Marx could not support his family. As a result, Engels came to play an outsized role in the life of the Marx household. As far as the Communist movement was concerned, Engels freely conceded that Marx was the senior figure in their partnership. Yet Marx became dependent upon the financial assistance of his well-off friend. For years, Engels was the guardian of the Marx family, ever ready to rush to its defense, even at real sacrifice to himself.

In the novel, Engels's readiness to subordinate his interests to those of Marx becomes a major theme. On one occasion, his devotion to his friend deeply affects his relationship with Mary and Lizzie. The consequences of this action are worked out through the course of the book. Lizzie must endure the defensive pride of Jenny, who, for all her ideological egalitarianism, remains uncomfortably aware of her former elevated social status and her current dependence on Engels. Yet Jenny cannot do what she did with Mary and refuse to acknowledge her. In her relations with Jenny, Lizzie becomes the feminine counterpart to Engels. Commonsensical and always ready to quite literally get her hands dirty, Lizzie becomes a problem-solving bulwark on which the ever-needy Jenny can lean. Initially exasperated with Jenny, Lizzie eventually begins to have great respect for her—she comes to sympathize with the travails of a woman united to a revolutionary.

Lizzie does not limit herself to the intricacies of managing a household staff or immersion in the subtle dramas of the Marx family circle. She starts searching for O'Malley, reputed to be living in London, because she has emotionally unfinished business with her first love. O'Malley had stopped drinking after Lizzie walked out and threw himself into the Irish struggle for independence, joining the Fenians, a secret organization dedicated to the armed struggle against British rule in Ireland. Lizzie learned of this while still living in Manchester and even gave O'Malley and some of his comrades shelter for a night at her home after an attempt to liberate some prisoners from the Manchester police. Finding O'Malley in London years later is difficult because he is a fugitive from the British authorities. To locate him, she must wend her way through the slums of London's East End, utilizing the street smarts that she has never lost.

For Lizzie, a reckoning with O'Malley is a judgement on the whole trajectory of her life that offers a way to evaluate the choice she made in living with Engels. The union with Engels has provided security and the trappings of a rise in station. She loves Engels, but she must share him with the memory of her sister, the Marxes, and his work. The promise of passion and adventure, O'Malley engenders nagging questions about what might have been. Ironically, O'Malley the Fenian is more of a revolutionary man of action than the Communist Marx and Engels, maneuvering for the overthrow of capitalism through books and platform speeches. Involving herself with O'Malley would put Lizzie at much greater risk than her association with the Communist movement.

By the end of the book, Lizzie finds herself caught in a web of dilemmas. She sees the implication of deeds far more clearly than the people around her. Though she was denied a formal education, she is a woman of deep feelings; the crux of the novel is her effort to sort these out. She finds herself juggling the demands placed on her by Engels, O'Malley, the Marxes, and her own conscience. To decide her future, she must make choices. To resolve these choices, she relies not on the ethical imperatives of nationalism or socialism, but on the promptings of her own moral compass.

McCrea brings his novel to a satisfying conclusion, resolving Lizzie's quest to do the right thing without doing violence to the historical record. This is no mean achievement. Readers will learn a good deal about the founders of Communism and nineteenth-century England. Lizzie becomes a truly memorable literary character, one that readers will find themselves thinking about long after they have set down the book. Critics were largely impressed by McCrea's debut effort and came to the same consensus, praising his success in giving a little-known figure such depth of character while also using this unique angle to provide greater insight into the personal lives of Engels and Marx. In a starred entry, the reviewer for *Publishers Weekly* wrote, "McCrea gives the illiterate Lizzie a vivid, convincing voice, sparkling with energy and not untouched by pathos." *Mrs. Engels* was long-listed for the 2015 Guardian First Book Award.

Daniel Murphy

Review Sources

Ciuraru, Carmela. "Review: New Novels by Paul Murray, César Aira and Others." Rev. of *Mrs. Engels*, by Gavin McCrea. *New York Times*. New York Times, 28 Oct. 2015. Web. 22 Feb. 2016.
Rev. of *Mrs. Engels*, by Gavin McCrea. *Publishers Weekly* 22 June 2015: 119. Print.
Sacks, Sam. "Fiction Chronicle: The Communist's Wife's Manifesto." Rev. of *Mrs. Engels*, by Gavin McCrea. *Wall Street Journal*. Dow Jones, 9 Oct. 2015. Web. 22 Feb. 2016.
Stidham, Jennifer B. Rev. of *Mrs. Engels*, by Gavin McCrea. *Library Journal* 1 Aug. 2015: 87. Print.
Stuart, Jan. "Faction." Rev. of *Mrs. Engels*, by Gavin McCrea. *New York Times*. New York Times, 20 Nov. 2015. Web. 22 Feb. 2016.
Wilkinson, Joanne. Rev. of *Mrs. Engels*, by Gavin McCrea. *Booklist* 1 Sept. 2015: 52. Print.

My Life on the Road

Author: Gloria Steinem (b. 1934)
Publisher: Random House (New York). 304 pp.
Type of work: Memoir
Time: 1930s–present
Locale: United States

Longtime feminist activist and author Gloria Steinem writes about how her unusual upbringing and years of travel have shaped her world view in her memoir My Life on the Road.

Principal personages:

GLORIA STEINEM, the author
LEO STEINEM, her father
FLORYNCE KENNEDY, her former speaking partner, a lawyer and civil rights and feminism activist
WILMA MANKILLER, her friend, a feminist activist who became a chief of the Cherokee Nation
BETTY FRIEDAN, an influential women's rights activist
HILLARY CLINTON, American politician who first campaigned for the Democratic presidential nomination in 2008

When Gloria Steinem, the eighty-one-year-old feminist activist and writer, was a child, she did not attend a regular elementary school. The schedule would have interfered with her father's intense wanderlust, which struck with a regularity the family otherwise lacked. During the summer, Leo Steinem ran a dance pavilion near a lake in rural Michigan. He hired big acts of the day, such as Duke Ellington and the Andrews Sisters, to play and invited locals to come and dance. But when the summer season ended, Leo loaded his family—Steinem, her older sister, and her mother, Ruth—into the family car and set out for either California to the west or Florida to the east. The family operated this way for years, though Steinem writes that her father embarked on each excursion as if it had occurred to him on a whim. "Sometimes this leave-taking happened so quickly that we packed more frying pans than plates, or left a kitchen full of dirty dishes and half-eaten food to great us like Pompeii on our return," she writes. To make money for gas and food, Leo sold antiques, cutting a well-worn trail of dealers across the country in every direction.

Steinem has written about her mother in the past. Her famous 1983 essay "Ruth's Song (Because She Could Not Sing It)" is a moving account of her mother's budding career in journalism, cut short by marriage; her constant anxieties about money and travel; and her subsequent poverty, mental illness, and death. But in Steinem's new book, a memoir called *My Life on the Road*, she explores her own wanderlust and complicated feelings about "home," finding that all roads lead back to her father.

My Life on the Road is not a standard, chronologically structured autobiography. While early chapters discuss Steinem's early life, subsequent chapters are arranged thematically, moving between poignant events and people in her life and the women's movement. One, "Talking Circles," discusses Steinem's trip to India in the 1950s, where she developed ideas about political organization that would sustain her career for more than fifty years. Another chapter, "Surrealism in Everyday Life," is a collection of strange anecdotes culled from taxi drivers (Steinem does not drive), flight attendants, and other people she has met along her travels. Some reviewers have noted that chunks of Steinem's book are essentially recycled from her previous works. (*My Life on the Road* is Steinem's first book in over twenty years; her last was *Revolution from Within: A Book of Self-Esteem*, published in 1992.) While *My Life on the Road* seems an appropriate vessel for all it contains—Steinem does appear to have quite literally spent her life "on the road"—the most successful passages are the ones in which she wrestles with what she has learned from the people she has known (her father, the late American Indian activist and Cherokee chief Wilma Mankiller, her one-time speaking partner Florynce Kennedy) and why she feels compelled to live in constant motion despite a deep yearning to settle down.

Steinem's parents separated when she was a preteen, and she and her mother moved, first to a small town in Massachusetts near where her sister was going to college, and then to a ramshackle farmhouse in Toledo, Ohio. Steinem became a caretaker for her mother, who suffered from delusions and depression. During her senior year of high school, her father took over as Ruth's caretaker, and Steinem went to live with her sister in Washington, DC. She worked on her first political campaign: Adlai Stevenson's unsuccessful 1952 presidential campaign, where she and other young female staffers were relegated to a back room whenever the candidate came to visit. (Stevenson was—very controversially at the time—divorced, and his strategists did not want him to be seen with any younger woman who could not plausibly pass as his mother.) After attending Smith College in Massachusetts, Steinem won a fellowship opportunity to travel to India. She spent two years in the country, arriving only a few years after the partition in 1947.

In India, Steinem traveled by railway, booking her ticket in carriages reserved for women only. She spent weeks with the women in her car, who welcomed her into their lives. It was her first inkling that there was power in bringing women together. After disembarking at an ashram in Kerala, in southern India, she was immediately drafted as a member of a peacekeeping team headed for a nearby rural village. She found herself invited into the women's quarters there and participating in talking circles. "It was the first time I witnessed the ancient and modern magic of groups in which anyone may speak in turn, everyone must listen, and consensus is more important than time," Steinem writes. She adds that talking circles, already a common practice in American Indian and African American communities in the United States, would give birth to the American feminist movement of which Steinem would become an integral part.

Upon returning from India, Steinem took a job as a journalist. She rarely got to report real news, being relegated mostly to celebrity profiles or style pieces, and she began to think critically about women and their role in the world. Eventually, she wrote a piece for *New York* magazine inspired by the civil rights movement, titled "After Black Power, Women's Liberation." In *My Life on the Road*, Steinem emphasizes her involvement with the civil rights movement and her support for nonwhite women within the feminist movement. Early in her career, she struggled with a paralyzing fear of public speaking and agreed to speak only with a partner; her first such partner was the electric Florynce "Flo" Kennedy, an African American lawyer, civil rights leader, and feminist activist. From the first, Steinem recognized that women of different races faced different challenges and sought to align herself with a diverse group of women in order to understand those challenges.

Gloria Steinem is an author and the cofounder of Ms. *magazine. As a longtime feminist activist, she has spent decades traveling around the world, speaking and organizing.*

The larger feminist movement was often not so inclined. Steinem recalls that Betty Friedan, author of *The Feminine Mystique* (1963), was vocal about focusing the movement on white, straight, college-educated women. Steinem herself describes an incident involving an op-ed piece she wrote for the *New York Times* in 2008, during the Democratic primary race between Senator Barack Obama and Senator Hillary Clinton, in which she appears to argue that gender is more restrictive than race. There was a swift and nasty backlash, which she remembers with woe.

Steinem's linear narrative splinters somewhere around her work with *New York* magazine, which makes her transition from writer to full-time activist a bit hazy. Subsequent chapters explore individual events or themes, such as her work on college campuses; another chapter is written entirely in bullet points. She writes in one chapter about her intense interest in American Indian culture, but a far more powerful section details the last days she spent with Mankiller, her close friend, when Mankiller was dying of cancer. While she is at her most reflective when recalling her childhood and teenage years, after that point, her narrative voice becomes more distant. Political events take center stage, while her personal life goes almost completely unexamined, to the disappointment of those reviewers who have been waiting for the iconic figure to get more personal in her writing. Steinem recalls romantic attachments in passing—she was married and then widowed in the early 2000s, yet her husband's name does not appear in the book at all—but devotes long passages to women like Mankiller and Kennedy. She even writes about how she and Mankiller planned to be buried together, ash mingling in ash. Her relationships with other women appear to be very important to her, but as Ann Friedman noted in a review of the book for the *New York Times*, Steinem does not explicitly say so—or what, more broadly, those relationships have meant in her life.

My Life on the Road is dedicated to Dr. John Sharpe, the late London doctor who performed an abortion for Steinem when she was twenty-two years old and en route to India. It was a decade before the procedure was legal in England, and Sharpe helped Steinem at considerable risk to them both. According to Steinem, he made her promise not to tell anyone his name, but also to make sure that she did exactly what she wanted with her life. The note strikes a powerful chord, a triumph over time in that Steinem can now celebrate her doctor (who is long dead) without recrimination. While Steinem has been criticized in the past for her singular focus on activism—she sold tickets to her own fiftieth birthday party to raise money for various political causes—this, ultimately, is her art. For her, storytelling is a political act. While she has little to say about current issues in the feminist movement—LGBT rights, campus sexual assault, the Internet as an organizing tool—she successfully frames her own story as a reminder of rights won and lost, and of the battles yet to be fought.

Molly Hagan

Review Sources

Blake, Meredith. "Gloria Steinem Revs Up Memories and Travels in *My Life on the Road* Memoir." Rev. of *My Life on the Road*, by Gloria Steinem. *Los Angeles Times*. Tribune, 5 Dec. 2015. Web. 13 Jan. 2016.

Friedman, Ann. Rev. of *My Life on the Road*, by Gloria Steinem. *New York Times*. New York Times, 13 Nov. 2015. Web. 13 Jan. 2016.

Klein, Julia M. "Gloria Steinem's Memoir Misses a Few Stops." Rev. of *My Life on the Road*, by Gloria Steinem. *Chicago Tribune*. Tribune, 22 Oct. 2015. Web. 13 Jan. 2016.

Roberts, Yvonne. "Reflections of a Tireless Campaigner." Rev. of *My Life on the Road*, by Gloria Steinem. *Guardian*. Guardian News and Media, 9 Nov. 2015. Web. 13 Jan. 2016.

Schuessler, Jennifer. "Review: *My Life on the Road*, Gloria Steinem's Journey as a Traveling Feminist." Rev. of *My Life on the Road*, by Gloria Steinem. *New York Times*. New York Times, 10 Nov. 2015. Web. 13 Jan. 2016.

My Struggle
Book 4

Author: Karl Ove Knausgaard (b. 1968)
First published: *Min kamp 4*, 2010, in Norway
Translated from the Norwegian by: Don Bartlett
Publisher: Archipelago Books (New York). 485 pp.
Type of work: Memoir
Time: 1987–88
Locale: Norway

Part autobiography, part confession, part fiction, My Struggle: Book 4 *is the fourth installment of an epic six-volume, 3,500-page work to be translated from Norwegian into English. In this entry, recent high school graduate and protagonist Karl Ove Knausgaard is hired to teach at a school in the far north of Norway.*

(Courtesy of Archipelago Books)

Principal personages:
KARL OVE KNAUSGAARD, "K. O.," the protagonist, a mildly fictionalized version of the author
SISSEL KNAUSGAARD, his mother, a recently divorced nurse and nursing teacher
DAD, his father, a teacher and an unnamed authoritarian figure
YNGVE KNAUSGAARD, his older brother
UNNI, his father's new girlfriend
FREDERIK, Unni's teenaged son
UNCLE GUNNAR, his father's younger brother
HILDE, his best friend and confidant
IRENE, one of his students, to whom he is attracted

It is a universally accepted fact of life that everything born must eventually die. Between the beginning and the end, the life of any organism is a constant struggle to feed, to mate, to survive. For humans, the road from birth to death is crossed by many paths, each leading to different outcomes, which present an infinite number of possibilities. It is impossible, as any moment in time is unfolding, to discern in advance which path taken will lead to a trivial or unmemorable event and which will have lasting impact and meaning. So the most rewarding course of action is to live every day as though it might be one's last and to savor every second, remembering everything in the smallest details, using all the senses, thereby delaying the inevitable indefinitely.

This, in essence, is the literary philosophy of author-protagonist Karl Ove Knausgaard in *My Struggle*, his massive, six-volume, semi-fictional self-examination. Published as *Min kamp* in Norway between 2009 and 2011, the individual volumes have been released one at a time as they have been translated into English (and more than twenty other languages). *My Struggle: Book 1* (2009; English trans., 2012) deals with the squalid demise of Knausgaard's alcoholic father when the author was in his early forties. *Book 2* (2009; English trans., 2013) moves back in time to the author's mid-thirties and details the breakup of one marriage and the beginning of a second, which produces several children. *Book 3* (2009; English trans., 2014) focuses on Knausgaard's childhood, from about the age of seven until the age of sixteen.

Book 4, originally published in 2010, takes up where the previous volume left off. It is 1987, and Karl Ove has graduated from high school and is trying to decide what to do with the rest of his life. A voracious reader of books by both Norwegian and American

(Asbjørn Jensen)

Karl Ove Knausgaard's first novel, Out of the World *(1998), received the Norwegian Critics Prize for Literature, the first time a debut work had been so honored. His second novel,* A Time for Everything *(2004), was nominated for the Nordic Council's Literature Prize and the Dublin Literary Award. Individual volumes of* My Struggle *have been nominated for multiple awards, and the first volume, published in 2009, won the Brage Prize.*

writers about young loners rejecting society—the latter including J. D. Salinger's *The Catcher in the Rye* (1951), Jack Kerouac's *On the Road* (1957), Hubert Selby Jr.'s *Last Exit to Brooklyn* (1964), and Ernest Hemingway's *The Garden of Eden* (1986)—Karl Ove also eagerly listens to contemporary music, smokes hand-rolled cigarettes, and drinks copious amounts of alcohol. At age nineteen, with little practical work experience, he manages to land a job teaching Norwegian, math, religion, and science at a small school in Håfjord, a village in the far north of Norway. Karl Ove hopes to earn and save enough money to travel through Europe before doing his compulsory military service and settling down. His hometown friends see him off as he boards a train heading north.

Håfjord has only about 250 inhabitants, who all know everything about one another. Karl Ove sets up in a furnished flat in a house, and several villagers stop by to welcome him. When school starts, he meets his fellow teachers and is introduced to the students in his small classes, most just a few years younger than himself. Karl Ove, like many male teenagers, thinks about sex frequently, and he becomes aroused in the presence of his young female students. Though he has boasted to his hometown friends of numerous sexual conquests, in truth he is still a virgin, a condition he desperately wants to change. During the course of the school year, Karl Ove will have multiple opportunities to lose his virginity, but all such encounters will be unsuccessful due to his unfortunate habit of becoming overstimulated in the presence of young women and experiencing premature ejaculation.

Because there is little to do in the village, Karl Ove begins writing during his spare time, and he produces a number of short stories. On weekends, he typically drinks until he blacks out. During weekdays, he does his best to educate his students, but he is ill prepared to be a teacher. When he attempts to be creative in class, the head teacher gently chides him, saying that most of his students are destined to become fishermen or to work at the nearby fish-processing plant and do not need much education beyond knowing how to read and write. Though it is a challenge, Karl Ove lasts out the year and heads south, where he has been accepted as a member of a writing academy.

Taken out of the context of the previous volumes, nothing much happens in *My Struggle: Book 4*. There is no real plot, simply a series of vignettes detailing Karl Ove's fumbling to fulfill his teaching assignments, his methods of self-entertainment in an environment with few leisure options, his efforts to write (which came to fruition a decade after the events described in this volume, when he published his first novel), and his embarrassingly futile attempts to sleep with a number of different willing women, who are by turns baffled, dismayed, or disgusted by his failure. The central story, concerning a particular year in the author's life, alternates lyrical observations of the wild landscape with scenes of wry humor.

Though autobiographical, *My Struggle* is also largely fictional, since it includes re-created conversations that could not possibly have been remembered verbatim and selectively omits other memories. The most interesting aspects of the memoir are the cathartic, Proustian associations engendered by mundane events that conjure nostalgic moments from the past to provide insight into the author's character. Like a dedicated diarist, Karl Ove obsessively reports on daily minutiae in intimate detail, and certain items spur extended flashbacks or brief flash-forwards that reveal facets of relationships with other individuals important to the author's life, some of whom (his father, his mother, his brother, his grandparents) have featured in previous volumes or will figure in forthcoming books. Words contained in a letter from a former girlfriend, for example, cause the author to envision past scenes with his sometimes-loving, sometimes-indifferent father, now separated from his mother and living with another woman. A phone call from a friend conjures the memory of a trip with a soccer team to Denmark, where he fell in love with a teenaged girl. The overall effect of apparently meaningless descriptions or lengthy digressions is strangely compelling and oddly inspiring. Readers who fall into syncopation with the rhythm of Karl Ove's compulsion to report fully on the good, the bad, and the ugly that he encounters will undoubtedly experience their own similar recollections. As a responsive chord is struck, the text will blur and the mind will wander as individuals cue up their own internal movies of past events, recalling poignant, forgotten moments of personal history.

Knausgaard does not always make it easy to follow where he leads. The first-person past-tense narration is continuous, without chapter breaks. Scene shifts—sometimes cutting to a different location on the same day, sometimes jumping to multipage dramatizations of incidents from the past or future—are usually indicated solely by an extra space between often dense paragraphs. Though the individual books are understandable on a stand-alone basis, it is probably helpful to read them in order.

My Struggle, though an unqualified commercial success (nearly 10 percent of all Norwegians have bought the work) and heaped with worldwide critical acclaim, has also been the subject of considerable controversy. First, because Knausgaard usually uses the real names of people in the books and has portrayed many in less-than-flattering fashion, he has been accused of invasion of privacy for subjecting his friends and family to humiliation. Some family members have threatened to sue the author and refuse to speak of or with him.

Second, the title of the series in Norwegian is *Min kamp*. This is uncomfortably close in sound, and identical in meaning, to Adolf Hitler's *Mein Kampf* (1925; *My Struggle*, 1933), the Nazi leader's autobiographical screed in which he blames Jews and Marxists for the problems of the world and outlines his plans for world domination. It is understandable that Norwegians might be sensitive to the similarity of the titles (though the two works have little in common beyond a focus on the lives of the respective authors), since, during World War II, Germany invaded and occupied neutral Norway with the collaboration of fascist Vidkun Quisling, who served as head of the Norwegian puppet state between 1942 and 1945. Quisling was executed for high treason and other crimes following the end of the war, and his name has since become a synonym for "traitor." It is likely that publication of the final volume of *My Struggle* will result in renewed outcries directed at Knausgaard's work, since it has been revealed that *Book 6* will contain an extensive biography of Adolf Hitler.

Jack Ewing

Review Sources

Blair, Elaine. "Looking after the Knausgaards." Rev. of *My Struggle: Book 4*, by Karl Ove Knausgaard. *New York Review of Books*. NYREV, 25 June 2015. Web. 27 Jan. 2016.

Garner, Dwight. Rev. of *My Struggle: Book 4*, by Karl Ove Knausgaard. *New York Times*. New York Times, 20 Apr. 2015. Web. 27 Jan. 2016.

Morrison, Blake. "*Dancing in the Dark*: Karl Ove Knausgaard's Teenage Years." Rev. of *My Struggle: Book 4*, by Karl Ove Knausgaard. *Guardian*. Guardian News and Media, 25 Feb. 2015. Web. 27 Jan. 2016.

Parker, Ben. "The Past Is Useless." Rev. of *My Struggle: Book 4*, by Karl Ove Knausgaard. *Los Angeles Review of Books*. Los Angeles Rev. of Books, 17 Aug. 2015. Web. 27 Jan. 2016.

My Sunshine Away

Author: M. O. Walsh
Publisher: G. P. Putnam's Sons (New York). 320 pp.
Type of work: Novel
Time: 1986–present
Locale: Baton Rouge, Louisiana

A man who grew up in Baton Rouge, Louisiana, delivers a confessional narrative of his teenage years to come to grips with the guilt he feels for exposing information about the rape of a young girl on whom he had a crush some twenty years earlier.

Principal characters:
THE NARRATOR, a resident of a Baton Rouge, Louisiana, suburb
KATHRYN, his mother
GLEN, his father
BARRY, his mother's brother
LINDY SIMPSON, his classmate and neighbor
JACQUES LANDRY, a neighbor who works as a psychiatrist
JASON LANDRY, a foster child living at the Landry home
ARTSY JULIE, a classmate and neighbor

Near the end of award-winning short-story writer M. O. Walsh's debut novel, *My Sunshine Away*, the narrator observes, "When people think of Louisiana, they think exclusively of New Orleans." Walsh may change that perception with his tale of adolescence, remembrance, and suburban life in the state's capital, Baton Rouge. He demonstrates that he is a highly capable novelist in this mesmerizing, modern southern gothic tale that mixes memory, desire, teenage angst, mystery, violence, and larger tragedies such as the Space Shuttle *Challenger* disaster and Hurricane Katrina.

The central story follows the life of an unnamed narrator growing up in Woodland Hills, a well-to-do subdivision of Baton Rouge. He falls in love at age eleven with his neighbor, an athletic girl named Lindy Simpson, who is a year older than him. Unlike most youthful crushes, however, the narrator's remains strong throughout his high school years. In the summer of 1989, when she is fifteen, Lindy is raped. Discovering the identity of the rapist occupies not only the local authorities but also the narrator. Although it becomes clear early in the story that he did not commit the crime, he sometimes speaks as if he is guilty—if not of the rape, at least of some transgression. His persistence in trying to uncover the perpetrator seems motivated by more than youthful infatuation for the victim. The book is one part coming-of-age novel, one part mystery; the narrator's quest to uncover the identity of Lindy's rapist draws readers into the book.

Because the rape occurred in his neighborhood, the narrator learns of it shortly after it occurs. He realizes this information should be kept private, but his desire to be admired by classmates leads him to tell others about the incident, driving a wedge between him and Lindy. The two remain estranged until a reconciliation more than a year later gives him hope that Lindy will finally look at him the way she looks at other boys. That opportunity is lost, however, when the narrator, acting on information provided by another teen, risks his own safety to gather information that would expose the rapist. Instead of being happy, Lindy is furious with him, especially since she knows he has targeted the wrong person. Lindy's parents move away, the two lose touch, and only a chance meeting years later gives the narrator fresh perspective on Lindy's perception of their teen years.

M. O. (Milton O'Neal) Walsh is an essayist and creative writer whose stories have appeared in numerous prestigious publications. His 2010 collection The Prospect of Magic *won the Tartt's Fiction Prize and was a finalist for the Eric Hoffer Award. He teaches creative writing at the University of New Orleans.*

(Used by permission of G. P. Putnam's Sons, Penguin Random House LLC.)

A simple plot outline does not do justice to this complex, evocative story. Told by the narrator who is now in his thirties, this retrospective covers other events that shaped his adult life, most notably growing up as the child of divorced parents and losing a sibling. Kathryn, the narrator's mother, does her best to raise him after his father, Glen, leaves her for a much younger woman. Glen is not out of the narrator's life, but his principled lectures on devotion and constancy leave the narrator cynical and depressed. Older sisters are almost absent until one, Hannah, is killed in an automobile accident and the other, Rachel, returns home to provide Kathryn some psychological support and comfort. The trauma of having to deal with these family matters further complicates the life of a teen who is already confused and emotionally wrecked because he has betrayed the girl he loves. In the midst of his troubles, the narrator receives unsolicited advice about love and life from his uncle Barry. Much of what Barry tells him sounds sensible, but the narrator's mother warns him that her brother is hardly one to be trusted, as he has been in trouble with the law and with creditors for years.

The suburban community Walsh creates is likely to strike a familiar chord with anyone who has grown up in such surroundings. Every neighborhood has its quota of oddballs, do-gooders, and solid citizens, and Woodland Hills is no exception. Lindy Simpson lives in a house close enough for the narrator to see from his bedroom window. She is the sunshine in the novel's title, the light of the narrator's life, but is ultimately more complex than the narrator's assumption of perfection would suggest. Among his other friends, Artsy Julie stands out as a kind of throwback to the hippie generation, and she plays an important role in helping the narrator come to some resolution about his feelings for Lindy when both are grown. Others fill typical roles as bullies, best friends, or casual acquaintances. Two characters, however, deserve special mention. The psychiatrist Jacques Landry is a monstrous man whose locked study holds deep and dangerous secrets. His penchant for taking in foster children, many of whom stay for only brief periods, leads to the introduction into the neighborhood of Jason, an older teen who remains in the Landry home despite his obvious hatred for his foster father. Both play key roles in the narrator's attempt to expose Lindy's rapist, although not in ways he (or any of the adults) expects.

Walsh's principal interest is in his unnamed narrator. Now in his thirties, the narrator says he is writing to try to understand his younger self and the world in which he grew up. While he works hard to appear reliable, he recognizes that as a teenager he was self-absorbed and may not have fully understood the importance of much of what he witnessed or heard about. As he admits, he pretended to know much more than he did—a trait that precipitated his tragic revelation to classmates that Lindy had been raped. Then, though he understood it was important, he did not know what the term "rape" meant, having heard it only in the context of the Louisiana State University football team being defeated. He also reveals how much he and his friends were voyeurs, spying on girls and adults. Teen boys are not the only voyeurs in the novel, however; Jacques Landry turns out to have a prurient interest in his neighbors and in the foster children he brings into his home. The revelation of Landry's activities is an important thread in this novel where multiple story lines intersect.

The ability of *My Sunshine Away* to capture and hold readers' attention is due in large part to Walsh's effective use of the first-person point of view. The narrator's willingness to expose his own shortcomings—some rather trivial, others more consequential—evokes empathy and draws readers into the tale. The concept of confession seems a most appropriate description of this story. The narrative is delivered with a certain sense of intensity and specificity of address, as if the narrator is writing to a particular person for whom his story may have special meaning. The older person looking back at his younger self explains why he feels compelled to offer his own life as a kind of cautionary tale to someone who has not yet reached the point where he or she may have to make the same kinds of choices the narrator did years earlier.

More than one reviewer has called *My Sunshine Away* a loving tribute to Louisiana. Walsh writes about his home state with authority and sensitivity, describing its lush natural terrain and alluding to its colorful history and traditions. There is a focus on food that borders on mania ("when we eat one meal we talk about the next"), and residents take every opportunity to enjoy their sports, recreational activities, and especially the constant rounds of parties and festivals, where excess is the norm. In fact, the title of the novel is a phrase from the Louisiana state song, "You Are My Sunshine," written by two-time Louisiana governor Jimmie Davis, who was also a country singer—which in itself suggests something about the nature of the state that Walsh celebrates. Walsh wants to redeem Louisiana, in the same way he redeems his narrator, from its "unfortunate past," for which many of its current tragedies (Hurricane Katrina among them) are seen as "payback." Although he does not push too hard, Walsh offers an apologia for Louisiana that counters some of the bad press the state has received for nearly a century.

In an era when so much fiction focuses on the outsider, *My Sunshine Away* is something of an anomaly. Walsh's principal character is a white male living in a relatively affluent suburb, the kind of protagonist one might expect to find in a John Updike novel. The story has a strong ring of authenticity, undoubtedly because Walsh grew up in Baton Rouge and underwent some of the same experiences as his narrator. *My Sunshine Away* is not, however, a simple roman à clef in which the author transposes life into art. It is a thoughtful narrative about the pangs and occasional joys of growing up in middle-class white America, told with exceptional skill and keen understanding of the lives of everyday people.

Laurence W. Mazzeno

Review Sources

Colvin, Beth. "Baton Rouge Featured Heavily in M. O. Walsh's Debut Novel *My Sunshine Away*." Rev. of *My Sunshine Away*, by M. O. Walsh. *Acadiana Advocate*. Capital City, 14 Feb. 2015. Web. 19 Jan. 2016.

Hickling, Alfred. "An Intense and Unsettling Debut." Rev. of *My Sunshine Away*, by M. O. Walsh. *Guardian*. Guardian News and Media, 23 July 2015. Web. 19 Jan. 2016.

Lemon, Alex. Rev. of *My Sunshine Away*, by M. O. Walsh. *Dallas Morning News*. Dallas Morning News, 6 Feb. 2015. Web. 19 Jan. 2016.

Mallette, Catherine. Rev. of *My Sunshine Away*, by M. O. Walsh. *Star-Telegram*. Fort Worth Star-Telegram, 4 Feb. 2015. Web. 19 Jan. 2016.

Maran, Meredith. Rev. of *My Sunshine Away*, by M. O. Walsh. *Chicago Tribune*. Tribune, 12 Feb. 2015. Web. 19 Jan. 2016.

Mycroft Holmes

Authors: Kareem Abdul-Jabbar (b. 1947) and Anna Waterhouse (b. 1954)
Publisher: Titan Books (London). 336 pp.
Type of work: Novel
Time: 1870
Locale: London, England; Trinidad

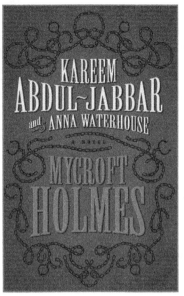

(Courtesy of Titan Books)

The novel Mycroft Holmes *presents a suspenseful Victorian-era transatlantic adventure, featuring the titular hero, the elder brother of Sherlock Holmes, in a mysterious case that seems to have supernatural overtones.*

PRINCIPAL CHARACTERS:

MYCROFT HOLMES, twenty-three-year-old, arrogant, muscular man, who is an assistant to the British secretary of state for war

CYRUS DOUGLAS, his friend who sometimes acts as his servant or valet, originally from Trinidad

GEORGIANNA SUTTON, his blond, blue-eyed fiancée, a teacher of poor boys

SHERLOCK HOLMES, his brother, a sixteen-year-old student at the Royal College of St. Peter

CHARLES PARFITT, a seventeen-year-old clerk and errand boy at his office

EDWARD CARDWELL, historical figure, who served as secretary of state for war (1868–74)

ADAM MCGUIRE, an American whom Mycroft encounters aboard the steamship Sultana

HUAN, the Chinese driver of a mule-drawn gig, friend of Douglas

LITTLE HUAN, Huan's nineteen-year-old son, a member of the Harmonious Order of Closed Fists

SIR ARTHUR CHARLES HAMILTON-GORDON, Baron Stanmore, historical figure, who served as governor of Trinidad (1866–70)

COUNT WOLFGANG HOHENLOHE-LANGENBURG, aristocrat, a distant relative of Queen Victoria

During his career, Scottish-born Sir Arthur Conan Doyle (1859–1930) was a prolific writer of historical, adventure, horror, and mystery novels; short stories; poems; plays; and nonfiction articles, books, and pamphlets. His best-known fictional creation is Sherlock Holmes, a private consulting detective who employs scientific methods and deductive reasoning. The character appeared in a total of sixty stories (five collections and four novels) between 1887 and 1927. Because the Sherlock Holmes stories focus mainly on the exploits of the detective, as chronicled by his companion and biographer, Dr. John Watson, little personal information about the detective is revealed throughout the series. However, in four stories—"The Adventure of the Greek Interpreter" (1893), "The Final Problem" (1893), "The Adventure of the Empty House" (1903), and "The Adventure of the Bruce-Partington Plans" (1908)—Sherlock's elder brother Mycroft either appears briefly or is mentioned in passing. Though details are scarce, a few salient facts about Sherlock's shadowy sibling have emerged. Mycroft has better powers of observation and deduction than Sherlock and a mammoth brain capable of remembering large quantities of data, but he has scant energy or ambition. He is a corpulent man with fat hands. He uses snuff. He lives in Pall Mall and is a member of the Diogenes Club—named for the Greek Cynic philosopher and truth seeker—which he cofounded. He holds a powerful, unnamed position in the British government. Beyond those few key points, the Conan Doyle–created Mycroft was a mystery.

(Courtesy of Titan Books)

Former basketball player Kareem Abdul-Jabbar is the all-time scoring leader of the National Basketball Association. He has written numerous articles and nonfiction books. Mycroft Holmes *is his first novel for adults. Anna Waterhouse has written for such films as* Power Play *(1994) and* Mission: Impossible II *(2000). She teaches screenwriting at Chapman University and the University of Southern California.* Mycroft Holmes *is her first novel.*

Devoted fans of Sherlock Holmes who thirsted for more information about the detective's elusive elder brother have had numerous opportunities over the years to satiate their curiosity. Mycroft Holmes has been depicted on radio, film, and television, usually as a secondary character in Sherlock Holmes stories; Mycroft appeared on screen as early as 1922. Likewise, readers have been able to learn more about Mycroft in novels, stories, parodies, and pastiches from such authors as Colin Dexter, Jasper Fforde, Laurie King, Quinn Fawcett, and Michael Mallory. He has also been seen in various incarnations in comic books and video games.

Coauthors Kareem Abdul-Jabbar and Anna Waterhouse present a fresh take on the character in *Mycroft Holmes* (2015), the first entry in what is planned as a series of novels. A sort of origin story that proposes to illustrate how the protagonist evolved into the character glimpsed in the Conan Doyle's tales, *Mycroft Holmes* is set in 1870. Facets of Mycroft's personality, the high-spirited energy of the novel, homage to the arcane and often bizarre nature of the Sherlock stories, a faithful adherence to the established Holmes canon, and a willingness to expand reasonably upon Conan Doyle's foundation are developed early.

Mycroft is a handsome, well-built, twenty-three-year-old Cambridge University graduate already admired for his abilities of keen observation and calculation, who has begun his civil service career as a trusted employee in the War Office. Mycroft is engaged to beautiful Georgiana Sutton, the daughter of long-established sugar planters in Trinidad. Hoping to win enough money to finance his wedding and a down payment on a home, he wagers heavily on his alma mater at the annual four-mile boat race between Oxford and Cambridge universities, then improves his odds against favored Oxford by arranging the rowers for maximum efficiency. The ploy works, and Cambridge wins. Mycroft, in company with his friend, Cyrus Douglas, owner of a local tobacco shop where Mycroft buys his cigars, collects winnings from a bookmaker. They are chased by a drunken mob of losing bettors intent on robbery and mayhem and have to gallop on horseback to escape.

The action soon switches from the familiar to the exotic. Mycroft's friend Douglas and his girlfriend Georgiana, both of whom hail from Trinidad, are concerned by unsettling, seemingly paranormal events (foreshadowed in a brief prologue) at home. People on the island have vanished and many children have been found dead, drained of blood; the *lougarou*, a legendary giant mosquito, is suspected. Around discovered bodies are the backward-facing footprints of *douens*, the spirits of children who died unbaptized. Georgiana, troubled and wishing to learn the fate of her parents, books passage to Trinidad. Mycroft, seeking to accompany his beloved, researches the situation and discovers that large sums of money have been sent from Luxembourg to Jamaica via the Bank of England. He convinces his superior, Secretary of State for War Edward Cardwell, that political trouble is brewing in the Caribbean, and is duly sent as an envoy to Trinidad. Before leaving, Mycroft visits his brooding teenage brother, Sherlock, who lends him a key piece of equipment: a walking stick containing a hidden sword. Mycroft collects Douglas, who dresses as a valet, and the two men board the steamship *Sultana*—the same ship Georgiana would use, since transatlantic vessels depart infrequently—for the eight-day voyage to Port of Spain, Trinidad.

After the ship embarks, Georgiana is nowhere to be found. However, Holmes and Douglas spot numerous unsavory types aboard, including American Adam McGuire. During foul weather, a group of thugs assaults Mycroft and his companion, who fend them off with martial skills. In the fight, Mycroft receives a deep gash on his face, which Douglas treats with an application from a first-aid kit. Soon afterward, Mycroft falls deathly ill. Nursing him, Douglas discovers that the medication applied was tainted with a toxic plant native to Trinidad. Holmes recovers by the time the ship reaches Trinidad, and as he leaves, the ship's captain gives him a list of eight names, including Adam McGuire, whose first initials spell out ARON BURR, a corrupted version of the name of an American vice president. Holmes speculates that another name beginning with "a," perhaps that of passenger Anabel Lynch, has been eliminated from the list.

At Port of Spain, Holmes and Douglas trail to a pub the men who attacked them, where their assailants fall dead after eating meat pies poisoned by toxins from a puffer fish, the handiwork of a well-known local poisoner. Holmes concludes whomever hired the thugs is covering his tracks. Holmes subsequently meets with the governor of the island and is afterward introduced to Douglas's friend Huan, and Huan's son

Little Huan, who board Holmes and Douglas in the Chinese section of town, among members of the Harmonious Order of Closed Fists.

The following day, Holmes, Douglas, and Huan visit the Sutton Plantation in search of the missing Georgiana. The plantation is not prosperous, as Mycroft's fiancée claimed, but rather has fallen into ruin. Mrs. Sutton, the only family member still alive, is aged beyond her years. She bemoans that she has not seen her daughter in many months, and shows Mycroft a stack of letters from Georgiana, addressed to Anabel Lynch Sutton. It becomes apparent that the Anabel Sutton aboard ship was Georgiana in disguise, and that Mycroft's fiancée has lied about many things.

As the story unfolds, Holmes and Douglas begin to unravel clues. The apparently supernatural events, such as the disappearing people, the blood-drained children, and the backward-facing footprints, are all part of an effort to frighten people away from certain locations on the island. The sinister reason is eventually uncovered, exposing a greater and more diabolical conspiracy involving prominent and ruthless people who are financed in their nefarious scheme by enormous amounts of laundered money from secret sources in Europe.

From start to finish, *Mycroft Holmes* is an enjoyable romp, faithful to the atmosphere, language, and morality of its original source material, most of which were presented as adventures with mysterious undertones. Though the story is complex, with a multitude of plot twists highlighted by explosions, hair-raising fights, feats of strength, and heroic derring-do, the presentation is in straightforward, readable third-person prose. As Mike Sager for *Esquire* notes, "The erudite Abdul-Jabbar has managed to weave elements of his far flung interests into a fascinating mystery narrative."

It is obvious, both from the finished result and from interviews conducted with the pair, that Abdul-Jabbar and Waterhouse—who previously collaborated on the screenplay of the NCAA Image Award–winning sports documentary *On the Shoulders of Giants: The Story of the Greatest Team You Never Heard Of* (2011)—had a great deal of fun in the process of forming an effective fiction-writing partnership. Abdul-Jabbar, the former professional basketball star who is a longtime aficionado of history as well as of crime and mystery fiction, concentrates on plot points, deftly punctuating a mostly serious narrative with humorous incidents. *Mycroft Holmes,* his adult-fiction debut, includes a major story line set in Trinidad. The setting serves as a tribute to the legends of the island from which some of Abdul-Jabbar's ancestors hail and also as a subtle reminder that author Conan Doyle was for much of his life fascinated by such topics as mysticism, spiritualism, telepathy, psychic powers, and clairvoyance. Anna Waterhouse, a script consultant and college-level screenwriting teacher, handles dialogue and characterization that rings true to the time period. The inclusion of a black man (Douglas) as a cherished colleague and a woman as a love interest provide opportunities to discuss Victorian attitudes toward racial and sexual roles in society—subjects generally overlooked or downplayed in Sherlock Holmes stories.

Jack Ewing

Review Sources

Hanson, Liv. "Mycroft Holmes by Kareem Abdul-Jabbar." Rev. of *Mycroft Holmes*, by Kareem Abdul-Jabbar and Anna Waterhouse. *Library Journal*. Library Journal, 19ʾAug. 2015. Web. 5 Dec. 2015.

Rev. of *Mycroft Holmes*, by Kareem Abdul-Jabbar and Anna Waterhouse. *Publishers Weekly* 29 June 2015: 44. Print.

Sager, Mike. "Kareem Abdul-Jabbar on his Forty-Five-Year Obsession with Sherlock Holmes." Rev. of *Mycroft Holmes*, by Kareem Abdul-Jabbar and Anna Waterhouse. *Esquire*. Esquire, 17 Sept. 2015. Web. 5 Dec. 2015.

The Nature of the Beast

Author: Louise Penny (b. 1958)
Publisher: Minotaur Books (New York).
384 pp.
Type of work: Novel
Time: Present day
Locale: Three Pines, Quebec, Canada

(Courtesy of Minotaur Books)

Armand Gamache becomes involved in a murder investigation that turns out to have national significance and connections to a previous case.

Principal characters:
ARMAND GAMACHE, a retired chief inspector of the Sûreté du Québec
LAURENT LEPAGE, a nine-year-old boy with creative imagination
AL LEPAGE, Laurent's father, a man with a hidden past
JEAN-GUY BEAUVOIR, son-in-law of the Gamaches, inspector for the Sûreté du Québec
ISABELLE LACOSTE, chief inspector, head of the Sûreté du Québec
JOHN FLEMING, a playwright with a sinister past known to Gamache

The Nature of the Beast, the eleventh book in Louise Penny's Chief Inspector Armand Gamache series, has garnered strong reviews. This is not surprising, as Louise Penny has won numerous honors, including five Agatha Awards. Though this book can be read on its own, a knowledge of the series will make the story line more understandable because Penny builds the book around previously established characters and events from earlier novels in the series.

One of the most intriguing aspects of the novel is the integration of a triple plot that entwines a murder in the small town of Three Pines, Quebec, with international intrigue and a piece of Gamache's own history. The story begins with Laurent Lepage, an imaginative nine-year-old boy, playing in the forest around Three Pines. While being pursued by imaginary enemy troops, the little "soldier" digs a hole for a hiding place. This hole reveals more than he could ever expect, and the child's previous penchant for tall tales pales in comparison to the story he carries to town about a gun as big as a house with a monster at its base.

When Laurent barges into the local bistro, interrupting a meal that Armand Gamache is sharing with his former assistant Isabelle Lacoste, no one is particularly concerned about anything more than the child's destruction of property as he swings his prized carved stick, which he imagines as a gun. Amused by the boy's inventive tale, Gamache takes him home to his hippie parents. Other than garnering a chuckle or a shake of the head, the idea of a huge gun hidden in the forest near the town is forgotten by the patrons of the bistro. However, the next day, Laurent's body is found on the side of the road, purportedly the result of a bicycle accident. As the town mourns the child's death, Gamache begins to doubt the reported cause of Laurent's death, and when he and a few others go searching for Laurent's stick, they find something that belies adult imagination. The search for Laurent's killer introduces both a number of suspects, including the child's own father, and the issue of how people grieve.

The book's secondary plot line results from the discovery made first by the child and later by the former chief inspector and his friends. Laurent had stumbled upon a monstrous creation: a huge missile launcher pointed south toward the United States. At the base of the gun is an etching of the Whore of Babylon and a Hebrew phrase about the end of the world. Gamache and his friends, along with Lacoste and Beauvoir, become actively involved in trying to figure out the mystery of this horrible machine. The story of twentieth-century Canadian scientist Gerald Bull pulls readers into the fearful account of Baby Babylon and Big Babylon, a set of almost prehistoric missile launchers that were designed to work without electrical technology. Gamache, Lacoste, and Beauvoir are pulled into a confusing web of cover-ups, national secrets, and international conspiracy as they try to understand how and why this weapon was built and then apparently abandoned so close to their peaceful home. A few new characters, two of whom claim to be from the Canadian government and one who is a retired researcher, add a layer of intrigue to this plot line.

The third thread in the story's plot revolves around the play that the local amateur theater is planning to perform. Antoinette Lemaitre, head of the theater group, has chosen a humorous play, but she has withheld the name of the playwright. When the playwright's name slips out during a casual gathering of friends, many of the players withdraw from the performance. The playwright, John Fleming, is a horrific serial killer with whom Gamache has a past. Though the novel raises the question of censorship based on authorship when the literature itself is not offensive, Penny skillfully pulls this link into the tangle of murder and weaponry presented in the other two threads of the book.

Before becoming a full-time writer, Louise Penny was a radio producer and a journalist. She is best known for the Inspector Gamache series, which includes eleven books.

After Antoinette is found murdered, the town starts to question her connection to Fleming, to the gun, and to Laurent's death. The idea of self-sacrifice emerges when it is revealed that Gamache, who also helps investigate Antoinette's murder, is one of only a small number of people who really understand the depth of Fleming's atrocious murders. This piece of the story line becomes more important than expected when the novel pulls to a close and Lacoste shifts her focus from the gun to the murders themselves.

In addition to creating a complicated, labyrinthine plot, Penny skillfully challenges readers to think about a variety of themes. The most obvious questions she introduces are those of morality in war and weapons development. As the secondary plot line develops, the idea of a weapon of mass destruction is introduced. She raises uncertainty in the readers regarding expectations of war and the lengths that governments and individuals might go to in building, hiding, or even selling weapons that could destroy thousands of lives.

The question of individual soldiers as weapons is also offered when Laurent's father, a man whom the town knows as a Vietnam War draft dodger, is suspected in his son's death. Al Lepage's true identity is exposed even as the man grieves the loss of his only child. Lepage's past renews the idea of Three Pines as a refuge, another strong theme in the novel. Since the town is close to the country's border with the United States, it served as a stopping point for military refugees during the Vietnam War, but Gamache and many others have found the town also to be a place where they can find peace. The universal message is that people can find asylum in a place, in others, and in acceptance of their own experiences. Hidden pain can be dealt with only when faced, and at least three characters find a way to move forward despite difficult pasts.

Finally, Penny complicates all three of the plot lines with the issue of distraction. Gamache faces the triple threat of insecurity, pain, and uncertainty when he allows the problems of the case to distract him from realizing where he belongs and what he should be doing. Involvement in the murder cases makes him question whether his retirement is the right choice, and offers of several different prestigious positions tempt him even while Reine-Marie, his wife, considers options for a retirement career.

A gifted storyteller, Penny infuses her work with humor and charm to keep the piece from becoming overwhelmingly suspenseful. Humor is found primarily in the character of Ruth Zardo, Three Pines' resident poet. This elderly woman's eccentric behavior, racy language, and pet duck give readers something to smile about in the midst of the heavy story. Familiar characters from previous books bring charm to the story. Returning to this piece are painter Clara, former psychologist and bookstore owner Myrna, and partners Gabri and Olivier, owners of the bistro and local bed and breakfast. The family ties between the Gamaches and son-in-law Jean-Guy Beauvoir add another touch of nostalgia to the series. The picture of friendships that can overcome tragedy, encourage humor, and help in understanding both the big and small issues in life adds to the allure of Penny's work.

Overall, reviewers hailed Penny's talented writing. From the enthralling plot to the humanity of the characters, the commentary from review sources such as the *Library Journal* and *Kirkus Reviews* on *The Nature of the Beast* has been positive. Penny's gift with prose as well as her ability to make readers question deeply held beliefs are integral to Armand Gamache's eleventh adventure. Borderline criticism of the novel from general readers suggests that this piece is missing the psychological exploration of the murderer, and that is somewhat relevant when considering the cases of Laurent Lepage and Antoinette Lemaitre; however, the tertiary plot with John Fleming brings a clear picture of the inhumanity of a murderer. In showing how inhumane Fleming is, Penny focuses on the humanity of characters such as Gamache, Beauvoir, and Lacoste. Most negative criticism of the book from reader reviews complained of the slow pace, the focus on the weapon itself, and the believability of the plot. Though there are times when the novel's pacing seems questionable, the sidebars are intriguing and important to the overall story. The plausibility of the weapon forms the basis of the other criticism, like that by Bill Ott in his *Booklist* review. The idea of a missile launcher the size of a house hidden in the woods outside a populated town may be far-fetched, but Penny tells readers in the afterword that her story was influenced by the real-life Canadian scientist Gerald Bull, who developed a massive missile launcher in the twentieth century.

Theresa L. Stowell

Review Sources

Biendenharn, Isabella. Rev. of *The Nature of the Beast*, by Louise Penny. *Entertainment Weekly* 9 Oct. 2015: 64–65. Print.

Lucas, Terry. "The Nature of the Beast: A Chief Inspector Gamache Novel." Rev. of *The Nature of the Beast*, by Louise Penny. *Library Journal* 1 July 2015: 55–58. Print.

Ott, Bill. Rev. of *The Nature of the Beast*, by Louise Penny. *Booklist* 15 July 2015: 39. Print.

Rev. of *The Nature of the Beast: A Chief Inspector Gamache Novel*, by Louise Penny. *Kirkus Reviews* 15 July 2015: 45. Print.

Rev. of *The Nature of the Beast: A Chief Inspector Gamache Novel*, by Louise Penny. *Publishers Weekly* 28 Sept. 2015: 85. Print.

Negroland

Author: Margo Jefferson (b. 1947)
Publisher: Pantheon Books (New York).
248 pp.
Type of work: Memoir, history
Time: primarily 1940s–80s
Locale: Chicago

Pulitzer Prize–winning critic Margo Jefferson recalls her childhood among the African American elite in her memoir Negroland. *The title, a word of her own devising, refers to the rarified world of black privilege in 1950s Chicago.*

Negroland, Pulitzer Prize–winning critic Margo Jefferson's newest book, is both a memoir of her childhood growing up in Chicago in the 1950s and a social history of America's black elite. The term "Negroland" is Jefferson's own, one she defines as "a small region of Negro America where residents were sheltered by a certain amount of privilege and plenty." Growing up, Jefferson was a resident of Negroland: her father, Ronald, was an influential pediatrician, her mother, Irma, a socialite. "Inside the race we were the self-designated aristocrats, educated, affluent, accomplished; to Caucasians we were oddities, underdogs and interlopers," she writes. Early on, Jefferson explains that she chose to use the word "Negro," for several reasons, among them, that the word was still widely in use when Jefferson was growing up, and, given its mutations throughout history, that it helped her understand how race is constructed. Jefferson traces mid-century Negroland back through its various iterations ("the colored aristocracy," "the blue vein society," "the old families," etc.), elucidates its hierarchies, and expounds, often painfully, on the positive and negative ways in which it has informed her identity and her understanding of the world.

Jefferson is a book and theater critic who formerly worked for the *New York Times*. She won the Pulitzer Prize for Criticism in 1995 and, in 2006, published the cultural critique *On Michael Jackson*. Jefferson's tone throughout *Negroland* is surprisingly immediate. She raises questions to the reader ("How does one—how do you, how do I—parse class, race, family, and temperament?"), doubles back on herself, and encourages herself to move forward. At the beginning of the book, Jefferson warns that the children of Negroland were taught never to "show off," unless it would benefit their family, social circle, and race. Jefferson was supposed to be gracefully and effortlessly good at everything, without drawing attention to her success. She was taught to keep private matters private, to be cautious with her trust, to never put herself in a vulnerable position where she might reveal weakness. Unfortunately, such a place is where memoir is born. Jefferson is scrupulous about her honesty in the book, interrogating herself even as she writes. The large swaths of social commentary are interesting but appear to serve as a warm-up—an important tie-in to Jefferson's personal history but also a way for her to justify talking about herself at all.

Jefferson was born in 1947, but she begins her narrative in the seventeenth century, stitching together biographies of various Negroland pioneers. There is the Angolan Anthony Johnson, who arrived in Virginia as an indentured servant in 1621 and later went on to marry, buy land, and become a slaveholder himself. But there is also Charlotte Forten Grimké, an intellectual and abolitionist from a wealthy Northern family who, though conflicted about her own ambitions, devotes her life to educating freed men and women. Throughout the book, Jefferson is candid about Negroland's complex and sometimes uneasy relationship to African American men and women further down the socioeconomic scale and, in these early vignettes, makes clear that that uneasiness was born long ago. Pioneering women particularly view the lower class as an inspirational calling—the National Association of Colored Women's Clubs' motto was "Lifting as We Climb"—but also a liability. Jefferson quotes Mary Church Terrell, an early civil rights activist and suffragist, who lamented "the lowly, the illiterate and even the vicious, to whom they are bound by the ties of race."

One begins to see the construction of the social pressure cooker into which Jefferson was born. The women of Negroland in the early twentieth century, like Jefferson's mother, were educated and as ambitious as was considered appropriate for women of the era. They were ladies, Jefferson writes, emphasizing the word, though being a lady was not as straightforward as it would seem. Being a lady in Negroland required a specific calibration of intelligence and social poise, an innate understanding of what one should and should not do—a conundrum that Jefferson describes as being "wholly normal and wholly exceptional." The rules of ladyhood were sometimes explicit; at others times, learned through humiliating trial and error. The women of Negroland were expected to behave like well-bred white women—only better—and look like them too. In one of *Negroland*'s most affecting passages, Jefferson catalogs and ranks the preferred hair types, skin tones, and nose and body shapes of the day. The lighter the skin, the better, Jefferson writes, adding that dark skin "often suggests aggressive, indiscriminate sexual readiness." Women wrestled with hot combs, creams, and oils to straighten curly or frizzy hair. Jefferson's mother wore her hair in spritely bob that recalled actress Claudette Colbert. When her older sister, Denise, started going to the beauty parlor to have her hair straightened as a teenager, she complained that the chemicals stung her scalp. Her hairdresser told her, "Beauty knows no pain." Broad and flat noses were scorned—better to have alluringly flared nostrils or a hooked nose that suggested American Indian ancestry—as were "unduly full" behinds or lips. Jefferson kept a running tally of her own perceived physical shortcomings and learned, from a young age, how to compensate for them. Her litany is punctuated by a photograph of Denise as a young girl staring intently at her own reflection in the bathroom mirror.

Maintaining one's physical appearance was nearly as exhausting as maintaining a proud, yet unobtrusive identity. Growing up, Jefferson was an avid reader, a pianist, and an actor. She and Denise read poems after school, delighting in nonsense rhymes like Lewis Carroll's "Jabberwocky." It was in the same spirit that Jefferson came across the Langston Hughes poem "Mother to Son." At first, the girls thought it was hilarious—the narrator drops her *g*'s and says "kinder" instead of "kind of." The speech was everything they had been taught to laugh at, but their mother was not laughing. She read the poem for them so that they could hear its pain. Looking back on that moment, Jefferson writes, "What are parents to do, when they've taken all steps to ensure that their children flourish in the world at large, to claim their right to culture and education, when suddenly this chasm of ignorance and inferiority opens up to swallow their cultivated little selves?" She adds, "How did these demons of scorn and mockery find their way into your children?"

With the exhilarating freedoms of the 1970s came more frustrations, more pressure, more self-lacerating doubts about how to present oneself. Jefferson and her friends embraced black culture and raced to distinguish themselves from the women they once were. After striving to emulate white beauty standards or culture, they now went out of their way to distance themselves from those things—but what should go and what should stay? The politics were tricky. So much so that, years later, a black friend guiltily confided to Jefferson that the death of actress Audrey Hepburn had been more significant to her personally than that of African American icon and Supreme Court justice Thurgood Marshall. In one chapter, Jefferson collects a number of what she calls "relativity tales," demonstrating the comedy of navigating identities. In one from the 1970s, Jefferson recalls her friend Shawn, a woman who had straight hair and wore an Afro wig. ("Many politically conscious black women with light skin and straight hair do the same," she writes of the time. "It's the only way to make sure people acknowledge their racial identity.") In a sweltering club in New Orleans, Shawn went to the restroom and removed her wig, shaking out her sweaty hair. Only then did she notice a woman standing next to her, also removing a wig and shaking out her hair—only the woman's hair was frizzy and natural, and her wig had straight hair: a direct inversion of Shawn and her wig. "Slowly, in near unison, they put their wigs back on and leave the bathroom in silence," Jefferson writes.

Margo Jefferson is a Pulitzer Prize–winning critic whose work has appeared in the New York Times, Harper's, Newsweek, *and* New York Magazine, *among other publications. She teaches writing at Columbia University. She is also the author of the book* On Michael Jackson *(2006).*

Jefferson also writes about her battle with depression, which also began around this time. The children of Negroland, particularly the girls, she writes, were not supposed to get depressed or think about suicide—but the enormous pressure and difficulty of maintaining "decorum" was certainly conducive to such distress. Depression was a privilege reserved for white women, the thinking went. "We were to be ladies, responsible Negro women, and indomitable Black Women," Jefferson writes. "We were not to be depressed or unduly high-strung; we were not to have nervous collapses. We had a legacy. We were too strong for that." In this way, Jefferson's own real depression also became, in her mind, a political act. She cites life-changing encounters with two plays—Adrienne Kennedy's *Funnyhouse of a Negro* (1969) and Ntozake Shange's *for colored girls who have considered suicide/when the rainbow is enuf* (1975)—that engaged this view. Jefferson, however, was serious. Each day she practiced contorting her body so that her head would fit in her oven—a nod to poet Sylvia Plath—and studied the construction of suicide notes. It is unclear exactly when Jefferson ended her fixation on death, or if she ever did.

The most intense passages of *Negroland* are written in short sketches, and Jefferson quickly moves on to the next subject. Other passages are written in the third person, as if Jefferson needed to step out of herself to talk about the event at all. *Negroland* can, at times, be difficult to follow. Jefferson jumps back and forth in time. She names some characters, refuses to name others, and, occasionally, changes her mind about it. But the more challenging aspects of the book appear to be attempts to keep it honest. Her life has been defined by her struggles with identity, and the same can be said of her memoir. Several times throughout the book, Jefferson repeats a mantra in which she says, "It's too easy to recount unhappy memories when you write about yourself. You bask in your own innocence. You revere your grief. You arrange your angers at their most becoming angles," she writes. "I don't want this kind of indulgence to dominate my memories."

Molly Hagan

Review Sources

Carroll, Rebecca. "Review: Margo Jefferson Reveals Life inside the Black Elite in 'Negroland.'" Rev. of *Negroland*, by Margo Jefferson. *Los Angeles Times*. Los Angeles Times, 9 Sept. 2015. Web. 10 Feb. 2016.

Garner, Dwight. "Review: 'Negroland,' by Margo Jefferson, on Growing Up Black and Privileged." Rev. of *Negroland*, by Margo Jefferson. *New York Times*. New York Times, 10 Sept. 2015. Web. 10 Feb. 2016.

Gay, Roxane. "Best Memoirs of the Year." Rev. of *Negroland*, by Margo Jefferson. *O: The Oprah Magazine*. Harpo Productions, 1 Sept. 2015. Web. 10 Feb. 2016.

Rev. of *Negroland*, by Margo Jefferson. *Kirkus Reviews*. Kirkus Media, 16 June 2015. Web. 10 Feb. 2016.

Obaro, Tomi. "*Negroland* Examines the 1950s Black Bourgeoisie." Rev. of *Negroland*, by Margo Jefferson. *Chicago Magazine*. Chicago Tribune Media Group, 26 Aug. 2015. Web. 10 Feb. 2016.

The Nightingale

Author: Kristin Hannah (b. 1960)
Publisher: St Martin's Press (New York). 440 pp.
Type of work: Novel
Time: World War II
Locales: Carriveau, France; Paris, France

(Courtesy of St Martin's Press)

The Nightingale *is a story of war and family. It follows a pair of sisters through the tragedies, violence, and heroism of life in France during World War II. Amid such significant events, it calls readers to focus on the meaning of family bonds.*

Principal characters:

VIANNE (ROSSIGNOL) MAURIAC, a schoolteacher in the small French town of Carriveau

ISABELLE ROSSIGNOL, a.k.a. Juliette Gervaise, her younger sister, a member of the French Resistance

RACHEL DE CHAMPLAIN, her best friend

WOLFGANG BECK, a German captain who billets at the Mauriac residence

JULIEN ROSSIGNOL, Vianne and Isabelle's father, a poet, and World War I veteran

GAËTAN, a fighter for the French Resistance

ANTOINE MAURIAC, Vianne's husband

SOPHIE MAURIAC, Vianne and Antoine's daughter

JULIEN MAURIAC, Vianne and Antoine's younger son, born after the war

SARA DE CHAMPLAIN, Rachel's daughter and Sophie's best friend

ARIEL DE CHAMPLAIN, Rachel's son

STURMBANNFÜHRER VON RICHTER, a German SS officer who billets at the Mauriac residence after the death of Captain Beck

The Nightingale begins in 1940, as war arrives in France for the second time in a generation. Vianne and her younger sister, Isabelle, came of age in a family splintered by the devastation of World War I. Their poet father, Julien Rossignol, returned from the front a shattered man. After their mother's death from tuberculosis, he left their upbringing to boarding schools and harsh caretakers. Now France and Germany are once again at war.

Vianne and her family live at the ancestral family home outside the small village of Carriveau. Her husband, Antoine Mauriac, a postman, is drafted into the French army. All Vianne can do is hope that he will not return as damaged as her own father did from World War I. Meanwhile, the rebellious Isabelle, who has spent her entire life in boarding schools, is expelled for the final time and returns to her father in Paris. The stories of Vianne and Isabelle are spun out throughout the novel. For the most part, their lives follow very different paths, but many of the greatest dramatic tensions of the novel arise when the two sisters find themselves together again in the same place. Though very different, Vianne and Isabelle both continue to struggle with the loss of their mother and the void left by their father's unloving demeanor. The pulsing tensions and affections among the three Rossignol family members tie the strains of the narrative together.

While the bulk of the story takes place during World War II, a few chapters intersperse a first-person narrative from 1995. The elderly and ill female narrator remains unidentified until the concluding pages of the book. It is easy to forget about this more modern narrative thread, since many chapters go by before the reader is again catapulted forward in time, but it is through this character that the final resolution of the novel is able to occur. Although the narrator offers some hints at the life that spanned the decades between the conclusion of World War II and 1995, some additional development might have better helped the reader accept the profound shift in personal circumstances implicit in the final resolution.

Kristin Hannah is the author of more than twenty books in a range of genres. Although The Nightingale *is unusual in her oeuvre, being a historical novel, it follows in her long interest of books that probe female family relationships.*

Vianne and Isabelle are introduced to the reader as opposites. Vianne is timid and emotionally vulnerable; though happily married to Antoine, she admits her own frailty, and she credits him for her ability to carry forward from day to day as a stable person. Prior to the birth of their daughter, Sophie, Vianne suffered a series of miscarriages and stillbirths, and she continues to mourn for her lost children. When Antoine is sent off to war, Vianne is confident that only the existence of Sophie will keep her breathing from day to day. She thrives in her domestic role, enjoying cooking and gardening, and generally stays close to home. Isabelle, by contrast, is outspoken, flashy in her beauty, and hard-edged in her personality. She cultivates her independence, having learned the hard way throughout her life that she can rely on neither her sister nor her father for support. She is rebellious and eager to make a name for herself. Carriveau is of little interest to Isabelle compared to the attractions of Paris, where her father owns a bookstore.

The opposite personalities of these two sisters complement each other perfectly over the arc of the narrative, revealing two sides of female heroism during war. Isabelle models heroism brashly and suffers the consequences of her great self-confidence as the novel progresses. Having tried out various roles within the resistance movement, she eventually comes into her own as a mountain guide and courier who spirits downed Allied fighter pilots over the Pyrenees to the British consulate in Spain. Using the assumed name of Juliette Gervaise and the code name the Nightingale (an English translation of her surname, Rossignol), she completes numerous successful runs, saving a large number of pilots. The authorities imagine the Nightingale to be a man, and this hero gains great notoriety on both sides of the battle lines. Vianne, meanwhile, remains in Carriveau throughout the war, attempting to quietly tend to her house, raise her daughter, and keep a low profile. Through a series of unfortunate circumstances, she too eventually decides to join the resistance. In her case, it is her love of children—and of her lifelong friend Rachel de Champlain—that provokes her to begin rescuing Jewish children as the Nazis' plan for genocide gradually becomes apparent. Vianne's work is unassuming and local, focused on the traditional female role of playing guardian to children; Isabelle's is public (though concealed), flagrant, and in direct contact with the military. Together their efforts suggest the breadth of means by which women found the capacity to fight back in a social context that allowed them little agency.

Having researched the history of female roles in the resistance during World War II, Kristin Hannah modeled the Rossignol sisters on the actions of several historical women from World War I and World War II in Belgium and France. Neither Vianne nor Isabelle is exactly derived from these historical figures, but the inspiration should nevertheless be acknowledged. Disappointingly, accounts of these real-life women do not appear in a forward or postscript, a decision that underplays the research that Hannah completed in order to write the novel. As the story allows the reader to grow close to the sisters through their heroic achievements, the reader should be made aware that their actions are not romanticized possibilities but rather real achievements carried out by women during wartime.

Though of less historical interest, much of *The Nightingale* centers on Vianne's work as mother and sole caretaker to her daughter, Sophie. As the novel progresses, Sophie grows from a young girl into a teenager. Aged by all that she has seen, Sophie appears older than she is. Though Vianne seeks to protect her daughter, she often finds that she does not know what to say or how to act, as she wants to be truthful to her daughter while also shielding her from the horrors around them. Although the relationship between Isabelle and Vianne is, ostensibly, the main focus of the novel, the one between Sophie and her mother seems to have the greatest intimacy and emotional interest. Indeed, the two share secrets unavailable to any other living soul, of the type to fuse them together for both of their lifetimes.

As should be expected from any novel set in Europe during World War II, there are many moments of deep tragedy in *The Nightingale*. The worst, though, are those that become personal. Here the reader's immersion in Vianne's social circle in Carriveau permits the atrocities of the Holocaust to take on a personal hue. Most heartrending is the story of Vianne's best friend and neighbor, Rachel, who is revealed to be Jewish about halfway through the book. Although it is difficult to read about Vianne and Sophie's suffering during the war, their plight is never as severe as that of Rachel, who struggles to care for her children, Sara and Ari. The story of this small family unit only becomes darker as the novel progresses.

Less satisfying are Vianne's relationships with two successive German officers. Wolfgang Beck, the first officer to lodge at Vianne's house, is a family man, characterized as good at heart but on the wrong side of the war. Though the two never consummate their mutual attraction, they are brought close as time passes. As the German position in the war disintegrates, Vianne's relationship with Beck becomes strained and comes to a violent conclusion. Beck is then replaced in the Mauriac household by a cruel SS officer, von Richter. His sexual abuse of Vianne is an almost inevitable act within the book, bringing into cruel clarity the dangerous quasi-romanticism of Vianne's relationship with Beck. Von Richter's rapes of Vianne set in motion other wheels of plot best left for the reader to discover, but these are not satisfactorily resolved, in part because of Hannah's decision to tell this story solely through the account of female voices, to the virtual exclusion of the male characters. Though less problematic, Isabelle's off-and-on relationship with the resistance fighter Gaëtan does not further the interest of the novel and, at times, slips it off course.

While it is not an intellectually hefty novel, *The Nightingale* offers readers the opportunity to follow the progression of World War II in France through the personal stories of a small cast of characters. Rather than attempting to grasp the vast scope of the human tolls of the war, Hannah reduces its monumental damages to these tragic and intimate stories. This approach runs the risk that readers may focus more on the personal dramas of these stories than on the ways in which they stand in for larger social and political aspects of the war. The female protagonist in the chapters set in 1995 furthers this particular possibility, as her reflections deal with the demons she has harbored over the decades since the war broke out around her. Still grappling with her own actions—and inactions—during the war years, she implicitly conveys the magnitude of suffering through the emotional damage of decades of reflection. However, if the pitfall of over-engagement in the personalities and lives of the characters can be avoided, *The Nightingale* brings great vividness to the realities of life in France during World War II.

Julia A. Sienkewicz

Review Sources

Burghardt, Linda F. Rev. of *The Nightingale*, by Kristin Hannah. *Jewish Book Council.* Jewish Book Council, n.d. Web. 25 Feb. 2016.

Landau, Arielle. "Kristin Hannah Makes It Easy to Relate to WWII Heroines in *The Nightingale*." Rev. of *The Nightingale*, by Kristin Hannah. *New York Daily News.* NYDailyNews.com, 7 Apr. 2015. Web. 25 Feb. 2016.

Rhule, Patty. "Kristin Hannah Takes on the Nazis in *Nightingale*." Rev. of *The Nightingale*, by Kristin Hannah. *USA Today.* Gannett, 8 Feb. 2015. Web. 25 Feb. 2016.

Nimona

Author: Noelle Stevenson
Publisher: HarperTeen (New York). 272 pp.
Type of work: Graphic novel
Time: Unknown
Locale: Unspecified medieval kingdom

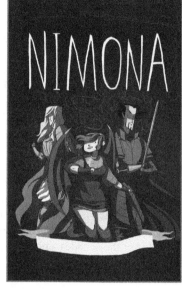

The celebrated online comic from writer and artist Noelle Stevenson, Nimona *revolves around a young shapeshifter who is the sidekick of an evil villain.*

Principal characters:
NIMONA, the energetic and shape-shifting
    evil sidekick of Ballister Blackheart
BALLISTER BLACKHEART, an evil villain who is
    not so terrible
AMBROSIUS GOLDENLOIN, a heroine who is not
    so heroic
THE DIRECTOR, the leader of the Institution
    for Law Enforcement and Heroics and Goldenloin's boss

Noelle Stevenson's award-winning *Nimona* began its life on the Internet. Stevenson already had an Internet following from a satirical art blog when she started *Nimona* as a biweekly web comic in 2012 (which she later used as her senior thesis). *Nimona* gained significant popularity and critical praise online; it was nominated for a Harvey Award for best online comics work and won the Slate Cartoonist Studio Prize for best web comic of 2012. In its book form, *Nimona* was a finalist for the 2015 National Book Award for Young People's Literature.

    The graphic novel itself is the story of Nimona, a prickly teenager who can shapeshift. The comic begins with Nimona knocking on the door of Ballister Blackheart, the supervillain of a medieval kingdom. Nimona tells Blackheart that she has arrived to be his evil sidekick. He is not interested until she turns into a shark, revealing a depth of possibilities for nefarious plans. As the story progresses, readers learn that the characters are not quite what they seem on the surface. This is one of the most intriguing aspects of the comic, particularly in the ways that Stevenson plays with hero tropes and gender roles. Ballister Blackheart, the villain, is only a villain because he was injured during a joust with his best friend, Ambrosius Goldenloin, while they both attended the Institution for Law Enforcement and Heroics. After his best friend shot off one of Blackheart's arms, Blackheart was kicked out of the Institution and "took the only other option available." He tells Goldenloin, "Choice? I never had a choice! The Institution needed a villain. That lot fell to me. I never chose it." Blackheart's bitterness motivates his villainy, but he occasionally stays from villain to hero as the distinction between good and evil becomes blurred.

As Nimona and Blackheart begin to work together, however, readers see major differences in their characters. Nimona is willing to do anything to win. She is not afraid of killing people—innocent or guilty—and her impulsive aggression often gets both herself and her new boss in trouble. Blackheart, on the other hand, is much more precise and scientific in his approach to vengeance. He plans out his attacks in detail and relies on scientific experimentation to make his point. For example, the two villains find out that the Institution for Law Enforcement and Heroics has been stockpiling a poisonous substance called "jaderoot." Though they do not know what the plans for the jaderoot are, they leak news of the stockpile to the public, and then Blackheart makes a poison that sets off a chain of undetermined illnesses that mimic that poison's side effects. The development of the antihero through these two characters in this series is one of its strongest aspects. Though it seems obvious that readers should dislike a character who is not only willing but eager to destroy others in self-interest, it is hard not to find the touchy teen and her calm boss likeable. Again, Stevenson bends the lines between good and evil: while Blackheart is likely acting to service his personal vendettas, he is also doing the general public a service by exposing the true nature of the powerful Institution.

Nimona is flawed, but also complex and full of contradictions. She is at one moment wide-eyed and playful, the next heroic and impulsive, another brooding and murderous. Though this is revealed within the first few panels of the novel, readers may find themselves amused by the continued antics of this teen. Her enthusiastic aggression, however, often gets her into trouble. In one action scene, she has shifted into dragon form to fight Goldenloin and his soldiers. While in this form, she is beheaded, leaving Blackheart grief stricken. Not even losing her head can stop this sidekick, though. She regrows a head, attacks the soldiers and Goldenloin, and rescues Blackheart.

Her backstory also gives her depth and makes her an empathetic character. She tells Blackheart that when she was six years old, her village that was attacked by raiders. She was out in the woods when she heard a voice coming from a hole in the ground. A witch was trapped and needed help. The witch turned the child into a dragon, so the witch could be carried out of the trap. At this point in the tale, Blackheart quipped, "Really, turn the six-year-old into a dragon? That was her idea?" The idea did turn out to be problematic. Once rescued, the witch departed, leaving Nimona in the form of a dragon. It took weeks for Nimona to figure out how to change back to human form, and by that time, her village had been burned to the ground and its residents, including her family, had been killed. She was left on her own and taught herself how to use her new powers of shape-shifting and take care of herself. Once more, Blackheart inserts irritation into the tale, responding, "I don't get it. The witch turned you into a dragon—why were you able to become other animals?" Nimona's response is simple: "The spell was slippery. She wasn't a very good witch." Nimona's story is not very good either, leaving room to doubt its veracity and Nimona's reliability.

Blackheart, too, is multilayered. Forced into the role of villain, he struggles with doing what is right and has set up a system of rules to keep his vengeance reasonable.

He rarely harms others and is frustrated with Nimona's lack of compassion. In one situation, they are robbing a bank, and he says to Nimona, "Just try not kill anyone, okay?" He also sends her out to make sure innocent bystanders are far enough away that no one will be hurt by his planned explosion using a supergun he created, a reflection of his interest in science. Besides being a villain, Blackheart is characterized as a mad scientist, allowing for even further antics for the two villains.

If a story is going to have a supervillain and his sidekick, then it must also have a hero. Ambrosius Goldenloin fills the role of superhero in the story. His superhero status is questionable, though, since readers are told early on that he blew Blackheart's arm off out of jealousy. Later, he is ordered by the Director to kill Nimona and Blackheart, and he bargains to kill only Nimona to save his old friend. Ultimately, though Goldenloin is revealed as a coward, readers also see him as a better friend to Blackheart than originally suggested.

These three characters are tied together by the themes of friendship, loyalty, individuality, and rescue. Blackheart and Nimona become more than boss and sidekick almost immediately. They quickly come to like and care for one another, and Blackheart's almost parental behavior further points to his good qualities. The enduring and complicated friendship and romance between Blackheart and Goldenloin is another illustration of the importance of this theme. Both relationships are tied into the issue of loyalty: loyalty to each other, to the kingdom, and to their own individuality. Nimona's is the most striking personality in the book and goes quickly from the sidekick to the driving force in the comic. Her strength, aggression, fear, and touchiness fight against each other to make her an unpredictable and intriguing antihero. Finally, everyone needs to be rescued at some point, and Nimona, Blackheart, and even Goldenloin do not disappoint in the way they surprise each other by saving the day.

One of the book's biggest strengths is the way that Stevenson plays with gender stereotypes and disregards them. The central conflict boils down to that between Nimona and the Director. Nimona is physically the strongest character in the story, and her personality traits are decidedly out of character for the typical female lead. Her punk hair and larger frame also defy the expectations for the appearance of a female comic-book hero. Blackheart and Goldenloin, ultimately secondary to Nimona, are both drawn with what might be considered feminine characteristics. Also, while there is a romantic subplot to the story, it is between the two male leads. Stevenson's disregard for gender norms and complex characterization of her heroes shows that *Nimona* is a character-driven piece that looks to change the perception of comic-book heroes.

Noelle Stevenson is an award-winning artist and writer who focuses on graphic novels and web comics. She attended the Maryland Institution College of Art and has worked for Disney, Marvel, and DC Comics. Nimona *was a 2015 National Book Award finalist.*

In addition to the well-developed characters and the engaging themes, *Nimona* has been lauded for a variety of other strengths. Among these positives are the science-fantasy elements. Blackheart's reliance on logic and science, along with his ability to develop poisons and weapons, point to science fiction, while the setting and Nimona's shape-shifting bring in fantasy elements. As noted earlier, Stevenson's dialogue is filled with snarky asides and gags; the graphic novel overall is quite funny, but the comedy ranges from downright silly to humor that is quite dark. The picaresque plot jumps readers from relationship to relationship and dastardly plan to dastardly plan in a reflection of Nimona's hyperactive persona. Stevenson is a skillful world-builder; she creates a cohesive medieval world where television and B movies live side by side with Renaissance fair clothing and attitudes. The genre crossover provides a further attraction for readers who enjoy satire, horror, fantasy, or science fiction.

Finally, it is necessary to consider the artwork in this graphic novel. Stevenson provides simple, clear panels with handwritten dialogue and colorful drawings. Though the color choices are often dark, leaning toward blacks, purples, and dark greens when Blackheart and Nimona are the central focus, Stevenson intersperses these somber-colored scenes with brighter colors for emphasis. Nimona's orange hair, for instance, lightens her intensity, while a selection of light greens provides instant recognition of television coverage of the villains' plots. The color contrast between Blackheart and Goldenloin, though not unexpected, adds an extra note to the story's plot as well.

Overall, Stevenson is a fresh voice that appeals to both young-adult and adult readers whose interests lean toward quirky superheroes and unexpectedly intense but enticing stories.

Theresa L. Stowell

Review Sources

Gaetano, Sian. Rev. of *Nimona*, by Noelle Stevenson. *Horn Book Magazine* May–June 2015: 120. Print.

Hicks, Faith Erin. "Drawn That Way." Rev. of *Nimona*, by Noelle Stevenson. *New York Times* 12 July 2015: BR20. Print.

Rev. of *Nimona*, by Noelle Stevenson. *Publishers Weekly* 23 Mar. 2015: 78. Print.

Robinson, Tasha. "Fun, Fast-Moving *Nimona* Is a Perpetual Surprise." Rev. of *Nimona*, by Noelle Stephenson. *NPR Books*. NPR, 19 May 2015. Web. 5 Jan. 2016.

432

Notes on the Assemblage

Author: Juan Felipe Herrera (b. 1948)
Cover art by: Juan Felipe Herrera
Publisher: City Lights Books (San Francisco). 104 pp.
Type of work: Poetry

(Courtesy of City Lights Publishers)

Notes on the Assemblage *is a full-length poetry collection with wide-ranging but largely political poems dealing with instances of injustice and calls to action.*

Like many of Juan Felipe Herrera's books of poetry, *Notes on the Assemblage* is sprawling in scope and activist in nature, speaking to injustices worldwide, giving voice to those who have died wrongful, often agonizing deaths and nudging readers to action. And while the list of atrocities is long—the presumed deaths of forty-three students from the Ayotzinapa Normal School in Mexico; migrant workers detained at the US border; the recent deaths of Eric Garner, Trayvon Martin, Michael Brown, Freddie Gray, and police officers Wenjian Liu and Rafael Ramos; the 1916 lynching of Jesse Washington in Waco, Texas; the beheading of Kenji Goto and Haruna Yakawa by ISIS in Syria; and the murder of nine African Americans at Emanuel African Methodist Episcopal Church in Charleston, South Carolina—Herrera manages to inspire hope.

Before hope, however, there is accountability, or the idea that people choose to be agents of change, and Herrera opens the book with "it can begin with clouds." On the surface, the poem seems ephemeral, almost wistful, but Herrera sets the stage for something more, something bigger, in selecting clouds as a metaphor for incidents of civil unrest and social injustice. He suggests that people should consider their place in the world and what they might do to effect change. As applied to the extensive list of murders and deaths in subsequent poems, the clouds are more than air and fluff. Readers are asked to consider "how they fray how they enter / then how they envelope the earth." As with any big news story, when it is first broadcast on TV or radio, everyone is shocked and everyone is talking, until the next shocking cloud rolls in and displaces the one before it. As Herrera explains in the poem,

> You can see this
> how it shreds itself so you can see this that
> is all there is then
> nothing again then you again and the clouds
> come to you and you pass.

People must choose to be present in these events, and unless they take a stand or take action, social injustice will continue, and the opportunity to effect change will be lost. Herrera plants this seed early in the book, and as the horrors unfold, readers imagine themselves at these events as possible agents of change rather than mere despairing observers. This is the beginning of hope.

The book offers more, however, than a winding road between social injustice and hope for the future. There are several tender elegies, such as the third section of the book, "Hard Hooks," which memorializes fellow writers and activists who have died— Wanda Coleman (1946–2013), Jayne Cortez (1934–2012), Phil Levine (1928–2015), Jack Gilbert (1925–2012) and José Montoya (1932–2013)—with revealing details and striking images that describe his relationship with each subject. Of particular note is "Los Angeles Barrio Sonnet for Wanda Coleman." Herrera, by declaring the poem a "Los Angeles barrio sonnet," refers to Coleman's in-

(Carlos Puma)

Juan Felipe Herrera is the first Latino poet laureate, both for the state of California (2012–14) and the United States (2015). He won the American Book Award for Face Games *(1987), the National Book Critics Circle Award for* Poetry for Half of the World in Light *(2008), and a Guggenheim Fellowship in Creative Arts (2010).*

novative use of the sonnet form, which she developed in her book *American Sonnets* (1994), and acknowledges her home base in Los Angeles, where she was especially known for her electrifying performances and her antipoverty and antiracism activism in her home community. Herrera paints an especially evocative portrait of Coleman as a "word caster of live coals of Watts and LA."

Another section, "i do not know what a painting does," includes ekphrasis to respond to art. Some poems respond to a specific piece of art, such as "Radiante (s)," which addresses Olga Albizu's 1967 painting of the same name. Others, such as "Tazmano" and "Fulgencio left Oaxaca toward El Norte," respond to the body of an artist's work (Alfredo Arreguín and Fulgencio Lazo, respectively). These poems include striking images and direct engagement with the artist, but it is the section's title poem, "i do not know what a painting does" that speaks to the process, the mysterious, almost unknowable quality that draws us to art.

While both of these sections include strong and admirable poems, it is the political poems that have the most depth and power in *Notes on the Assemblage*. "White Dove—Found outside Don Teriyaki's," for example, tells the seemingly simple story of an injured dove in need of care. The speaker notices the injured dove and takes it home, cares for it, becomes its protector, and determines that "if I release her she is going to / stumble then Jack Hawk will shred her so / I'll keep her in the cage—I tell myself." The caged dove is a metaphor for how easily protection turns into imprisonment, despite the best intentions. While the speaker recognizes that the bird should be freed and would be happier freed, he is unable to do so, worrying that the bird will be hurt by other natural forces.

In the final poem in the book, the moving "Poem by Poem," dedicated to the nine people murdered in a South Carolina church during prayer, Herrera speaks to the power of poetry, not only as a call to action but as action itself. "Poem by // poem / we can end the violence," Herrera writes. He emphasizes the responsibility of each individual within the community to answer the call and to stop the escalating violence: "You have a poem to offer / it is made of action—you must / search for it . . . give your life to it." Herrera encourages readers to have empathy for people unlike themselves:

> when the blood come down
> do not ask if
> it is your blood it
> is made of 9 drops
> honor them
> wash them stop them
> from falling.

Stylistically, Herrera continues to build upon his early influences. He utilizes the long lines, the listing and layering of images of Walt Whitman and Allen Ginsburg, and each poem gains power and momentum through these techniques. Poems such as "Half Mexican" speak to the constraints of labels, how being thought "half" essentially means not being truly either Mexican or American and results in "the half against itself." The listing of images in the following lines helps propel the poem forward and reveals a visceral frustration:

> Slavery, sinew, hearts shredded sacrifices for the continuum
> Quarks & galaxies, the cosmic milk that flows into trees
> Then darkness
> What is the other—yes

Herrera also incorporates his signature use of anaphora, repetition at the beginning of multiple successive clauses, lines, or verses, evident in older poems like "Blood on the Wheel" from *Border-Crosser with a Lamborghini Dream* (1999), in which he repeats the phrase "Blood on the . . . " at the beginning of line after line. Herrera largely follows this construction through much of the poem, giving it the incantatory feel of litany. In *Notes on the Assemblage*, his use of anaphora is much more subtle. The phrases are generally shorter, used more infrequently, and dispersed more sporadically throughout the poem. In poems such as "song out here," Herrera repeats "if I could sing" at the beginning, in the middle, and at the end of the poem, and he repeats "it's gonna be alright" three times in a row two-thirds of the way through the poem. He employs this convention in several poems, including "Borderbus" and "Almost Livin'

Almost Dyin,'" and it provides a haunting echo, something readers hear, question, and anticipate.

If there is one criticism, it would be Herrera's resistance to punctuating his poems, making them sometimes difficult to parse and necessitating several re-readings to determine his intended phrasing and message, though after a few attempts, his intentions become clear. Herrera most likely hopes to slow readers down to help them visually secure the images and encourage greater understanding. In "Ayotzinapa," for example, lines 3–5 read:

> it was a protest for our school that is all rural teachers nothing
> more nothing less we were protesting for funds that is all we were
> surrounded by police

After a couple of reading passes, it is clear that the lines should be read: "it was a protest for our school that is all rural teachers, nothing more, nothing less; we were protesting for funds, that is all. We were surrounded by police." However, if readers could have that degree of clarity on the first read, rather than the second or third, their understanding may be greater and the power of the poem more evident. This is especially important when reading the poem as opposed to listening to it. Undoubtedly Herrera relies on his immense performance skills when reciting the poem in person to get his ideas across.

Nevertheless, *Notes on the Assemblage* is an important book and worthy of the near-unanimous accolades it has received. Craig Morgan Teicher, reviewing the book for National Public Radio, starts his assessment by declaring Herrera "at the top of his game." Rigoberto González, reviewing for the *Los Angeles Review of Books*, stated that the lesson Herrera provides is "how to close the space between those who suffer and those who can respond to that suffering." These poems provide a lesson in empathy. They provide a lesson in acting on that empathy. They provide a much-needed and powerful lesson.

Marybeth Rua-Larsen

Review Sources

Berman, Barbara. "Notes on the Assemblage by Juan Felipe Herrera." Rev. of *Notes on the Assemblage*, by Juan Felipe Herrera. *Rumpus*. Rumpus, 2 Oct. 2015. Web. 28 Dec. 2015.

Gonzalez, Rigoberto. "Juan Felipe Herrera's Global Voice and Vision." Rev. of *Notes on the Assemblage*, by Juan Felipe Herrera. *Los Angeles Review of Books*. Los Angeles Review of Books, 23 Sept. 2015. Web. 28 Dec. 2015.

Hoffert, Barbara. "Notes on the Assemblage by Juan Felipe Herrera: LJ Review." Rev. of *Notes on the Assemblage*, by Juan Felipe Herrera. *Library Journal* 1 Sept. 2015: 102. Print.

Lund, Elizabeth. "A New Collection from the Poet Laureate and Other Best-Poetry Books." Rev. of *Notes on the Assemblage*, by Juan Felipe Herrera. *Washington Post*. Washington Post, 18 Aug. 2015. Web. 28 Dec. 2015.

McHenry, Eric. "Poetry." Rev. of *Notes on the Assemblage*, by Juan Felipe Herrera. *New York Times* 27 Dec. 2015: BR26. Print.

Teicher, Craig Morgan. "From Mexico Kidnappings to Eric Garner, Herrera Writes Poetry of the Moment." Rev. of *Notes on the Assemblage*, by Juan Felipe Herrera. *NPR Books*. NPR, 16 Sept. 2015. Web. 28 Dec. 2015.

On the Move

Author: Oliver Sacks (1933–2015)
Publisher: Knopf (New York). Illustrated. 397 pp.
Type of work: Autobiography
Time: 1930s–2010s
Locales: United States, England

(Courtesy of Graywolf Press)

On the Move offers Oliver Sacks's own story of his life as a gay man, a bodybuilder, a swimmer, a motorcyclist, a writer, and one of the most distinguished doctors of his era. Sacks, who was enormously interested in the human brain, shared his knowledge with millions of readers in a series of widely read books.

Principal personages:
OLIVER SACKS (1933–2015), British-born doctor, scientist, and medical writer
THOM GUNN (1929–2004), British-born poet; his longtime friend
JONATHAN MILLER, British physician, media figure, and play director; his longtime friend
FRANCIS CRICK (1916–2004), pioneering British scientist most famous for codiscovering the double helix structure of DNA

The millions of readers who have helped make Dr. Oliver Sacks one of the best-selling medical and scientific writers of all time will naturally be interested in learning more about the man who produced such popular books as *Awakenings* (1973), *The Man Who Mistook His Wife for a Hat* (1985), *Seeing Voices* (1989), and *Musicophilia* (2005), among many others. Even many persons who have not actually read much, if anything, by Sacks will know his name. He was, after all, respected as not only a writer but also an important scientist in his own right. Thus, an autobiography by Sacks, who passed away in 2015 from cancer at age of eighty-two, shortly after the book's publication, can expect to attract a wide readership.

Sacks lived an undeniably interesting life. Born to prominent Jewish physicians in Britain in 1933, the year that Adolf Hitler took power in Germany, Sacks was one of many children who had to be evacuated from wartime London to rural England to escape German bombing. Yet he says little about the war or its immediate aftermath, focusing instead on his late teens and early twenties, by which time he had already developed a strong interest in science, motorcycles, and other young men. His father took the latter information quietly and tolerantly, but the reaction of Sacks's mother provides one of the most shocking moments in this book and in his life: after hearing the news, "she came down with a face of thunder, a face I had never seen before. 'You are an abomination,' she said. 'I wish you had never been born.' Then she left and did not speak to me for several days." Later their relationship resumed. Sacks's mother never mentioned the matter again and never apologized. "But her words," Sacks says, "haunted me for much of my life and played a major part in inhibiting and interjecting with guilt what should have been a free and joyous expression of sexuality."

Readers hoping for a fuller treatment of this issue from one of the most significant scientists of the twentieth century will be disappointed. Sacks says little about his life as a gay man, partly because he was largely closeted and partly because—for reasons he never quite explains—he went without sex for much of his life. Sexually active during his twenties and thirties, in 1972, he ceased having sex for thirty-five years. In the decade before his death, he finally met and fell in love with a much-younger man, but again Sacks says almost nothing about this aspect of his existence.

The book as a whole is not especially revealing about Sacks himself. He discusses his varied interests in motorbikes, swimming, traveling, and weightlifting; in fact, anyone who is familiar with Sacks mainly from photographs taken during his old age may be surprised to see the photo of him sitting, thick-thighed and smiling, during his youth in a leather jacket and astride a massive motorcycle. And such readers may also be surprised to see photos of him taken around the same time at Muscle Beach in Venice, California, or the picture of him in his late twenties lifting six hundred pounds from a squatting position to win a California state record. Given his physical and mental accomplishments, Sacks had every reason to be enormously self-confident. But instead he depicts himself as a shy, quiet, diffident, somewhat awkward person (at least in his early years and into his twenties and thirties), disappointed in love and eventually spiraling into heavy drug use in the 1960s. This revelation of his drug addiction may be another major surprise for many readers, but again Sacks does not go into much detail. His tone throughout the book is even, measured, understated, and even somewhat underwhelming.

Oliver Sacks was a neurologist widely known for his writings about his patients and his other medical and scientific interests. His highly acclaimed books include The Man Who Mistook His Wife for a Hat, Seeing Voices: A Journey into the World of the Deaf, *and* An Anthropologist on Mars.

Both Sacks and the book come most alive when he is recounting his various scientific discoveries, including his early work on migraine headaches and his increasing interest in various aspects of the brain and various mental aberrations. One is reminded repeatedly throughout this autobiography that much of what we know about the proper functioning of the brain results from learning about all the many ways in which it can *mal*function. Poignantly, one of Sacks' own brothers suffered from a severe mental illness, and so one can easily see why studying the brain had such personal relevance to Sacks. One senses in Sacks an enormous curiosity about the various patients he treated, but one also senses enormous compassion for them as well. Sacks emerges from this book as not only highly intelligent but also highly sensitive, capable of truly appreciating other people, whether they were severely handicapped or world famous.

As Sacks began to write about his interests in different kinds of patients and conditions, he achieved more and more prominence of his own. His books were sometimes turned into films; his articles were published in leading magazines; his activities were sometimes featured in filmed documentaries; and he became, in short, something of a celebrity, both within the world of science and outside it. Many pages of this book are spent recounting the writing of Sacks's earlier volumes, and these sections of the autobiography will be especially interesting to readers already familiar with those earlier texts. Sacks clearly loved being a writer, but some readers of the present volume may wish that the writing displayed here were itself more consistently compelling. Little in the present book suggests that Sacks was a master of English prose, capable of creating memorable sentences or spinning fascinating yarns. There is, as some reviewers have suggested, a seemingly "rushed" quality to the present book, as if Sacks, realizing that death was looming, was in a hurry to turn notes into chapters as quickly as possible. Anyone picking up this book as a first book by Sacks may be disappointed. Anyone already a fan of his writing will probably welcome the chance to learn about his life, no matter how laconically that life is described.

Partly, perhaps, because Sacks was so insecure for so much of his life, he may have felt the need to emphasize his accomplishments as his life came to a close. This book may strike some readers as partly a catalog of all the famous people he knew, all the various honors he received, and all the various opportunities his best sellers created for him in other media. Of course, part of the real interest of his life will lie, for most readers, precisely in learning about all the intriguing personalities he met during the course of his eighty-two years, including the stage director Jonathan Miller, the poet Thom Gunn, the cartoonist Al Capp, the diplomat Abba Eban, the actor Robin Williams, the Harvard scientist Stephen Jay Gould, and the Nobel Prize–winning scientist Francis Crick, one of the codiscoverers of the double helix structure of DNA.

These people and many other prominent figures come into and out of Sacks's life at different points along the way, and he usually has nothing but good things to say about them. There is, in fact, little of the gossip and few of the kinds of revelations one might expect to find in a book of this sort. On the evidence of this volume, Sacks was an extraordinarily even-tempered man who got along with almost everyone and who could see the good in practically every person he ever met. This trait made him (at least by his own account) an admirable human being, but it makes this book somewhat less than consistently interesting. Sacks seems to have had few enemies, and there is almost no score settling in the pages of this volume. He seems, in general, to have lived and to have died a happy man. And, just as readers will learn little about the deeper details of his life, so they will learn almost nothing of any compelling interest about his final years and months. He leaves his life as he lived it: with great poise and equanimity.

Two surprises await the reader in the book's final pages. First, Sacks reveals that at one point the pain he was suffering from sciatica was so "overwhelming that I could no longer read or think or write and, for the first time in my life, thought about suicide."

But the matter is raised only to be instantly dropped, perhaps because Sacks, even in an autobiography, felt too reserved to dig deeper. Second, in the final pages Sacks reveals that in 2008, shortly after turning seventy-five, he began to fall in love with a person he identifies only as "Billy." Sacks tells us almost nothing about Billy, although a photo reveals that he was middle-aged when he met Sacks, and an offhand comment allows any reader with access to the Internet to track down the person's name and accomplishments. According to Sacks's 2015 obituary in the *New York Times*, he was survived by his partner of six years, the writer Bill Hayes. "It has sometimes seemed to me," Sacks says late in this book, "that I have lived at a certain distance from life." Sacks claims that this tendency changed when he met Billy, but many readers may feel that this habit of keeping a distance from his own experiences affected even the reticent, reserved nature of this autobiography. Although the book does reveal a few items that may surprise some readers, it does not delve into details and is, overall, a book much like the man who wrote it, who was friendly and intelligent, but also restrained and taciturn.

Robert C. Evans

Review Sources

Appignanesi, Lisa. Rev. of *On the Move*, by Oliver Sacks. *Guardian*. Guardian News and Media, 17 May 2015. Web. 30 Nov. 2015.

Forbes, Peter. Rev. of *On the Move*, by Oliver Sacks. *Independent*. Independent, 14 May 2015. Web. 30 Nov. 2015.

Koven, Suzanne. Rev. of *On the Move*, by Oliver Sacks. *Boston Globe*. Boston Globe Media Partners, 25 Apr. 2015. Web. 30 Nov. 2015.

McAlpin, Heller. "Oliver Sacks' 'On the Move' A Memoir of an Extraordinary Life." Rev. of *On the Move*, by Oliver Sacks. *Los Angeles Times*. Tribune Publishing, 30 Apr. 2015. Web. 30 Nov. 2015.

Self, Will. Rev. of *On the Move*, by Oliver Sacks. *Guardian*. Guardian News and Media, 8 May 2015. Web. 30 Nov. 2015.

Shilling, Jane. Rev. of *On the Move*, by Oliver Sacks. *Telegraph*. Telegraph Media Group, 22 June 2015. Web. 30 Nov. 2015.

Solomon, Andrew. Rev. of *On the Move*, by Oliver Sacks. *New York Times Sunday Book Review*. New York Times, 11 May 2015. Web. 30 Nov. 2015.

The Only Ones

Author: Carola Dibbell (b. 1945)
Publisher: Two Dollar Radio (Columbus, OH). 368 pp.
Type of work: Novel
Time: Near future
Locales: Queens, New York City, New York; upstate New York; New Jersey

(Courtesy of Two Dollar Radio)

Set in a dystopian America crippled by worldwide pandemics, The Only Ones *is an examination of motherhood presented through the story of an uneducated young woman who unwittingly becomes the mother of an infant cloned from her own plague-resistant cells.*

Principal characters:
INEZ "I" KISSENA FARDO, a "hardy" (plague-resistant) woman
ANI FARDO, her clone and unofficially adopted daughter
RAUDEN SACHS, a veterinarian working to produce animal and then human clones
RINI JAFFUR, the client who initially wants to purchase I's cloned embryos
JANET DELIZE, Rauden's assistant

In *The Only Ones*, Inez "I" Kissena Fardo, a young woman who knows almost nothing about her origins, travels from the zone-restricted boroughs of the former New York City to an upstate "farm," where a man named Rauden Sachs has hired her for biological tissue and egg harvest. Rauden, a former veterinarian and now unauthorized geneticist and biologist, is traumatized when he learns what I has had to do in order to survive her young life thus far. However, he is ecstatic when he realizes that she is a "Sylvain hardy," or an individual who has been exposed (in many cases deliberately) but has not succumbed to the viruses and pathogens that have been decimating the world's population in the twenty years since the first pandemic, known simply as the "Big One."

At first, I is content to have steady meals and a safe place to stay with Rauden and his colleagues. Rauden uses an underground broker to come to an agreement with Rini Jaffur, a wealthy woman who lost all four of her children to the various plagues that have swept the globe. Rini initially hopes to fertilize I's eggs with donated sperm and carry one or more fetuses to term herself, but when this does not work, Rauden talks Rini into cloning I's cells directly. Because Rini still cannot carry the embryos to term herself, the group ultimately attempts to grow them in artificial wombs. By the time the only surviving fetus is born, however, Rini has changed her mind, after forcing I to promise that she will raise the child herself. Worried that I and Ani's relationship may draw the attention of one of the cult fringe groups that will kill those who are suspected to be "unnatural," Rauden allows I to take Ani back to Queens after he and Janet attempt to teach I the basics of caring for a baby.

I and Ani are able to eke out an existence by foraging through the many intact residences that the plagues have left behind. Although I worries that someone will notice Ani and report her to the authorities, she finds that the few people who encounter Ani are in fact fascinated by the sight of a now-rare baby and ultimately end up contributing helpful supplies. The years pass with occasional visits to Rauden's farm so that he can harvest additional eggs and tissue samples from I. Meanwhile, I is extremely protective of Ani and therefore terrified when she receives official notice that she should bring the now five-year-old to the school that the

(Nina Christgau)

A well-known rock-and-roll critic, Carola Dibbell has had short stories published in the New Yorker, Paris Review, *and elsewhere.* The Only Ones *is her first novel.*

government is attempting to reopen in her neighborhood. However, I feels heartened when she sees, for the first time, several other children who are near Ani's age. Indeed, the first day of school is an emotional scene for all involved, particularly when people without their own children show up to witness so many youngsters in one place at the same time. From that point on, I works odd jobs to pay for Ani's educational needs, but she also spends time pondering how to make sure that she and Ani are actually separate people. In particular, I is determined that Ani will never have to experience the same kind of life she did, selling blood, teeth, and tissue samples to stay alive.

Unfortunately, as time passes, I's secret becomes harder to keep, especially from Ani. I remains handicapped by ignorance, believing that because Ani is her clone, she is destined to lose her guardian when she is ten years old, just because I did. In addition, Ani's intellectual development is initially slow, making it difficult to find a school that can teach her effectively. I finally gets Ani enrolled in a particularly good school in a dome-protected area of the city, but the other children consider Ani an outcast and refuse to socialize with her. Increasingly, Ani resents I and demands to know more about her origins.

Although the concepts of cloning and a post-plague society are not new, this novel is quite original, particularly in its distinct narrative style. I is completely uneducated, has a limited vocabulary, and utilizes poor and inconsistent grammar. She also tends to use present and past tense almost interchangeably, giving the impression that while she does recognize the passage of time, she has a survivor's mentality and lives "in the now." In addition, although I eventually gains a great deal of insight into her life and her relationship with Ani, she often does not understand what is happening around her until months or years after the fact. In spite of this narrative challenge, author Carola Dibbell skillfully manages to convey to the reader exactly what is happening, in many cases by having Rauden explain to his colleagues why I is genetically special or by having I refer to incidents of which she is reminded without knowing why. In many ways, I's narrative voice is reminiscent of that employed in Peter Heller's *The Dog Stars* (2012), in which the main character's bout with a super-flu plague has affected his mental processes. In both novels, the narrative style is jarring at first but soon becomes transparent to the reader because it remains perfectly consistent and is logically derived from the character's particular circumstances.

In addition to *The Dog Stars*, *The Only Ones* shares a literary tradition with two classic post-plague dystopian novels: *The Handmaid's Tale* (1985), by Margaret Atwood, and *Earth Abides* (1949), by George R. Stewart. Like *The Handmaid's Tale*, Dibbell's novel centers on a young woman who is of great value to the human race because she retains a rare capacity to viably reproduce, even if not by traditional means. Similarly, as in *Earth Abides*, Dibbell creates a post-disaster generation whose outlooks and priorities are so different from those of present-day North Americans that they seem almost alien. *The Only Ones* takes this point a step further by emphasizing the differences between I's and Ani's priorities, even though they are genetically identical clones separated by only twenty years.

Within the framework of the cloning and plague tropes, perhaps the two most prominent themes in this novel are those of parenthood and identity, which here are irrevocably intertwined. At the beginning of the novel, I is not particularly self-aware, although she observes others' behavior because she finds it interesting to see what will happen. She even notes, upon meeting Rauden, that he seems uncomfortable calling her "I," suggesting that he too may have difficulty attributing an individual identity to her aside from her value as a Sylvain hardy. However, once the responsibility for raising not just an infant, but a clone of herself, is thrust upon her, I is constantly forced to wonder if she and Ani are the same person, and whether that would be a positive or negative thing. Most profoundly, near the end of the novel, I concludes that while her specific feelings for Ani are completely unique, in that she would not feel the same about any other clone of herself, she understands that the nature of those feelings is actually universal in the human experience. Jason Heller, in a review for NPR, lauded Dibbell's use of the relationship between I and Ani to prompt significant reflection on the part of the reader, writing, "When Ani goes through a typical childhood phase of mimicking everything Inez says, it eerily drives home the point that the two of them share the exact same genetic material, which raises even bigger questions: How much are we products of our parents versus products of our environment? Or is the fault in thinking that we're products at all?"

The only area in which *The Only Ones* is somewhat unclear is the nature of Ani's generation's developmental problems. For instance, one of Ani's fellow students has a condition, recognized in this future world, that causes children to walk backward instead of forward; Ani begins to emulate this behavior, much to I's chagrin. Years later, Ani explains to I that these children are walking backward because they do not know if they are coming or going, but it is not entirely clear to the reader how literally to take this statement. In addition, Ani and many other children can literally get lost in a small enclosed room and be unable to find the door. Once the schools are reestablished, teachers use magnets to keep the students from getting lost, but neither the condition nor the coping mechanism is clearly defined. Metaphorically, these conditions seem to point to a "lost" generation, caught at the point where technological regression may have halted but forward progress has not yet been achieved.

Refreshingly, for a novel in which billions have died and the remainder are often forced to scavenge for life's basic necessities, this story and its dystopian portrait of humanity are not as grim as the reader may initially expect. Although Rauden and I have reason to fear the Knights of Life, who take it upon themselves to raid any facility trying to "unnaturally" produce farm animals, let alone humans, most of the people that I encounters seem willing to help each other, or at least stay out of each other's way. Further, while it is natural that I assumes a certain selflessness when she takes on parental responsibility for Ani, it is particularly heartening that her neighbors are willing to make sacrifices for the sake of the child as well. In contrast to a world in which overpopulation is a likely future threat, any viable child in this fictional future is a precious resource that benefits all of society.

Ultimately, *The Only Ones* is an emotionally satisfying narrative about identity, love, and both personal and species-level survival. In a review for *Library Journal*, Barbara Hoffert called the book "a deft study of human identity, desperation, and longing." I realizes that she cannot control Ani's life or choices, even if Ani chooses to do the same things from which I was determined to shield her. I also learns that the work she and Rauden have done together over the years, both with Ani and with some later batches of cloned embryos that may or may not have survived out in the world, has resulted in a level of intimacy that in some ways surpasses that of conventional lovers. In addition, I finally learns more about her own origins, allowing her to draw some surprisingly sophisticated conclusions about life, fate, and personal choice.

Amy Sisson

Review Sources

Heller, Jason. "*The Only Ones* Puts a Heartbreaking Spin on Dystopia." Rev. of *The Only Ones*, by Carola Dibbell. *NPR*. NPR, 19 Mar. 2015. Web. 26 Feb. 2016.

Hoffert, Barbara. Rev. of *The Only Ones*, by Carola Dibbell. *Library Journal* 1 Mar. 2015: 82. Print.

Rev. of *The Only Ones*, by Carola Dibbell. *Publishers Weekly* 12 Jan. 2015: 32. Print.

Oracle: Poems

Author: Cate Marvin (b. 1969)
Publisher: W. W. Norton (New York). 96 pp.
Type of work: Poetry
Time: 1960s to 2010s
Locale: United States

Oracle is the third book of verse by Cate Marvin, a prize-winning poet who teaches at the College of Staten Island, City University of New York, and Lesley College. The poems in this collection deal with numerous topics, including dogs, relationships, and memories of high school.

(Courtesy of W.W. Norton & Co.)

One of the first things that will strike many readers of Cate Marvin's *Oracle* is its sheer inventive richness. Marvin composes one interesting line after another. She is a veritable font of similes and metaphors as well as of intriguing images, striking rhythms, and alternating registers and voices. Her poetry is lively, engaging, and often funny. Sometimes the effect of her verse is overpowering, as if one were trying to take sips from a fire hose, but at its best her work achieves real coherence and poise. And even when it does not, it is hardly ever uninteresting. There is almost always something going on in a Marvin poem to keep a reader intrigued (even if sometimes a bit mystified). These are high-energy poems that reward close reading.

Consider, for example, the opening lines of a poem titled "I'll Be Back":

> Walking very quickly makes it quite impossible
> to note the lousy perfection of stars. It's why I walk
> as if everything from me might be snatched should
>
> I slow down, as if even the stars might be whisked
> out from the fumes of sky.

These lines exemplify many typical traits of Marvin's style. Here, as so often, a first-person speaker is emphasized: "I" is one of the most common words in Marvin's lexicon, giving her verse a strong sense of immediacy, a distinctive voice, and a forceful credibility. The first-person narrators are, however, often not Marvin herself; how much, if any, of the collection is drawn from Marvin's own life is unclear.

This poem begins in action, opening with a verb, and thus typifying the often energetic tone of Marvin's writing. The phrasing is generally clear and colloquial, but it never becomes entirely predictable. One soon learns to expect, in a Marvin poem, surprises lurking just around each shift from one word or line to the next. The words "lousy perfection," for example, have the force of an oxymoron or paradox, leading the reader to wonder exactly what they mean as a description of stars. They also exemplify Marvin's tendency to challenge conventions and disrupt any sense of predictability. Another example of this is the clever but understated way she undercuts the kind of phrasing one might have expected in line 3. Rather than saying "might be snatched from me," she instead says "from me might be snatched," emphasizing the verb and catching readers a bit off guard.

(© Rex Lott)

Cate Marvin is the author of three books of poetry: Oracle *(2015),* Fragment of the Head of a Queen *(2007), and* World's Tallest Disaster *(2001). She is the winner of the Kate Tufts Discovery Prize, a Whiting award, and various other prizes.*

As this poem illustrates, Marvin often uses stanza divisions but also often ignores them: her stanzas frequently consist of predictable numbers of lines with predictable shapes or lengths, but she often spills the sense of the phrasing over the edge of each stanza, moving smoothly from one section into the next. Punctuation rarely occurs at the ends of her lines, and her regular use of enjambment gives her verse a strong sense of flow. Her writing resembles prose without being merely prosaic. Rhythm is important in much of her verse, as in the heavily accented first syllables of the opening three words here ("Walking very quickly"), which give the poem's opening an energy that mimics its subject matter. She also has a good ear for sounds, as in the "l," "k," and "y" sounds in those three words as well as in the brevity of the words themselves. Her words here are generally short (one or two syllables at most), so that when longer, more complicated terms such as "impossible" and "perfection" do appear they stand out and command attention. This same alertness to sound can be heard in the sudden shift to "I slow down" in line 4, where each word is not only monosyllabic but also heavily accented. Again, the very rhythm of the verse mimics its sense. Marvin's gift for metaphor appears here in the memorable reference to "fumes of sky," one of many slight details that suggest an urban atmosphere—a setting that becomes clearer and more explicit as the poem develops.

Marvin's unusual syntax and word choices sometimes seem designed to slow the reader down and make them reread the line in order to tease out its meaning. For example, later in "I'll Be Back," she writes, "thunder claps, cracks / my own house in half." "Claps" might at first seem a noun but then only makes grammatical sense as a verb. The effect is complex: to make sense of this line, readers must read that word twice, so that Marvin gets double effectiveness from one word: what at first seems a thing then seems an action.

The pages of Marvin's book are alive with one striking phrase after another, including references to an "ear (pinched with a plain pearl)," rain that "runnels its hasty murks down drains," and the statement from a speaker, looking back on high school, that "I was known to be dumb, detentioned, a kill myself kind of girl." One poem abruptly begins by saying, "Angel, I'm drilling an edge of the island for oil"; later it mentions someone who "thinks she's trading up prayers"; later still it describes how a "ferry ruts the docks"; and finally it concludes with the speaker saying, "I am punching your molecular code into my / forever panel. I speak the language of locks." The poems are sometimes hard to follow and may sometimes seem too long, but they are almost always intriguing, line-by-line. Often it is difficult to see how things all add up, but readers will instantly perceive that Marvin has real skill with words and a splendid ability to concoct phrases. For instance, the poem "Thoughts on Wisteria" describes the titular plant as "a vine that centuries into a tree," and then immediately follows this with "It is terrible sweet" (not "terribly" sweet), which suddenly moves the poem into an altogether different tone of voice from the rest of the passage. This poem is one of the more directly accessible in the book as a whole; often Marvin's phrasing seems far more surreal than it does here. A poem titled "Why I Am Afraid of Turning the Page" begins, for example, with these lines:

> Spokes, spooks: your tinsel hair weaves the wheel
> that streams through my dreams of battle. Another
> apocalypse, and your weird blondness cycling in
> and out of the march: down in a bunker, we hunker,
> can hear the boots from miles off clop.

Part of the fun of reading Marvin is her sheer joy in sound effects. This passage is full of interesting sounds: wordplay, alliteration, internal rhyme, and the wonderfully postponed and strongly emphatic verb "clop." On the spectrum of poetic styles, Marvin falls closer to Wallace Stevens than to Philip Larkin, and one does not usually finish her poems feeling that one has learned anything especially memorable about life. But expecting Marvin to provide that sort of pleasure may be expecting the wrong thing. The poems seem to grow out of her private experiences and her highly personal imagination without often quite leaving either place entirely. They do not so much speak "to" readers as speak "about" the poet (or at least the poet's speakers). Clear communication is not the main purpose; rather, they seem designed to give the mind and language a workout. Yet one does not feel that Marvin is being completely self-indulgent. Often she seems to be playing, and play is often fun—both to watch and to participate in. Thus, a poem ("Epistle, Many-Pronged") that seems to begin on a serious note soon turns silly, at least for the time being:

Mortification, I've known your corpse lips.
I've undone your pants, reached in to make
balloon animals. Once I twisted you a pink
and silver rabbit-eared hat. You squeaked,
I swore I'd someday Swinburne you.

The poem continues, memorably referring in passing to an "origami hothouse of /
hatreds," to a plant that "grew untended, loved being a weed-beast," and to the way
"seeds germinate in the dark, in the same way / a sack of potatoes will grow raw hairs
inside / the cabinets that sit beneath our kitchen sinks." All these phrases, once read or
heard, are hard to forget, and perhaps that is enough.

Marvin has a way not only with words but also with forms. Nowhere is this talent
for formal experimentation more obvious than in a long poem titled "My First Husband Was My Last," which displays a dazzling, even dizzying array of formal patterns
as it shifts from short lines ("If not for this one fond thought. / Trees wave their violent
weight") to longer lines ("Yet, we had much in common. We were both / nocturnal as
bats. We both smoked furiously"), back to short lines, and then to unusually long lines,
and so on. On the page, the poem looks interesting, and reading it reveals Marvin's
usual striking imagery and linguistic inventiveness, showing her to be a poet who
merits attention.

Robert C. Evans

Review Sources

Billey, K. T. Rev. of *Oracle: Poems*, by Cate Marvin. *Thethe Poetry*. THEthe Poetry
Blog, 20 July 2015. Web. 21 Feb. 2016.
Gailey, Jeannine Hall. Rev. of *Oracle: Poems*, by Cate Marvin. *Rumpus*. Rumpus, 8
Aug. 2015. Web. 21 Feb. 2016.
Hoffert, Barbara. Rev. of *Oracle: Poems*, by Cate Marvin. *Library Journal* 15 Mar.
2015: 110. Print.
McDonough, Max. Rev. of *Oracle: Poems*, by Cate Marvin. *Adroit Journal*. Adroit
Journal, Winter 2016. Web. 21 Feb. 2016.
Rev. of *Oracle: Poems*, by Cate Marvin. *Publishers Weekly*. PWxyz, 16 Feb. 2015.
Web. 21 Feb. 2016.
St. John, Janet. Rev. of *Oracle: Poems*, by Cate Marvin. *Booklist Online*. Booklist, 1
Mar. 2015. Web. 21 Feb. 2016.

Ordinary Light

Author: Tracy K. Smith (b. 1972)
Publisher: Alfred A. Knopf (New York). 349 pp.
Type of work: Memoir
Time: Late twentieth and early twenty-first centuries
Locales: California, Alabama, Massachusetts

Tracy K. Smith's first published work of prose describes her childhood and young adulthood, focusing on her relationship with her mother and dealing with matters of spirituality, race, and sexuality. It was short-listed for the 2015 National Book Award for Nonfiction.

(Courtesy of Alfred A. Knopf)

Principal personages:
TRACY, the author and protagonist
KATHRYN, her mother
FLOYD, her father
CONRAD, her older brother
MICHAEL, her older brother
WANDA, her older sister
JEAN, her older sister

The title of poet Tracy K. Smith's memoir reflects her intention to record the ordinary. In this respect it differs from so many tell-all examples of the genre, which serve up the sensational and the salacious for a voyeuristic reader. Smith draws a picture of her childhood and young-adult years, painstakingly wielding her pen to sketch both light and shadowed memories. In a starred review for *Booklist*, Donna Seaman summed up the work as "a gracefully nuanced yet strikingly candid memoir about family, faith, race, and literature."

Each of the five sections of the work offers glimpses of Smith's life in one or more of these areas, bookended by her mother's death from colon cancer just after Smith graduated from college. The segments are numbered; each has between five and seven titled chapters that move at a magisterial pace. The first section situates the reader in a loving family of seven (the perfect number, as Smith, the baby who is eight years younger than her closest sibling, is told). It covers Smith's memories until second grade. The next section covers her life from second to fifth grade, and the remaining sections cover junior high, high school, and college. In each section Smith reflects on the difficulties of both loving her mother and separating from her and her conservative Christian faith.

Some readers may be put off by the slow pace or by incredulity about Smith's memories of her life as a preschool child. One hundred and fifty pages into the book, the memoir is nearly half completed, and Smith is still only in fifth grade. Clearly, her earliest memories hold great importance.

This work can be paired with some of the poems in Smith's award-winning poetry collection *Life on Mars* (2011), in which Smith grieves her father's death and recalls his grief for his own father. In a complementary fashion, *Ordinary Light* serves as a prose elegy for her mother. The five-page prologue, titled "The Miracle," recounts in poignant detail her mother's death. The reader is given to understand that this event is key to both the memoir and Smith's life as a young woman. Kathryn Smith is her youngest child's touchstone, to be bonded with or fought against, even beyond her death. While Smith's father, a former military man, leaves the family during the week to work in Silicon Valley as an engineer, her mother is always there. In fact, after Smith runs into difficulties at school during second grade, her mother quits her job teaching life skills to adults, saying that it is not important.

While studying ballet as a child, Smith begins to sense the emotional depths of adulthood. She tells herself, "One day I will house a tremendous heartache. One day I will reel with a singular ecstasy." Years later, she does indeed find that tremendous heartache in various romantic relationships and remembers that prescient insight.

Smith gradually learns what it means to be an African American girl. When she is five years old, her mother makes her a ghost costume for Halloween, even though Kathryn does not approve of the holiday. She fashions a pointed hood for the costume, turning her daughter into a small Ku Klux Klan member and discomfiting the neighbors, until young Tracy asks to take it off because it is hot.

Kathryn Smith grew up in the Deep South, and she has stories to tell of her life during the civil rights movement of the 1960s. She returns to Alabama regularly to visit family, taking Tracy and her siblings to meet their aunts and cousins, as well as the formidable Mother. As the youngest child, Smith misses her chance to meet some of the most beloved characters in Kathryn's stories, who have died by the time she is old enough to visit. The realities of her relatives' hard life—her grandmother still cleans for a white family—upset young Tracy.

Even as a child in a gifted program in relatively progressive California, Smith fields supposedly innocent questions from white classmates such as, "Don't you wish you were white?" These queries help Smith affirm her satisfaction with being who and what she is. However, she does not always fit in with the African American community; using what her father calls "proper English" creates a gulf between her and some of the other African American students, as does making grades good enough to get into a program for gifted children. Later, at Harvard University, Smith goes through a militant phase, reading the works of James Baldwin, Ralph Ellison, Langston Hughes, Zora Neale Hurston, and Richard Wright. Her speech becomes full of phrases that reflect her reading: the black community, women of color, white power structure. She wears her hair in dreadlocks.

Smith's wrestling with conservative Christianity is another motif in the memoir. Steeped in the Baptist faith of her family, when she is only three, Smith tells her mother that she wants to ask Jesus into her heart. This simple faith does not always serve her as she grows up and begins to reconcile her faith with what she learns in school or experiences in her relationships. As Mariam Williams wrote in her review for the *National Catholic Reporter*, "Tracy's questions about God and religion are always quietly present, too, as is her uneasiness about her belief."

Tracy K. Smith is the author of three collections of poetry. Life on Mars *(2011), her third collection, won the 2012 Pulitzer Prize for Poetry. In 2014, she received the Academy of American Poets Fellowship. She is the director of Princeton University's creative writing program.*

As a child, Smith decides to read the New Testament book of Revelation to try to understand the belief that Jesus Christ will soon return and take believers back to heaven. She struggles with the lurid details that she was taught to interpret literally, but concludes, "Even though such images repelled me, I couldn't not believe; it wasn't an option. Belief was stitched into me, soldered to my bones. It was almost as though I was born believing, as though I had believed even before I was born."

Her family's faith demands sexual abstinence before marriage; Smith watches as an older brother violates that command and hurts his parents by doing so blatantly. The high school–aged Smith rebukes her brother, using the same language her father used on her years earlier for not completing her homework before Sunday evening. At the same time, she realizes she is "someone lying carefully in wait, biding her time, determined . . . to do the very same thing as the person she blame[s]: to grow up and leave home and live her own life honestly, unapologetically, doing exactly as she please[s]."

In college, Smith determines that God is bigger than who and what she had been taught to believe. Furthermore, despite actions that her mother would have disapproved of, Smith is convinced that God is still present in her life—abiding, as she puts it, waiting patiently for her. She is, however, afraid to claim her own faith until, in the epilogue, her children are born and she begins praying, not only for them but also for herself, that she will be the mother they need. Thus, the memoir comes full circle.

Smith was one of two black female poets who published memoirs during spring 2015, the other being Elizabeth Alexander, whose memoir *The Light of the World* covers the loss of her husband and her devotion to their two teenage sons. In 2007, Alexander, who is ten years Smith's senior, interviewed Smith for the website Poets. org; even then, Smith admitted to being "quite obsessed with 'ordinary' lives."

Memoirs typically include reconstructed scenes and (possibly imagined) dialogue. However, as Mariam Williams points out, Smith "is guilty of telling much more than she shows, a tactic memoir writers allegedly use to protect themselves from the shame of baring all," particularly in the parts of Smith's memoir dealing with sex. Part of Smith's telling includes the repeated questioning of her past self, flagellating herself for things she has done and not done. She takes herself to task for her sometimes-judgmental attitude, her lack of initial concern about her mother's illness, and her refusal to face the facts of her mother's coming death. To Smith, being young is not an excuse; she is haunted by her self-absorption and desire for independence, qualities that characterize many adolescents. These questions may be a substitute for the self-reflection of an older, wiser self that is characteristic of many contemporary memoirs: *then I thought/did; now I think/do.*

Throughout the work, Smith reminds her readers, using beautiful language and imagery, that she is first and foremost a poet. She describes listening with her father to recordings of popular musicals on the reel-to-reel player "while the giant spools spun slowly around like the eyes on a robot." Later, with permission, she takes her mother's bottle of perfume with her to college and sometimes wears the expensive fragrance; in retrospect, she muses, "Maybe I was the idea of her younger self, the one I sometimes tried to reach with my thoughts, the one who would surely have wanted to live in that delicate exhalation of jasmine and new grass and, deeper under the surface, a living kind of heat. Like a young woman's wish, if such a thing could be weighted to the skin."

Judy A. Johnson

Review Sources

Bass, Patrik Henry. "No Ordinary Love." Rev. of *Ordinary Light*, by Tracy K. Smith. *Essence* Apr. 2015: 61. Print.

Pinckney, Darryl. Rev. of *Ordinary Light*, by Tracy K. Smith. *New York Times*. New York Times, 28 Apr. 2015. Web. 15 Feb. 2016.

Seaman, Donna. Rev. of *Ordinary Light*, by Tracy K. Smith. *Booklist* 1 Feb. 2015: 18. Print.

Williams, Mariam. "New Memoir Explores Middle-Class Blackness in the Post–Civil Rights Era." Rev. of *Ordinary Light*, by Tracy K. Smith. *National Catholic Reporter*. Natl. Catholic Reporter, 3 June 2015. Web. 15 Feb. 2016.

Orhan's Inheritance

Author: Aline Ohanesian
Publisher: Algonquin Books (Chapel Hill, NC). 352 pp.
Type of work: Novel
Time: 1915, 1990s
Locale: Turkey, Los Angeles

(Courtesy of Algonquin Books)

Orhan's Inheritance *is Aline Ohanesian's debut novel. It describes the events of the Armenian genocide—long denied by the Turkish government—and explores its effects on survivors and future generations.*

Principal characters:
ORHAN TÜRKOĞLU, a young resident of Istanbul who inherits his grandfather's rug business
SEDA "LUCINE" MELKONIAN, an Armenian American woman who inherits Kemal's house
KEMAL TÜRKOĞLU, Orhan's grandfather, Seda's childhood love
MUSTAFA TÜRKOĞLU, Kemal's son, Orhan's father
FATMA TÜRKOĞLU, Kemal's sister
ANI MELKONIAN, Seda's niece who is dedicated to telling the story of the Armenian genocide

Orhan's Inheritance is a novel in which nothing is quite what it seems. It traces the history of the troubled relationship between the Armenians and the Turks. In the process, it demands that the reader acknowledge the reality of the Armenian genocide at the hand of the Turks, an oft-forgotten event long dismissed by the Turkish government as part of the broader conflict of World War I rather than a systematic campaign against one ethnic group. At the same time it takes a nuanced view of such a controversial subject and the way it touches ordinary people. Ultimately, it is a story of family secrets and the long reach of the past.

The novel opens with ninety-three-year-old Kemal Türkoğlu's dead body being found in a vat of blue dye in the courtyard outside the family home in Sivas Province, Turkey. The dye is somewhat fitting since Kemal is a noted kilim rug maker and blue is considered the color of death. Yet he has not accidentally drowned, as his head and face are not dyed blue. How he died and why he is in the vat of dye is a mystery. His grandson Orhan, a successful businessman in Istanbul and a former photographer once politically exiled from the country, learns that Kemal's will is equally mysterious. Orhan has inherited the rug business, but Kemal's home—which has been in the family for nearly a century—is left to Seda Melkonian, an elderly Armenian woman living in a senior facility in Los Angeles, California.

Orhan is a decent young man and feels compelled to inform Seda of her inheritance and convince her to sell the home back to his family. He is also curious about the role she plays in his family's history because he has never heard of her. So Orhan travels to Los Angeles and attempts to get Seda to share her story with him. Hesitant at first, once she sees his grandfather's sketches she is more than willing. Ultimately, she shares her story—which is deeply entwined with the story of the genocide—with Orhan. As the story unfolds, Orhan has no choice but to put a face to the horrors and possibility of an actual planned extermination of the Armenians at the hands of the Turks, something he never learned of growing up.

Ani, Seda's niece, is not interested in the inheritance, or in Orhan for that matter. She is an Armenian activist and wants people to

(Raffi Hadidian)

Aline Ohanesian studied history before becoming a novelist. She has attended the Bread Load Writer's Conference and the Squaw Valley Writer's Conference. The critically acclaimed Orhan's Inheritance *(2015) is her first novel.*

see her exhibition of photos and stories of the genocide survivors. She wants their stories to live on after their deaths and for their experience to be acknowledged by the Turkish government. At first, Orhan sees her devotion to this cause as an unhealthy way of living in a past that is not hers while dealing with pain that was never hers. Ohanesian gradually reveals that such a trauma can indeed be intergenerational and that all people are the product of the experiences of those who came before them. Pain and other emotions are personal and yet also a key aspect of history.

It is while listening to the survivors' tales that Orhan begins to return to his former passion for photography, at last seeing the exquisite detail in the faces and bodies that speak of their experience. The meeting with Seda and Ani changes his life in more ways than one. Of course, he is changed by what he learns of his family history and the ways in which Seda and Ani are a part of that. He is also changed by the realization that what happened to the Armenians matters to him. The injustice done to them beginning in 1915 has permeated his family life even without his knowledge of it. It has shaped his worldview and his future and will continue to do so, with the new knowledge he has gained playing an integral part.

Ohanesian's writing is strong. Her characters are well defined and well developed. Their backstories are important to this historical novel, and it is evident that Ohanesian has given considerable thought to the details of each one. The motivations ascribed to the characters are highly believable. The framework of Seda telling her life story and Ani providing historical context also helps to effectively evoke different senses of the Armenian experience as they were forced to flee their homeland. Both the personal histories of survivors and the modern perspective on history are invaluable in facing the past. Ohanesian develops the stories slowly enough for the entire impact to strike her reader. Once the stories are told, there is no turning back. It is clear to all that the past must be dealt with in some way. It cannot be ignored.

Historical novels with multiple plot lines can be complicated, and this is no exception. There is an ebb and flow to the telling, with people appearing in some parts of the narrative and not in others as the situation dictates. Ohanesian does an outstanding job of keeping the reader's interest as she spins this tale, clearly and effectively switching between Orhan's point of view in the 1990s and Seda and Kemal's experience in 1915. She makes it possible for the reader to learn along with Orhan, grappling for the truth when there is something that is not yet clear. The overall effect is to create a novel that has an important but painful topic at its heart and is accessible and engaging despite the difficult subject matter.

In part, this novel is engaging due to the multidimensional figure of Orhan. He is a likable but imperfect young man and becomes a complex character who provides a relatable entry point for the reader, who grows along with him. His concerns and actions are consistent, and his personality well fleshed out. At first he does not know much about history and is not that concerned at his ignorance. Yet he does not want to treat anyone badly, not even an old Armenian woman he has never heard of. He wants to respect his grandfather's will and the woman named in it while protecting his family's interests as well. And, along with the reader, he finds himself drawn to hear and understand what happened to Seda and Kemal in their past. Once he has been opened to a history that makes him question his very identity, Orhan—and the reader—must decide how to move forward.

Ohanesian, a second-generation Armenian American herself, based this novel in part on the story of her grandmother's own experience during the Armenian genocide. Her grandmother had pulled her aside when she very young to tell her a story she otherwise never spoke of. After the telling it was never mentioned again. Yet the story stuck with Ohanesian, and as an adult she became further interested in relaying it, fascinated by the intersection of a trauma that was in some ways too devastating to be effectively put in words and fiction's power to affect one's outlook. She combined the essence of her own family history with extensive historical research in order weave a fictional narrative that could explore coming to terms with something as complex as a forgotten genocide.

Orhan's Inheritance met with significant critical acclaim upon its release. Most reviewers agreed that Ohanesian indeed effectively tackled the issues surrounding the Armenian genocide, praising her nuanced examination even if she takes a definite side in what can be a contentious debate over the subject. As Lynn Neary wrote in her NPR review, "Ohanesian examines what happened from different perspectives, but she makes no pretense of objectivity. She believes this was genocide and that what happened should never be forgotten." The work was also hailed as a testament to the Armenian spirit and lauded for introducing readers to an event that they may previously have known little about. Critics praised the novel's heartfelt and realistic portrayal of both horror and hope, and many applauded Ohanesian's take on identity, history, and loyalty as both highly personal and broadly universal concerns. As Anderson Tepper wrote for the *New York Times Sunday Book Review*, "*Orhan's Inheritance* is itself a lament disguised as a romance, a narrative in which the reclamation of a family home, the weaves of carpets, even the scent of a handkerchief come to represent a private version of a much larger historical tragedy."

A reviewer for *Kirkus Reviews* summed the book up as "a novel that delves into the darkest corners of human history and emerges with a tenuous sense of hope." As the story of the past unfolds, each character adding to the growing narrative, each also becomes aware of the larger picture. This is not a novel in which the point-of-view character tells his or her story in a sort of isolation from the greater narrative of the world at the time. The characters are very much aware of what is happening to the people around them. They are reacting to situations as narrow as a family secret and as broad as a genocide. Orhan's growth comes as he realizes that to ignore the truth cannot protect him from the effects of that knowledge. His entire life—and everyone else's lives—are part of the aftermath of earlier events, whether one knows it or not.

Gina Hagler

Review Sources

Neary, Lynn. "'Orhan's Inheritance' Is the Weight of History." Rev. of *Orhan's Inheritance*, by Aline Ohanesian. *Weekend Edition Saturday*. NPR, 18 Apr. 2015. Web. 3 Feb. 2016.

Rev. of *Orhan's Inheritance*, by Aline Ohanesian. *Kirkus Reviews* 29 Jan. 2015: 321. Print.

Panossian, Nayiri. Rev. of *Orhan's Inheritance*, by Aline Ohanesian. *Armenian Weekly*. Hairenik Assn., 7 Apr. 2015. Web. 3 Feb. 2016.

Tepper, Anderson. Rev. of *Orhan's Inheritance*, by Aline Ohanesian. *New York Times*. New York Times, 5 June 2015. Web. 3 Feb. 2016.

Our Souls at Night

Author: Kent Haruf (1943–2014)
Publisher: Alfred A. Knopf (New York). 179 pp.
Type of work: Novel
Time: Present
Locale: Holt, Colorado

Addie Moore, a widow, and Louis Waters, a widower, have lived on the same street for decades. When Addie approaches Louis one day with an unexpected proposal, they embark on a new relationship that changes both of their lives. Our Souls at Night *marks the final installment in Kent Haruf's series of novels about the residents of a fictional small town called Holt in eastern Colorado.*

(Courtesy of Alfred A. Knopf)

Principal characters:
ADDIE MOORE, a seventy-year-old widow who lives alone
LOUIS WATERS, her neighbor, a widower
GENE MOORE, her son, the father of Jamie
JAMIE MOORE, her six-year-old grandson
HOLLY WATERS, Louis's daughter
RUTH, her elderly neighbor
CARL MOORE, her deceased husband
DIANE WATERS, Louis's deceased wife

Like all of his novels, Kent Haruf's *Our Souls at Night* takes place in the fictional small town of Holt, Colorado. Haruf, who was born in Colorado, has often been lauded as one of the state's finest novelists. Published posthumously, *Our Souls at Night* is a quiet love story between two aging people who have lost their spouses many years before. Addie Moore and Louis Waters, now both in their seventies, have long lived just one block apart from each other on Cedar Street—unremarkable with its elm trees, green lawns, and two-story houses. Like so many neighbors in Middle America, Addie and Louis have never been close, but one day Addie appears at Louis's door with "a kind of proposal." "I wonder if you would consider coming to my house sometimes to sleep with me," Addie ponders aloud. Addie assures Louis that she is not talking about sex. Rather, she seeks companionship and the warmth of another body to help her get through the lonely nights. Louis is receptive but hesitant; he worries aloud that he might snore. Thus begins the humble, humorous, and heartbreaking story of Addie and Louis's relationship.

However unconventional Addie's initial proposition, what follows between Addie and Louis at times resembles the most conventional of courtships. The two proceed carefully with one another, asking the types of questions people ask when they are first becoming acquainted. On their first night together, Addie shows Louis around her home. They each casually mention their deceased spouses as a kind of formality, but they refrain from saying too much. Later, they climb delicately into bed together. Addie asks Louis what he does before he goes to sleep, which is a question that is somehow polite and intimate at the same time, but notably, in addition to making polite conversation, Addie and Louis risk a stripped-down honesty with each other. Louis confesses that it is strange for him to be in Addie's bed and that he is glad he never knew Carl, Addie's husband, very well, or he would not feel as good as he does about being with her. Addie tells Louis that being together is, for her, "a good kind of new." Much of the novel consists of plainspoken conversations like this one—conversations that are, for both Addie and Louis, seemingly ordinary yet profoundly unprecedented.

Like any relationship, Addie and Louis's friendship becomes more complicated as they continue to spend time together. To begin, the town starts talking. Dorlan Becker from Louis's men's group asks how Louis has "so much energy." A store clerk makes a series of rude comments to Addie comparing finding items in the store with being able to "find any good man." Addie and Louis forge ahead, however, and decide not to care about what members of their small-minded town think of them.

As Addie and Louis continue talking together in the dark each night, they reveal more to the other about their lives. Haruf develops Addie's and Louis's characters gradually and quietly; readers learn of past mistakes, losses, and regrets. In the process, Addie and Louis become more real to readers as readers begin to see them in the full context of their lives. Louis tells Addie about how he temporarily left his wife, Diane, and daughter, Holly, for another woman, Tamara. He confesses, to the surprise of readers, that he regrets hurting Tamara more than he regrets hurting his wife. He also confesses that he missed his chance to be "something more than a mediocre high school English teacher in a little dirt-blown town." In this moment, readers see and begin to understand Louis through his flaws and in his deepest desires. Addie, too, reveals her secrets to Louis, telling him about the tragic loss of her daughter, Connie, who as a very small child was struck by a car. As Addie recounts the raw, painful details of that day, readers are drawn in to her vulnerability. At the end of the scene, Louis recalls that he never came with Diane to visit Addie and her husband after the accident, and he confesses that his absence was due to a failure of character. In a profound moment of forgiveness, Addie simply says, "Well, you're here now," to which Louis responds, "This is where I want to be now." Addie and Louis's exchange illustrates what might be a central claim of the book—that no matter our age or stage in life, it is possible to radically change the way we think and in the process radically change our lives and that it is possible to not only be forgiven by those we feel we have harmed, but also learn to forgive ourselves. As Louis himself says with respect to his relationship with Addie, "It's some kind of decision to be free. Even at our ages."

While Addie and Louis's relationship eventually becomes sexual, Haruf does not fixate on this trajectory. The true drama of the novel centers on the emotional risks that Addie and Louis choose to take with each other. Sex is certainly bound up with it all, but it is not what moves the plot. In decentering sex, Haruf is able to explore other forms of vulnerability, risk, and connectedness that are the basis of complex relationships.

Throughout the novel, Haruf subtly explores the challenging nature of family relationships. Louis's daughter, Holly, is not shy about telling him that she does not approve of his relationship. Addie's family life also begins to affect her new relationship when her son, Gene, calls one day to tell her that he and his wife are having marital problems and that his business is going under. Gene asks whether his son, six-year-old Jamie, can come stay with Addie for a while. When Jamie arrives, Addie must learn how to negotiate her various roles as mother and grandmother, roles that have defined much of her life, and her new role as Louis's partner. What Addie and Louis soon discover is that they can create a new family together. Louis teaches Jamie how to garden, play baseball, and camp. Together the three adopt a dog. In caring for Jamie together, Louis and Addie grow closer.

Through the most ordinary exchanges between characters, Haruf reveals with clarity and grace the nature of intimacy. Intimacy occurs in moments of generosity—sharing one's bed with the troubled grandson of your partner, for example—and acceptance—acknowledging, for example, that in order to be with the person you love, you must embrace and even share in their responsibilities to the other people in their life. At the end of the novel, Louis and Addie are forced to make the most difficult choice of all, one that tests their commitment to each other and their resilience in the face of what is more often than not a cruel and precarious world.

Critics have long praised Haruf for his sparse but accurate-feeling depictions of the people and the landscape of Middle America. Through his use of compressed prose, Haruf brings characters to life that are immediately relatable and human. Haruf rose to fame with the publication of *Plainsong* (1999), a best-selling novel about the intertwining stories of the residents of Holt and of a romantic relationship between two high school teachers. The novel was a National Book Award Finalist. In *Our Souls at Night*, which was published posthumously, Haruf continues his tradition of writing quiet stories about the ordinary lives of people living in small-town America. In *Our Souls at Night*, Haruf lucidly evokes the landscapes of Colorado's Eastern Slope—the "clear icy water, with brook trout holed up in the hollows below the rocks" higher up in the Rocky Mountains and the hot, dry, bare, and treeless country of the plains down below

Kent Haruf wrote six novels, all of which take place in the fictional town of Holt, Colorado. He was the recipient of a Whiting Foundation Writers' Award, the Mountains & Plains Booksellers Award, and the Wallace Stegner Award. Haruf died in November 2014 at the age of seventy-one.

where the town of Holt is situated.

The precarious, ephemeral nature of all life is an underlying theme of the book. *Our Souls at Night* remains attentive to the particulars of the material world—wet summer rain, night air, cool creek water, and human flesh and hair. Haruf often captures his characters in moments of joy or pain in the natural, physical world. For example, at one point, when Addie and Louis are picnicking by a local creek, they take off all of their clothes and lay back in the cool water together. "I don't even care if someone sees us," Addie exclaims. Here readers see the characters simply rejoicing in being alive together. Haruf often intersperses the vibrant, physical present time of the novel with his characters' fleeting, dreamlike memories of the past, underscoring the way in which living one's life, even in the most joyful, embodied moments, is always a living in anticipation of, and through, loss. Addie and Louis are sweet and sometimes funny in their advancing age, but they are far from caricatures: they are fully realized characters that seem to readers like real people who have lived long and complicated lives. *Our Souls at Night* is a moving depiction of the process of coming to love someone amid the ordinary pressures, obstacles, and losses that constitute much of modern life. It is a deeply satisfying final novel by a great writer of the American West.

A. Lewandowski

Review Sources

Charles, Ron. "Kent Haruf's Posthumous Novel Offers a Tender Look at Love in the Twilight." Rev. of *Our Souls at Night*, by Kent Haruf. *Washington Post*. Washington Post, 19 May 2015. Web. 1 Feb. 2016.

Dallas, Sandra. "'Our Souls at Night,' Kent Haruf's Last Novel." Rev. of *Our Souls at Night*, by Kent Haruf. *Denver Post*. Digital First Media, 24 May 2015. Web. 1 Feb. 2016.

Freeman, John. Rev. of *Our Souls at Night*, by Kent Haruf. *Boston Globe*. Boston Globe Media Partners, 12 June 2015. Web. 1 Feb. 2016.

Hopley, Claire. Rev. of *Our Souls at Night*, by Kent Haruf. *Washington Times*. Washington Times, 28 May 2015. Web. 1 Feb. 2016.

Le Guin, Ursula K. "Happiness at the End of Life." Rev. of *Our Souls at Night*, by Kent Haruf. *Guardian*. Guardian News and Media, 27 May 2015. Web. 1 Feb. 2016.

Silber, Joan. Rev. of *Our Souls at Night*, by Kent Haruf. *New York Times*. New York Times, 5 June 2015. Web. 1 Feb. 2016.

Outline

Author: Rachel Cusk (b. 1967)
Publisher: Farrar, Straus and Giroux (New York). 256 pp.
Type of work: Novel
Time: Present
Locale: Athens, Greece

Rachel Cusk blurs memoir and fiction in her new novel Outline, *about an author teaching a writing workshop in Athens, Greece.*

Principal characters:
FAYE, a recently divorced writer
SEAT NEIGHBOR, an aging Greek shipping magnate who sits next to her on a flight from London
RYAN, another teacher at the workshop; an Irish short story writer
ANNE, a new teacher at the workshop; a Scottish playwright

(Courtesy of Farrar Straus & Giroux)

Rachel Cusk's new novel *Outline* does not lend itself easily to description. In it, a recent divorcee named Faye travels from her home in London to teach at a writing workshop in Athens, Greece. Cusk, a well-regarded if controversial figure in British fiction, explores reality and illusion in her narrative, which consists of a handful of conversations between Faye and the various characters she meets on her trip. Faye is a woman adrift, and her own story is told in the negative image the stories of others leave behind. The shape of the novel becomes clear toward the end of the book, when Faye meets a Scottish playwright named Anne. Anne has just arrived at the apartment in Greece that Faye is vacating, and when Faye wakes up on the day of her departure, she encounters Anne sitting on the couch eating honey out of a jar with a spoon. Anne is also newly divorced, but more recently, was robbed and almost killed by her assailant. The incident left her unable to interact with the world as she once did, compounding the problems caused by her divorce, which left her scrambling for the remaining shards of her previous, single identity. Anne tells Faye that she eats compulsively and is thrown into an existential crisis by even the most casual interaction. If a drink with a friend can be summed up by the word "friendship" alone, Anne wonders what else the interaction is worth. But on the plane, she said, she struck up a conversation with the man sitting next to her, a diplomat. She began asking him question after question about his life, "and the longer she listened to his answers, the more she felt that something fundamental was being delineated, something not about him but about her . . . she began to see herself as a shape, an outline, with all the detail filled in around it while the shape itself remain blank. Yet this shape, even while its content remained unknown, gave her for the first time since the incident a sense of who she now was."

Cusk published her first novel, *Saving Agnes*, to great acclaim in 1993. A slew of novels followed—Cusk was named one of *Granta*'s best young novelists in 2003—as well as several memoirs, including *A Life's Work: On Becoming a Mother* (2001) and *Aftermath: On Marriage and Separation* (2012). These two books in particular, the first about giving birth to her daughter and the second about her divorce from photographer Adrian Clarke, elicited violent reactions from readers. Her critics found her willfully distasteful and narcissistic; her fans praised her for refusing to censor even her most brutal instincts. Those instincts, however, left Cusk exposed at precisely the moment she was most vulnerable. She stopped writing for three years, not interested in writing fiction anymore but fearing the reaction to any further venture into nonfiction. In *Outline*, Cusk charts new territory in both form and genre. *Outline* is a novel—sort of. Like other popular books, including Elena Ferrante's Neapolitan novels, Karl Ove Knausgard's *My Struggle*, and Ben Lerner's *10:04*, Cusk's book is both autobiographical and fictional. But Cusk's real achievement is her form, which is, perhaps, singular in contemporary fiction. Faye is known entirely through her interactions with others. If Cusk, as an author and narrator, was once overexposed, *Outline* renders her almost completely invisible.

Rachel Cusk is a novelist and memoirist whose previous works include Saving Agnes *(1993), which won the Whitbread First Novel Award, and the controversial memoir* Aftermath: On Marriage and Separation *(2012).*

When *Outline* begins, Faye is rushing to meet a plane. She recalls her earlier conversation with an eccentric billionaire, who wants her to help him write his autobiography, and almost immediately falls into another conversation with her seatmate, a wealthy Greek shipping magnate. Cusk never gives him a name; Faye refers to him only as "my neighbor," recalling this meeting on the plane. As the narrative continues, and Faye spends more time with her neighbor, his title becomes increasingly inadequate in proportion to their relationship. It is as if, Cusk seems to suggest, Faye is trying to keep him at arm's length despite their growing intimacy. When they first meet, he tells her about his childhood in Athens and about the dissolution of his first marriage—and then the dissolution of his second and third. Faye is a careful listener, and almost supernaturally perceptive and well spoken. Of course, as Cusk subtly reminds us, readers are getting Faye's version of events. Faye relates most of her conversations in paraphrase, attuned to the narrative structures of her neighbor's stories, which she often criticizes, not only internally but aloud. When her neighbor recounts a story about his second wife, for example, Faye points out that it invariably shows him and his children in a positive light, while the ex-wife shows up only in situations that make her look worse.

Faye's conversations are never a mere exchange of pleasantries. All of them, even those in which she first meets her students (none of whom count English as their first language), are revealing and often bafflingly intimate. When Faye asks her students to go around the table and say their name and something they noticed that morning, one woman says that she passed an open window through which she heard someone playing the D minor fugue from Johann Sebastian Bach's *French Suites*. The song, she said, was familiar to her because she used to play it when she had dreams of becoming a professional musician. To hear someone else play it, she said, filled her with a profound sense of loss. Another student, inspired by the first, tells the class about the time she heard her husband singing a song in the shower, and knew immediately that he was being unfaithful to her. That morning, she said, she met his mistress. The woman is precise in her descriptions—the orange she was juicing in the kitchen, the piece of artwork that her husband used as a soap dish—as if writing a novel out loud. In fact, each character in *Outline*—though it is most apparent in the classroom scenes—seems to be voicing or demonstrating a philosophical query about storytelling and fiction, daring the reader to believe that these characters are real and that they are really saying these things. ("Is it surely not true," says the piano-playing student to another, "that there is no story of life; that one's own existence doesn't have a distinct form that has begun and will one day end, that has its own themes and events and cast of characters?") One student gives voice to this hesitation to suspend one's disbelief: she calls Faye a lousy teacher and asks for a refund.

A running bit of humor—and sharp piece of social commentary—is how little Faye's friends and acquaintances ask her about her own life. Ryan, Faye's colleague and a fellow visiting writer, spends an entire interaction talking about himself and his writing woes before turning to leave, asking, almost by way of parting, "Are you working on anything?" Cusk's style is spare and precise, but also lightly satirical, as if written with a raised eyebrow. Many eyebrows are raised at marriage and how people describe their romantic partnerships in general. Ryan and his wife are very calculated (his own word) about their arrangements. They are totally equal partners in child care, and allow one another sufficient independence. Faye's seat neighbor's second and third wives were less committed to equality. Variously indulgent and prudish, they were always measured against her neighbor in that they gave him either too much or not enough of what he wanted—though what he really wanted from them, he cannot say. "More life," he says once, adding "more affection," but he is unable to articulate his desires any further.

Elaine Blair, writing for the *New Yorker*, points out that Cusk's narrative features only one scene in which dramatic action supersedes conversation. In this scene, Faye's neighbor attempts to kiss her while they are out on his boat. Faye rebuffs him somewhat harshly, later telling her friend that she could not believe it, that she never even saw it coming despite going on several dates with him. Her reaction is revealing, though it only reveals how far adrift Faye really is. Her friend asks if she liked the man, and she says that she can only describe her feelings toward him as "absolute ambivalence." "I had become so unused to thinking about things in terms of whether I liked them or whether I didn't that I couldn't answer her question." As Blair points out, Faye's true want (perhaps her need) is unclear; she must have derived something positive from her interactions with the man if she continued to spend time with him of her own volition. Cusk gently asks the reader to consider the point Anne the playwright later makes explicit. Perhaps, despite his age, ugliness and relative lack of self-scrutiny, Faye's neighbor "delineated" something in her. Perhaps she just wanted him to keep talking.

Molly Hagan

Review Sources

Blair, Elaine. "All Told." Rev. of *Outline*, by Rachel Cusk. *New Yorker*. Condé Nast, 5 Jan. 2015. Web. 16 Jan. 2016.

Julavits, Heidi. Rev. of *Outline*, by Rachel Cusk. *New York Times*. New York Times, 7 Jan. 2015. Web. 16 Jan. 2016.

Mcalpin, Heller. "There's Nothing Sketchy about This Outline." Rev. of *Outline*, by Rachel Cusk. *National Public Radio*. NPR, 13 Jan. 2015. Web. 16 Jan. 2016.

Myerson, Julie. "Rachel Cusk's Greek Chorus Enthralls and Appalls." Rev. of *Outline*, by Rachel Cusk. *Guardian*. Guardian News and Media, 6 Sept. 2014. Web. 16 Jan. 2016.

O'Rourke, Meghan. "Seeing Is Not Believing." Rev. of *Outline*, by Rachel Cusk. *Slate*. Slate Group, 2 Feb. 2015. Web. 16 Jan. 2016.

Peterson, Britt. "Mommy Meanest." Rev. of *Outline*, by Rachel Cusk. *New Republic*. New Republic, 3 Feb. 2015. Web. 16 Jan. 2016.

Purity

Author: Jonathan Franzen (b. 1959)
Publisher: Farrar (New York). 563 pp.
Type of work: Novel
Time: 1960s–2010s
Locales: East Germany, California, Colo-
rado, Bolivia

Jonathan Franzen's fifth novel, Purity, *combines intimate tales of mothers and marriages with political intrigue.*

Principal characters:
PURITY "PIP" TYLER, a twenty-four-year-old
intern with massive college-loan debt
PENELOPE TYLER/ANABEL LAIRD, her frustrat-
ingly mystical, mountain-living mother
ANDREAS WOLF, the CEO of a social justice
website who grew up in Soviet-era East
Germany
TOM ABERANT, a magazine editor with a turbulent romantic past
LEILA HELOU, a Pulitzer Prize–winning journalist at Tom's magazine as well as Tom's
longtime girlfriend

(Courtesy of Farrar Straus & Giroux)

Jonathan Franzen, the author of the widely lauded 2001 novel *The Corrections*, is one
of the most recognizable figures in contemporary literary fiction. In 2010, he published
a novel called *Freedom*, about a nuclear family during the George W. Bush presidential administration in the early 2000s. Like *The Corrections* before it, *Freedom* was
widely praised as an all-encompassing social novel, capturing what it meant to live in
the United States—or at least what it meant to belong to a liberal, American, upper-
middle-class, white family—in the early twenty-first century. Like the United States
itself, the Berglund family of *Freedom* faces a crossroad. Compromise and regret define the relationship between parents, Patty and Walter, and their children, Joey and
Jessica, who already seem adrift as teenagers. Franzen writes swathes of the novel
from each character's point of view, folding into the narrative mix a discourse on en-
vironmentalism, criticisms of the Iraq War, and a running exploration of what freedom
really means.

Franzen's fifth novel, *Purity*, is similar to *Freedom* in style, structure, and intention; it follows the members of a loosely connected family, each of whom narrates
a section of the book and is somehow disillusioned by modern life. Politically and
socially, the narrative takes aim at big banks, Silicon Valley, WikiLeaks, social media,
and the Internet itself. The novel asks reader to consider, in different circumstances,
what it really means to be pure.

Critical reception for *Purity* was largely positive, although many reviews were filtered through the prism of Franzen's controversial public persona. In the past, Franzen has engaged in public spats with Oprah Winfrey (he refused to participate in her book club but later apologized) and Pulitzer Prize–winning *New York Times* critic Michiko Kakutani (he once called her "the stupidest person in New York City"). He has been described by various people, fairly and unfairly, as an arrogant sexist and as a Luddite after he criticized novelist Salman Rushdie for using Twitter. Franzen has become almost comically divisive; he is an enthusiastic birder, but he published an article in the *New Yorker* in April 2015 that had even the National Audubon Society angry with him. This is all to say that for Franzen, more so than for other modern novelists, his literary output is viewed as an extension of his personality. (Curtis Sittenfeld, in her review of *Purity* for the *Guardian*, likened reading the novel to watching a Julia Roberts movie in that the viewer is more conscious of Roberts's presence than of the character she portrays, writing "it's impossible to read this novel without its author's reputation looming on the periphery.") For example, *Purity* was criticized for its portrayal of women—some saw disturbing correlations between one toxic relationship in the book and Franzen's well-documented former marriage to writer Valerie Cornell—and its suggestion that the Internet is the modern-day equivalent of a totalitarian regime. At nearly six hundred pages, *Purity* is somewhat overstuffed. Some moments, as writer Roxane Gay noted in her review of the book for *All Things Considered*, read as "self-indulgent nonsense." Nevertheless, the book as a whole is quite good, and many critics consider it better than *Freedom*.

The novel has several central characters. The first one the reader meets is a twenty-four-year-old girl named Purity, or Pip for short. (The allusion to Charles Dickens's 1861 classic *Great Expectations* is purposeful; Purity has her own "great expectations" of which she is unaware.) Pip grew up with her hippie mother in a tiny cabin in the Santa Cruz Mountains. They were, and are still, extremely poor, and after taking out loans to pay for college at the University of California, Berkeley, Pip is deeply in debt. She lives in a squatter house with a few antinuclear activists in Oakland and works for a shady Silicon Valley start-up that has something to do with solar energy. Pip's moral compass is pointed in the right direction, though she herself is a bit aimless. "Pip wanted to do good," Franzen writes, "if only for lack of better ambitions."

Pip has no real friends and her corrosive loneliness leads her to push potential ones away. But after a chic, German houseguest named Annagret singles her out as special, she is inspired—at Annagret's urging—to apply for a paid internship in Bolivia with the Sunlight Project. The Sunlight Project is a social-justice organization that publishes leaked and classified information, and its leader, the magnetic Andreas Wolf, is a celebrated global figure. Wolf is similar to Julian Assange, the controversial editor of WikiLeaks, but he is not a fictional stand-in for him; Wolf is actually described as a superior version of Assange—whom one character refers to as "an autistic megalomaniac sex creep." Wolf, who is so famous that a film is being made about his life, takes a surprising interest in Pip via e-mail. Pip loves the attention, but she has some reservations. She is also afraid to leave her needy mother. Pip loves her mother—her relationship with her mother informs her relationships with others—all the while knowing that her mother keeps from her the identity of Pip's father and her own real name. In the end, Pip is persuaded to go to Bolivia because she thinks Wolf can help her procure this information.

The next section of the book is told from Wolf's perspective. In his fifties, Wolf was born and raised in Soviet-era East Germany.

Jonathan Franzen is an award-winning novelist and essayist. His 2001 novel The Corrections *won the National Book Award and was a finalist for the Pulitzer Prize for Fiction. In 2010, Franzen published* Freedom *to critical acclaim.* Purity *is his fifth novel.*

His father was a high-ranking member of the government and his mother, Katya, was a celebrated professor. Like Pip—though for wholly different reasons—Wolf's turbulent relationship with his mother informs his relationship with the rest of the world. He is a golden child—wildly intelligent, handsome, and given every advantage in a country built on not handing out advantages—but he is reckless and emotionally abusive. He feels that deep down he is corrupted and becomes obsessed with exorcising that corruption. This need defines his relationship to both a young and earnest Annagret and even the creation of the Sunlight Project itself. His complex backstory is also framed by the story of a crime. This crime, readers will come to realize, is the central point from which all other plotlines in the book radiate—including one involving an American woman named Leila, the narrator of the third section of Franzen's novel.

Leila is a Pulitzer Prize–winning journalist who works for an investigative news magazine in Denver. She is working on a story involving a nuclear warhead and an incriminating Facebook photograph that she acquired from her new intern, Pip. Leila is the longtime girlfriend of Tom Aberant (the fourth central character in the book), the editor of the news magazine for which she works. Tom, the reader is told, is a very good man, which makes it all the more surprising (as subsequent sections reveal) that his story runs parallel with Wolf's—only his bête noire is not his mother but his former wife Anabel. Tom and Anabel's relationship, as told by Tom in a personal autobiography (a device Franzen also used in *Freedom*), is by turns funny and sickening. Their tortured tale also plays a part in the web of secrets, lies, conspiracies, and coincidences that make up the formidable plot of *Purity*.

Franzen is a highly skilled writer. He employs classic elements of structure to satisfying effect, which is to say that readers are eager to turn the page wondering what will happen next. In the hands of another writer, *Purity* might collapse under the weight of its Dickensian ambition. *Purity* is sprawling in its scope—far more so than *The Corrections* or *Freedom*—it traverses half the globe and covers over sixty years in time, but Franzen never seems to stray too far from his intended purpose. The book's thematic elements are presented with the same clarity as the plot, though these elements are messy in and of themselves. Franzen is writing about purity, but the word has a host of different meanings in his hands. For instance, Tom and Andreas both run organizations viewed from different angles as the apex of truth, but both men harbor dark secrets from the past. Do their present endeavors—the newsgathering, the publishing, the renouncing of others—make them pure? (And does that, Franzen nudges the reader, kind of sound like a Soviet regime?) Modern tech companies use large, sterile words that bespeak connection, truth, pure democracy—but those words mask a more complicated meaning.

In other instances, relationships are put under a harsh light. Tom writes the story of his relationship with Anabel to purify himself for Leila; Anabel denounces her father's fortune (and her father himself) for the impure way for which the money was acquired; Andreas becomes an outspoken feminist—pure and unyielding in his beliefs—as penance for preying on young girls in his own youth, but most particularly for a terrible incident involving a girl that looked, not coincidentally, a little bit like his mother. Franzen, who has always taken a critical interest in relationships between mothers and children, even seems to wonder how anyone can be purely oneself when one has a mother at all. Finally, the novel itself contributes to its own theme: the book's reception is tainted by the fact that it was written by Franzen, a man about whom so much is known and who has been judged in the public eye and found wanting by many. It is true, as Nell Zink suggested in her tongue-in-cheek review for *n+1* magazine, that if readers love Franzen they will love *Purity* and vice versa, but this would be an unfair assessment all by itself. *Purity* is a good book, warts and all.

Molly Hagan

Review Sources

Crain, Caleb. "Jonathan Franzen Strikes Again." Rev. of *Purity*, by Jonathan Franzen. *Atlantic*. Atlantic Media Group, 1 Sept. 2015. Web. 2 Nov. 2015.

Kakutani, Michiko. "'Purity,' Jonathan Franzen's Most Intimate Novel Yet." Rev. of *Purity*, by Jonathan Franzen. *New York Times*. New York Times, 24 Aug. 2015. Web. 2 Oct. 2015.

Scholes, Lucy. "Jonathan Franzen's Purity: Is It the Great American Novel?" Rev. of *Purity*, by Jonathan Franzen. *BBC*. BBC, 1 Sept. 2015. Web. 6 Nov. 2015.

Sittenfeld, Curtis. Rev. of *Purity*, by Jonathan Franzen. *Guardian*. Guardian News and Media, 26 Aug. 2015. Web. 6 Nov. 2015.

Zink, Nell. "Early Thoughts on *Purity* by Jonathan Franzen." Rev. of *Purity*, by Jonathan Franzen. *n+1*. n+1 Foundation, 15 July 2015. Web. 6 Nov. 2015.

Refund

Author: Karen E. Bender
Publisher: Counterpoint (New York). 256 pp.
Type of work: Short fiction

The thirteen stories in Karen E. Bender's first story collection, Refund *center on modern Americans suffering the fallout from the 2009 recession.*

(Courtesy of Counterpoint)

Most of the generally good reviews of Karen Bender's first short-story collection focus on what *Los Angeles Times* reviewer Meredith Maran calls the "stresses, strivings, and moral lapses" money engenders, especially set against the backdrop of the 2008 financial crash and the 2009 recession in the United States. Only Caitlin Macy in the *New York Times* rightly points out one of the flaws in these stories—Bender's tendency to move too quickly to a "universalizing remark"—her desire to "inject profundity," which sometimes has the opposite effect of leading the reader away from the story to the contemplation of "Big Themes."

In the opening story, "Reunion," the narrator, Anna Green, and her husband, like many couples in this collection, are perplexed by their economic downfall, but are trying to get on with it. This is a high school reunion story, and as in most such stories, this one focuses on how classmates have met with success or failure. Also, as usual, in such stories, Anna is looking for her first love from high school, a skinny kid named Warren Vance who had plans to be a TV news producer and a real estate tycoon. When she sees him, he looks as though he has been inflated like a balloon. To add to the "ripped from the headlines" context of the story, while Anna is at the reunion, one disgruntled classmate starts shooting at everyone.

Later, she meets Vance at his run-down real estate office in an industrial area, and he tells her a glowing story of his success and offers her a money-making real estate deal if she will come up with $5,000. However, a week later, her credit card bill arrives listing items for steaks, airline tickets, and over $3,000 worth of watches. Vance's real estate office has disappeared and he is gone. This rather conventional story ends with a bitter-sweet resolution as Anna falls asleep by her husband, having whispered to him the sexual intimacy she had whispered to Warren Vance when she met with him.

"Theft" focuses on another con artist, this one an eighty-two-year old woman named Ginger Klein, who solicits funds for nonexistent charities. The story begins when a doctor tells her that she is suffering from dementia and does not have long to live. Not wanting to die in her apartment, she books an Alaska cruise so at least she will be found by someone. Ginger's backstory is calculated to elicit the reader's sympathy, or at least, an understanding of her heartless bilking of innocent people out of their money. At age fifteen, she arrived in Los Angeles with her seventeen-year-old sister, Evelyn, who taught her how to swindle others. Their mother had died of tuberculosis and their father had left them for a stripper. The sisters dupe victims by telling extravagant tales of woe, deformed babies, and murdered husbands—that is, until Evelyn leaves Ginger for a man, forcing her to fend for herself.

The basic theme of the story is suggested by Ginger's knowledge that her great gifts are her "awareness" and her ability to project herself into the identity of others—both her victims and the imposters she pretends to be—sometimes imagining she has become the other person. The story ends with Ginger losing contact with reality, feeling the vibrations of the ship's motor in her throat as it moves north through the clear, chill water.

(Jonah Siegal)

Karen E. Bender's stories have appeared in Best American Short Stories and The Pushcart Prize. Her collection Refund *was a finalist for the 2015 National Book Award. She is also the author of two novels,* Like Normal People *(2000) and* A Town of Empty Rooms *(2013), and the coeditor of collection of essays,* Choice *(2007).*

"Anything for Money" is a concept story, moving inevitably to a predictable realization that money cannot buy everything. The central character, Lenny Weiss, is executive producer of a popular game show he created named *Anything for Money*, which has made him one of the most powerful men in Hollywood. His backstory is of a boy who grew up in Chicago in the 1940s and whose mother moved them to Los Angeles when his father died.

He is sixty-five at the time of the story, and his wife has left him, taking away his daughter, Charlene, who has become an alcoholic. He is living alone in a mansion in the Santa Monica Mountains, Charlene, who is now in a rehabilitation clinic, sends his twelve-year-old granddaughter Aurora to live with him. The key thematic issue in the story is what Lennie has mastered, and what Aurora wishes to learn—how to become a success. Naturally, the answer to that question is the title of his hit show—being willing to do anything for money.

When the child develops a fatal heart problem and requires a transplant in order to survive, Lenny pledges $20 million for a new hospital wing in order to get her moved to the beginning of the donor list and sets up a special episode of his show calling for people who are willing to give up their heart for $5 million. The story ends with a scene in his garden as Aurora tells him about all the things she has stolen and has been given over the years, as if by taking them, she could keep part of the people they belong to. Thus, it seems inevitable that Lenny asks her for something of her own—a trivial thing that means nothing in terms of money, but everything in terms of personal worth.

In "The Third Child," a paradigmatic story of the effect of the failing economy, Jane, a freelance editor, and her husband, strapped for money, have moved from Boston to a small town in South Carolina. As in many stories in the collection, the language is often highly generalized: "They had longed for this, from the first lonely moment of their childhoods when they realized they could not marry their fathers or mothers." The third child of the title is Mary Grace, the eight-year-old daughter of a neighbor, but also the unborn child with whom Jane has learned she is pregnant. Jane gets an abortion, and the story ends in a poignant scene with her son and Mary Grace selling lemonade and counting their riches over and over.

"The Loan Officer's Visit" is another paradigmatic generalized story, about a woman's newly discovered awareness of her parents, who visit her and her husband after many years—the fulfillment of a desire that has "illuminated" her life. During the visit, she sees her parents as younger, at different ages. At the end of the visit, she wonders why she had moved away, why they had not come to see her earlier, and how long they would have on earth together. She wonders how long it would take her to go visit them, how long it would be before they died, and how long it would take for the tracks from her car tires disappear and it would be as if none of this had ever really happened—all generalizations not clearly justified by the story.

"Refund" begins with another generalized couple—in their late thirties, sunk in debt, having failed to make a living on their painting. They sublet their apartment, which is six blocks north of the World Trade Center, to get needed money for their son's private school. Less than two weeks after they leave, the Trade Center towers go down, and their tenant wants a refund. The couple return to a stack of bills and constant e-mail demands from their former tenant for a refund, including $1,000 for every nightmare she has had since the attack. This is a story of a couple caught, as many of Bender's couples are, by lack of money, but it is also tied in to the Twin Towers disaster.

"This Cat" is a whimsical, yet potentially tragic, story of a forty-four-year-old woman who, after buying a cat for her two children, cuddles the animal, feels a familiar fullness in her breasts, and squeezes a droplet of milk out of one nipple. When she tells her gynecologist about it, she is put through a number of painful tests on her breasts. When the cat mysteriously dies, the story ends with the mother and her children burying it in the backyard, and the phone ringing, which she worries is the hospital calling with the results of her tests—a rather predictable ending to a story based on an intriguing metaphor.

"A Chick from My Dream Life" is a characteristic sister-identification story, about a twelve-year-old narrator named Sally, whose eleven-year-old sister Betsy has one hand with no fingers, which makes her "possess" the parents in a way Sally does not. Sally is jealous of the special nature the hand gives Betsy, even as she pities her. Throughout the story, Sally has mixed feelings about her sister's deformity. When Betsy touches a boy's arm with her bad hand, Sally thinks she had never wanted so much to be her. The story ends with a scene on the beach when Betsy tells a group of boys that her name is Sally, and they begin to chase her. She takes Sally's hand with her good hand, and it fits so perfectly, it has never fit so well, and they run with the boys calling "Sally, Sally," as they run after Betsy—making the identification between the two girls complete.

"The Sea Turtle Hospital" is written from the point of view an assistant elementary school teacher on a day when a shooter enters the school. In spite of the horrors of such scenarios in modern America, the narrator takes a rather flippant attitude toward it all. For example, she thinks one boy, a biter, could go, while another, her best reader, could be saved first. In a previous lockdown at a nearby school, a tenth grader brought out a hammer and started "whacking" his classmates. Consequently, when the senior teacher begins to sing "If I Had a Hammer," the narrator thinks it is a "poor choice." However, Bender's use of this example is in itself a questionable choice, meant to make the reader laugh at a potentially tragic situation.

The story shifts to a student, Keisha Jones, whom no one has come to pick up and with whom the narrator identifies. Keisha is upset, not because of the shooting, but because she has not brought her permission slip for going to the sea turtle hospital the next day. Predictably, the narrator, who obviously needs her own lesson in loneliness because her boyfriend has left her, decides to take the girl to see the sea turtles, saying she wants them to have something new and gorgeous on their minds.

When they do see the turtles, naturally Keisha feels sorry for their condition, especially for a pitiful blind turtle, whom she thinks is too big for the tank he is in. She makes the teacher promise to get him a larger tank. However, reality sets in when the two get to Keisha's apartment and find a number of parked cars, including one police car looking for the missing child. As the narrator and Keisha talk about their grandiose plans for the turtle, the narrator feels that the sky seemed to be "holding back something invisible and enormous"—a generalized metaphor more conventional than significant.

This collection of stories was shortlisted for the National Book Award. However, these stories are somewhat predictable in their structure and conventional in their methods—receiving good reviews mainly for the timeliness of their subject matter and themes.

Charles E. May

Review Sources

Brady, Michael Patrick. Rev. of *Refund*, by Karen E. Bender. *Boston Globe*. Boston Globe Media Partners, 14 Jan. 2015. Web. 29 Dec. 2015.

Maran, Meredith. Rev of *Refund*, by Karen E. Bender. *Los Angeles Times*. Los Angeles Times, 23 Jan. 2015. Web. 29 Dec. 2015.

Macy, Caitlin. Rev. of *Refund*, by Karen E. Bender. *New York Times*. New York Times, 22 Mar. 2015. Web. 29 Dec. 2015.

Rev. of *Refund*, by Karen E. Bender. *Kirkus*. Kirkus Media, 22 Oct. 2014. Web. 29 Dec. 2015.

Rev. of *Refund*, by Karen E. Bender. *Publishers Weekly*. PWxyz, 10 Nov. 2014. Web. 29 Dec. 2015.

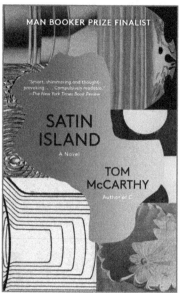

Satin Island

Author: Tom McCarthy (b. 1969)
Publisher: Alfred A. Knopf (New York), 192 pp.
Type of work: Novel
Time: Early twenty-first century
Locales: London, England; various cities in Western Europe

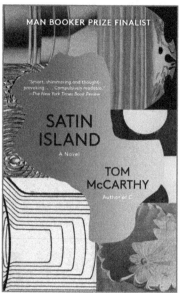

(Courtesy of Alfred A. Knopf)

In Satin Island, *renowned writer and avant-garde thinker Tom McCarthy explores the problem of creating genuine intellectual and social meaning, as well as relationships, in the context of a society defined and governed by a corporate monoculture.*

Principal characters:
U., the narrator and a corporate anthropologist
PEYMAN, his boss and the head of the Company
MADISON, his lover
DANIEL, his colleague
PETR, his friend
TAPIO, Peyman's right-hand man

Tom McCarthy's latest book is a relentless interrogation of the effects of technology, networks, and the production of meaning and relationships in the twenty-first century corporate landscape. *Satin Island* is a novel that resists with ferocious intensity the conventional structures of the genre, and this resistance defines the story and all of its forms as the plot, setting, characters, and relationships emerge as faint shadows and remain barely discernible throughout. The building blocks of narrative have been stripped down below the bare essentials. The result, which is clearly deliberate in light of McCarthy's much-praised avant-garde practice of rejecting conventional narrative forms, is to force readers to question how meaning is created and consumed in the brave new world of corporate supremacy. The effect of this required interrogation is one of disorientation and even frustration as readers wait in vain for some sort of clarity—for characters, events, or relationships—to hang on to. For some, these disconcerting effects might overshadow the narrator's occasionally insightful theoretical ruminations; other readers might ultimately appreciate the book's refusal to let itself off the hook, as it ruthlessly embodies its obsessive themes of meaningless repetition, complex network structures, and corporate dominance over consumer culture to the point of hollowing out human relationships along with the key art form intended to represent them.

Eschewing the expected structures of a novel, McCarthy introduces his main character as a man who calls himself U. and is a classically trained anthropologist whose talents serve not academia but the Company, a global branding-type consultancy whose name is never revealed. U.'s involvement with the Company in part suggests the unknowability of corporate secrecy and power but also its generic nature. Like so many overgrown corporations, the Company's primary significance lies in its power to produce and control consumers by manufacturing meaning for products. U.'s job as corporate anthropologist is to supply this meaning, which he fulfills, dwelling in a basement office, by pondering things such as the symbolism of breakfast and by folding critical theory into the rips and creases of blue jeans, all in service of helping other companies sell more stuff. But to U., this meaning at first seems to be genuine as he quotes his boss, "We dealt, as Peyman liked to say, in narratives," an ironic announcement in a novel that works so hard to resist almost everything about narrative, particularly its implicit promise of coherence.

Accordingly, there are some events and even more patterns in this story but no real plot. The novel opens with U. stranded at the airport in Turin, Italy, as he is trying to return to London. While he waits, he ponders the airport's status as a hub and a connection point, which leads him to other types of connectors and implicitly signals his own role as connector, serving to connect bits of knowledge in his anthropological work. He begins to notice the patterns of sounds, people, and images around him: two boys chase each other throughout the airport and video screens show repeated images of football replays, a bombing in the Middle East, and an aerial shot of an oil spill. He then receives a celebratory text from his boss, Peyman, announcing that the Company has won a major contract called the Koob-Sassen Project. Then he receives another text with the same message from another colleague, then another. He receives a Skype call from his lover; the chasing boys and screen images repeat and are reflected over and over again on the surfaces of the glass shops and luxury goods lining the airport. These patterns, which initially seem to be U.'s chance observations as he waits for his flight, actually signal the novel's themes of repetition, connection, and networks and how they come to make (or not make) meaning.

Tom McCarthy's previous books include Remainder *(2005),* Tintin and the Secret of Literature *(2006),* Men in Space *(2007), and* C *(2010).* Satin Island *and* C *were both short-listed for the Man Booker prize.*

Aside from his contributions to the Koob-Sassen and other company projects, U. has been assigned by Peyman to produce some sort of ultimate meaning in the form of the Great Report, which Peyman declares will be "The First and Last Word on our age." This task, ultimately abandoned, prompts U. to collect dossiers on the various items and phenomena that interest him: the oil spills, newspaper obituaries, alien sightings, tattoos, the death of a parachutist whose equipment failed, and so forth. McCarthy punctuates this scavenging with U.'s theories, experiences, and occasional daydreams where readers learn of the work that launched U.'s rising star, the meaning of the Company's logo, the rituals of Vanuatans, and more.

The sparse events emerge in exactly the same way as U.'s ruminations, as repetitive loops: U. periodically looks in on his colleague Daniel, and they watch scenes of traffic jams in Lagos or other random patterns; he meets his friend Petr for drinks but frequently ends up tuning out of their conversations; he regularly meets his lover, Madison, but renders the meetings in the dry language of corporate reports ("Later that evening, I saw Madison again. Again we had sex. Afterwards, lying in bed, I found my mind drifting, once more, among images of oil."). He meets with Peyman, whose absurd pronouncements and escalating praise of U.'s contributions to the Company, which remain undisclosed, become ever more incomprehensible. Beyond these opaque vignettes, which are rigidly confined to U.'s limited, exterior observation, the reader knows virtually nothing about these characters or of U. himself. McCarthy does use certain events to toy with the possibility of change or development in these relationships, such as when U. finally hears the story behind why Madison once found herself in the Turin airport, or when his friend Petr becomes ill. But like U.'s attempt to write the Great Report, these details yield meaning that either makes no sense or that undermines the possibility of coherent narrative, a point driven home by the speech at Petr's funeral service, which bears no resemblance whatsoever to his actual life.

McCarthy's patterns of disjunction become increasingly ironic, as, for example, U. eventually realizes the futility of attempting the Great Report, and Peyman heaps praise on U. for the wild success of the Koob-Sassen project, despite U.'s minuscule or perhaps even nonexistent role. It seems that this irony is the novel's most consistent mode as it exposes all its various repetitions as ultimately fruitless: U.'s endless theorizing, investigations, and ruminations, his meetings with people that never bring understanding or develop into deeper relationships, the Company's opaque victories—all of these, the reader eventually understands, will remain incomprehensible or hollowed out and generic. The novel's repetitions find meaning, ultimately, in their refusal to offer relatedness or closure.

The problem this creates is clear enough. If readers are meant to know U., the few characters he interacts with, and the Company as nothing other than generic cogs spinning uselessly in the corporate monoculture to which they are hopelessly subject, and if U.'s intellectual pursuits are ultimately shown to be fruitless and a parody of knowledge and its uses and pleasures, it becomes difficult for readers to care much about any of these things. This is not to say that the novel is problematic because it rejects traditional forms such as realism, empathy, developed characterization, and resolution; great modernists such as Samuel Becket and Franz Kafka created masterpieces by making use of some of the same techniques that McCarthy relies on, such as deliberately obscure characters. But *Satin Road* struggles to compel the reader's attention perhaps because it relies too heavily on deconstructing conventions that previous writers have already challenged.

There is, in fact, a countervailing irony to the novel's ponderous deconstruction in McCarthy's marked invocations of literary tradition. Besides offering a clear nod to Kafka's protagonist K. in the modernist novel *The Castle* (1926), the single-letter-as-name U. is also meant to be read as "you," suggesting U. as an Everyman and thus veering back toward allegory, the most conventional of medieval forms. Likewise, the nameless "Company" has no specific identity but rather represents the monoculture that corporate dominance has ushered in. The Company does not just stand for every company; it *is* more or less every other company. Even if these allegorical hints are meant to deliberately signal an alarming return to some sort of primitive chaos, they are self-consciously embedded in literary traditions spanning from the Middle Ages to the twentieth century, and these traditions mark the novel as deeply informed by literary convention. Even Peyman and his desire for the Great Report descend from Edward Casaubon, the deluded reverend from George Eliot's nineteenth-century novel *Middlemarch*, who believes he can write the Key to All Mythologies as the scholarly last word on mythological origins. But if both Casaubon and Peyman fail in their pursuit of ultimate, absolute knowledge, McCarthy, unlike Eliot, cuts short any hint of promised closure or edification, both formally and thematically.

This is as it should be given the novel's total commitment to breaking traditional rules. But beyond the deliberate ruptures of form, the fruitless and repetitive pursuit of knowledge and social meaning in the face of corporate dominance is also a familiar topic. Is this novel's parodic, avant-garde treatment of this theme enough to engage readers? For some, it will be, especially given the increasing global influence of corporations and their increasingly intrusive cultural prescriptions and surveillance. Yet, the popularity of realistic modes in twenty-first century fiction suggests that other readers may prefer fiction rooted in more traditional modes and conventions, which perhaps offers a far more effective challenge to the cultural repetition and alienation that McCarthy portrays so intensely and with such impressive comprehension.

Ashleigh Imus, PhD

Review Sources

Lasdun, James. Rev. of *Satin Island*, by Tom McCarthy. *Guardian.* Guardian News and Media, 11 Mar. 2015. Web. 6 Jan. 2016.

Mewshaw, Marc. "An Effort to Map Humanity Goes Awry." Rev. of *Satin Island*, by Tom McCarthy. *Atlantic.* Atlantic Monthly Group, 18 Feb. 2015. Web. 30 Jan. 2015.

Turrentine, Jeff. Rev. of *Satin Island*, by Tom McCarthy. *New York Times.* New York Times, 20 Feb. 2015. Web. 6 Jan 2016.

White, Duncan. Rev. of *Satin Island*, by Tom McCarthy. *Telegraph.* Telegraph Media Group, 29 July 2015. Web. 6 Jan. 2016.

Scattered at Sea

Author: Amy Gerstler (b. 1956)
Publisher: Penguin Books (New York). 96 pp.
Type of work: Poetry

Scattered at Sea is a collection of poetry by the award-winning writer Amy Gerstler. The poems in this collection are often light, witty, and humorous, but some are on serious subjects and are frequently somber and thoughtful in tone.

(Courtesy of Tyrant Books)

Even the drawings included in Amy Gerstler's new collection of poems, *Scattered at Sea*, suggest that this will be a lighthearted, whimsical book—one more concerned with clever phrasing and facetious conceits than with probing, profound thoughts or with weird technical experiments. Gerstler's book is typically lighthearted, accessible, and often funny. To say this, however, is not to suggest that its tone is uniformly bright. Physical sickness, mental decline, weakness, aging, and the inevitable fact of death all play dark roles in this volume, giving it a kind of substance it might otherwise lack and making its celebrations of sheer joy all the more appealing. The book is not concerned merely with making jokes or displaying wit, although both are often welcome. *Scattered at Sea* is hedged round with shadows that enhance its usual brightness.

One of Gerstler's key talents and techniques is concocting lists. Individual sentences often involve listed phrases, individual poems often involve listed sentences, and long poems often involve listed sections. Often the lists exhibit clever, unexpected, or simply random juxtapositions, and all the listing suggests both the fecundity of Gerstler's imagination and the general ease with which she expresses her inventive ideas. Sometimes the wit seems strained, as if Gerstler is trying a bit too hard to by play the clown by seeming absurd or shocking. But for the most part, her poems are entertaining and sometimes something more.

Typical of her style and methods is a poem titled "Kissing," which opens with:

> Kissing occurs in skirmishes, wallops, or big gulps.
> Pressing lips to lips or lips to objects jolts both souls.
> Is kissing particular to mammals? Have you ever watched lizards or insects kiss?
> Can you imagine kissing our grave, bearded waiter?

Its diction is characteristically simple and clear; its structure poses no problems; it abounds in metaphors and similes; and its tone is both lighthearted and inviting. Constructed as a lengthening list, it begins in the first line by presenting a list within a list. The use of listing suggests Gerstler's desire to be comprehensive, to see whatever she is describing (or considering) from multiple points of view. No sooner does she make one assertion than she makes a further, complicating assertion, so that her thinking seems open-minded and comprehensive. Even the listing at the end of the first line suggests sudden shifts in perspective: "skirmishes" suggests a small fight, "wallops" implies a vigorous blow struck by one individual against another, and then "big gulps" switches the metaphorical register entirely. The first two words seem paradoxical (by associating kissing with fighting), while the third seems almost literal and over the top at the same time. The whole line associates kissing with enormous energy and strong emotions, while the line also displays Gerstler's interest in sound effects, including alliteration, assonance, or the two in combination, as in "wallops, or big gulps."

Line 2 begins by emphasizing physical contact but ends by suggesting that humans are more than bodies. The whole line again exhibits Gerstler's joy in playing with sounds, especially in the simultaneously alliterative and assonantal (and heavily accented) phrase "objects jolts both souls." Then, no sooner does Gerstler establish a pattern of declarative sentences in the first two lines than she suddenly switches to two questions. These unexpectedly put the ball into readers' courts, making them think rather than allowing them to sit back as passive spectators. The first question might seem seriously thought-provoking; the second seems more oddly playful. More questioning continues in line 4, but the addressee seems less the reader (or readers) in general than some particular person sitting across from the speaker even as she speaks. Then, just as suddenly as the poem shifted from declarations to questions, declarations abruptly resume.

Almost nothing about this poem seems predictable. The speaker's active mind implies the need for active, engaged readers. With line 5, a list of three metaphors commences. Gerstler's metaphors often seem both convincing and suggestive. Thus, a kiss usually *does* deliver "a long awaited verdict," implying that thought and deliberation have indeed gone into the decision to engage in one of the first serious kinds of physical and emotional intimacy. In addition, kissing can in fact metaphorically map "a hazardous passage," providing the first entrance into a potentially serious relationship, with all the emotional risks and psychological dangers relationships often entail. Kissing can genuinely be a response to "deliverance from dangers," and it can also be a "prelude to wounding," emotionally and mentally. Even in this one line, then, Gerstler can imagine opposed perspectives. The whole poem rapidly shifts from one viewpoint to another, provoking or confirming thoughts all along the way.

Many of the same methods that appear in "Kissing" appear in other of Gerstler's poems. Lists are almost inevitable, but the lists often vary in kind. There are, for instance, lists of similes, as in a poem titled "In Search of Something to Worship, My Eyes Lighted on You":

Other faces

> formed and burst beneath his roughedup
> public one, surfacing like battered cargo
> postshipwreck, or like alternative verdicts
> rising in the minds of a tired jury,
> or like the stowaway radiance that shone
> through his clothes . . . .

Sometimes there are lists of adjectives, as in a poem titled "Womanishness," which begins with lines that read as if they might have been written by a female Gerard Manley Hopkins: "The dissonance of women. The shrill frilly silly / Drippy prissy pouty fuss of us."

In lines like these, Gerstler's sheer playfulness shines through, as does her pleasure in the joy of producing clever sounds. Other poems employ the kind of list making used in "Kissing" but achieve almost chanting rhythms, such as a lyric titled "Cursing of the Party Responsible for Her Suffering," which consists of ten lines like these: "May his scalp sizzle, blister, and itch. / May his nose run like the Amazon. / May his lips swell to melons."

And so on. It is easy to imagine how effective Gerstler's poems would sound if recited at a poetry reading. They are poems that almost demand a crowd of listeners and a social performance. Funny as they often are on the page, they would seem even funnier as scripts for a stand-up comedian. They will remind many readers, in many ways, of poetry's ancient history as an originally oral (and aural) art.

As *Scattered at Sea* evolves, it becomes increasingly somber. "Merrythought" deals, somewhat comically but finally poignantly, with the death of a man who left behind two lovers (who talk at his hospital bedside) as well as a daughter who also happens to be his nurse. A poem titled "Childlessness" is splendidly tender. "Ancestor Psalm" is nostalgic without being sentimental, while "On Buying a Walker" is both funny and touching and even, finally, irreverent. "The Suicide's Wife" ends with the title character

Amy Gerstler is the author of seven previous books of poetry. Bitter Angel *(1990) won the National Book Critics Circle Award.* Scattered at Sea *was a finalist for the 2015 National Book Award.*

finally managing to capture a bat (trapped and flapping desperately inside her house) and then releasing it into the night air,

> into the trees
> where the lawn peters out
> where the idea that at death
> something is liberated
> can flap blackly away.

One the most moving texts—a long prose poem titled "He Sleeps Every Afternoon"—recounts a loved one's gradual loss of memory and identity and ends as follows: "It's still him, I tell myself every day. Still alive. Still in there. His sense of humor is mostly intact. He recognizes me. He knows who he is. Remembering many recent events. Except for the staples in his scalp he looks great." The word "many," which implies "not all," typifies the frequent subtlety of Gerstler's writing—the way she often manages to suggest much by saying little.

Poems such as "What I Did with Your Ashes" combine seriousness and humor (that poem's opening line is "Shook the box like a maraca"), while the poem titled "It Was a Splendid Mind" employs an entirely new approach to listing to suggest the flotsam and jetsam of an aging parent's mental decline. By the final section of the book, however, the tone becomes more optimistic, more hopeful, and even grateful. In a sense, the book moves from joyous fun to stoic, good-humored sadness, and then finally to a kind of deeper joy rooted in sheer gratitude for life and for feeling alive. Typical of this closing change in tone is a brief poem titled "Miraculous," in which the title is also the first word. Here, again, is the master technique of listing, both of adjectives ("Miraculous," "astonishing," "Incredible") and of "that" clauses. Also present are the chanting rhythms and heavy emphases on key words. Here, too, is the typical stress on illness and death, but also a focus on awakening, recovery, and, at the end, simple beauty.

The first few lines create some sense of mystery, but by the poem's second half, meanings are clearer. It is indeed astonishing that "waking *ever* follows hibernation" (emphasis mine). And it is, if not "Incredible" (7), then at least something to be deeply thankful for that recovery often follows illness. If earlier poems are tinged with senses of decline, mortality, and sadness, and if poems before those (from the earliest parts of the book) sometimes run the risk of seeming flippant, poems such as this one (which dominate the volume's final portions) seem celebratory, both gracious and grateful. Reading *Scattered at Sea* is like following an inverted arc of emotions, one that begins high, bends lower, but then finally moves back upward again. This is a book with many pleasures to give and much to appreciate.

Robert C. Evans

Review Sources

Brodeur, Michal Andor. "'Breezeway' by John Ashbery and 'Scattered at Sea' by Amy Gerstler: Something's in the Air." Rev. of *Scattered at Sea*, by Amy Gerstler. *Boston Globe*. Boston Globe Media Partners, 27 June 2016. Web. 3 Feb. 2016.

Hoffert, Barbara. Rev. of *Scattered at Sea*, by Amy Gerstler. *Library Journal*. Library Journal, 1 May 2015. Web. 3 Feb. 2016.

Lennon, Jeff. Rev. of *Scattered at Sea*, by Amy Gerstler. *Rumpus*. The Rumpus, 24 July 2015. Web. 3 Feb. 2016.

Rev. of *Scattered at Sea*, by Amy Gerstler. *Publishers Weekly* 15 June 2015: 62. Print.

Willis, Wendy. "Wild Minds, Only in Fragments." Rev. of *Scattered at Sea*, by Amy Gerstler. *Los Angeles Review of Books*. Los Angeles Review of Books, 3 June 2015. Web. 3 Feb. 2016.

The Sculptor

Author: Scott McCloud (b. 1960)
Publisher: First Second Books (New York). 496 pp.
Type of work: Graphic novel
Time: Present day
Locale: New York City

The Sculptor, a graphic novel that follows the last days of a struggling artist, is an exploration of the meaning of art and life by one of America's best-known comics theorists.

Principal personages:
DAVID SMITH, a sculptor
MEG, his love interest
UNCLE HARRY, Death personified as his great-uncle
OLLIE, a gallery manager and his childhood friend

Many artists perceive the act of creation as a pathway to immortality. Art satiates the human desire to be remembered by providing artists with a tangible representation of their voice and identity that is capable of enduring long after they are gone. In interviews, American author and cartoonist Scott McCloud has said that he believes the artist's struggle for immortality is without purpose; eventually the passage of time will erode the memories of even the world's most famous artists. To McCloud, there is something compelling about an artist who understands the futility of art and still chooses to engage in the struggle of creation.

McCloud, who has been described as the "Aristotle of comics," has been creating comic art for over thirty years. He is best known as the author of the comic-book series *Zot!* (1984–90) and the much lauded, instructional nonfiction titles *Understanding Comics* (1993), *Reinventing Comics* (2000), and *Making Comics* (2006). In his graphic novel *The Sculptor*, McCloud asks the question: is a chance at artistic greatness worth the price of an artist's life?

In order to explore the significance of artistic greatness, McCloud employs a protagonist who aspires to achieve it. David Smith is a young sculptor whose fifteen minutes of fame have already passed him by. When McCloud begins David's story on his twenty-sixth birthday, he is broke and without friends or family. Just as it seems that he is out of options and will have to leave New York City and his career in art behind, David has two encounters that change the trajectory of his life.

The first encounter is reminiscent of the German legend of Faust. As David sits alone in a restaurant on his birthday, he encounters Death incarnate as his great-uncle Harry. Harry proceeds to tell David his future: he will fall in love, get married, and have children. Although he may continue to create art, his life will ultimately be one of security, love, and family rather than fame and success. David is horrified by the mundane nature of Harry's premonition. When Harry asks him what he would give for his art, David replies that he would give his life. Harry then temporarily bestows David with the superpower to sculpt any material with his hands and mind, stipulating that if he likes it, he will have two hundred days to use it before he dies.

David is walking through the city in disbelief about Harry when he encounters his second twist of fate. A beautiful angel descends from the sky and assures David that everything will be all right before kissing him and disappearing. While David believes this to be another supernatural event, it turns out to be nothing more than an elaborate piece of street theater. However, the event introduces him to Meg, the actor who played the angel and the woman with whom he will eventually fall in love.

McCloud uses both of these encounters as introductions to *The Sculptor*'s main themes of artistic ambition, mortality, and love. Throughout the rest of the narrative, it is these three forces that shape David's actions and growth as a character. The breadth of these themes suggests that McCloud is attempting to ensure that readers can relate to David's story. Although artistic ambition may initially seem specific to artists, it is universal in the fact that it is rooted in the human desire to be remembered as someone who matters.

As the sun rises and the next day begins, David's superpower awakens. Upon learning that he can manipulate metal with his bare hands and therefore he is no longer inhibited by a lack of tools or material, David runs through the streets of New York, yelling that he is the master of the universe. Back in his apartment, he begins sculpting a large block of granite into the image of Meg as the angel. Harry appears and asks him if he accepts the deal of having two hundred days to live with this superpower before dying. Without hesitation, David agrees.

In many ways, the set up to David's story is derivative of a standard superhero origin story. Like most superheroes, David is alone in the world after most of his family has died tragically. He is then granted superpowers, which enable him to change the course of his life. McCloud, who is best known as a comics theorist, may have embraced this standard superhero story line deliberately. Not only does it enable *The Sculptor* to pay homage to the annals of graphic novels it aspires to join, but by setting David's story up with familiar narrative elements, McCloud imbues his readers with a false sense of security. When McCloud later breaks away from narrative expectations, he draws his readers in further.

The clearest example of McCloud deviating from the standard graphic-novel narrative is David's use of his superpower. Despite David's ability to sculpt anything, David's work is never considered genius. After spending the first six weeks with his new superpower sculpting and thus immortalizing significant memories of his life, David invites gallery manager and childhood friend Ollie over to view his work. While Ollie is overwhelmed by David's collection, he is not impressed and states that it lacks a singular vision. The critics who attend a later showing agree, comparing David's work to the contents of a Polynesian gift shop. Feeling defeated, David begins ruminating about how the world will go on as if he had never existed. He then tries to take his own life by jumping in front of a subway car, but he is pulled back by Meg and one of her friends.

David's relationship with Meg is perhaps the most clichéd element of *The Sculptor*. After Meg saves David in the subway, she allows him to move in with her until he gets back on his feet, and it is not long before he is in love with her. McCloud employs Meg as David's antithesis. A bike messenger and aspiring actor, she is warm and kind. Where David obsesses over his own artistic greatness, Meg spends her time taking care of others. Although she does not reciprocate his feelings right away, Meg eventually falls for David and their relationship diminishes his perception of the importance of his initial goal.

In his remaining days, David and Meg help each other survive and grow. He does not allow her to push him away when she sinks into a state of depression, and she teaches him to stop putting so much stock in the opinion of others. Meg, who believes that everyone dies and is eventually forgotten, is a stand-in for McCloud's own philosophy on art. McCloud has said that artists should create because they feel a need to produce art, not because they want to send a message or persuade people. By shackling themselves to the goal of greatness, and thereby perceiving the opinion of others as a metric of success, artists ultimately doom themselves.

Scott McCloud is an American cartoonist, comics theorist, and award-winning author. A lecturer on the power of visual communication, McCloud is best known for his instructional nonfiction titles Understanding Comics *and* Making Comics.

Once David embraces Meg's advice to stop caring about the critics, he is artistically liberated. He begins wandering the streets of New York by night, sculpting the concrete, gridiron, and brick of the city into trompe l'oeil figures. His new approach to sculpting is similar to the work of a graffiti artist such as the infamous Banksy, performed anonymously and with the intention of sparking discussion. Despite his work getting public attention, David's style continues to be described as childish and unfocused by the critical community. This does not stop him from creating, however. As his two hundred days run out and his feelings for Meg grow, David discovers that his wants have changed and wishes that he had chosen a life of love, family, and security instead of his superpower.

From the beginning of *The Sculptor*, McCloud sets up David's fate to be one that ends in irony. Earlier in the graphic novel, McCloud reveals a seminal moment in David's life through a flashback in which his father makes him promise that he will make a name for himself. This event perfectly encapsulates the futility of David's ambition. David can never make a name for himself because he already shares his name with the American abstract expressionist David Smith, one of the most famous sculptors of the twentieth century. At best, David can only become famous as "the other David Smith." Ultimately, McCloud concludes that making a name for oneself is not important. It is only a life with meaning that is worth living and meaning can come from work or relationships.

Although the critical reception of *The Sculptor* has been mixed, its visual storytelling and artistic technique have received widespread positive reviews. Many critics have commended the graphic novel's panels, which are inked in black and blue and boast strong line work and perspective. In his *New York Times* review, Stephen Burt praises McCloud's masterful skill in shaping the plot and characters through his drawings alone. Similarly, Kriston Capps of the *Atlantic* describes McCloud's visual storytelling technique as "unimpeachable" and argues that *The Sculptor* is as instructive as his nonfiction title *Making Comics*. Beyond his meticulous panel sequences and page layouts, McCloud is also successful in engaging his readers by using a cinematic aesthetic. Like a film director, McCloud establishes tone and atmosphere through his choice of lighting and color. He uses close-ups, cutaways, and expressive faces to convey his characters' emotions as well as the weight of their experiences. Additionally, McCloud maintains a sense of steady pacing by spreading important moments out over several panels. This allows the readers' eyes to move quickly through the sequences with complete certainty of the plot.

While *The Sculptor* has almost universally been declared a visual triumph, its written narrative has been met with more uneven critical response. The most common criticism has been that Meg's character embodies the "Manic Pixie Dream Girl" film trope and thus lacks any real depth. This stock female character, originally defined by film critic Nathan Rabin, is beautiful, eccentric, and whimsical, and comes into the life of the male protagonist to teach him about what is really important, while seeming to lack any inner life of her own. Meg possesses all of these qualities. McCloud attempts to make her three-dimensional by revealing that she is manic depressive; however, her imperfections do not compensate for the fact that her character operates solely to teach the male protagonist a valuable life lesson. In addition to Meg's character being cliché, some critics have argued that the plot of *The Sculptor* is formulaic. However, these alleged flaws stem in part from the fact that McCloud borrowed heavily from his own life. The character of Meg is based on his wife Ivy and the predictable shift in David's goals is a reflection of the change in what McCloud wanted for his own life after he met Ivy. Once the semiautobiographical context of *The Sculptor* is established, it becomes easier to overlook the story's shortcomings. Ultimately, *The Sculptor* is an engaging read that explores the timeless themes of art, mortality, and love in a modern context.

Emily E. Turner

Review Sources

Capps, Kriston. "Scott McCloud's *The Sculptor* Proves Just How Much Graphic Novels Can Do." Rev. of *The Sculptor*, by Scott McCloud. *Atlantic.* Atlantic Monthly, 5 Feb. 2015. Web. 15 Nov. 2015.

Harvey, Doug. "The Sculptor." Rev. of *The Sculptor*, by Scott McCloud. *Comics Journal.* Fantagraphics, 16 Mar. 2015. Web. 15 Nov. 2015.

Lehoczky, Etelka. "A Comics Creator Muses on Art and Life in 'The Sculptor.'" Rev. of *The Sculptor*, by Scott McCloud. *NPR Books.* Natl. Public Radio, 5 Feb. 2015. Web. 15 Nov. 2015.

Smart, James. "The Sculptor Review—Scott McCloud's First Graphic Novel in a Decade Examines Art and Commerce." Rev. of *The Sculptor*, by Scott McCloud. *Guardian*. Guardian News and Media, 12 Feb. 2015. Web. 15 Nov. 2015.

The Secret Chord

Author: Geraldine Brooks (b. 1955)
Publisher: Viking (New York). 320 pp.
Type of work: Novel
Time: Ca. 1000 BCE
Locale: Israel

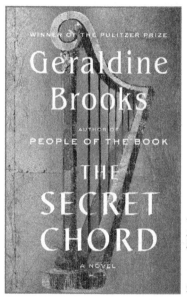

(Courtesy of Viking)

Pulitzer Prize–winning author Geraldine Brooks's novel The Secret Chord *is historical fiction based on the Bible. It tells the story of David, king of Israel, through the eyes of the prophet Natan.*

Principal characters:
NATAN, a prophet
DAVID, a king

In the Bible, a shepherd boy named David defeats the giant Goliath and goes on to become the king of Israel. In the first and second books of Samuel—the prophet who anointed both David and his predecessor, Saul—David comes across as a conflicted individual, a devout follower of God but also a terrible sinner. Beguiled by David's complexity, and inspired by the legend of his beautiful playing of the harp, Pulitzer Prize–winning novelist Geraldine Brooks set out to tell a fictionalized version of David's life through the eyes of his prophet, Natan. (Brooks uses name transliterations from the Tanakh, the canonical Hebrew Bible; Samuel becomes Shmuel, Solomon becomes Shlomo, Nathan becomes Natan, and God is referred to simply as "the Name.")

The book begins in David's court, well into his reign. David is getting old. Once a great warrior, he is beginning to show his age on the battlefield. After a particularly close call, David's nephew, a general named Yoav (Joab), asks the king to stay home. A proud man, David is deeply humiliated. In his shame he calls for his prophet, Natan, the only man who could ever speak truthfully to him without punishment. As Brooks describes him, Natan is merely a vessel of the Name, a divine voice that speaks through Natan to its chosen one, David. But Natan is also a man who has learned to wield his powers carefully for the larger good—and, occasionally, for his own benefit. On this occasion, Natan comes to the king with only his power of persuasion. So many great rulers have been lost to time, he muses. He recalls when, as the young son of a vintner, he came across shards of a great monument to a long-forgotten king in his cellar. Statues are not enough, Natan says, but a story written down might stand the test of time. David agrees and gives Natan a surprising task. David does not want to tell his own story; he wants Natan to seek out the people from his life, particularly those whom he has wronged, and record what they say.

So Brooks begins her tale of David's life, carefully interwoven with the sad backstory of Natan, who, as a child, witnessed the murder of his father by none other than David himself. That the fates of the two men should, in that moment, become irrevocably intertwined is a biblical irony that Brooks handles with the care of a realist. Most men around David think that Natan spoke the words of the Name that day to save his own skin.

Brooks has a talent for finding meaningful gaps in known stories and exploiting them to artistic success. Her most famous novel, *March* (2005), which won the Pulitzer Prize for fiction in 2006, is told from the point of view of the absent patriarch of the March family in Louisa May Alcott's *Little Women* (1868–69). The girls are at home with their beloved Marmee while Mr. March is fighting in the American Civil War, sending falsely cheery letters back to his "little

(© Randi Baird)

Geraldine Brooks is an award-winning novelist originally from Australia. Her works include the novel March, which won the 2006 Pulitzer Prize for fiction, as well as People of the Book *(2008) and* Caleb's Crossing *(2011).*

women." Brooks was criticized for rearranging history in *March* to suit her own narrative purposes, and she faced similar criticism after the publication of *The Secret Chord*. Brooks concedes in her afterword that there is a lack of historical evidence that David existed at all, though she argues that she cannot imagine a people who "would invent such a flawed figure for a national hero." Regardless of historical record, she hews closely to the biblical telling of David's life—so closely, in fact, that she seems trapped by it, unable to render *The Secret Chord* as a novel separate from the legend.

The most compelling passages in *The Secret Chord*, the title of which is taken from a lyric in the Leonard Cohen song "Hallelujah," are those told from the points of view of the women in David's life. The first person Natan interviews for his history of David's life is Nizevet, David's mother. (Nizevet, elsewhere Nitzevet, is named in the Talmud but not in the Bible.) As a young boy, David was not permitted to live with his family because his father, Yishai (Jesse), thought he was illegitimate. In truth, David was, through a farcical turn of events, his father's son, but in keeping with the customs of the time Nizevet was unable to speak up and say so. The knowledge of David's conception torments Nizevet as her husband sends the boy out into the fields as a shepherd, hoping that he will be eaten by lions. This torment does not end when a prophet anoints David as a "chosen one"; rather, it only makes Nizevet feel her shame more intensely, though she has done everything in her limited power to protect her son. The elderly Nizevet whom Natan meets in the book continues to bear the burdens of her foolish husband and brash sons, hidden away on a compound outside the kingdom.

Another woman who lives at the whims of the men around her is Mikhal (Michal), David's first wife, who is destined to spend her miserable life as a political pawn. The daughter of King Shaul (Saul), she must share David, whom she at first truly loves, with her brother Yonatan (Jonathan). David and Yonatan's relationship is both sexual and mutually reverential, throwing into stark relief David's meager one-sided relationship with his wife. Mikhal betrays her father to help David, but when she is not around, David hardly gives her a second thought. At the time, Mikhal tells Natan, she did not care. "I loved enough for both of us," she says, though subsequent events have made her bitter. Natan's complicity in her fate troubles him so much that he puts off going to see her, though they live in the same compound. Mikhal's anger toward David makes the story immediate and real. Natan (and the Name) makes much hay over several major crimes that David commits later in his life, but Brooks makes it clear that David, while also a hero, has committed many smaller crimes and that his status is diminished by the many cruelties he has inflicted on the women in his life.

Occasionally David is repentant for his behavior, though he is notably similar to his father in that pride prevents him from ever truly making good on his mistakes. Years after Yishai banished David from his house, believing David to be illegitimate, Nizevet finally found the courage to reveal David's true origins, yet Yishai's behavior did not change; he was too embarrassed to admit he was wrong, so he did nothing. Likewise, when it becomes clear that David demanding Mikhal's return to the kingdom, ripping her away from her husband and children, was a mistake, rather than correct himself, David digs deeper into his cruelty—and, worse, calls it kindness. Later, David's only daughter, Tamar, is subject to her father's brutal apathy after being tortured and raped by David's son Amnon, her half brother. David is unable to punish his son but is too ashamed to see his daughter, so he sends her away, never to be seen again.

Brooks occasionally delves into the politics of David's court from the perspective of his wives, including the famous Batsheva (Bathsheba), who found herself married to David after he raped her and killed her husband, Uriah the Hittite. Batsheva fears David but, in Brooks's telling, grows bolder after the birth of her son Shlomo (Solomon). She conspires with Natan, who is Shlomo's teacher, to make sure that David names the boy king before he dies. Natan has similar conspiratorial dealings with Tamar's mother, Maacah; having foreseen the fall of the family, he assures her that Tamar's assault will be avenged, though he cannot tell her how. David's wives, like most people in the kingdom, are afraid of Natan, but they are also among those most likely to seek him out, perhaps because they live their lives at the mercy of others and demand to know if their submission will be rewarded.

Narratively speaking, it makes sense that Brooks would choose to tell David's story from Natan's perspective, as the book of Nathan is one of the great lost books of the Bible. Still, for one familiar with the Bible, Brooks's Natan reveals little that is not already known. Brooks wrote *March* from the one perspective conspicuously missing from *Little Women*; readers knew what life was like for Marmee and the girls at home, but what was it like for their father at war? In *The Secret Chord*, Natan is merely a vessel for the story of David. As portrayed by Brooks, he has no want or need outside of serving the king.

Aside from the lack of conflict in Natan himself, the next most conspicuously missing perspectives in David's story are those of the women in his life. Outside of several interviews and passing interactions with Natan, their perspectives never assert themselves into a point of view. With the biblical story told the way it is, there is less negative space for Brooks to play in, though she makes the most of what she is given. Her prose is lyrical and precise; even stomach-turning scenes of battle are described with poetry and verve. Her descriptions of Israel circa 1000 BCE, from the dusty roads to the watered wine, are subtle yet real. *The Secret Chord* is detailed and well wrought, but it still manages to leave too much unsaid.

Molly Hagan

Review Sources

Hoffman, Alice. "Geraldine Brooks Reimagines King David's Life in *The Secret Chord*." Rev. of *The Secret Chord*, by Geraldine Brooks. *Washington Post*. Washington Post, 28 Sept. 2015. Web. 8 Feb. 2016.

Jaffe, Meredith. "Portrait of a Humanised King David." Rev. of *The Secret Chord*, by Geraldine Brooks. *Guardian*. Guardian News and Media, 7 Oct. 2015. Web. 8 Feb. 2016.

McEvoy, Marc. "*The Secret Chord* by Geraldine Brooks Shows a Bible Hero's Human Flaws." Rev. of *The Secret Chord*, by Geraldine Brooks. *Sydney Morning Herald*. Fairfax Media, 3 Oct. 2015. Web. 8 Feb. 2016.

Newhouse, Alana. Rev. of *The Secret Chord*, by Geraldine Brooks. *New York Times*. New York Times, 22 Oct. 2015. Web. 8 Feb. 2016.

Olidort, Shoshana. Rev. of *The Secret Chord*, by Geraldine Brooks. *Chicago Tribune*. Tribune, 8 Oct. 2015. Web. 8 Feb. 2016.

The Sellout

Author: Paul Beatty (b. 1962)
Publisher: Farrar, Straus and Giroux (New York). 288 pp.
Type of work: Novel
Time: Present
Locale: Dickens, California

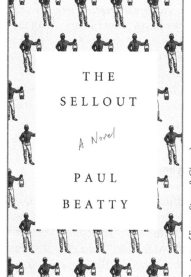

(Courtesy of Farrar Straus & Giroux)

Paul Beatty's new novel, The Sellout, *is a caustic, absurdist take on race and cultural identity in America as told through the eyes of a man who brings back slavery and segregation in an effort to save his town.*

Principal characters:
BONBON "THE SELLOUT" ME, a farmer turned slaveholder
F. K. ME, his father, a social scientist with literary aspirations
HOMINY JENKINS, a former child star of The Little Rascals, his slave
FOY CHESHIRE, F. K.'s frenemy, a former television personality and a writer who bowdlerizes classic texts

Paul Beatty's novel *The Sellout* is a brutal satire that centers on an African American man named BonBon and his quest to save his South Los Angeles suburb through outrageous means. BonBon lives in an "agrarian ghetto" called Dickens. He farms the same plot of land on which he was raised by his unorthodox social scientist father, growing superior strains of both watermelon and weed. Little BonBon was the subject of many of his father's hare-brained experiments; recalling an early one, he narrates,

> When I was seven months, Pops placed objects like toy police cars, cold cans of Pabst Blue Ribbon, Richard Nixon campaign buttons, and a copy of *The Economist* in my bassinet, but instead of conditioning me with a deafening clang, I learned to be afraid of the presented stimuli because they were accompanied by him taking out the family .38 Special and firing several window-rattling rounds into the ceiling, while shouting, "N——, go back to Africa!" loud enough to make himself heard over the quadraphonic console stereo blasting "Sweet Home Alabama" in the living room.

BonBon's father was also a counselor known around town as the "N——— Whisperer" due to his ability to calm desperate men and women who "needed to be talked down from a tree or freeway overpass precipice." (After one such incident, BonBon asked what he had said; his father responded, "I said, 'Brother, you have to ask your-self two questions, Who am I? and How may I become myself?' That's basic person-centered therapeutics. You want the client to feel important, to feel that he or she is in control of the healing process. Remember that s——.")

The Sellout, as one can see, is not for the easily offended. Nevertheless, BonBon—improbably, given another experiment utilizing electric shocks—makes it to young adulthood physically unscathed, though he is emotionally and culturally adrift. His one real friend is an elderly black man named Hominy Jenkins, "the last surviving member of the Little Rascals." The Little Rascals/Our Gang were a group of children who starred in comedy shorts beginning in the late 1920s. At the time, people praised the series for featuring African American characters, but the depictions of those char-acters were grossly racist. In the book, Hominy is the former understudy for a charac-ter named Buckwheat, played in real life by William Thomas Jr. and famously paro-died by comedian Eddie Murphy.

BonBon and Hominy, alongside BonBon's crush and later first girlfriend, Marpes-sa, spend afternoons together watching reruns of the Little Rascals. Hominy, perhaps taking a cue from Thomas, is proud of his work, clinging to it and its racism as a pillar of his identity. Later, he takes this identity to its illogical extreme, asking BonBon, who saves his life after he tries to commit suicide, to take him in as a slave. BonBon is horrified, but after the disappearance of Dickens, enslavement seems to be the only thing that will make Hominy happy, so he agrees to play the role of master. Among Hominy's self-imposed tasks is standing in BonBon's front yard as a human lawn jockey—hence the book's cover design.

The disappearance of Dickens happens literally overnight. One day, carloads of ag-ing white fans are knocking on Hominy's door; the next day the visits stop. Signs de-noting the town's location are removed from roads and maps, making what was once a place a mere space. The erasure enrages BonBon, who begins scheming to bring the town back. BonBon is a de facto leader of Dickens after the death of his father, who was shot by police at a routine traffic stop.

In addition to his work as a social scientist and counselor, BonBon's father also led a regular round table at a local doughnut shop called the Dum Dum Donut Intellectu-als. One of the Dum Dums, a blowhard named Foy Cheshire, got rich after stealing BonBon's father's idea for a children's television show. He went on to host several news programs with titles that swapped the word "fact" for "black," the most recent of which was called *Black Checker*. Less successful now, Foy churns out abridgements of classic novels; in his version of Mark Twain's *Adventures of Huckleberry Finn* (1884), titled *The Pejorative-Free Adventures and Intellectual and Spiritual Journeys of African-American Jim and His Young Protégé, White Brother Huckleberry Finn as They Go in Search of the Lost Black Family Unit*, he replaced the N-word with the word "warrior," and the word "slave" with the phrase "dark-skinned volunteer." (Lesser titles in Foy's oeuvre include his bowdlerization of George Eliot's famous novel *Middlemarch Middle of April, I'll Have Your Money—I Swear* and the Charles Dickens classic *Measured Expectations*.) Foy is also the one who bestows BonBon with his derogatory nickname, the Sellout, for his refusal to abide by the rules of the politically orthodox Dum Dums.

Amid this kaleidoscope of characters, BonBon and Hominy tend to satsumas of unearthly quality, segregate the local middle school, and—in celebration of Hominy's birthday—post a "Whites Only" sign in the front seats of a city bus. (BonBon pays a white actor to board the bus so that Hominy might have the satisfaction of offering her his seat.) Their efforts, satsumas and the rest of their harvest aside, almost land Bon-Bon in jail and take him all the way to the Supreme Court, where an African American justice—a nod to the famously tight-lipped Justice Clarence Thomas—breaks his silence to implore, "N——, are you crazy?"

Explaining the plot of Beatty's novel is like explaining the punch line of a joke. As other reviewers have noted, synopses fail to communicate particular force of Beatty's story, his tone, or his humor. *The Sellout* is viciously sharp satire forged in the flame of a modern culture that claims to be "postracial." Beatty examines concepts of identity and authenticity in the era of cultural appropriation, the first black US president, the killings of unarmed black men such as Michael Brown, Eric Garner, and Freddie Grey at the hands of police, and the Black Lives Matter movement. Late in the narrative, BonBon recalls seeing a black comedian berate a white couple for laughing inappropriately at his jokes, which he deemed "our thing." Looking back, BonBon wonders what constitutes "our thing," and that question pervades the novel. Referencing the anecdote in his *Los Angeles Times* review, Kiese Laymon concluded, "*The Sellout* firmly situates itself between white supremacy and black love, between thick anti-blackness and communal black innovation. It is a bruising novel that readers will likely never forget, especially those readers with the stomach to imagine and the will to remember the mystery and enduring thump of 'our thing.'"

Beatty is a writer and poet well known for his 1996 novel *The White Boy Shuffle*, a fish-out-of-water satire about a young black poet that similarly targets such issues as racial identity, modern culture, and multiculturalism. He was also the editor of a 2006 anthology of African American humor called *Hokum*, which was referenced by critics Dwight Garner and Kevin Young in their separate reviews for the *New York Times*. Beatty, Young noted, is part of a rich tradition in African American comedy of "break[ing] open the private jokes and secrets of blackness (one of which is that Being Black Is Fun) in a way that feels powerful and profane." Beatty constructs an absurd and satirical universe, one in which Foy wrangles such prominent figures as President Barack Obama, Colin Powell, and Condoleezza Rice to attend a Dum Dums meeting, but also utilizes classic principles of comedy to deploy his sharply observed jokes. He rattles off lists of offenses that explode at the end; one such list, of particularly hurtful slights suffered by poor people and people of

Paul Beatty is a novelist and poet whose previous work includes The White Boy Shuffle *(1996),* Slumberland *(2008), and an anthology of African American humor called* Hokum *(2006). The Sellout was a finalist for the National Book Critics Circle Award in Fiction and was named one of the top ten books of 2015 by the* New York Times.

color at the hands of California, includes "Propositions 8 and 187, the disappearance of social welfare, David Cronenberg's [film] *Crash*. . . ."

The Sellout, adhering to half of the famous maxim, aims to afflict the comfortable, and it succeeds. Though it is occasionally difficult to follow logically, the larger story leaps off the page with a surprising amount of heart for a comedy with such a pronounced a nihilistic streak. BonBon is a man in search of himself who becomes the unlikely leader of a movement. Like the protagonist of *The White Boy Shuffle*, a poet who is accidentally anointed the "savior of the blacks," BonBon is content with his weed (he has a best-selling strain called "Anglophobia") and his surfboard until the deaths of his father and the city of Dickens force him to confront and then inhabit his identity in a new way. Of course, in Beatty's demented world, BonBon's tactics include erecting a fake state-of-the-art, whites-only middle school across the street from a failing black and Latino middle school to unite the students against a common enemy, but the truth of BonBon's quest remains the same. Beatty's comedy is delightfully vulgar, but recalling those whom BonBon and his father counseled off a ledge, it finds its roots in real pain. "Who am I?" and "How may I become myself?" are just two of the many urgent questions Beatty raises in his incendiary novel, but they are as good a place as any to start.

Molly Hagan

Review Sources

Garner, Dwight. "Review: *The Sellout*, Paul Beatty's Biting Satire on Race in America." Rev. of *The Sellout*, by Paul Beatty. *New York Times*. New York Times, 26 Feb. 2015. Web. 13 Feb. 2016.

Hsu, Hua. "No Compromises." Rev. of *The Sellout*, by Paul Beatty. *New Yorker*. Condé Nast, 31 Mar. 2015. Web. 12 Feb. 2016.

Laymon, Kiese. "Review: Paul Beatty's Bruising, Satirical *Sellout* Is Driven by Black Voices." *Los Angeles Times*. Tribune, 26 Feb. 2015. Web. 11 Feb. 2016.

McMurtrie, John. Rev. of *The Sellout*, by Paul Beatty. *SFGate*. Hearst Communications, 4 Mar. 2015. Web. 11 Feb. 2016.

Seidel, Matt. "The Inanity of American Plutocracy: On Paul Beatty's *The Sellout*." Rev. of *The Sellout*, by Paul Beatty. *Millions*. Millions, 9 Mar. 2015. Web. 11 Feb. 2016.

Young, Kevin. Rev. of *The Sellout*, by Paul Beatty. *New York Times*. New York Times, 9 Apr. 2015. Web. 12 Feb. 2016.

Seveneves

Author: Neal Stephenson (b. 1959)
Publisher: William Morrow (New York). 880 pp.
Type of work: Novel
Time: The near future and five thousand years later
Locales: Postapocalyptic Earth, the International Space Station

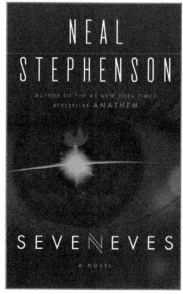

(Courtesy of HarperCollins)

Seveneves *chronicles the blowing up of the moon and then the inevitable destruction of Earth. The book follows the human race's painstaking, clinical decisions on how to preserve life in an outer-space setting, detailing who would be chosen to live aboard the space station and why.*

Principal characters:
DOCTOR DUBOIS "DOOB" JEROME XAVIER
    HARRIS, an astronomer and popular TV personality
JULIA BLISS FLAHERTY, the president of the United States
DINAH MACQUARIE, a robotics specialist
IVY XIAO, the commander of the space station
MOIRA CREWE, a geneticist
SEAN PROBST, a business mogul

Author Neal Stephenson has developed a loyal following of readers who enjoy novels with an emphasis on the science aspect of science fiction. His readership has come to expect a heavy dose of "hard science" in his speculative fiction. If a futuristic device is mentioned, then Stephenson's fans want to know how the item was researched, patented, built, manufactured, and distributed. They appreciate the minutiae and expect the speculative technology to be conveyed as potentially possible and eventually close at hand. They do not want fantasy but rather books that deal with imminent realities and alternate possibilities. As Stephenson himself once said in a 1999 interview for *SF Site*, "The science fiction approach doesn't mean it's always about the future; it's an awareness that this is *different.*"

In *Seveneves*, Stephenson has fashioned a book that begins with a literal bang. On the very first page, the moon meets a terrifying fate that will have generational consequences for the hapless residents on Earth: "The moon blew up without warning and for no apparent reason. . . . Later it would be designated A+0.0.0, or simply Zero." Right away, readers see that Stephenson will be placing his characters in harm's way, but their potential survival or imminent deaths will be treated with a clinical, scientific mind-set. The moon has broken into hurling, clashing, colliding pieces, but its devastating destruction has been analyzed and categorized in a bureaucratic, bloodless way. Indeed, Stephenson's ability to showcase a horrifying event and not have it degrade into hysterical, full-blown "bad" science fiction—a monster movie meets a disaster flick—is the best part of the novel, but this lack of sentimentality is also what received the most negative and unflattering remarks from reviewers.

Acclaimed novelist Neal Stephenson has won some of science fiction's most renowned honors, including the Hugo Award (for The Diamond Age, *1995) and several Locus Awards (for* The Diamond Age; Cryptonomicon, *1999;* The System of the World, *2004; and* Anathem, *2009), and has been nominated for Campbell, Clarke, and Nebula Awards as well. He also has worked as an adviser for Blue Origin, a company developing a piloted, reusable suborbital rocket, and is the chief futurist for Magic Leap, a virtual-reality start-up.*

Stephenson has populated the novel with many intelligent characters, and it is these brainy folks who offer earthlings the best chance to continue the preservation of the human race into the future. The rational and clear-thinking characters know that there will be a limited number of people able to be sent to live aboard the International Space Station. This logistical consideration provides ample opportunity for Stephenson to talk about how a space station can be expanded to allow for an influx of additional residents. The construction of pods and the machinations of airways and telecommunication links are intricately explained. The engineering know-how is chronicled, and the blueprint for each advancement is explored.

Beyond the chance to construct a supersized and superfunctioning satellite station, the premise of planning a controlled migration of people offers the author the chance to talk about the follies involved in trying to recreate a race of people in a new and startlingly different environment. This is one of the core themes at the heart of *Seveneves*: in the pursuit of keeping humanity alive, many humans lose all sense of what it means to be humane. When attempting to start all over, it is not just the best values that are promoted and imitated. Stephenson shows how venal, petty, self-serving, and separatist attitudes can also thrive when people are given the opportunity to rebuild and reestablish a new life for humanity. When offered a second chance, many people will merely use it as a way to pursue their self-interests in a more manic and dangerous way.

One of the heroes of the novel is a popular celebrity scientist known as Doc Dubois, or Doob, blatantly modeled after real-life celebrity scientist Neil deGrasse Tyson. Doc Dubois has managed to acquire a powerful presence on Earth, due to his enormous number of Twitter followers and his lectures that are popular with zillionaire technocrats and wealthy housewives alike. He is the voice of reason that dubs the fiery apocalypse that is about to storm down upon Earth as the "Hard Rain." He becomes the initial mentor for scared humanity and a character whom readers can cheer for and feel empathy toward. Many of the other characters who inhabit the doomed Earth and then the space station are mere archetypes; critics pointed out that Stephenson did not fully delineate their flesh-and-blood characteristics.

To counterbalance the selfless heroes, Stephenson provides selfish villains. Among the ranks of the devious is the willful and calculating president of the United States, Julia Bliss Flaherty. Despite an agreement not to send politicians into the safety of the space station, Flaherty manages to finagle her way into the ranks of the saved. In fact, the driven, determined president will end up becoming one of seven matriarchs from which the future race of human beings will stem.

Since the novel focuses on the aftermath of planetary annihilation—billions and billions of earthlings have been incinerated—the repopulation of a new race of people is both necessary and time sensitive. Interestingly, the fiery vanishing of the home planet is one of the most beautifully detailed passages in the massive novel, containing the most romantic and poetic descriptions: "Right now the light was orange because the Earth was on fire. . . . Earth looked as if some god had attacked it with a welder's torch, slashing away at it and leaving thin trails of incandescence. . . . [Ivy] fancied she could almost feel the warmth radiating from the planet."

With all of Earth's inhabitants destroyed, a crucial next step is to follow the biological imperative: to reproduce. Rather than through a romantic or traditional mating liaison, Stephenson has his characters attain that goal in the most sexless, scientific way possible. Most of the outer-space survivors are decimated in a series of events, but the goal has not been altered: "eight humans remained alive and healthy. . . . [Ivy] then called a meeting of the entire human race: Dinah, Ivy, Moira, Tekla, Julia, Aïda, Camila, and Luisa." That meeting comes to be known as the Council of the Seven Eves.

In a nod to feminism and female empowerment, Stephenson has concocted a world that is now without men. The chance to create future citizens is left to the machinations of seven women—the Seven Eves—who are now the sole salvation for future generations. Rather than worrying that the absence of men means their fertility plans are now futile, the women are saved by technology, as Moira explains:

> There is a process known as parthenogenesis, literally virgin birth, by which a uniparental embryo can be created out of a normal egg. It's been done with animals. The only reason no one ever did it with humans is because it seemed ethically dodgy, as well as completely unnecessary given the willingness of men to impregnate women every chance they got.

The brave new world of *Seveneves* then propels itself forward five thousand years into the future. Reviewers were vocal about disliking the fact that any characters that the readers have grown to care about are no longer alive. This jump into a far-distant reality happens not quite two-thirds of the way through. What follows is more than three hundred pages of what many critics felt is an overextended epilogue. Humanity now comprises seven distinctly different tribes or "races" of people: the descendants of the original Seven Eves, who have lived separately from one another, not commingling, cohabitating, or copulating. These new races have divided themselves into two separate states identified by color, the Red and the Blue—eerily reflecting election maps in the present-day United States, where the country is discussed in terms of these color distinctions (red for Republicans, blue for Democrats). The Red and Blue factions treat one another as Cold War cohabitants; they eye one another suspiciously, engage in espionage against one another, demean one another culturally, and occasionally break out into saber-rattling and land-grabbing threats. Yet these new people have one mission in common: after detecting one or more possible life-forms upon Earth, the progeny, all three billion of them, "embark on yet another audacious journey into the unknown . . . to an alien world utterly transformed by cataclysm and time: Earth."

Many reviewers were displeased with this segregation of the progeny, saying that they were surprised that Stephenson would imply that a willful decision to be aloof, to stay with one's genetic-sequence siblings and remain so strongly in the mold of the women who begat them five thousand years earlier, would not fly in the face of progress. They were astonished that over the massive span of time, nary a single descendant dared to integrate and expand their gene pool. Critics pointed out that it was as if personality traits and instincts had become part of DNA, and these latest descendants were still individually bound by the Seven Eves.

An argument can be made that Stephenson is recording the way modern-day humanity has separated itself into different factions that are continually invading one another, waging war, and seeming even during peacetime to prefer the company of like-minded and similar-appearing folks to the new, the different, and the foreign. It is no mere coincidence that Stephenson has given these new races of people a shared origin story that has nods to two biblical precedents. The seven procreating women are named for Eve, the first woman of Earth in the book of Genesis; and when the geneticist Moira explains the proposal for parthenogenesis to the seven candidates, she compares it to a "virgin birth," mirroring the New Testament's depiction of the birth of Jesus Christ. Yet when the seven races talk about the centuries that have preceded their existence, they are paying tribute to the heritage of their tribes' origin stories, sharing in a commonality of their culture. Since the Seven Eves produced their descendants in the same way, during the same trying times, perhaps the new earthlings will realize this sameness and build a better, more cohesive planet for the next generations.

A hopeful element could be construed in this, were it not for Stephenson's ending. When a representative from each of the races is asked to discover if there were any survivors on Old Earth (OE) after the ages-old "Hard Rain," this group of recruits, called the Seven, does encounter postapocalyptic civilizations. One group known as Pingers survived by living in submarines in ocean trenches, while others, termed Diggers, created a subterranean world in mines. The novel concludes with alliances with OE dwellers that seem to portend the possibility of future rifts, divisiveness, and misunderstandings, rather than hope for unity, waiting on the horizon.

Stephanie Finnegan

Review Sources

Gilsdorf, Ethan. Rev. of *Seveneves*, by Neal Stephenson. *Boston Globe*. Globe Media Partners, 19 May 2015. Web. 17 Feb. 2016.

Poole, Steven. "*Seveneves* by Neal Stephenson—a Truly Epic Disaster Novel." Rev. of *Seveneves*, by Neal Stephenson. *Guardian*. Guardian News and Media, 13 May 2015. Web. 17 Feb. 2016.

Sheehan, Jason. "*Seveneves* Blows Up the Moon—and That's Just the Beginning." Rev. of *Seveneves*, by Neal Stephenson. *NPR Books*. NPR, 21 May 2015. Web. 17 Feb. 2016.

Wolfe, Gary K. Rev. of *Seveneves*, by Neal Stephenson. *Chicago Tribune*. Tribune, 14 May 2015. Web. 17 Feb. 2016.

Wolk, Douglas. "Neal Stephenson's *Seveneves* Is Moonstruck by Nerdiness." Rev. of *Seveneves*, by Neal Stephenson. *Los Angeles Times*. Tribune, 29 May 2015. Web. 17 Feb. 2016.

Yu, Charles. Rev. of *Seveneves*, by Neal Stephenson. *New York Times*. New York Times, 27 May 2015. Web. 17 Feb. 2016.

The Shepherd's Crown

Author: Terry Pratchett (1948–2015)
Publisher: HarperCollins (New York). 288 pp.
Type of work: Novel
Time: The Century of the Anchovy
Locales: The Chalk, Lancre, Ankh-Morpork

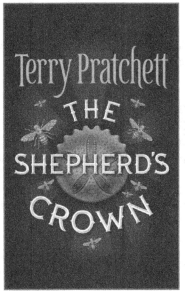

The final novel in Sir Terry Pratchett's long-running Discworld universe and the fifth in the Tiffany Aching series, The Shepherd's Crown *book centers on Tiffany's official entrance into adulthood with the death of Granny Weatherwax.*

Principal characters:

TIFFANY ACHING, a teenage girl who is elected unofficial leader of the witches

GRANNY WEATHERWAX, the unofficial leader of the witches

NANNY OGG, a friend of Granny Weatherwax and mentor to Tiffany

ROB ANYBODY, the leader of the Nac Mac Feegles, or Wee Free Men, a group of blue "pictsies"

GEOFFREY SWIVEL, a runaway who becomes the first male witch under Tiffany's tutelage

PRESTON, a medical student and Tiffany's love interest

The Shepherd's Crown is the fifth book in the Tiffany Aching series, which, in turn, is a part of Pratchett's forty-one books set in the Discworld. In this final book, Tiffany Aching has reached early adulthood, and she has come a long way from the nine-year-old girl readers met in *The Wee Free Men* (2003). Though *The Shepherd's Crown* can be read as a standalone book, fitting it into its own series, if not the whole Discworld fantasy realm, makes it stand out as an important conclusion to Pratchett's prolific career. To understand the way this book works as a farewell piece for not only the series but for Pratchett himself, it is necessary to first establish its place in the Aching subseries of Pratchett's Discworld.

The Wee Free Men introduces readers to Tiffany Aching, the bright, inquisitive daughter of a shepherd in the Chalk, a hilly region of the Discworld. In this beginning story, Tiffany learns not only that she is a witch but that her grandmother, Granny Aching, was probably an unacknowledged witch as well. Along with being introduced to the possibility of being magically inclined, Tiffany finds out that there are other fantastic beings, some of whom want to cause problems for her world and others of whom will become her lifelong friends.

(Used by permission of HarperCollins Publishers)

The second book, *A Hatful of Sky* (2004), follows eleven-year-old Tiffany as she begins her formal witch training as an apprentice with Miss Level, an established witch. In this installment, Tiffany is possessed by a hiver, a demonic entity that attempts to change her personality into something hateful. With the help of the Wee Free Men, she overcomes the evil, releasing the personalities that the hiver has claimed and freeing herself of its influence.

Wintersmith (2006), the middle installment, finds Tiffany's corner of the Disc thrust into eternal winter when the twelve-year-old witch unwittingly joins a ceremonial dance that is supposed to mark the end of the season. As Tiffany enters the dance, she replaces the Summer Lady, and the Wintersmith thinks he is in love with her. Tiffany learns to accept responsibility for her immature actions as she discovers that being a witch is more about observing and caring for people than about anything fantastic.

Sir Terry Pratchett was a prolific author of more than seventy books, including forty-one novels in the Discworld comedic fantasy series. He was best known for this best-selling series, which contains books for both adults and younger readers.

The main story line of the fourth book, *I Shall Wear Midnight* (2010), follows the death of the baron of the Chalk and the impending marriage of his only son, Roland. Tiffany struggles with Roland's marriage plans since she and Roland had been an unofficial couple for several years. While she comes to terms with the reality that she and Roland would never have lasted, she is pursued by the Cunning Man, the evil spirit of a witch-hunter. The baron's death and Roland's marriage teach Tiffany several more lessons about adulthood that help her overcome the Cunning Man and prepare her to become the leader she will need to be in *The Shepherd's Crown*, when the witches' unofficial but universally acknowledged leader, Granny Weatherwax, dies and leaves her in charge of not only the Chalk but the nearby highland kingdom of Lancre as well. It is fitting that this final tale of the Discworld teaches readers how to mourn for those who have lived a good life—a last lesson, as many critical reviews of the novel argued, left by Pratchett for his fans in the death of one of his most favorite characters.

The Shepherd's Crown begins with one of three main plotlines that will intertwine throughout the novel. Granny Weatherwax has come to the end of her long life, so she cleans her cabin, dresses in her best clothing, and props a note to Nanny Ogg on her chest. As she prepares to leave the world, Granny Weatherwax and Death converse about her life. Death (who always speaks in capital letters) tells her, "YOU ARE TAKING THIS VERY WELL, ESME WEATHERWAX." She responds, "It's an inconvenience, true enough, and I don't like it at all, but I know that you do it for everyone, Mr. Death. Is there any other way?" His answer could serve as an epitaph for Pratchett as well:

NO, THERE ISN'T, I'M AFRAID. WE ARE ALL FLOATING IN THE WINDS OF TIME. BUT YOUR CANDLE, MISTRESS WEATHERWAX, WILL FLICKER FOR SOME TIME BEFORE IT GOES OUT—A LITTLE REWARD FOR A LIFE WELL LIVED. FOR I CAN SEE THE BALANCE AND YOU HAVE LEFT THE WORLD MUCH BETTER THAN YOU FOUND IT, AND IF YOU ASK ME, said Death, NOBODY COULD DO ANY BETTER THAN THAT.

Indeed, Granny Weatherwax's life of caring for others and her insight into the world around her have left those in her little environs ready to accept a new leader in Tiffany Aching. Though Tiffany is honored by Granny Weatherwax's trust in her, she runs herself ragged with the desire to fulfill the needs of all the people under her mentorship, as well as those in her own home region of the Chalk. She is constantly flying back and forth between the two areas, attempting to keep up with an impossible load.

Tiffany's inability to sufficiently carry such a burden is tied into the secondary and tertiary plots, which have caught much critical attention. The secondary plot is built around the fairy realm. With the loss of Granny Weatherwax, the boundary guardian, the doors between the fairies and the human world are once again weakened. Since the fairies have grown bored with inactivity, they break through to wreak havoc on the hapless humans around Lancre and the Chalk. The queen of the fairies, who was defeated by the nine-year-old witch in *The Wee Free Men*, understands the dangers of venturing back into the Disc, and fear of the onslaught of iron machinery strengthens her reserve; however, her followers do not care that the world is changing, and in a lack of foresight, one elf lord overthrows the queen. Tiffany discovers the injured queen, takes her in, and teaches her what it is like to be human.

The third plotline introduces sixteen-year-old Geoffrey Swivel, the underappreciated third son of a baron who is good with goats. Geoffrey's interest in intellectual pursuit results in his father's disregard, so Geoffrey takes his pet goat, Mephistopheles, and heads out into the world. When he finds Tiffany, his destiny is set: he will begin training to become the first male witch the world has seen—a reversal of the roles in Pratchett's third Discworld novel, *Equal Rites* (1987), as many reviewers have noted, in which a young girl becomes the world's first female wizard. Through Geoffrey's gentle ministrations, the people around Lancre will receive the same kind of care that Tiffany can give only to the place where she knows she belongs, the Chalk. Tiffany's maturation throughout this piece can be seen as she begins to grab onto Nanny Ogg's advice from *I Shall Wear Midnight*: "Human being first, witch second; hard to remember, easy to do."

Throughout the novel, characters undergo a series of minor but significant changes and events. For example, Tiffany's relationship with Preston, a young man with whom she began a romantic affiliation in the fourth book, is reaffirmed, but it is strained by the distance between the two and their desires to pursue their chosen careers. Preston is in the city of Ankh-Morpork training to become a doctor, while Tiffany is torn between Lancre and the Chalk. Neither feels free to leave their duties at this point in their lives, so they have to come to a decision to do what they need to do at the moment. Tiffany's leadership role also allows her to encourage her friend Roland's wife, Letitia, to take over some of the witching duties in the Chalk, something the previously untrained witch does with little hesitation. Tiffany's friends the Nac Mac Feegles, a constant presence in the stories, appear in this novel as well, with the clan matriarch Jeannie providing Tiffany with wise counsel and Rob Anybody, Jeannie's husband and Tiffany's champion, continuing to guard the girl. The inclusion of the six-inch-tall, blue, kilted pictsies throughout the series has provided many points of comedy, and they continue to lighten the heavier tone of this final story.

In the afterword, Pratchett's assistant, Rob Wilkins, notes that as *The Shepherd's Crown* is Pratchett's final novel, written while he was suffering from early-onset Alzheimer's disease, it has not been edited and rewritten as much as Pratchett would have preferred. Wilkins tells readers, "*The Shepherd's Crown* has a beginning, a middle, and an end, and all the bits in between. Terry wrote all of those. But even so, it was, still, not quite as finished as he would have liked when he died." The circumstances of Pratchett's own life and health are likely why, as several critical reviews have noted, the book feels unpolished or unfinished. Regardless, *The Shepherd's Crown* maintains Pratchett's unparalleled humorous banter, connection to mythology and archetype, and sense of downright fun. The final image of Death, presented shortly after Granny Weatherwax's departure from the Disc, captures the overall feeling of most fans' reactions, not just to the novel but to Pratchett's own death: "And far away, in someplace unthinkable, a white horse was being unsaddled by a figure with a scythe with, it must be said, some sorrow."

Theresa L. Stowell

Review Sources

Dirda, Michael. "*The Shepherd's Crown* Review: The Final Discworld Novel." Rev. of *The Shepherd's Crown*, by Terry Pratchett. *Washington Post*. Washington Post, 28 Aug. 2015. Web. 20 Dec. 2015.

Norton, Eric. Rev. of *The Shepherd's Crown*, by Terry Pratchett. *School Library Journal* Oct. 2015: 106. Print.

Robinson, Tasha. "*The Shepherd's Crown* Tells Terry Pratchett Fans How to Mourn Him." Rev. of *The Shepherd's Crown*, by Terry Pratchett. *NPR*. NPR. 2 Sept. 2015. Web. 20 Dec. 2015.

Rev. of *The Shepherd's Crown*, by Terry Pratchett. *Kirkus Reviews* 15 Sept. 2015: 105. Print.

Welch, Cindy. Rev. of *The Shepherd's Crown*, by Terry Pratchett. *Booklist* 1 Oct. 2015: 74. Print.

Slade House

Author: David Mitchell (b. 1969)
Publisher: Random House (New York). 256 pp.
Type of work: Novel
Time: 1979–present
Locale: London, England

David Mitchell's Slade House *is a haunted-house tale told through a series of interlocking short stories. An offshoot of Mitchell's previous novel* The Bone Clocks *(2014),* Slade House *finds its characters battling two evil, immortal twins for their souls.*

Principal characters:
NATHAN BISHOP, a lonely young boy in 1979
GORDON EDMUND, a divorced cop in 1988
SALLY TIMMS, a shy college student in 1997
FREYA TIMMS, Sally's older sister, a journalist in 2006
NORAH GRAYER, a Victorian twin with evil psychic powers
JONAH GRAYER, Norah's twin brother, also with evil psychic powers

Award-winning author David Mitchell's novel *Slade House* is a classic ghost story featuring a haunted house, soul-sucking evil twins, and portraits that try to escape from their frames. Told in five chapters—or rather, five separate but interlocking short stories—Mitchell's tale centers on a mysterious apparition called Slade House that appears every nine years in a narrow alley behind the Fox and Hounds pub.

For the reader, Slade House is at first very real. In "The Right Sort," the book's first story, readers know just as much as the house's first hapless victim, a young boy named Nathan Bishop. It is 1979, and Nathan and his mother, Rita, have been invited to a party thrown by the mysterious Lady Grayer. Rita does not know Lady Grayer personally, but her name alone signifies a kind of prestige. Rita and Nathan have hit hard times; Rita is trying to salvage her career as a concert pianist while raising Nathan, who is nerdy and painfully introverted. Following Lady Grayer's directions, they find Slade House through a tiny entrance in an impossibly small brick alley. Beyond an iron door is a lush and summery garden—a first hint that something is not right, because it is October—and a graceful Victorian manor. Slade House is all the more beautiful to Nathan because, unbeknownst to his mother, he slipped two of her Valiums before leaving the house. His experience of the garden party is a very strange one, but he attributes it to the pills. Jonah, Lady Grayer's young son, seems to know too much about Nathan, and time seems to be moving very strangely. First the boys are sitting by the pond; then they are under a tree, and then they are playing tag. Jonah Grayer and his twin, Norah, eventually prey on Nathan, and he becomes a portrait hanging in the hall at Slade House.

Slade House started in an unlikely place. Mitchell first published "The Right Sort" as a stand-alone story in 140-character segments on Twitter. Self-reference is something that Mitchell has been known to use, and the story drew heavily from the world he created in his 2014 novel, *The Bone Clocks*, in which immortal forces of good and evil vie for power by inhabiting the bodies of living beings. The evil Anchorites do more and worse: they eat souls. The Grayer twins of Slade House are Anchorites who lure victims to their home to eat. The first story of the Grayer twins was so popular on Twitter that Mitchell wrote an entire book around it.

Mitchell is a literary fiction writer with a penchant for fantasy and science fiction. His most famous novel to date is *Cloud Atlas* (2004), a sprawling sextet of novellas spanning five centuries. By comparison, the scope of *Slade House* is small. Indeed, at about 250 pages, it is Mitchell's shortest novel to date.

Critics praised Mitchell's masterful storytelling in *Slade House*, though some took issue with the novel's few moments of exposition. In order to explain the Grayer twins' motives, Mitchell gives much of the explanation to the twins in large chunks of dialogue. After each successful entrapment, the twins engage in backstory- and jargon-laden exchanges in front of their guest and soul-meal. In the second chapter, for example, Norah says,

> The operandi works provided out birth-bodies remain here in the lacuna, freeze-dried against world-time, anchoring our souls in life. The operandi works provided we recharge the lacuna every nine years by luring a gullible Engifted into a suitable orison. The operandi works provided our guests can be duped, banjaxed and drawn into the lacuna. Too many *provided*s. . . . Yes, our luck's held so far. It can't hold forever, and it won't.

Some reviewers found this a bit much. Others, such as Ron Charles of the *Washington Post*, found the novel "devilishly fun." In his exuberant review for NPR, Jason Sheehan poked fun at the mystery and horror tropes that Mitchell so earnestly engages with, writing that the book's elements seem to have popped out of "Ghosty McGuffin's Magical Nonsense Generator." *Slade House*'s contrivances, however, are a small price to pay for its story. Discussing Mitchell's work in the July 5, 2010, issue of the *New Yorker*, critic James Wood wrote that *Cloud Atlas* was a success because each novella contained within the novel was strong enough to stand alone. A similar comment could be made about *Slade House*, in that the protagonist of each story is fully realized outside of their connection to a horror story. This is what makes the book at times so terribly sad and poignant, occasionally in ways that surprise the reader.

The stakes are high; once the Grayers get their hands on a victim—or rather, once the victim has ingested food or drink laced with the magical substance known as "banjax"—that person cannot be saved. But it is the Grayers' method of entrapment that makes each subsequent parting worse. The twins lure each of their victims (every one psychically special in a way that makes them "Engifted," and thus the ideal nourishment) into the magical "lacuna" of the house, which can be transformed to reflect any setting that suits their purpose and will best attract their intended victim. Young Nathan, dragged to a garden party with his struggling pianist mother, is drawn in when Norah dangles the opportunity for Rita to play for a famous musician and for Nathan to make his first real friend. Later, the twins treat Nathan to an illusory visit with his beloved father, who has moved to Rhodesia (present-day Zimbabwe) with his new wife.

Gordon, a lovelorn cop, is lured to Slade House in 1988 under the pretext of sex. Having been so easily entrapped, he stumbles across a room in the attic where Rita Bishop appears to be held captive. (Gordon recognizes her because he was originally in Slade Alley to follow up on the Bishops' disappearance.) Rita is menacing and practically mad with grief. Often in the horror movies that Mitchell draws from, viewers know just enough about a character to follow him or her through a story, but the more the audience knows about a character, the longer they live. Mitchell flips this principle. He puts the reader inside the mind of each victim, even imbuing their compatriots—such as Rita—with hopes and dreams, making them more than mere collateral damage.

For Sally Timms, a shy, overweight college student who visits Slade House nearly twenty years later, Norah and Jonah evoke the cruelty of Sally's high school years, leading her to believe that her crush has taken a real interest in her. In Sally's story—titled "Oink, Oink," after her adolescent nickname—an amateur society of ghost hunters seeks out Slade House based on the rumors that circulated following the disappearances of Nathan and Rita in 1979 and Gordon in 1988. Gordon had reported the existence of a manor in an alley behind the dusty Fox and Hounds pub; after his disappearance, the station was surprised to find that no such manor existed.

David Mitchell is an award-winning novelist who has twice been short-listed for the Man Booker Prize. His books include Cloud Atlas *(2004),* Black Swan Green *(2006), and* The Bone Clocks *(2014). He lives in Ireland.*

The merry band of ghost hunters, led by the nephew of the last person to see Rita and Nathan Bishop alive, traipses down narrow Slade Alley looking for ghosts but find instead a college Halloween party. The party is the last thing the group hoped to find, but, not wanting the night to be a total waste, they jump right in. Now that ghost hunting is off the table, Sally is free to chat up Todd, a quiet, punkish second-year student on whom she has developed an enormous crush. With his gentle encouragement, Sally spills her guts to Todd—only to come to a terrible realization about their relationship after a heart-stopping attempt to escape the house.

Sally's story is made all the more heartbreaking by Mitchell's uncanny narration. He slips into the voice of an alienated teenage girl with ease, just as he parrots a hyperintelligent small child and a lonely cop. But it is the wish-fulfillment aspect of each story that allows Mitchell to deliver larger truths alongside the thrills and chills. In the fourth story, "You Dark Horse You," Sally's older sister Freya agrees to meet a man named Fred Pink—the last person to see the Bishops alive—at the Fox and Hounds.

Freya is driven by a savage guilt over the disappearance of her little sister, with whom she did not have the best relationship. She has spent the last nine years trying to find out what happened to Sally, holding out hope that she is still alive. "Sometimes I envy the weeping parents of the definitely dead you see on TV," Freya narrates. "Grief is an amputation, but hope is incurable hemophilia: you bleed and bleed and bleed. Like Schrödinger's cat inside a box you can never ever open."

The emotional mechanics of the story—Freya's grief, Sally's loneliness, Nathan's desire to see his father—are what propel *Slade House*, though the Grayers are the ones pulling the levers of the plot. The twins are out-and-out villains and, in keeping with the horror tropes that Mitchell uses throughout, are not incredibly complex. Though the Grayers appear the most consistently, it is their victims who are the most compelling aspects of *Slade House*.

Molly Hagan

Review Sources

Charles, Ron. "David Mitchell's *Slade House*: A Ghost Story That Began Haunting Twitter." Rev. of *Slade House*, by David Mitchell. *Washington Post*. Washington Post, 15 Oct. 2015. Web. 16 Feb. 2016.

Forbes, Malcolm. Rev. of *Slade House*, by David Mitchell. *Financial Times*. Financial Times, 23 Oct. 2015. Web. 16 Feb. 2016.

Garner, Dwight. "Review: David Mitchell's *Slade House* Plunges into a Battle of Immortals." Rev. of *Slade House*, by David Mitchell. *New York Times*. New York Times, 22 Oct. 2015. Web. 16 Feb. 2016.

Jensen, Liz. "Like Stephen King in a Fever." Rev. of *Slade House*, by David Mitchell. *Guardian*. Guardian News and Media, 29 Oct. 2015. Web. 16 Feb. 2016.

Sheehan, Jason. "It's Coming from inside the House. . . *Slade House*, That Is." Rev. of *Slade House*, by David Mitchell. *NPR*. NPR, 28 Oct. 2015. Web. 16 Feb. 2016.

So You Don't Get Lost in the Neighborhood

Author: Patrick Modiano (b. 1945)
First Published: *Pour que tu ne te perdes pas dans le quartier*, 2014, in France
Translated from the French by: Euan Cameron
Publisher: Houghton Mifflin Harcourt (New York). 160 pp.
Type of work: Novel
Time: 1945–2013
Locale: France

So You Don't Get Lost in the Neighborhood *is a novel about memory, mystery, and how the mind deals with pain from the past. Jean Daragane, a mystery writer, must contend with a con man, his intriguing sidekick, and a host of characters from childhood memories as he navigates the privileges and pitfalls of forgetting the past.*

(Courtesy Houghton Mifflin Harcourt)

Principal characters:

JEAN DARAGANE, an aging mystery writer living in isolation with a very limited memory of his childhood and past

GILLES OTTOLINI, a con man who finds Jean's misplaced telephone notebook and inquires about a man from Jean's past

CHANTAL GRIPPAY, Gilles's girlfriend and sidekick

ANNIE ASTRAND, Jean's childhood caretaker

"Almost nothing. Like an insect bite that initially strikes you as very slight. At least that is what you tell yourself in a low voice so as to reassure yourself," begins the English translation of French Nobel Prize winner Patrick Modiano's novel *So You Don't Get Lost in the Neighborhood*. This opening, directed toward "you" but spoken by no one, is an apt metaphor for how *So You Don't Get Lost in the Neighborhood* approaches personal identity, history, and how the two intertwine, solidifying or unraveling the mental stability of a person in one fell swoop.

Jean Daragane is an elderly writer living a solitary life in present-day Paris when he receives a mysterious phone call. The man on the line, who the reader soon finds out is Gilles Ottolini, an expert but petty con man, claims to have found Jean's personal address book holding many of his contacts from the last thirty years at a train station a week before. Though Jean has little need for the book—he had hardly even realized it was gone—he agrees to meet Gilles at a café the following day to retrieve it. During the meeting Jean notes to himself that the other man has the persistence of an insect, echoing the first line of the novel and hinting at Gilles's part in unlocking Jean's memories. The thawing of the past comes slowly at first, and then there is a great rush.

When he returns the notebook, Gilles mentions that he glanced through the pages and is interested in information about one of the men listed inside, one Guy Torstel. Though Jean has no memory of Torstel, it emerges that he used the name in one of his novels early on in his career. Gilles is investigating a news item he read about from long past involving Torstel and a murder. The implication is that Gilles has come to blackmail Jean through his connection to the event. Jean's efforts to remember send him on an odyssey through the past, one that threatens to uncover dark events from his childhood in the shadow of World War II.

Patrick Modiano is the widely acclaimed author of novels, memoirs, and hybrid works that have been translated from his native French into over thirty-five languages. In 2014 he received the Nobel Prize in Literature.

Modiano, whose work is known for examining the complex atmosphere of postwar France, takes what appears to be a traditional mystery tale and uses the tools from that genre's kit to create something fresh, exciting, unexpected, and devastating. He baits-and-switches his audience by setting up Gilles and his partner, Chantal, as stereotypical villains only to change their roles so greatly that readers may be left wondering where they started in the first place. Instead of playing into a standard plotline where Gilles somehow weaves his way into Jean's past and becomes part of the story, Gilles is quickly revealed to be a con man after money, looking for ways to cash out and move on. Chantal becomes a temporary confidante, sympathetic to Jean's isolation and his protector against Gilles's games. She is the one to turn the narrative toward the unexpected by providing Jean with key pieces to the past.

The use of the telephone both figuratively and literally weighs heavy on the novel. Noted is that Torstel's number is merely seven digits, a relic of an older phone number system, and so must be at least thirty years old. Though Jean's phone has long sat derelict in his apartment, it now connects him to the outside world, particularly in the form of Chantal and Gilles, with each of the early chapters beginning with a sudden call to his flat. The first chapter ends with Jean going over the numbers in his recovered address book, noting that none of them mean anything to him any longer and that important numbers he had memorized would no longer connect to the people they once did. This reflection on the passage of time provides insight into Jean's character and sets up the exploration that is about to come, with the mysterious Torstel providing the impetus.

Instead of focusing on the potential threat of Gilles, Jean begins to revisit his long forgotten novel, *Le Noir de l'ete,* of which he does not own a single copy, and investigates the inclusion of Guy Torstel in that tome. His mention is quick, hardly worth noting, but the short scene is significant nonetheless. Here lies the true brilliance of Modiano's work. Through a patchwork of dreamlike sequences, Jean begins to explore and undercover his painful past, which leads right to Annie Astrand, his caretaker in childhood after his birth parents abandoned him. In an envelope given to him by Chantal, Jean uncovers some small passport-sized portraits but does not recognize the boy in them, only to realize sometime later that the boy is him. This and other small details that lead to the book's climax are like a collection of talismans meant to protect Jean as he weaves through the labyrinthine landscape of his past, with each creating the sense of a sort of mirror to hazy memories.

Modiano expertly links together concise, simple sentences to elaborate Jean's existential journey. The language is at once as straightforward as a classic noir mystery and highly literary. For example, while looking at his childhood photograph Jean wonders: "Was it something that embarrassed him, an exhibit, to use the legal language, and which he, Daragane, had wanted to erase from his memory? He experienced a sort of giddiness, a tingling sensation at the roots of his hair." The reader can almost see the flickering of Jean's brain on the page and cannot help but feel a sense of paranoia: how easily can the past be forgotten and what has been forgotten in their own life? The ease with which Jean has lost the ability to recognize himself as a child is alarming and also warns the reader not to take anything at face value. The story is dealing with a narrator who does not know himself to be unreliable, but indeed is.

The novel takes three paths: the first placed in the present as Jean stumbles along his path to realization; the second from the period when he was composing his book *Le Noir de l'ete*, remembering that he once tracked down Annie and visited some of the settings from his childhood; and the third—and perhaps the most important—following the track of his childhood, leading toward the revelation all of the narrative pieces are slowly joining to reveal. What is striking about all three paths is Modiano's evocation of Paris and other regions of France as backdrops for the plot. Weaving through seasons, historical periods, and times of day—the first part of the book seems to take place mostly at night, while the later portions offer more variation—the novel seamlessly presents a landscape that at times soothes the tension of Jean's journey and at others offers a dark subtext never far removed from the lingering touch of the war. Gritty realities are presented plainly and through various lenses (for example, Annie was a dancer at a local club, and the reader gets to see Jean's reactions to that lifestyle as a child), furthering the themes of remembrance and the role of narrative itself.

Despite its brevity—the book clocks in at a slim 160 pages—a thrilling and stirring story is unveiled, no doubt due to Modiano's skill as a novelist. Hailed by some critics as the Marcel Proust of his age, Modiano readily acknowledges the influence of World War II on his psyche and writing. *So You Don't Get Lost in the Neighborhood* was received as a worthy entry in his extensive catalog of works exploring that haunting influence. Many reviewers noted that the book was satisfying despite—or because of—the many ways in which Modiano toys with the reader, providing tantalizing glimpses and deep layers of context and meaning without providing any easy answers. One could argue that his writing, focusing so heavily on the World War II and postwar period in which Europe struggled with the burden of memory, is a way of commemorating the past while also examining the nature of non-memory.

The publication of *So You Don't Get Lost in the Neighborhood* also came at a time when a wider audience was just beginning to discover Modiano's works, especially in the English-speaking world, following his 2014 reception of the Nobel Prize. The efforts of translator Euan Cameron won significant praise right alongside critical acclaim for the writing itself. With a mounting number of his titles being translated and reviewed each year, Modiano's is an essential voice to audiences around the world interested in the universal themes of memory, identity, and storytelling. "To being with, it is almost nothing, the crunch of the tyres on the gravel, the sound of an engine growing fainter, and you need more time to realize that there is no-one left in the house apart from you," Modiano writes, an image of realization that could easily be applied to the most significant moments in both one's personal history and the past at large.

Melynda Fuller

Review Sources

Eleveld, Mark. Rev. of *So You Don't Get Lost in the Neighborhood*, by Patrick Modiano, trans. Euan Cameron. *Paste*. Paste Media Group, 8 Oct. 2015. Web. 8 Feb. 2016.

Rev. of *So You Don't Get Lost in the Neighborhood*, by Patrick Modiano, trans. Euan Cameron. *Publishers Weekly*. PWxyz, Sept. 2015. Web. 8 Feb. 2016.

Tonkin, Boyd. Rev. of *So You Don't Get Lost in the Neighborhood*, by Patrick Modiano, trans. Euan Cameron. *Independent*. Independent Digital News and Media, 11 Sept. 2015. Web. 8 Feb. 2016.

Ulin, David L. "Patrick Modiano's Many Detours into Echoes, Longings and Tension." Rev. of So You Don't Get Lost in the Neighborhood, by Patrick Modiano, trans. Euan Cameron. *Los Angeles Times*. Los Angeles Times Media Group, 18 Sept. 2015. Web. 8 Feb. 2016.

The Soul of an Octopus
A Surprising Exploration into the Wonder of Consciousness

Author: Sy Montgomery (b. 1958)
Publisher: Atria Books (New York). 272 pp.
Type of work: Science, nature, memoir
Time: 2011–13
Locales: Boston, Massachusetts; Cozumel, Mexico; Seattle, Washington; Mooréa, French Polynesia

(Courtesy of Atria Books)

In The Soul of an Octopus, *acclaimed naturalist Sy Montgomery examines the psychological and physical world of the octopus. The probing book reveals how exploring the intelligence and personalities of octopuses can yield surprising insights about human consciousness.*

Principal personages:
SY, the narrator, a naturalist
WILSON, the New England Aquarium's most experienced octopus volunteer
BILL, the senior aquarist of the New England Aquarium's Cold Marine Gallery
ANNA, a teenage volunteer at the New England Aquarium

In interviews, naturalist Sy Montgomery has expressed her concern that humans are on the cusp of destroying the earth. Consequently, it is a critical time to be researching the natural world and improving the way that animals are understood. In *The Soul of an Octopus*, Montgomery embraces this task by investigating one of the planet's least understood creatures through the practice of immersive journalism. Classified as an invertebrate, mollusk, and cephalopod, the octopus is special in that it has the capacity for self-awareness. In *The Soul of an Octopus*, Montgomery sets out to explore octopus consciousness and determine if it is at all comparable to the human experience.

As a naturalist writer, Montgomery employs a unique blend of personal observations, history, and zoological research. When stating scientific facts, she conveys her own sense of awe rather than maintaining an objective tone. This imbues the narrative, and subsequently her readers, with a sense of revelation and excitement. In *The Soul of an Octopus*, Montgomery leverages this style to establish the breadth and complexity of the research into octopus consciousness. She begins the narrative with a description of how physiologically different octopuses are from humans: they have three hearts and blue blood; their mouths are in their armpits, and they taste through the suckers that cover their eight limbs. It is because of this alien physicality, Montgomery posits, that octopuses represent the mysterious "other" to humans.

While half a billion years of evolution have resulted in distinct anatomical differences between humans and octopuses, both species have developed the capacity for consciousness. In order to better understand the nature of octopus consciousness and how it differs from that of humans, Montgomery began conducting regular research sessions at the New England Aquarium in Boston, Massachusetts. Her first interaction with a giant Pacific octopus named Athena is depicted as a revelatory, sensory experience. When Montgomery puts her arms into Athena's tank, she is surprised to learn how friendly and gentle the octopus is. Athena greets Montgomery by wrapping several of her limbs around Montgomery's hands and forearms. By using her suckers, which are composed of chemoreceptors, to taste Montgomery, Athena is attempting to get to know her better.

(David Scheel)

Sy Montgomery is a naturalist, documentary screenwriter, and the author of more than twenty nonfiction books, including the national best seller The Good Good Pig *(2006).*

Montgomery meets Athena on three occasions before the octopus dies unexpectedly. Surprised at her profound emotional response to this news, Montgomery realizes that she had started to think of Athena as a friend. Her nascent belief that octopuses are distinct individuals is furthered in the months that follow as she continues conducting observations at the New England Aquarium. By familiarizing herself with a number of different giant Pacific octopuses over an extended period of time, Montgomery is able to conclude that octopuses are in fact conscious beings with unique personalities. Defining consciousness as the ability to think, feel, and know, Montgomery demonstrates the cognitive ability of octopuses by relaying incidents of their curiosity and playfulness. She cites their tendency to change color depending on their mood as evidence of their capacity for emotion. Finally, she shares how her colleague at the New England Aquarium, a seasoned volunteer named Wilson, has successfully taught octopuses to solve puzzles, which she presents as evidence of their higher intelligence.

Montgomery attempts to dispel any doubt regarding octopuses' sense of self-awareness by pointing to their capacity to recognize others as individuals. She states that not only octopuses are capable of distinguishing one human from another with their eyes and suckers, but they also like certain people more than others. To support this argument, she recounts stories of octopuses that have repeatedly ignored or squirted specific people they disliked. Additionally, she describes how the New England Aquarium octopuses are often leery of strangers but capable of building trusting relationships with their keepers, such as Wilson and senior aquarist Bill Murphy.

As she relays her findings, Montgomery works to foster a sense of respect for each

of her research subjects as individuals. One way she achieves this is through the organization of the text. Of the eight chapters that make up *The Soul of an Octopus*, four
are named after the octopuses she worked directly with: Athena, Octavia, Kali, and
Karma. She also provides detailed descriptions of each octopus's personality. Where
Athena was named after the Greek goddess of war because of her fiery demeanor, her
successor, Octavia, was known for being more shy and reserved. Meanwhile, Kali
was outgoing and mischievous, and Karma was capricious. Additionally, Montgomery
aims to deepen readers' empathy toward octopuses as conscious beings by drawing
parallels between the octopuses' lives and the lives of their keepers. When Octavia
succumbs to senescence, for example, Montgomery notes that this occurs at the same
time that Wilson is forced to seek hospice care for his wife.

Arguably the most prevalent theme within *The Soul of an Octopus* is how much
octopuses can teach people about themselves. In her conclusion, Montgomery argues
that Athena, Octavia, Kali, and Karma have transformed her life by providing her with
a deeper understanding of her own consciousness. Equally important, she implies, is
the emotional impact octopuses can have on people. For Anna, a teenaged volunteer
with autism to whom *The Soul of an Octopus* is dedicated, Octavia was a source of
comfort after her best friend committed suicide. Anna found that not only could she
could express her emotions better when she was around Octavia, but she also felt a
sense of purpose when she was with the octopuses. According to a formerly homeless
man whom Montgomery encountered at the Seattle Aquarium, the sight of octopuses
can provide inner peace.

Montgomery presents the progression of her research over time as a journey comprising different octopuses, aquariums, and oceans. To capture the feeling and significance of this journey, she often employs religious analogies and language. The
act of touching and embracing an octopus, for example, is presented as a passageway
to peace and bliss. Similarly, she compares the experience of watching octopuses to
meditation or prayer, writing, "Once we [plunged our arms into the water], we entered
what we called Octopus Time. Feelings of awe are known to expand the human experience of time availability. . . . Meditation and prayer, too, alter time perception."

In order to observe wild octopuses in their natural habitat, Montgomery travels to
the Cozumel National Marine Park in Mexico. While underwater, she feels as though
she is becoming a part of the "*animus mundi*," or "all-extensive world soul shared by
all of life." When she finally surfaces, she weeps with joy. After traveling to Mooréa,
an island in French Polynesia, for another scuba expedition, Montgomery finds herself
in a local temple that was once dedicated to the octopus. There, Montgomery contemplates the meaning of souls and whether octopuses have them. She concludes that if
she has a soul, octopuses must have them too.

Ultimately, Montgomery uses religiosity to establish a sense of holiness around the
natural world. She has stated that when octopuses and other animals are believed to
have souls, they are granted a level of sacredness and respect. While her conclusions
may initially seem speculative and radical, Montgomery's beliefs regarding octopuses'
consciousness are in line with mainstream animal science. In 2012, an international
group of leading neuroscientists signed the *Cambridge Declaration on Consciousness*.

Amid the vast collection of mammals and birds determined to be as self-aware as humans, there was one invertebrate listed: the octopus. Similarly, Montgomery's prose fits well within the canon of naturalist literature. Like Henry David Thoreau, she uses nature as both a pathway to spiritual discovery and a tool to better understand human existence. Montgomery is also similar to Thoreau in that her writing calls attention to the issue of nature preservation.

The Soul of an Octopus has been a popular success, becoming one of the first ever books about an invertebrate to reach the top ten of the *New York Times* Best Seller list of animal books. Critically, too, the book received largely positive reviews, leading to it becoming a finalist for the National Book Award. Much praise for Montgomery's work has been directed at her in-depth exploration of the physical and emotional world of the octopus. Many critics point to Montgomery's assemblage of research and personal experience as being transformative in its ability to change readers' perceptions of octopuses. In a review for *New Scientist*, Phil McKenna argued that as a book, *The Soul of an Octopus* has the unique ability not only to educate readers on a subject they knew little about before but also to completely change the way they see the world. Similarly, William O'Connor wrote for the *Daily Beast* that Montgomery is highly convincing in her argument for octopuses being more complex and intelligent than people tend to believe.

In addition to its enlightening qualities, *The Soul of an Octopus* has also been commended for its beautiful prose. Montgomery's depictions of the octopuses are detailed and have an arguably lyrical quality. Reflecting on her first experience with the octopus Athena, for example, Montgomery describes how her "hands and forearms are engulfed by dozens of soft, questing suckers." By using both sensual language and emotion to describe her experiences with the octopuses, Montgomery deviates from standard clinical science writing. The end result is a narrative that engages readers on a deeper, more human level.

Not all reviewers found Montgomery's affecting prose beneficial to the narrative, however. Some have criticized her tendency to anthropomorphize her subjects. In a review for the *Wall Street Journal*, Jennie Erin Smith wrote that Montgomery fails to escape the pervasive "anthropocentric fallacy" that animals valuable first and foremost for their "humanoid qualities, or for what they supposedly teach us about ourselves." Although Montgomery states outright that projecting human feelings onto subjects is a "cardinal sin" in the study of animal science, she regularly describes octopuses as having personality traits or actions that are distinctly human. While this tendency may be bothersome to some, as a whole it works to serve Montgomery's primary supposition, which is encapsulated in the memoir's title: octopuses have souls and, therefore, are akin to humans. At times, anecdotes of Montgomery's enchantment with her subjects may become slightly repetitive, but this shortcoming is ultimately compensated for by the book's engrossing scientific elements. The end result is a well-balanced, fascinating read.

Review Sources

Davis, Melissa. "*The Soul of an Octopus*: Book Charts Seasons of a Cephalopod." Rev. of *The Soul of an Octopus: A Surprising Exploration into the Wonder of Consciousness*, by Sy Montgomery. *Seattle Times*. Seattle Times, 28 May 2015. Web. 22 Dec. 2015.

King, Barbara J. "The Watery World of Cephalopod Intelligence." Rev. of *The Soul of an Octopus: A Surprising Exploration into the Wonder of Consciousness*, by Sy Montgomery. *Times Literary Supplement*. Times Literary Supplement, 17 June 2015. Web. 22 Dec. 2015.

McKenna, Phil. "*The Soul of an Octopus*: Getting to Know an Intelligent Mollusc." Rev. of *The Soul of an Octopus: A Surprising Exploration into the Wonder of Consciousness*, by Sy Montgomery. *New Scientist*. Reed Business Information, 10 June 2015. Web. 22 Dec. 2015.

O'Connor, William. "Does an Octopus Have a Soul?" Rev. of *The Soul of an Octopus: A Surprising Exploration into the Wonder of Consciousness*, by Sy Montgomery. *Daily Beast*. Daily Beast, 22 May 2015. Web. 22 Dec. 2015.

Smith, Jennie Erin. "Eight Arms to Hold You." Rev. of *The Soul of an Octopus: A Surprising Exploration into the Wonder of Consciousness*, by Sy Montgomery. *Wall Street Journal*. Dow Jones, 22 May 2015. Web. 22 Dec. 2015.

A Spool of Blue Thread

Author: Anne Tyler (b. 1941)
Publisher: Alfred A. Knopf (New York).
  368 pp.
Type of work: Novel
Time: Twentieth and twenty-first century
Locale: Baltimore

A Spool of Blue Thread *continues Pulitzer Prize–winning novelist Anne Tyler's exploration of families and quirky people. It was short-listed for the 2015 Man Booker Prize.*

Principal characters:
ABBY WHITSHANK, a retired social worker
RED WHITSHANK, her husband, owner of the
    family construction business
DENNY, Abby and Red's son
AMANDA, one of Abby and Red's daughters
JEANNIE, one of Abby and Red's daughters
STEM, Abby and Red's adopted son, who moves in with them in their old age
LINNIE MAE WHITSHANK, Red's mother
JUNIOR WHITSHANK, Red's father

(Courtesy of Alfred A. Knopf)

Anne Tyler's first novel, *If Morning Ever Comes*, was published in 1964, when Tyler was a new college graduate. Since then she has published an additional nineteen novels, plus short stories. Considered a Southern writer, with a debt to both Eudora Welty and Reynolds Price, under whom she studied at Duke University, Anne Tyler typically focuses her attention on ordinary families and misfits within those families. Baltimore, the city in which Tyler has lived for most of her adult life, is the setting for all her novels. *A Spool of Blue Thread*, Tyler's twentieth novel, delivers what readers have come to expect in her work, in terms of characters, theme, setting, and tone.

The novel is told in four sections. Part 1, by far the largest segment of the book, is entitled "Can't Leave Till the Dog Dies." Initially set in 1994, and then continuing in 2012, the first section tells the story of the family that Red and Abby, in their seventies, have created. It also chronicles Abby's slow decline and Red's increasing physical frailty. The second part is titled with a quotation from *Wizard of Oz*, "What a World, What a World," the words of the Wicked Witch of the West as she is dying. In this section, which takes place in the late 1950s and 1960s, the reader watches Abby fall in love with Red, who has already fallen for her. The third section, which focuses on the relationship of Red's parents during the 1930s, is entitled "A Bucket of Blue Paint." Denny's story is taken up in part 4, "A Spool of Blue Thread," following the events in part 1. The reverse chronological structure, according to Charles Finch for *USA Today*, gives the novel "an infusion of intensity and energy."

The book centers on two love stories that have become family lore. One is the story of Red's parents, Junior and Linnie Mae. In the third segment, the reader discovers that they have vastly different accounts of their courtship and marriage. The first love story that appears is of the second generation, their son Red and Abby. "It was a beautiful, breezy, yellow-and-green afternoon," Abby repeatedly begins telling this tale of the day she fell in love with Red, only to stop at that juncture.

Although Tyler maintains that her writing is not autobiographical, it is worth noting that her mother, a social worker, died of Alzheimer's disease and her father, a year later, died of heart disease. Abby is seventy-two in the first section of the book, the age Tyler herself was when she completed the novel.

Anne Tyler has written twenty novels, some of which have been adapted into feature films. In 1985 The Accidental Tourist *won the National Book Critics Circle Award for fiction.* Breathing Lessons *was awarded the 1989 Pulitzer Prize for fiction.*

The novel is a kaleidoscope of all sorts of love within a family and all the permutations of love over time. After Red and Abby have a dispute about the way Denny, their prodigal son, should have been treated, Red says, "Sometimes I rue and deplore the day I married a social worker." Tyler later comments, "At such moments, they hated each other." The reader finds both love and conflict among siblings, with Amanda phoning Denny to give a lecture that ends with, "But most of all, Denny, *most* of all: I will never forgive you for consuming every last little drop of our parents' attention and leaving nothing for the rest of us." Still, Denny returns to the family home after this outburst.

Tyler's third-person narrator offers several possible interpretations of these love stories. To the Whitshanks, the family narratives are joined by the theme of patiently waiting for what they should have: the house, the wife. Alternatively, writing for the British journal *New Statesman*, Leo Robson suggests that the theme of envy dominates the main stories of both married couples, as Tyler writes an outsider would perceive. Tyler herself may favor this explanation; twice in the book characters from different generations point out that quality in someone else. Had anyone known the families deeply, which was not the case, Tyler says they might have recognized yet another point—both stories led to disappointment. Not noticing this disappointment, Tyler writes, may have been "just further proof that the Whitshanks were not remarkable in any way whatsoever." A third love story, between Red's sister, Merrick, and Walter Barrister III, confirms these ideas of patient waiting, envy, and disappointment. Trey was first engaged to a friend of Merrick's, and the marriage, though a source of wealth, does not bring Merrick either happiness or children.

This insistence that the family is ordinary is part of Tyler's familiar bag of tricks. Tyler highlights the universal, ordinary nature of this family, saturating the work with details that conjure an era and characters. Indeed, the creation of memorable characters is one of Tyler's strengths as a writer. For example, Abby "insisted on natural childbirth, breast-fed her babies in public, served her family wheat germ and home-brewed yogurt, marched against the Vietnam War with her youngest astride her hip, sent her children to public schools. Her house was filled with her handicrafts—macramé plant hangers and colorful woven serapes." In fewer than fifty words, Tyler economically conjures an earth mother of the 1960s. A retired social worker, Abby is the center of the family, with a big heart that widens the family circle into an ellipsis. She invites people who have nowhere else to go to join her family for what are known as her "orphan dinners." These meals are a source of embarrassment and resentment to her children, even after they are grown.

Tyler is also noted for her hapless male characters, which appear in several of her works. In this novel, Denny, a shape shifter of a son who glides in and out of Abby and Red's lives, as well as out of college and relationships, is that hapless male, a pointed contrast to his hardworking contactor father and brother. A brief, perplexing call from him in which he announces that he is gay, even though it turns out that he is not, provides the opening gambit of this novel, showing how he affects the others in the family and how they fret over him.

Tyler also lavishes attention on characters who appear only once in the story. One of Abby's "orphans," an immigrant whom she met in the supermarket, appears for Sunday dinner "wearing a heavy belted dress and stockings that looked like Ace bandages." Her treatment of such a characters is reminiscent of Shakespeare's minor characters, who are just as complex and interesting as the main characters.

Tyler is a master at rendering the small conflicts of daily life between the characters and generations. Food, which plays a significant role in the novel, is one source of conflict. Tyler sneaks in references to food, a minor character in the book, the way mothers may sneak vegetables into favorite meals. For example, she tells us that when the children were young, they rejected Abby's healthy food as much as they could, preferring hot dogs and white bread. They also hated it when Abby was in charge of school picnics, because she provided healthy fare. After Stem, his wife, Nora, and their boys move in, Nora takes over the cooking, making separate meals for her children if they refuse to eat the food she has prepared for the rest of the family. This coddling of children upsets Abby, as do the unfamiliar casseroles and succotash Nora cooks.

After Red has a heart attack and Abby experiences memory failure and begins wandering, sometimes getting lost in her own neighborhood, Denny comes home to care for them. His action creates another cycle of conflict and competition, however, because he arrives just after Stem and his family have moved into the house. After discussing the situation, the grown children ultimately determine that a retirement community would be best for Red and Abby.

This decision creates further conflict and tension, because Red's father built the house, using only the finest materials. Although originally commissioned and purchased by another man, the house has always belonged to the Whitshanks, in Junior's mind at least. The house is a character itself, demanding attention, becoming a burden (among other things, it lacks air conditioning), disappointing even Junior, who tinkered endlessly with the house and yard. Tyler comments on Junior's use of the phrase "In this house" when making pronouncements, "So 'this house' really meant 'this family,' it seemed. The two were one and the same."

Critics vary in where they would place Tyler and her writing among fiction writers. Leo Robson is impressed by Tyler's "comic naturalism," using contemporary family life as a means of "getting inside the 'ordinary', in the sense not of bland but of typical, common, universal." He places Tyler's work in the family saga subgenre, tracing the development of the family saga to the nineteenth-century French writer Émile Zola. He considers Tyler as linked with modern writers such as Joanna Trollope, Marilynn Robinson, and John Updike. The family saga tales in this novel are not many generations long, however; Junior and Linnie Mae's story takes place in the 1930s, and the romance between Abby and Red begins in the 1960s.

In contrast, Finch suggests that Tyler belongs with other domestic writers such as Laurie Colwin and Adam Gopnik, though because of the occasional tours of the darker side of life, she may more accurately be compared to Canadian writer Alice Munro. Others, noting that Tyler's work is always focused on domestic situations and the ordinariness of life, spiced with humor, liken her to Jane Austen.

Though *A Blue Spool of Thread* was short-listed for the prestigious Man Booker Prize, critical reception for the novel has been mixed. For Donna Seaman, writing a starred review in *Booklist*, *Blue Spool* is not only written in prose "as transparent as ice," but it is also an attack on unfair presuppositions readers may unconsciously hold about age, gender, race, and class, thus giving the book some weight that many fictional works do not have. Not every reviewer was complimentary, however; the influential critic Michiko Kakutani, commenting in *New York Times*, considered the work to be a mere recycling of previous plot ideas and themes "in the most perfunctory manner imaginable."

Despite the occasional negative reviews, Tyler fans throughout the world seem ever eager to embrace the imperfect families that Tyler creates. As Heller McAlpin, writing for National Public Radio, explained, "You don't read Anne Tyler to have your worldview expanded, or to be kept awake at night anxiously turning pages. You read, instead, for the cozy mildness, the comfort of sinking into each new warmhearted, gently wry book."

Judy A. Johnson

Review Sources

Finch, Charles. "Anne Tyler Unspools a Gem." Rev. of *A Blue Spool of Thread*, by Anne Tyler. *USA Today*. Gannett, 10 Mar. 2015. Web. 2 Oct. 2015.

Hoffert, Barbara. "LibraryReads: Anne Tyler." Rev. of *A Spool of Blue Thread*, by Anne Tyler. *Library Journal* 15 Feb. 2015: 134. Print.

Kakutani, Michiko. "Ordinary People, Wayward Son." *New York Times*. New York Times, 5 Feb. 2015. Web. 14 Sept. 2015.

McAlpin, Heller. "Cozy 'Blue Thread' Is Unabashedly Domestic." Rev. of *A Blue Spool of Thread*, by Anne Tyler. *NPR*. NPR, 10 Feb. 2015. Web. 6 Oct. 2015.

Robson, Leo. "Generation Game." Rev. of *A Blue Spool of Thread*, by Anne Tyler. *New Statesman* 13 Feb. 2015: 48–50. Print.
Seaman, Donna. Rev. of *A Blue Spool of Thread*, by Anne Tyler. *Booklist* 1 Dec. 2014: 23–24. Print.

The State We're In
Maine Stories

Author: Ann Beattie (b. 1947)
Publisher: Scribner (New York). 224 pp.
Type of work: Short fiction
Time: Early twenty-first century
Locale: Maine

(Courtesy of Scribner)

The State We're In: Maine Stories is Ann Beattie's collection of short stories either set in the state of Maine or loosely connected to it. When looked at more deeply, however, the title of the book can be seen as a metaphor for the society's "state of mind."

In the 1970s and 1980s, Ann Beattie ranked with such writers as Raymond Carver, Tobias Wolfe, and Bobbie Ann Mason as being primarily responsible for what was widely called a "Renaissance of the American Short Story." Critical reaction to her early story collections such as *Distortions* (1976), *Secrets and Surprises* (1978), *The Burning House* (1982), and *Where You'll Find Me* (1986) was largely positive, labelling her the spokesperson for the generation of the 1960s and praising her for her accurate portrayal of that generation's passivity.

Beattie's realistic–minimalist technique focused on subtle emotional conflicts that cannot be expressed directly but that must be evoked by a seemingly trivial object or by an apparently irrelevant character. It is a technique pioneered by Anton Chekhov and mastered by James Joyce and Raymond Carver. It explores human complexity not by internal monologue or reflection, but by concrete situations and details that seem simple and ordinary but clustered together embody a profound psychological, subtly symbolic significance.

Beattie's previous collection of stories, *Follies* (2005), departed from her famous so-called minimalism style and engaged in a kind of literary play with a variety of parodies and comic voices. Her large collection of previously published stories, many of which date to the 1970s, appeared in 2011 and evoked nostalgia for her earlier work.

Publishing a collection of new short stories after ten years of silence might suggest that Beattie has been working on them and reworking them for a decade. However, as Beattie told a *New Yorker* interviewer, she wrote eighteen stories in the summer of 2014, threw out three, and realized that the remaining stories could form a book. If *The State We're In* is that book, then reviewers had reason wonder how the once meticulous and demanding Ann Beattie could have written all fifteen stories in one summer and rather randomly tossed them together in this book.

Los Angeles Times reviewer David Ulin said that these most recent stories are developed incrementally, "almost anecdotally." However, as Ulin reminds readers, there is a difference between art and anecdote. The problem with an anecdotal structure is that it is wandering, rambling, loose, and lacking in any kind of unified significance. The details appear thrown in simply because the writer happened to think of them at that particular point in the composition and did not bother to edit them out. Ulin justifies Beattie's incremental structure by claiming that they are a welcome rejection of that old short-story cliché, the Joycean "epiphany," arguing that Beattie's eschewal of the epiphany makes her stories more demanding of the reader by making her characters more real. Mary Pols, in her review in the *New York Times*, is perhaps closer to the truth when she claims that there is a "willful vagueness" to almost all the stories that veer off on so many tangents "the train of thought rushes past the station."

The stories in *The State We're In* are loosely connected by locale, primarily in the south of Maine, where Beattie and her husband spend half the year. Three stories are more closely centered on a teenage girl named Jocelyn, who is sent to summer school in Maine by her mother who either has had surgery or just wants the child out of the way for a while. Jocelyn is staying with her uncle Raleigh and her Aunt Bettina Louise Tompkins, who are dubbed BLT, "hold the mayo." In the first story in the collection, "What Magical Realism Would Be," we discover that Jocelyn hates summer school because her teacher Ms. Nementhal has assigned ten papers; she is having particular difficulty with one on the magical realism of Gabriel García Márquez.

Although written in third person, the language of the story reflects the voice of the girl, beginning, "Writing essays was retarded. It completely was." The story also features an old Beattie signature of referring to contemporary popular culture phenomena, such as Amazon Prime, the availability of certificates to perform marriages over the Internet, Mr. Rogers and his parody on *Saturday Night Live*, the television series *Breaking Bad*, and two separate references to Ben Affleck's getting thrown out of a casino in Las Vegas for counting cards.

Of course, the title, *The State We're In* refers both to the geographical location of the stories and, as reviewers like to point out, to some cultural or existential state of mind. In the story "Duff's Done Enough," the Beattie narrator explains that all writers will explain that the world is full of stories, and you can't find the "inevitable" one, "be-

Ann Beattie won the PEN/Malamud Prize for the Short Story in 2000 and the Rea Award for the Short Story in 2005.

cause so many needles appear in so many haystacks. Most writers spend their entire careers . . . considering endless piles of hay, praying . . . that a needle will prick their finger." She also reminds us that the actions she describes, such as a married man getting involved with a transgender person, are not the kind of actions we usually expect to find happening in Maine.

Some stories are more like short exercises. "The Fledgling" recounts when the narrator saved a small bird and then recites facts or observations as they occur to her. Other stories appear to be excuses to describe idiosyncratic details, such as "Aunt Sophie Renaldo Brown," which tells of a woman who wears a push-up bra inside of which she puts two metal wire champagne cork baskets to suggest large protruding nipples.

It is an image the narrator niece keeps coming back to as she self-consciously wonders how to tell the story, which ultimately seems to be about the aunt having breast cancer. In "Adirondack Chairs," the narrator criticizes the chairs because they ruin women's stockings and make you spill your drink, and you have to sit in them awkwardly while pretending they are comfortable, "with the seats so tilted so deeply backward that your knees sprang up like a ventriloquist's dummy."

"Yancy," a story admired by several reviewers, is about a seventy-seven-year-old female poet who is visited by an agent of the Internal Revenue Service to investigate whether a room she has deducted as a work space for her writing is actually used for that purpose. The poet has a daughter named Ginger, who is married to another woman, and a dog who has been with her for thirteen years. Indeed, she introduces the story with the dog, which gives the story its name, but she reassures the reader that she does have a topic of conversation other than the dog—the visit from the IRS agent, who, it turns out, is very nice and tells her about his own life. He has a daughter who wants to be a playwright. His wife forgot to pick him up at the hospital after he had his appendix out because she was having a drink. He asks her to recommend a book of poetry for him to read, which leads to a little discussion of the poetry of James Wright. The woman recites, and the story quotes in its entirety Wright's poem, "Lying in a Hammock at William Duffy's Farm in Pine Island, Minnesota." Even though she has started to wonder impatiently when the man is going to leave, the woman abruptly asks him to move in with her, which he politely declines.

"Silent Prayer" is a very brief story that evokes a bit of Beattie in her prime. It is mostly a dialogue between a man and his wife about how "couples talk to each other. . . . But there's no way to find out. You can't believe what you see in movies on TV or in books, least of all the so-called reality shows." The conversation between the two seems to have no direction or central focus, except the wife is left feeling that what she does is less important that what her husband does. However, after she watches him leave for his business trip, the story ends with lines that remind us of early Beattie stories: "Please let the plane not crash, she thought, going weak in the knees. This was a habitual thought. More or less like prayer."

"Missed Calls" focuses largely on a conversation between a writer and a famous photographer's wife about a visit Truman Capote once made to her home. The woman's one Truman Capote story is that while he was visiting he used the phone several times and left dollar bills on which he signed his name. The story then comes together when the visiting writer dumps her own problems on the woman about her goddaughter who has just told the family she has no intention of graduating from college. Howard Norman in the *Washington Post* singles out "Missed Calls" for special praise, suggesting it goes beyond its initial appeal to eavesdropping on "high-toned" gossip by going into serious inquiry about art, although he fails to explain what that serious inquiry is.

The final story in the collection, "The Repurposed Barn," returns to the teenager Jocelyn whose mother has returned with her boyfriend to pick her up. Readers find out the answer to the pressing question of whether Jocelyn finished writing the papers assigned to her and what kind of grade she got on them. Jocelyn revises her essay as a piece of fiction—even though she thought that journalism was "cool" and fiction was "sort of retarded"—about a couple who buy two Elvis lamps and argue about them for five years. While driving around with the lamps in the back seat, they have an accident and are killed and go to Heaven. God will not let Elvis in, but the lamps start singing and God relents. The paper gets Jocelyn a B. The Beattie story ends informing us that Jocelyn is seven weeks pregnant, leading the narrator to proclaim: "Jocelyn became Everywoman. That's where the story ends." And that is also where Ann Beattie's new collection of stories ends.

Charles E. May

Review Sources

Broening, John. Rev. of *The State We're In: Maine Stories*, by Ann Beattie. *Denver Post.* Digital First Media, 16 Aug. 2015. Web. 9 Jan. 2016.

Kanner, Ellen. Rev. of *The State We're In: Maine Stories*, by Ann Beattie. *Miami Herald.* MiamiHerald.com, 7 Aug. 2015. Web. 9 Jan. 2016.

Pols, Mary. Rev of *The State We're In: Maine Stories*, by Ann Beattie. *New York Times.* New York Times, 4 Sept. 2015. Web. 9 Jan 2016.

Rev. of *The State We're In: Maine Stories*, by Ann Beattie. *Kirkus Reviews.* 1 June 2015. Web. 9 Jan. 2016.

Ulin, David. Rev. of *The State We're In: Maine Stories*, by Ann Beattie. *Los Angeles Times.* Los Angeles Times, 7 Aug. 2015. Web. 9 Jan. 2016.

Step Aside, Pops

Author: Kate Beaton (b. 1983)
Publisher: Drawn and Quarterly (Montreal), 160 pp.
Type of work: Graphic novel, current affairs, history
Time: Various
Locale: Various

(Courtesy of Drawn & Quarterly)

Step Aside, Pops *is the second collection of Kate Beaton's popular webcomic* Hark! A Vagrant, *featuring subtle yet funny commentary on topics ranging from obscure historical figures to superheroes to modern-day movie stars.*

What do *Wuthering Heights*, Janet Jackson, and Wonder Woman have in common? All have been rendered with grace, wit, and more than a bit of verve by comic artist Kate Beaton in *Step Aside, Pops*, the second hardcover collection of her *Hark! A Vagrant* webcomic.

Since starting *Hark! A Vagrant* in 2008, Beaton has become one of the most successful representatives of the online comics boom. Her webcomic and website are wildly popular, and the occasional presence of her drawings in the *New Yorker* magazine acts as the ultimate legacy media vindication. In a crowded field, where anyone with an Internet connection and a pen can start their own webcomic, Beaton's work makes itself known both in style and substance. *Step Aside, Pops* is no exception.

Like the rest of Beaton's oeuvre, *Step Aside, Pops* resists easy categorization. A former student of history and anthropology who once worked in a maritime museum in Victoria, Canada, Beaton's interests tend toward the historical, but one is just as likely to find her interpretations of pop culture, classic literature, music, or bizarre artistic ephemera from yesteryear in the pages of this collection. Uniting these disparate topics is a penchant for esoteric specificity. One series of strips chronicles the tormented relationship between Mexican president Benito Juárez and Emperor Maximilian, who traveled in the 1860s to Mexico on behalf of the Austrian Empire and with the support of Napoleon III and the French army to declare himself emperor. Beaton portrays Maximilian as an overly earnest naïf. ("I mean, no, Maximilian, you can't rule Mexico, but we feel really bad about having to execute you!" she writes beneath the strips.) Juárez, meanwhile, is eternally chagrined, at least until he inevitably has Maximilian executed and regains control of his country. ("Do not weep for me, my subject," Maximilian says to comfort Juárez, even as the president sends him to his death.) The characterizations may be exaggerated, but the history is real, and it is rich fodder for Beaton's talent for mining comedy from the unlikeliest of places.

Almost incidentally, in the process of being thoroughly entertained, the reader also learning new and interesting things. In a review for NPR, Amal El-Mohtar singled out the unique blend of subversion and reverence, instruction and insurrection that characterizes *Step Aside, Pops*, noting that she "was especially impressed by Beaton's capacity for teaching while being equal parts funny and considerate of her subjects." Referencing several obscure historical figures celebrated in the collection—Tom Longboat, Ida B. Wells, Katherine Sui Fun Cheung—El-Mohtar wrote, "I marveled over the fact that I'd never heard of these amazing people—but marveled more at the fact that Beaton managed to tell jokes while being fiercely respectful of their struggles and achievements."

It is obvious where Beaton's sympathies lie, and it is not with Western history's old, white, and overwhelmingly male canon. As

Kate Beaton is a former history student and the author of Hark! A Vagrant, *a popular webcomic.* Step Aside, Pops *is the second printed collection of her work, which has also been featured in the* New Yorker.

Sean Rogers wrote in the Toronto-based *Globe and Mail*, "Her princes and generals look silly, at best, in their perches of power, and often seem dangerously ignorant." Beaton's retelling of the story of Lady Shalott and Lancelot involves the knight relieving himself in the middle of the road. Pop-culture heroes do not fare much better: her Superman is a muscular busybody who is prone to thrusting his curly-haired head into Lois Lane's second-story windows unannounced and asking, "LOIS ARE YOU IN TROUBLE?" Backing out, he explains, "I saw you on the phone . . . just thought something was going on." Here, career woman Lois Lane is the hero, and the attention from Clark Kent and his alter ego is just getting in the way. As Beaton explains, "If Lois isn't kicking ass, taking names, and winning ten Pulitzer Prizes an issue, I don't even want to hear about it."

Lois is one of several feminist heroes in a work full of impassioned feminism. The cover image is a spoof on nineteenth-century illustrations depicting women on early bicycles, called velocipedes, which served as means not just of transportation but also of greater freedom and liberation for women. Victorian illustrations of the time emphasized and satirized the "scandal" of such an activity; in her cover for *Step Aside, Pops*, Beaton then satirizes the original satire. The focus of the cartoon is a woman who is perched on a velocipede with her arms crossed, one leg up and resting on the handlebars. Inside the book, the "awful velocipedestrienne" appears again with a lit cigarette in her mouth as she rides about in full Victorian garb, jaw thrust out in defiance. "You see me rollin up pops," she warns, "you step aside." A mustached man, a foppish proxy for the patriarchy, calls her a "public nuisance." In the final frame, another woman, dressed in the era of the 1920s, walks with a cigarette in her mouth and an old-time phonograph on her shoulder, much like a twentieth-century boombox. "Ain't give a damn," she states, while a male onlooker exclaims, "Bloody unbelievable."

The jutted jaw of the velocipedestrienne (a word, Beaton notes on her website, that she did not make up) captures the rebellious spirit that animates *Step Aside, Pops*. "You sense . . . a fierceness—it's close to anger—just beneath the surface," noted *Guardian* reviewer Rachel Cooke. Beaton's Wonder Woman is not all beatific smiles and heroism. Instead, she slouches over a bar, suffering a moment of existential dismay as a fellow patron heaps superficial adulation on her. On the surface, it is comical to see a female superhero renowned for her grace and composure just as frustrated as so many other women, but it also speaks to a frustration with the societal roles available to women as well as to the stereotypes heaped upon them.

At her most biting, Beaton lampoons "straw feminists" by conjuring a pair of hairy-legged women who hiss with forked tongues that "all men are garbage" and who burn bras and terrorize children. In this manner, *Step Aside, Pops* is a hilariously over-the-top takedown of a particularly insidious cultural caricature of feminism and of anyone who harbors the belief that feminists spend their time lecturing young women about why they should want all men to be dead. Just as important is the subtler feminist bent that pervades the rest of Beaton's work. Her twist on the Cinderella tale involves the titular heroine acquiring a bulging bodybuilder physique when her fairy godmother decides to "take it to the limit." It is hard to tell whether Beaton is deliberately inverting the gender expectations of the princess or if she is simply wanting to connect Cinderella up with a muscular prince who has apparently ripped the sleeves off of all his formal attire.

Artistically, this collection tends toward the simple and expressive. Pens and simple ink washes are Beaton's preferred tools, and though some online strips are in color, this collection is strictly black and white. While the art lacks a sense of formality and polish, it does not lack skill. Beaton knows how to capture the visual essence of a character, whether it be Ben Franklin's louche charm or the pug-like visage of French revolutionary Georges Jacques Danton, and she has an instinctive grasp of just how much detail is needed to get her joke across to her audience.

The majority of Beaton's comic strips are brief, three-panel affairs, often presented in loose series organized around a particular theme. There is just enough dialogue and illustration to convey the joke before moving on to the next one. Given Beaton's roving intellect, this may be for the best, but the collection shines when it breaks free of her traditional boundaries. One notable example is an extended commentary answering the question, Whatever happened to the young men of Janet Jackson's "Nasty" song? Beaton's answer is a ten-page free-form comic telling the story of a young man who is haunted by Jackson's dismissal. He returns home one day, dejected, to find an eviction notice. "NASTY!!" it scolds. Homeless now, he is passed by a woman and her child. "Don't look, son," the woman says, "he's nasty." Soon he is taken in by St. Jude's Home for the Nasty—and this is just the midway point in a surreal narrative that spans more than forty years.

Several other standouts are similarly centered on bits of artistic ephemera from the past, such as the covers of Nancy Drew books, Halloween-themed postcards, or old broadsides. The results are silly and surreal, but they are a welcome demonstration of Beaton's artistic and creative agility. In the *Globe and Mail*, Rogers warned that readers may begin to see the "easy formula" of "old-timey topic plus new-fangled slang equals shtick"—but if diminishing returns are in the offing, they are not here yet. "Founding Fathers (in a Mall)" imagines the United States' preeminent statesmen faced with such modern marvels as a singing novelty fish. "America was born of blood for this," Jefferson says to Adams, as an animatronic bass belts the chorus of "Rock around the Clock." If the collection suffers from any major flaw, it is that every now and then, the jokes rely a bit too much on the reader's outside knowledge. By and large, Beaton's ability to reward casual readers and students of history and literature such as herself is remarkable, but sometimes, such as in the *Wuthering Heights* strips, she risks presuming a bit too much reader knowledge.

Taken as a whole, *Step Aside, Pops* is a triumph, embodying an idiosyncratic perspective of the sort that would have struggled to find an audience in traditional media. Thanks to its genesis as a webcomic, *Step Aside, Pops* was able to gather an audience before it was even published. Now, in print, it has the chance to prove to even more people that intelligent, feminist comic strips about velocipedestriennes, peasants, and little-known revolutionaries are worth reading about, not only for their insight and subtle edge, but also for their sheer entertainment.

Kenrick Vezina

Review Sources

Carroll, Tobias. Rev. of *Step Aside, Pops*, by Kate Beaton. *Paste*. Paste Media Group, 15 Sept. 2015. Web. 31 Dec. 2015.

Cooke, Rachel. "Hairy Heroines and Fierce Laughs." Rev. of *Step Aside, Pops*, by Kate Beaton. *Guardian*. Guardian News and Media, 14 Sept. 2015. Web. 31 Dec. 2015.

El-Mohtar, Amal. "*Step Aside, Pops* Lampoons History with Humor and Wit." Rev. of *Step Aside, Pops*, by Kate Beaton. *NPR*. NPR, 18 Sept. 2015. Web. 31 Dec. 2015.

Rogers, Sean. "Review: Kate Beaton Explores New Avenues in the Very Funny *Step Aside, Pops*." Rev. of *Step Aside, Pops*, by Kate Beaton. *Globe and Mail*. Globe and Mail, 18 Sept. 2015. Web. 31 Dec. 2015.

The Story of My Teeth

Author: Valeria Luiselli (b. 1983)
First published: *La historia de mis dientes*, 2013, in Mexico
Translated from the Spanish by: Christina MacSweeney
Publisher: Coffee House Press (Minneapolis). 195 pp.
Type of work: Novel
Time: 1945–2013
Locales: Mexico and the United States

The Story of My Teeth *is an experimental novel about Gustavo "Highway" Sánchez, a legendary auctioneer who excels at storytelling. Told in six parts, with a seventh part added for the English edition, the narrative uses unconventional methods, like assigning allegories to teeth on an auction block, to tell the story.*

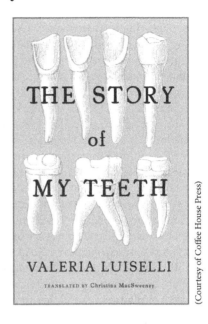

(Courtesy of Coffee House Press)

Principal characters:
GUSTAVO "HIGHWAY" SÁNCHEZ SÁNCHEZ, narrator, legendary auctioneer, and storyteller
FLACA, his wife
SIDDHARTHA, their son
VORAGINE, his friend and an artist

Valeria Luiselli's novel *The Story of My Teeth* is a collaboration between the author and workers at a juice factory in Mexico. The story follows legendary auctioneer Gustavo "Highway" Sánchez Sánchez from birth to death in a series of experimental chapters, originally written as a series of chapbooks.

Like any great story starring an epic character, Highway's begins with a colorful start. He says of his birth, "I was born in Pachuca, the Beautiful Windy City, with four premature teeth and my body completely covered in a very fine coat of fuzz." He goes on to say he's "grateful for that inauspicious start because ugliness, as my other uncle, Euripides Lopez Sanchez, was given to saying, is character forming." He has other endearing and myth-building qualities that he shares by way of formal introduction to the reader: he can imitate Janis Joplin after two rums, interpret Chinese fortune cookies, float on his back, count to eight in Japanese, and stand an egg upright on a table like Christopher Columbus. Each detail is small, but when told in his confident, comical tone, they come across as a unique amalgam of characteristics that make him come to life on the page.

The story is told in six sections, all disparate but connected by the character Highway: The Story (Beginning, Middle, and End), The Hyperbolics, The Parabolics, The Circulars, The Allegorics, and The Elliptics. (A final chapter, The Chronologic, is a chronology of events in Highway's and Mexico's life, beginning in 1938 and ending in 2013.)

The first section, The Story, provides the reader with a standard biography of Highway. Told in a first-person narrative style, the chapter sets up the remainder of the book in tone, style, and setting. The reader learns of Highway's young life and the afternoons he spent entertaining Azul, his boss's wife when he was eight years old and working his first job at a newspaper stand. Azul was frequently caught in a tryst with another man, and young Highway would interrupt them in order to play games with her through the afternoon. Highway's beginnings as a collector are explained, and the reader learns of his first collection: his father's discarded fingernails, which he collects in envelopes.

Photo of Valeria Luiselli
Author: *The Story of My Teeth*
Publisher: Coffee House Press
Photographer Credit: Alfredo Pelcastre
(Use of photo must carry credit)

(Alfredo Pelcastre)

Valeria Luiselli was born in Mexico City and raised in South Africa. Her previous works include a collection of essays called Sidewalks *(2013) and the novel* Faces in the Crowd *(2014). She was included in the 2014 National Book Foundation's 5 under 35 award and has received numerous other awards and recognitions.*

His mentally abusive wife Flaca is introduced, as is their son, Siddhartha, and finally Luiselli describes how Highway becomes a legendary auctioneer and a collector of strange objects from his later-in-life travels around the world. This first chapter provides the background that allows the following chapters to be nearly self-contained. Highway's teeth, which he claims once belonged to Marilyn Monroe, are also introduced early in the book, and while they are literally a part of Highway, since they have been implanted in his mouth, they are very much a character in their own right.

Dealing heavily in the philosophies of some of Luiselli's favorite writers. Each chapter has its own epigram with another semiotics-themed quote from a different philosopher. The first chapter begins with an epigram from J. S. Mill:

> A man may have been named John because that was the name of his father; a town may have been named Dartmouth, because it is situated at the mouth of the Dart. But it is no part of the signification of the word John, that the father of the person so called bore the same name; nor even of the word Dartmouth, to be situated at the mouth of the Dart.

Thus, this quote sets up the crux of Highway's own philosophy: It is not the object that holds importance. Rather, the significance is in the importance that is placed upon the object. Highway uses this as a mantra of sorts throughout his days as an auctioneer.

Highway was long estranged from his son Siddhartha when an auction for a local church about to fall into financial ruin reunites the pair, however malevolently. Highway has amassed a large collection of items and a house where he stores them all. Father Luigi Amara, the parish priest of Saint Apolonia's, approaches Highway seeking his skills as an auctioneer and suggests he could auction off part of his large collection to benefit the ailing parish. It is 2011, and the economic crisis has hit Highway as well as the rest of Mexico and the world. He agrees that this would be a good way to pare down his collection, make some money, and seek a piece of spiritual salvation at the same time.

While perusing his collection, Highway decides that he will auction off the ten best teeth that he kept after he had the Marilyn Monroe teeth implanted in his mouth years earlier. The chapter is called The Hyperbolics because Highway intends to attach a story, "an elegant surpassing of the truth," of a great writer or philosopher to each tooth. He includes Plato, Augustine of Hippo, Rousseau, and even Virginia Woolf as the subjects of his stories, and Father Luigi agrees to the plan, though we are given the impression he does not fully understand Highway's intended use of hyperboles: "The hyperbole is an effective means of transmission of the great power of the Holy Spirit," he asserts. The lot of teeth is just one tooth that is still in Highway's mouth. He therefore auctions himself off, and Siddhartha buys his father for 1,000 pesos.

Alongside the epigrams introducing each chapter is a saying from a fortune cookie closing out the chapter. While the epigrams provide for the reader a philosophical insight into Highway, the fortunes foreshadow what is to come and provide further insight into what just took place. "The Hyperbolics" ends with the fortune, "Demented is the man who is always clenching his teeth on that solid, immutable block of stone that is the past."

The next chapter, The Parabolics, finds Highway without his teeth and in an art gallery. He is being tormented by demented clowns voiced by his son. This begins the tragic downturn of a once robust man. The final chapter, The Elliptics, is told by Voragine, a young artist whom Highway meets and invites to stay in his house. The two become close, and Highway asks Voragine to promise to tell his story. Though this section is perhaps the most straightforward, it is also the most poignant. The reader sees the culmination of Highway's life's work in the breath of one chapter.

It is easy and perhaps helpful to approach *The Story of My Teeth* as an art project as much as a novel. In 2013, Luiselli was commissioned by Mexico's Galería Jumex to create a fictional work that would appear in the catalog for an exhibition called *The Hunter and the Factory*. Luiselli explains in the afterword of *The Story of My Teeth*, "The idea behind the exhibition, and my commission, was to reflect upon the bridges—or the lack thereof—between the featured artwork, the gallery, and the larger context of which the gallery formed part."

Funded by Grupo Jumax, the juice factory where the workers who collaborated with the writer are employed, the Jumax Collection is considered one of the world's most important contemporary art collections. Luiselli saw the commission as an opportunity to write for, rather than about, the factory workers, and she wanted the piece to act as an allegory about the art world.

Starting with an initial installment printed in a chapbook format, Luiselli sent the work for the factory workers to read aloud in a weekly discussion group with a curatorial assistant. They responded with comments and criticisms, which Luiselli would apply to the next round of writing, and many of the stories in the book came from the workers themselves. She wrote as Gustavo "Highway" Sánchez Sánchez, revealing her identity only at the end when in a recording of her reading her final work. Luiselli refers to the work as a collective "novel-essay."

The Story of My Teeth won praise from most major critics and outlets, including from the *New York Times*, where Jim Krusoe said, "*The Story of My Teeth* is playful, attentive and very smart without being for a minute pretentious. It's Walter Benjamin without tears—sunnier, more casual and more nimble. Luiselli is an exciting writer to watch, not only for this book, but also for the fresh approach she brings to fiction, one that invites participation and reaction, even skepticism—a living, breathing map." *The Story of My Teeth* was included on many best-of book lists in 2015 and further cemented Luiselli's place as a major new literary voice and nodded toward the current Latin American literary renaissance.

Melynda Fuller

Review Sources

Bady, Aaron. "Bolaño's Teeth: Valeria Luiselli and the Renaissance of Mexican Literature." Rev. of *The Story of My Teeth*, by Valeria Luiselli. *Los Angeles Review of Books*. Los Angeles Review of Books, 4 Dec. 2015. Web. 28 Jan. 2016.

Felicelli, Anita. Rev. of *The Story of My Teeth*, by Valeria Luiselli. *Rumpus.* The Rumpus, 29 Sept. 2015. Web. 28 Jan. 2016.

Katz, Amanda. "Dickens + MP3 ÷ Balzac + JPEG." Rev. of *The Story of My Teeth*, by Valeria Luiselli. *Slate.* The Slate Group, 9 Sept. 2015. Web. 28 Jan. 2016.

Kellogg, Carolyn. "Valeria Luiselli's 'The Story of My Teeth' Is a Collision of Storytelling, Lying and Art." Rev. of *The Story of My Teeth*, by Valeria Luiselli. *Los Angeles Times*. Los Angeles Times, 17 Sept. 2015. Web. 28 Jan. 2016.

Krusoe, Jim. Rev. of *The Story of My Teeth*, by Valeria Luiselli. *New York Times*. New York Times, 11 Sept. 2015. Web. 28 Jan. 2016.

Mcalpin, Heller. "'Story of My Teeth' Covers Art, Identity and Dental Adventures." Rev. of *The Story of My Teeth*, by Valeria Luiselli. *NPR*. NPR, 14 Sept. 2015. Web. 28 Jan. 2016.

The Story of the Lost Child

Author: Elena Ferrante (b. 1943)
First published: *Storia della bambina perduta*, 2014, in Italy
Translated from the Italian by: Ann Goldstein
Publisher: Europa Editions (New York). 464 pp.
Type of work: Novel
Time: 1980s–2010s
Locales: Italy, France, United States

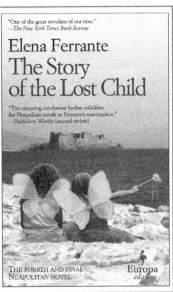

"One of the great novelists of our time."
—*The New York Times Book Review*

Elena Ferrante
The Story
of the Lost Child

"This stunning conclusion further solidifies the Neapolitan novels as Ferrante's masterpiece."
—*Publishers Weekly* (starred review)

THE FOURTH AND FINAL NEAPOLITAN NOVEL

Europa
editions

(Courtesy of Europa Editions Inc)

The Story of the Lost Child is the fourth and final installment of the Neapolitan novels, an internationally successful series published by Elena Ferrante. The final book continues the story of lifelong friends Elena Greco and Raffaella Cerullo.

Principal characters:

ELENA "LENÙ" GRECO, the narrator, who has been best friends with Lila (Raffaella) since childhood

RAFFAELLA "LILA" CERULLO, her closest friend since meeting at the age of six

PIETRO AIROTA, her husband, now separated

DEDE, her daughter with Pietro

ELSA, her daughter with Pietro

NINO, her current lover and Lila's former boyfriend

IMMA, her daughter with Nino

GENNARO, Lila's son with her former husband

ENZO, Lila's partner

TINA, Lila's daughter with Enzo

Through four books and over fifteen hundred pages, the pseudonymous Elena Ferrante has been chronicling the lives of Elena (Lenù) Greco and Raffaella (Lila) Cerullo in her collection known as the Neapolitan novels. The books, including the fourth and final installment, *The Story of the Lost Child* (2015), are narrated by Elena and have followed the now-grown women from grade school and first crushes to their first major division, when Lila is forced to quit her studies in fifth grade while Elena is encouraged and allowed to continue; to first marriages and betrayals; and middle age and motherhood. The previous novels include *My Brilliant Friend* (2012), *The Story of a New Name* (2013), and *Those Who Leave and Those Who Stay* (2014), and deal with the periods of childhood, late adolescence and young adulthood, and adulthood and parenthood, respectively.

With her signature style—quick, casual sentences that impose an immediacy on the plot development and the characters—Ferrante delivers a devastating concluding portrait that builds upon the themes of friendship, sacrifice, loss, identity, and the limits of love in her final volume. Ferrante is a writer unafraid of employing techniques that would seem cliché in less capable hands. A striking example is the ending of each volume: a dramatic cliff-hanger frequently closes the action of the novel, and often the end of each short chapter meets a similar fate, so much so that the experience of reading a Ferrante novel is one of being swept into the drama of the plot, pausing to reflect only when Elena, the character, or Ferrante, the novelist, offers such a moment.

The material covered in the Neapolitan series previously appeared in shorter works that began to be published in the early 1990s. Ferrante quickly rose to fame in her native Italy and across the European continent before also gaining a literary reputation in the United States. *The Days of Abandonment* (2005), perhaps her most loved and respected work to date, builds a foundation for the themes of motherhood and feminism that she picks up in the Neapolitan novels, particularly in the final installment. But, while her first books are shorter stand-alone novels, the Neapolitan series could be, and often is, considered one long novel. As Rachel Cusk wrote in her *New York Times Book Review* about the similar story lines appearing in the shorter early novels and the Neapolitan series, "'Do you want the long answer or the short?' is the customary divide between explanations versus outcomes in the retelling of events. Ferrante gives us both the long answer *and* the short, and in doing so adumbrates the mysterious beauty and brutality of personal experience."

At the opening of *The Story of the Lost Child*, having just left her husband, two small daughters, and Naples behind at the conclusion of the third novel, Elena is traveling to a conference in Montpellier, France, with a man named Nino, Lila's former boyfriend, whom Elena has loved since childhood. Lila is living in Naples, in the old neighborhood, and has begun a successful computer-programming and consultancy business. The relationship between the two is strained. *The Story of the Lost Child* covers perhaps the smallest period of time, but delivers the biggest emotional impact, as the relationship between Elena and Lila evolves further into something that mirrors sisterhood more than friendship.

Through the Neapolitan saga, the dueling personalities of Lila and Elena have been the base of emotional resonance. As the lives of the two women have progressed, so have the complicated feelings they have for each other, their home, their lives, and their ambitions. While Elena aspired to become a part of the intellectual set, to be educated and modern, to find a balance between the life of a feminist and mother and wife, Lila has passed through her life without a true direction; however, she exudes a raw talent that is admirable and threatening, whether she is working within the boundaries of artistic expression, business, or motherhood.

Lila's ease has long caused Elena to question her own talent as a writer; Elena frequently references a story written by Lila when they were children called *The Blue Fairy*, a tale that has haunted her through her adult life. To Elena, that story was the first mark of true brilliance in her friend, and she, though a respected writer, feels she will never write anything as good—in fact, she sees traces of this early tale in her first novel. Ferrante commented in a rare interview with the *Paris Review* in 2015 about the relationship of writing between the two characters: "We'll never know if Lila's few texts really have the power that Elena attributes to them. What we do know is, rather, how they generate a sort of model that Elena tries to follow all her life. She tells us something about that model, but that's not what matters. What matters is that, without Lila, Elena wouldn't exist as a writer."

In this final installment, the duality of the two friends reaches a fever pitch. Finding themselves well into their thirties, both living in Naples and pregnant at the same time, the friends visit the same doctors, holding hands during their exams. Lila's body reacts violently to the pregnancy, while Elena feels happiness in the midst of the experience. They give birth to daughters a few months apart, and eventually Elena moves into an apartment in the neighborhood of their violent youth, a floor above Lila, where they begin to take part in an almost communal form of childrearing.

Elena is quickly folded back into this shadowy world and feels at once threatened and inspired. Having just sold another novel to her publisher in Milan, Elena wants to be close to the source of her material, the old neighborhood, in order to create an authentic, raw voice and tone in her work. She also feels that she needs to be closer to her source of inspiration, Lila. Her daughters, who have enjoyed a privileged life-style since infancy, are immediately disgusted by their new surroundings, but Lila captivates them both and becomes a surrogate mother of sorts. Her daughter Tina and Elena's daughter Imma become inseparable, mirroring the lives of their mothers.

Another standout detail of the Neapolitan series has been the continued presence of a supporting cast of characters. Readers find in *The Story of the Lost Child*, as with the other volumes, that the persons have not changed. They remain enmeshed in each other's lives. In fact barely a day seems to go by that they do not impact each other's lives in some way. As Elena struggles to find her place in her old world, she is also able to offer insights into the lives of those who stayed from the unique perspective of an insider who got out. She is no longer as intimidated by the violent Solara brothers and she is able to show the reader how the lives of the women she was friends with as a child are by comparing theirs to hers. Ferrante also shows the complexities of attempt-ing to return to the past through these relationships.

Though the supporting characters offer a captivating world of their own, it is the friendship between the two main characters that holds the reader's attention most. The series features a circular structure and begins in the first book with Elena and Lila both in their sixties, just as Lila has disap-peared completely. Ferrante is not mysteri-ous about what causes the final break in Lila's psyche—the title of the final book says it all. Elena says in the first pages of *My Brilliant Friend*, "It's been at least three decades since she told me that she wanted to disappear without leaving a trace, and I'm the only one who knows what she means. . . . I take it for granted that she has found a way to disappear, to leave not so much as a hair anywhere in this world." The final pages of *The Story of the Lost Child* provide

Elena Ferrante is the Italian author of the novels The Days of Abandonment *(2005),* Troubling Love *(2005), and* The Lost Daughter *(2008), in addition to the* Neapolitan series.

the clues to and finer details of the final years before Lila's disappearance. Uncontrollable anger and a condition Lila describes as "dissolving boundaries" have marked her psychology since childhood, and with the publication of a short novel, *A Friendship*, Elena alienates her longtime friend.

As with Ferrante's other Neapolitan novels, *The Story of the Lost Child* was received to critical acclaim and instantly became a *New York Times* best seller. It has been echoed widely that it is one of the great feminist novels of the twenty-first century, and Ferrante's style and storytelling capability has often been compared to both Jane Austen and Marcel Proust. Because she has always written under a pseudonym, Ferrante's anonymity has given the work an elevated sense of mystery, and because of this anonymity it could be argued that she is able to speak more widely about the lives of women, through the twentieth century and today. In her review of the book for National Public Radio, Maureen Corrigan also emphasizes the final book's addition to the entire story's clever evaluation of the "darker currents of female friendships." Ultimately, the Neapolitan series, including its finale, *The Story of the Lost Child*, is an important work offering unique insight into the lives of its female characters and society.

Melynda Fuller

Review Sources

Acocella, Joan. "Elena Ferrante's New Book: Art Wins." Rev. of *The Story of the Lost Child*, by Elena Ferrante. *New Yorker*. Condé Nast, 1 Sept. 2015. Web. 14 Dec. 2015.

Biggs, Joanna. "I was Blind, She a Falcon." Rev. of *The Story of the Lost Child*, by Elena Ferrante. *London Review of Books*. LRB, 10 Sept. 2015. Web. 14 Dec. 2015.

Corrigan, Maureen. "*Lost Child* Wraps Up Ferrante's Neapolitan Series with 'Perfect Devastation.'" Rev. of *The Story of the Lost Child*, by Elena Ferrante. *NPR*. NPR, 10 Sept. 2015. Web. 14 Dec. 2015.

Cusk, Rachel. Rev. of *The Story of the Lost Child*, by Elena Ferrante. *New York Times*. New York Times, 26 Aug. 2015. Web. 14 Dec. 2015.

Shulevitz, Judith. "The Hypnotic Genius of Elena Ferrante." Rev. of *The Story of the Lost Child*, by Elena Ferrante. *Atlantic*. Atlantic Monthly Group, Oct. 2015. Web. 14 Dec. 2015.

A Strangeness in My Mind

Author: Orhan Pamuk (b. 1952)
First published: *Kafamda bir tuhaflık,* 2013, in Turkey
Translated from the Turkish by: Ekin Oklap
Publisher: Alfred A. Knopf (New York). 599 pp.
Type of work: Novel
Time: September 1968–October 2012
Locales: Istanbul, Turkey; Konya, Turkey

(Courtesy of Alfred A. Knopf)

The ninth novel by Nobel Prize–winning author Orhan Pamuk, A Strangeness in My Mind *is a love story that unfolds over the course of decades. As in Pamuk's other works, this novel centers on life in Istanbul.*

Principal characters:
MEVLUT KARATAŞ, a street vendor living in Istanbul
RAYIHA, the woman who becomes his wife despite a mistaken identity at the start
SÜLEYMAN, his cousin who tricks him into writing to Rayiha rather than Samiha
SAMIHA, Rayiha's younger sister, the girl to whom Mevlut thought he was writing
MUSTAFA, his father

A Strangeness in My Mind tells the story of Mevlut Karataş, an accepting, yet not simplistic, Everyman who sees the gift in even the worst of occurrences. He comes to Istanbul with his father in the late 1960s at the age of twelve, lives through tumultuous times, and finds he is ultimately content to pursue a way of life that is all but forgotten.

That Mevlut is not an intellectual bright light is potentially underscored by the ease with which he can be tricked. Key among these incidents is the one in which he sees a girl he instantly loves, writes to her through a trusted intermediary for three years, elopes with the girl under cover of darkness, and discovers in the process that he is not eloping with the girl he thought. The reader soon learns that Süleyman, the one who has delivered the letters and facilitated the elopement, has tricked Mevlut the entire time because he wants the pretty girl for himself. Then again, Mevlut finds a true love and partner in Rayiha. They are happily married even as Süleyman is frustrated to learn that Samiha will not have him. In the end, the question lingers: Is Mevlut a fool, or is he someone who has the ability to find and pursue the good in a situation?

One enduring image in *A Strangeness in My Mind* is of Mevlut walking the streets at night, calling out his wares for sale. "Booo-zaaaaa . . . Goooood boozaaaaa," he wails. And his calls are answered by those who are melancholy for a simpler time when boza, a fermented beverage with a very low alcohol content, was sold on the street, along with the yogurt products that are now sold in containers from coolers in stores. They lower baskets or wait while he trudges upstairs to deliver their beverage, complete with roasted chickpeas and cinnamon on top for old times' sake.

Orhan Pamuk is the recipient of the 2006 Nobel Prize in Literature. His many novels focus on life in Istanbul and the relationship between Muslims and the West, as well as the changes that have taken place in Istanbul during his adolescence and adulthood.

The people in Mevlut's world come from a variety of backgrounds and occupations. Much like in Garth Risk Hallberg's *City on Fire* (2015), a sprawling story about New Yorkers in the 1970s, the characters in *A Strangeness in My Mind* connect through one single character—in this case, Mevlut. Sometimes Pamuk switches from third-person limited narration of Mevlut's life to first-person accounts from other characters, more directly influencing what the reader believes of them. They also occasionally speak directly to the reader, breaking the "fourth wall" to implore that things that would be injurious to their reputations be left out of the narrative. Dwight Garner points out in his review for the *New York Times*, "The humor in this novel . . . flows freely. The narrators interrupt and contradict one another as if they were talking heads in an early Spike Lee movie." Their observations of life add nuanced layers to the overall effect. As in all things, the unflappable Mevlut does not stand in the way of this. Instead, his story is told in what is described by reviewers repeatedly as Dickensian detail that traces his life from his first moments in Istanbul until his final appearance.

A Strangeness in My Mind was well received and sold well. It continues the exploration of Istanbul that informs Pamuk's body of work. He has lived all but three years in Turkey, spending more than sixty in Istanbul. If his books are love songs to a city, this novel is one with more than a hint of *huzun* (melancholy), as Garner notes. For some, the mood was too much, reducing the book to an overly long tale that tried to be an epic. For others, the huzun was just right, bringing to light a sad tale of long-gone people and times.

A Stranger in My Mind is not a page-turner. Garner notes that he "mostly turned its pages with polite interest rather than real desire. This novel hits its low points in its too frequent nods toward its title, to the strangeness in Mevlut's mind." As it does, the reader is left to wonder if the strangeness is the result of the turmoil of politics and religion, the fast-paced urban development and casting aside of traditional venues and values, or Mevlut's own lack of insight into the events of his time. Is that due to disinterest, the inability to synthesize the disparate pieces, or the lack of a need to do anything other than exist as he is—the Everyman who walks the streets of the city selling boza at night? It is enough to keep the reader turning and looking for a clue as to what exactly constitutes the strangeness in Mevlut's mind.

Readers are also left to ponder the themes of the juxtaposition between tradition and modernity, and conformity and hypocrisy, which, Adam Kirsch notes, Pamuk does through the use of boza. What is more traditional than a beverage that was the favorite of the Ottomans? Why bring it into the modern age at all? And if boza had an alcohol content at all, how was it that the Muslims of the time could claim to be in conformity with all of the laws they espoused? It is a grand example for the sort of confusion that arises in the face of a bevy of traditions and clashing conventions moving toward what is perceived as modernity.

Pamuk does not just keep to the events that occur in Istanbul. He writes about global events such as the fall of the Berlin Wall and the September 11 terrorist attacks, as well as about the last half-century of Turkish history. Kirsch writes that it is not just Mevlut's "inner serenity and his profound sense of place" that allow Pamuk the opportunity to delve into these events. "Mevlut remains on the edge of all this action; like a novelist, a peddler sees life from outside, at an angle. But that allows him to see it more vividly and poetically than most people." Writing for the *Guardian*, critic Angela Chen agrees. "It is precisely neutrality (or apathy) that allows Mevlut to 'go everywhere' and hear the voices of both the city's extreme left- and right-wing ideologues—and, by extension, let Pamuk explore Istanbul's politics and history even as he insists that he does not write novels with strong political messages."

Indeed, Mevlut is an unlikely hero. He is described throughout the novel in many less than favorable ways. In his review of the *New York Times*, Martin Riker cites a number of them: "Mevlut stands out as the most sentimental, purest of heart and humblest of aspiration. If he were an archetype, he would be the wise fool. His cousin Suleyman thinks him an inexplicable simpleton; his communist friend Ferhat says 'he's a bit of a weirdo, but he's got a heart of gold'; his sister-in-law calls him 'cute as a little boy.'" Yet, Riker comments and others agree, none of these interpretations of Mevlut comes close to capturing the essence of this observer of life.

By selecting a protagonist who is at once familiar and unfamiliar to any urban dweller, Pamuk has created an opportunity for the reader to go along for the ride without the need for judgment or deep reflection. Mevlut's actions may not be those the reader would take, but they are not actions that cause the reader to question Mevlut's character or motives. Over and over again, Mevlut is portrayed as a man who understands that there is a rhythm to life that carries all along with it. It is not that it is useless to resist; it is that there is room for more than one interpretation and more than one reality to exist in the same space. Yes, Mevlut has been tricked into marrying the wrong sister. Equally true is the fact that Mevlut is happy in his marriage. He has the capacity of open acceptance. As Alberto Manguel writes in his review for the *Guardian*, "His attitude is not one of resignation, but of gratitude for unexpected gifts. Mevlut's life is one of ongoing generous recognition and marveling acceptance of such revelations."

Ultimately, the reader comes to understand that the strangeness in Mevlut's mind is his appreciation of the city and its scope. When he covers the city at night on foot to sell his boza, he is part of both the history and the ongoing struggle of the day. He explains, "The light and darkness inside his mind looked like the nighttime landscape of the city. . . . Walking around the city at night made him feel as if he were wandering around inside his own head." This may be a less than satisfactory conclusion to those who will ultimately view Mevlut as an unambitious man. For those who catch the glimmer of a satisfied and happy man at peace with his choices and the occurrences of his life, it will be a satisfactory conclusion—even as it is one coated in *huzun*.

Gina Hagler

Review Sources

Chen, Angela. "'A Book Is Not Its Plot': Orhan Pamuk on New Novel A Strangeness in My Mind." Rev. of *A Strangeness in My Mind*, by Orhan Pamuk. *Guardian*. Guardian News and Media, 12 Nov. 2015. Web. 22 Feb. 2016.

Garner, Dwight. "Review: Orhan Pamuk's 'A Strangeness in My Mind.'" Rev. of *A Strangeness in My Mind*, by Orhan Pamuk. *New York Times*. New York Times, 20 Oct. 2015. Web. 22 Feb. 2016.

Kirsch, Adam. "'A Strangeness in My Mind' Review: Orhan Pamuk's Love Letter to Turkey." Rev. of *A Strangeness in My Mind*, by Orhan Pamuk. *Washington Post*. Washington Post, 19 Oct. 2015. Web. 22 Feb. 2016.

Manguel, Alberto. "A Strangeness in My Mind by Orhan Pamuk Review—An Encyclopedia of Istanbul." Rev. of *A Strangeness in My Mind*, by Orhan Pamuk. *Guardian*. Guardian News and Media, 2 Oct. 2015. Web. 22 Feb. 2016.

Riker, Martin. Rev. of *A Strangeness in My Mind*, by Orhan Pamuk. *New York Times*. New York Times, 23 Oct. 2015. Web. 22 Feb. 2016.

A Stranger's Mirror
New and Selected Poems, 1994–2014

Author: Marilyn Hacker (b. 1942)
Publisher: Norton (New York). 320 pp.
Type of work: Poetry

A Stranger's Mirror offers twenty-five new poems by the distinguished poet Marilyn Hacker, plus a generous selection of previous works. It illustrates Hacker's command of varied subjects, styles, and forms.

Marilyn Hacker

New and Selected Poems

1994-2013

A Stranger's Mirror

(Courtesy of W.W. Norton & Co.)

Readers already familiar with the poetry of Marilyn Hacker will be happy to hear that so much of it (including roughly two dozen new works) has been collected in *A Stranger's Mirror: New and Selected Poems, 1994–2014*. Unlike most volumes of poetry, this one is thick and thorough, with far less wasted white space than most new books of poems. Poems often fill whole pages, and the chance to compare and contrast some of Hacker's newest work with some of her old writings is an added bonus. The book is a welcome reminder of why Hacker has such a distinguished reputation as a poet. Reviews for Hacker's collection have been generally positive and have spoken to its range of both emotion and format, the latter often borrowed from other cultures and languages. As Grace Shulman writes for the *Kenyon Review* "It is a commonplace that good poems can bridge cultures even when the cultures themselves continue to be at loggerheads. Marilyn Hacker's new poetry collection . . . fulfills that promise."

Hacker's new poems exhibit many of the same characteristics of her previous one. She often submits herself to various formal challenges, as in the initially clotted rhyme words and persistent anaphora of "Casting Out Rhymes," which shifts to an even more complex pattern near the end. This poem is followed by "Pantoum in Wartime," which uses a complex Malay verse form to explore perceptions of the war-torn Middle East. Another such work, titled simply "Pantoum," explores similar perceptions in a similar setting, while "October Sestina" employs one of those highly intricate devices of rhyme that professional poets often love but that many readers may sometimes find more trouble than they are worth. That poem is followed by "Sapphics in Winter" (self-consciously using yet another distinct form of verse) and "Alcaics for a Wedding," a poem that employ a kind of verse first used by an ancient Greek from Mytilene.

Thus, Hacker is willing once again to attempt various kinds of intricate sound patterns, which many other contemporary poets disdain. Far from being "free," her

newest verse occasionally runs the risk of seeming almost too complicated for its own good, as if
the need to rhyme in innovative and exceedingly
complex ways was the main impetus behind the
poem rather than some important perception that
the poet wanted to preserve and pass on to readers.
Philip Larkin (mentioned briefly by Hacker) once
suggested that preserving a vivid experience and
re-creating it both in and for the reader was the
main impulse of poetry. In Hacker's best poems,
one senses this impulse at work and often sees it
successfully achieved. In many of the new poems,
however, the complex rhyme schemes can sometimes seem more a distraction than a means of
intensifying the experience. Furthermore, sometimes the experiences themselves seem so remote
from the ordinary life of most of Hacker's readers
that the poems appear more exotic than inviting or
accessible.

(Courtesy of W.W. Norton)

*Marilyn Hacker is an award-win-
ning poet and translator whose
mostly autobiographical works
often combine colloquial phrasing
with formal experimentation. She
is a professor at the City University of New York.*

There is much to be said for poetry that challenges readers and stretches their imaginative horizons—poetry that forces them to see new things in new ways. Hacker's
interest in Middle Eastern wars and turmoil would seem tailor-made for a poet with
her demonstrably keen talents of detailed observation and memorable phrasing. For
instance, apparently referring to refugees, she at one point writes, "A doctor, an actress, an engineer / wrestle with the rudiments of grammar / disillusioned, stumbling in
a new language, / hating their luck, and knowing they are lucky." That last line catches
superbly the paradox of needing to flee an embattled country: being an exile is un-
lucky, but exiles feel fortunate simply to be alive. The new poems are full of moments
like this—moments when Hacker renders, in precise, memorable words, experiences
that most of her readers can only imagine.

In poems like "Pantoum in Wartime," the relentless repetitions of words and
rhythms sometimes have a hypnotic effect. Finally, however, it seems difficult to
know, precisely, what that poem is about or what it all means. This seems even truer
of the mystifying "Fugue on a Line of Amr bin M'ad Yakrib," although even such poems contain memorable moments: "And in that memory there is a mountain, / Above
it, a reddish hawk that swooped and soared alone." What, exactly, these lines have to
do with the rest of the poem is not an easy question to answer, but they are certainly
vivid in and of themselves. Hacker's new verse sometimes alternates between lines
that seemingly mean something to the poet (but that may seem forbidding to readers)
and lines that suddenly snare one's attention, if only because of the sheer beauty of the
imagery and sound. Thus, one section of a poem titled "Paragraphs" begins as follows:

> You'd have no one coming to Vermont
> for art camp, to the mill that does not mill

> grain any longer, though the bannered air will flaunt
> high above the Lamoille
> River, blue-green vistas your argument
> (despite gimcrack guttings) can't discount.

Readers will likely find the meaning of this stanza hard to decipher. The poem seems written mainly to and for Hacker (and perhaps a personal friend). The poem ends, however, with a stunning reference to a "history . . . paragraphed / in wind-heft, cord-wood, winter, water, green"—a statement beautifully memorable because it is so vivid, so concentrated, so rhythmic, and so rich with striking sound and images.

Hacker is in the unenviable position of all important poets: competing with an earlier version of herself. Some of her earlier poems are so rich, so compelling, and so successful that most of the new works inevitably fall somewhat short by comparison. Take, for instance, a poem included in an earlier book, published in 2001:

> I'm four, in itchy woolen leggings,
>
> the day that I can't recognize the man
>
> down at the park entrance, waving,
>
> as my father. He has ten
>
> more years to live, that spring. Dapper and balding
>
> he walks toward me; then I run toward him, calling
>
> him, flustered by my flawed vision.
> Underfoot, the maples' green-
>
> winged seeds splay on mica-specked octagons.
> His round face, thin nose, moustache silvered gray
>
> at thirty-eight look (I think now) Hungarian.
>
> I like his wood-smell of two packs a day
>
> as he swings me up to his shoulder
> and I say, things look blurry far away
> —one Saturday, two years after the war.

There are so many things to admire about such a poem. The poem is partly about the speaker's inability to perceive clearly, especially from a distance. (Perhaps she is beginning to need glasses.) Paradoxically, however, perceiving clearly from a distance is precisely what she does so well in this poem. Every detail of this past encounter with her father is vividly re-created, and readers can instantly "relate" to it in ways they might be able to relate to some of Hacker's more recent poems. Part of the power of the poem is the way Hacker quickly foreshadows the father's fate: readers learn that he has only "ten / more years to live," a fact that gives added poignancy to the rest of the poem. This is a work not simply about remembering a father but about remembering a father who was doomed (the speaker now realizes) far before his time.

No sooner does she mention his death, however, than she mentions their meeting is, ironically, in a park in springtime—a place and a season normally associated with joy, youth, and life. But the father is not romanticized: no sooner does she call him "Dapper" than she reveals that he was "balding"; already, at age thirty-eight, he was beginning to look older than he actually was. He "walks" calmly toward her; she runs excitedly toward him: each character in this little anecdote behaves exactly as one might expect, in archetypal ways to which most readers can connect. There is some subtle wordplay in the almost-rhyme of "balding" and "calling"—an effect typical of Hacker at her best, with her often wonderful ear for echoed sound. One notes, for instance, the combined (but not excessive) assonance and alliteration of line 7, the splendid juxtaposition of the almost-rhyming "green-" and "winged" in lines 8 and 9, and the ways lines 10, 12, and 14 do rhyme, as if to subtly signal the approaching end of the poem.

The maple seeds suggest new life, while the father's "moustache silvered grey" already suggests approaching death. The parenthetical phrase "(I think now)" reiterates the theme of passing time while also quickly explaining how the speculation about his age and nationality is not coming from a four-year-old. Then one encounters the splendidly ironic reference to "his wood-smell of two packs a day," which simultaneously associates him with nature and, perhaps, with cancer: it is easy now to imagine how and why he died within ten years of this walk in the park. Also, the implicitly grim reference to his smoking habit is juxtaposed with his relatively youthful strength, swinging his little girl "up to his shoulder" with all the ease of a vital man. But these joyous images are darkened by her realization (and ours) that he will be dead by the time she is fourteen.

This, like so many of Hacker's works, is a wonderful poem. Hacker's poem slightly resembles a sonnet (reminding readers that Hacker is in fact one of this era's best sonneteers), but nothing in the title calls undue attention to the form, and the form itself seems anything but self-conscious or artificial. Simply to have written one poem as good as this is an impressive achievement. To have written as many as Hacker has done over a lengthy lifetime of writing only confirms one's gratitude for her long poetic career and her steadfast presence among us.

Robert C. Evans

Review Sources

Huston, Karla. Rev. of *A Stranger's Mirror: New and Selected Poems, 1994–2014*,
    by Marilyn Hacker. *Library Journal*. Library Journal, 15 Feb. 2015. Web. 27 Nov.
    2015.

Ostriker, Alicia. "Love as Fierce as Death." Rev. of *A Stranger's Mirror: New and
    Selected Poems, 1994–2014*, by Marilyn Hacker. *Women's Review of Books*.
    Wellesley Centers for Women, 1 July 2015. Web. 27 Nov. 2015.

Schulman, Grace. "Strangers and Friends." Rev. of *A Stranger's Mirror: New and
    Selected Poems, 1994–2014*, by Marilyn Hacker. *Kenyon Review Online*. Kenyon
    Review, 2015. Web. 27 Nov. 2015.

Seaman, Donna. Rev. of *A Stranger's Mirror: New and Selected Poems, 1994–2014*,
    by Marilyn Hacker. *Booklist*. Booklist, 1 Jan. 2015. Web. 27 Nov. 2015.

Van Buren, Ann. Rev. of *A Stranger's Mirror: New and Selected Poems, 1994–2014*,
    by Marilyn Hacker. *Rumpus*. Rumpus, 17 June 2015. Web. 27 Nov. 2015.

Submission

Author: Michel Houellebecq (b. 1958)
First published: *Soumission*, 2015, in
  France
Translated from the French by: Lorin
  Stein
Publisher: Farrar, Straus, and Giroux (New
  York). 246 pp.
Type of work: Novel
Time: 2022
Locale: Paris, France

A dystopian satire of the future of France,
Submission *is the sixth novel by the contro-*
versial French author Michel Houellebecq.

Principal characters:
FRANÇOIS, the narrator, a literature professor
  at the Sorbonne
MYRIAM, his former girlfriend
MARIE-FRANÇOISE, his colleague
ROBERT REDIGER, president of the Sorbonne

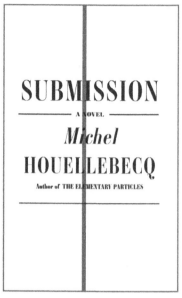

(Courtesy of Farrar Straus & Giroux)

Throughout the course of his literary career, Michel Houellebecq has built a reputation for being a provocateur. Often considered the most famous French novelist of
his generation, Houellebecq has incited controversy by depicting contemporary society, religion, and sex in an unforgiving and offensive light. However incendiary
his previous novels may have been, Houellebecq's *Submission* (2015) was met with
an unprecedented amount of notoriety because of its association with tragic national
events. *Submission*, which imagines a future where France is governed by Sharia law,
was released on the same day that two Islamic terrorists attacked the offices of the
French satirical magazine *Charlie Hebdo*. Despite Islam playing a central role in the
plot, *Submission* is not intended as a polemic against the religion. Instead the novel
aims to criticize the values of modern French culture, which Houellebecq posits is on
the verge of collapse.

  Originally published under the French title of *Soumission*, *Submission* is the story
of François, a forty-four-year-old literature professor in the midst of an existential crisis. Simply put, François is bored; he no longer enjoys teaching at the Sorbonne or se-
ducing his students. His life has become a cycle of mediocrity and microwave dinners.
François's only real relationship is the one he has with the work of the nineteenth-
century French novelist Joris-Karl Huysmans. Huysmans was the focus of François's
doctoral thesis and the only author he continues to read. Houellebecq's decision to
incorporate Huysmans as an integral part of François's story is significant for several

reasons. For one, it allows Houellebecq to pay tribute to an author for whom he has declared his admiration in interviews. The high regard in which he holds Huysmans is likely because the two share a pessimistic view of society; Huysmans's work focused on "humankind's endless stupidity," and Houellebecq's novels express a similar disdain. Furthermore, Houellebecq integrates Huysmans into the narrative in order to utilize the author's life as a framework for François's story. Like François, Huysmans spent his life at an unfulfilling day job, enjoyed a small amount of success, and eventually faced a crisis of faith in his middle age.

When *Submission* begins, it is 2022—an election year. In the context of *Submission*'s 2015 publication date, François's story is set in the near future. Houellebecq has arguably chosen this futuristic time frame with deliberation; it is far enough away for readers to believe that significant changes have occurred in France's sociopolitical landscape, but close enough to 2015 that François's world is familiar and needs no explanation. Houellebecq depicts life in 2022 France as no different than 2015 with one exception: both far-right and Muslim political parties have risen to the mainstream. As the conservative, xenophobic National Front makes unprecedented gains in the polls, a moderate Islamic party becomes the increasingly viable political ally to leftists like François and his peers who typically vote for the Socialist Party. In the weeks leading up to the election, François and his colleagues are slightly uneasy about how the elections will affect their lives but are otherwise described as indifferent and supine. They are depicted negatively because the primary purpose of *Submission* is to criticize these alleged intellectuals and demonstrate how their behavior will facilitate the downfall of French society.

To illustrate the shortcomings of this social class of politicians, academics, and journalists, Houellebecq employs François as their pathetic, navel-gazing representative. François spends most of his time ruminating on the lack of physical pleasure in his life. Like many of Houellebecq's protagonists, he is a misogynist who only views women in terms of their sexual viability. He has a relatively positive opinion of his former girlfriend Myriam only because she is hypersexual and beautiful. Meanwhile, when an older female colleague named Marie-Françoise mentions that she is married,

Michel Houellebecq is a French novelist, literary critic, poet, and filmmaker known for his controversial critiques of modern French society. His novel The Elementary Particles *(1998, trans. 2000) was an international best seller.*

François is shocked that such an unattractive individual could even be a woman, let alone a woman that a man would want to marry. While François's general behavior is repugnant, it is his treatment of women that arguably solidifies his wantonness to readers. Ultimately, the protagonist of *Submission* is a lowly character because Houellebecq has a poor opinion of humankind.

When the National Front wins a majority of the vote, the other political parties scramble to form a coalition in order to obstruct the far-right party from ruling the parliament. To this end, the Socialists form an alliance with the Muslim party and appoint Ben Abbes the president of France. Although this event is met with some surprise by François and his peers, there is ultimately no resistance to the new Muslim government and the changes it will implement on secular France. The formation of the coalition is arguably the catalyst to what *Submission* poses as France's doomed future. However, Houellebecq does not point to Islam as the source of dystopia. Instead, he insinuates that the French are responsible for their own fate of cultural subjugation. To demonstrate just how possible a France under Sharia law could be, Houellebecq depicts the cultural changes that ensue once Ben Abbes is in power as gradual and organic developments. Women's skirts become longer. Halal menus, which are in accordance with the Muslim diet, start appearing in restaurants. Then, after several months, the changes become more dramatic. Ben Abbes solves the unemployment crisis by offering French women a stipend to leave the workforce to stay with their families. Polygamy soon becomes commonplace.

Eventually, François receives a letter in the mail saying that the Sorbonne has been purchased by Saudi investors and any university staff members who do not convert to Islam will be asked to retire. In return they will immediately start receiving their pension. When François loses his job, the existential void in his life becomes too overwhelming to bear. It is at this point in the narrative Houellebecq begins to align François's story more closely to the trajectory of Huysmans's life. This is a fact that is not lost on François. He remarks that Huysmans, after years of feeling discouraged by the state of humankind, reluctantly converted to Catholicism. However, a trip to the same monastery that Huysmans visited does not achieve the same thing for François. Instead, he abandons the effort to connect to something bigger than himself after dismissing a transcendent, spiritual moment with the statue of the Black Madonna of Rocamadour as an episode of low blood sugar. When he returns to Paris, François meets the new president of the Sorbonne, Robert Rediger. A Muslim convert with a disarming smile, Rediger quickly charms François with his intelligence, beautiful young wives, and luxurious home. After the two share a lengthy conversation about how Europe once was the pinnacle of world culture but "committed suicide," Rediger proposes that Islam is the next logical evolution in society. He offers François a copy of his book on Islam and a proposition that if he converts, he can have his old job back with triple the pay. François spends the remainder of *Submission* attempting to decide.

Although the tone of *Submission* is decidedly melancholic, the novel has been labeled a satire. This designation is one that can be applied to many of Houellebecq's previous works, including his breakout novel, *Particules élémentaires* (1998; *The Elementary Particles*, 2000), in which he suggests that France's unfettered economic liberalism and sexual libertinism would eventually lead to the two worlds literally merging. As evident in *The Elementary Particles*, satirical narratives do not depict the humorous elements of human life but rather the absurdities if they were taken a step further. Just as satirist Jonathan Swift posed in *A Modest Proposal* (1729) that because the English treated the Irish as animals, the next logical step would be eating their babies, Houellebecq suggests in *Submission* that the French intellectual class is so willing to protect their elitism that they would forgo their secular, Enlightenment values for Islam if it guaranteed power and young wives.

As a writer, Houellebecq has consistently proven to be a polarizing force among critics. *Submission* fits neatly within this tradition. In both France and the United

States, the controversial subject matter of *Submission* has garnered mixed reviews. A frequent criticism among the novel's detractors has been Houellebecq's depiction of women. In his interview with the *Paris Review*, Houellebecq addressed this controversy by stating that "a feminist is not likely to love this book." His admission is an acknowledgment of both François's perspective, in which women are good only for sex or housework, and the novel's passive portrayal of French women who acquiesce to the oppression of Sharia law without a fight. In her *National Public Radio* review, Heller McCalpin writes that she hopes women will not take this "insulting scenario" lying down. *Slate*'s Lydia Kiesling praises Submission as "elegantly written" and "mesmerizing," but notes that she is angry about Houellebecq's misogyny as well as other literary critics' reluctance to acknowledge it.

Submission has also been met with accusations of Islamophobia. This criticism should be expected given Houellebecq's litigious history with Islam. In 2001, Houellebecq gave an interview to *Lire* magazine in which he accused Islam of being "the dumbest" religion. The author was subsequently met with charges of provoking racial hatred by three separate Islamic organizations. He was acquitted the following year. Although some critics have claimed that the dystopian scare story at the heart of *Submission* incites Islamophobia, most have argued that Houellebecq never actually portrays Islam in a negative light. In the end, Houellebecq's narrative is more Francophobic than Islamophobic in its depiction of France's leftist intellectuals.

The most common praise for *Submission* has been that it is a much-needed "novel of ideas." True to this philosophical genre of fiction, which includes works such as Albert Camus's *Stranger* (1942) and Fyodor Dostoyevsky's *Crime and Punishment* (1866), *Submission* is thematically rich and unrelenting in its quest to scrutinize the state of modern French society. Mark Lilla writes for the *New York Review of Books* that *Submission* is a "classic novel of European cultural pessimism" and that Houellebecq is successful in creating a narrative that explores the dangers of societal weariness and indifference. Similarly, Adam Gopnik argues in his *New Yorker* review that Houellebecq is a satirist "worth reading" and praises the author's deftness in depicting both the contemporary consumer culture that he abhors and the "apocalypse" it will allegedly bring. Despite its controversy, *Submission* is a deeply thought-provoking novel that refuses to compromise its central message for the sake of readers' comfort.

Emily E. Turner

Review Sources

Gopnik, Adam. "The Next Thing." Rev. of *Submission*, by Michel Houellebecq. *New Yorker*. Condé Nast, 26 Jan. 2015. Web. 31 Jan. 2016.

Kiesling, Lydia. "The Elegant Bigotry of Michel Houellebecq." Rev. of *Submission*, by Michel Houellebecq. *Slate*. Slate Group, 6 Oct. 2015. Web. 31 Jan. 2016.

Knausgaard, Karl Ove. "Michel Houellebecq's, 'Submission.'" Rev. of *Submission*, by Michel Houellebecq. *New York Times*. New York Times. 2 Nov. 2015. Web. 31 Jan. 2016.

Lilla, Mark. "Slouching toward Mecca." Rev. of *Submission*, by Michel Houelle-
becq. *New York Review of Books.* NYREV, 2 Apr. 2015. Web. 31 Jan. 2016.
McCalpin, Heller. "Don't Take 'Submission' Lying Down." Rev. of *Submission*, by
Michel Houellebecq. *NPR Books*. NPR, 20 Oct. 2015. Web. 31 Jan. 2016.
Preston, Alex. "Submission by Michel Houellebecq Review—Satire That's More
Subtle than It Seems." Rev. of *Submission*, by Michel Houellebecq. *Guardian.*
Guardian News and Media, 8 Sept. 2015. Web. 31 Jan. 2016.

Surrounded by Friends

Author: Matthew Rohrer (b. 1970)
Publisher: Wave Books (Seattle). 112 pp.
Type of Work: Poetry

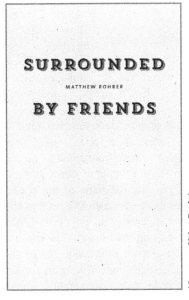

(Courtesy of Wave Books)

Surrounded by Friends is the newest book of poems by Matthew Rohrer, author of numerous previous volumes. This book is understated in tone and phrasing, modest in ambition and topics, and appealing in its accessibility, its lightheartedness, and its emphasis on connections with others, including various poets of the past.

The poems collected in Matthew Rohrer's new book are minimalist in almost every sense of the word. They tend to be small in size, short in line lengths, and sparing in their use of punctuation. Metaphors and similes are rare; regular rhythms are mostly absent; and rhyme is avoided almost altogether. The diction of individual words and phrases is simple, plain, and easily accessible, even when the overall meanings of the poems are often less than lucid. These are stripped-down poems: imagistic, impressionistic, associative, and often lacking in the kinds of clear syntax favored in much traditional verse. Lines and images often shift unpredictably from one focus to another, as if the speaker is offering raw experience and brief snapshots of reality rather than attempting anything more developed or ambitious. All of this is intentional. Rohrer is not trying to write a different kind of poetry and failing at the task; instead, he is doing things his own way (with some obvious debts to William Carlos Williams and Gertrude Stein). A poem titled "Pavilion of Leaves" is a good example of his style:

> Central Park in a
> pavilion of leaves
> with extra sauce
> for midday
> is only a snack
> and a photograph
> of cold cherries
> like a young woman's
> legs softly peeling
> after burning
> a pennywhistle

in the distance
with the piping children's
voices which are
distant peace
in a breeze
two white butterflies
trying so hard

(Courtesy of Matthew Rohrer)

To ask about the references to (and relevance of) "extra sauce" and "cold cherries" is to ask for a more conventional kind of poem than Rohrer wants to write. Instead, one is left praising the parts of the poem that *do* seem more conventional, such as the memorable metaphor "a / pavilion of leaves" and the striking final image. The poem creates a larger, overall impression out of a series of smaller ones, and it is up to readers to decide if the impressions amount to much more than that. Perhaps a series of impressions is enough.

Matthew Rohrer is the author of numerous books of poetry, including A Hummock in the Malookas *(1995),* Satellite *(2001),* A Green Light *(2004),* Rise Up *(2007),* They All Seemed Asleep *(2008),* A Plate of Chicken *(2009), and* Destroyer and Preserver *(2011).*

Various series of impressions, in any case, are mostly what Rohrer provides, as in another poem ("A Little Rain") set in a park:

Everything beneath the roof
of trees is sticky
from the trees. Trade éclairs
on a bench because
Does my ass look big?
Everything in the park is reflected
back to beauty. If I find
a moneylender I'm going
to kiss him. The water
comes from lions. It goes
back to water. In a puddle
a sparrow soaks himself
then hops away
to roll in dust. A man
turns and says *Look
at yourself young man
official society
will never trust you*

(he is not speaking to me)

(a little rain blows under the trees)

There is something to be said for the modesty of poems like this. Their tone is understated, and they have no great (or at least obvious) "points" to make. They do not seem relevant to much besides or beyond themselves. They stake no great claims and take no great risks. They do not expect much of readers except an openness to the speaker's random observations—observations that *do* often cohere into a general mood or feeling. The fact that the poems are often so accessible is something to be praised, as is the fact that they involve experiences to which most people can relate. There are no verbal pyrotechnics, and if the phrasing, shifts, and images are sometimes surreal (as with the reference to kissing "a moneylender"), the poems are nonetheless sufficiently realistic to seem relevant to most readers.

One often notices, in Rohrer's poems, a preference for the abstract and general rather than the specific. Thus, in the poem just quoted, the word "Everything" is used twice; the word "beauty" is used once; the abstract noun "park" appears; and the abstract verb "reflected" ties all the other general ideas together: "Everything in the park is reflected / back to beauty." This is the sort of thing almost anyone might say when contemplating the scene the speaker describes—a fact that keeps Rohrer's language close to common speech but sometimes also makes his phrasing seem less than sharply vivid. The observation that everything "beneath the roof / of trees is sticky / from the trees" is memorable partly because of the metaphor ("roof") and partly because of the tactile precision of "sticky." The fact that the trees are simply "trees" (rather than "oaks" or "elms") and that everything is "Everything" (rather than, say, "The green wooden bench") is just further evidence of Rohrer's frequent preference for the general rather than the particular.

As the poems already quoted suggest, Rohrer often sets his lyrics in natural surroundings (a fact that will already make them appealing to many readers), but his settings are also often urban as well. And, as the two poems about parks also demonstrate, sometimes one setting implies the other. Residents of New York City, where Rohrer lives, are especially likely to appreciate the local color of many of these lyrics, but the same is probably true of residents of any other large urban area. Among Rohrer's other ideal readers are likely to be young couples with children and even, perhaps, children themselves. Thus, the following poem ("There Is Absolutely Nothing Lonelier") might easily turn up someday in a grade-school textbook:

> There is absolutely nothing lonelier
> than the little Mars rover
> never shutting down, digging up
> rocks, so far away from Bond Street
> in a light rain. I wonder
> if he makes little beeps? If so

> he is lonelier still. He fires a laser
> into the dust. He coughs. A shiny
> thing in the sand turns out to be his.

One thinks of R2-D2 or WALL-E, those beloved robotic stars of the big screen, and one wonders if this poem may have been written, in fact, for the speaker's (presumably also the poet's) young daughter, who turns up elsewhere in this volume. The speaker's double use of the adjective "little," along with the attempt at endearing personification, runs the risk of seeming maudlin, but perhaps sentimentality is better than the faux sophistication and hard-edged cynicism found in other recent books by other notable poets. One senses, in Rohrer's book, that he (or at least his speaker) is a loving father and husband capable of genuinely caring about other people, including the women in his life. Other recent prominent books of poetry cannot make the same claim, reveling instead in example after example of sadomasochistic sex that ultimately add up to nothing (see, for instance, Simeon Berry's 2015 book, *Monograph*). In contrast, Rohrer is capable of writing a tender lyric such as this ("The Emperor"):

> She sends me a text
> she's coming home
> the train emerges
> from underground
>
> I light the fire under
> the pot, I pour her
> a glass of wine
> I fold a napkin under
> a little fork
>
> the wind blows the rain
> into the windows
> the emperor himself
> is not this happy

Here again there is a risk of sentimentality, but there is also a beguiling normalcy about the events and emotions. Moreover, both the title and the closing lines link the poem to traditional Chinese verse. The allusion and the general technique remind one of Ezra Pound's tender "The River-Merchant's Wife: A Letter." Pound's poem benefits from its complexity, its rich imagery, and its subtle use of implication. Rohrer's poem seems much plainer, but to compare the two works is really not fair to Rohrer. The mere fact that he writes so openly about a loving relationship is admirable, especially in today's sometimes deliberately bizarre poetic "scene," and the final two lines help protect the poem from seeming too mushy. They remind readers that Rohrer is dealing with an ancient topic that transcends cultural differences, and they exemplify, too, his interest elsewhere in this book in cross-cultural dialogue, in echoes and even translations of poems from other times and places.

One unusual feature of this collection, in fact, is implied by its title: many of the "friends" it refers to are poets from the distant past, including the Japanese writers Kobayashi Issa (1763–1828), Yosa Buson (1716–84), and Matsuo Bashō (1644–94). One of a number of pieces titled "Poem Written with Issa" reads as follows:

> Phone on my stomach
> waiting to see
> whether she texts me back
> the night shifts
> across the earth
> like a blanket
> that's too small
> under the summer rain
> the skinny cat leaps up
> the moon on her hands

Of the various poems "written with" another poet, this is one of the most straight-forward: the imagery is effective and consistent (the blanket simile seems especially memorable) and the mood is unified throughout. Rohrer here manages to "update" a traditional kind of verse by alluding to the phone and texting, but except for those two details the poem might easily have been written by Issa himself. Sometimes Rohrer has fun with these poems, as when he writes in one of them that "The children ate cereal / under a gloomy sky, and sadly, / the girl loves her mother / more than she loves me." Later, another poem in the "written with" series begins as follows: "Spring break / in a dim room / with a glass of wine / is what it is. / A drunk wrecked / my truck." The wit of including the cliché that something "is what it is" suddenly wrenches the tone of the poem from seriousness to comedy, while the reference to the wrecked truck further undercuts the mood established in the first three lines. In poems like this, Rohrer juxtaposes different registers and tones of voice in ways that can spark a smile while also, perhaps, undermining the unified effect of the work. To say this, however, may be to criticize Rohrer unfairly for displaying a wittiness he obviously values. Poets need not always be serious, and, in fact, part of the appeal of this volume is the way the speakers often mock themselves. On the evidence of this collection, Rohrer is not a self-important egotist; there is a winning humility to many of the lyrics. They are mostly modest poems, displaying no need to shock or scandalize their readers—no need to put the poet at center stage, fully spotlighted, to call attention to himself or to any odd or kinky quirks (as in the poems of Simeon Berry). One leaves Rohrer's book with the impression that he does indeed (as the book's title implies) value friendship and is probably a good friend himself, as well as a good husband and dad. The personality that the book suggests is at least as appealing as any particular poem the book contains.

Robert C. Evans

Review Sources

Dabbene, Peter. Rev. of *Surrounded by Friends*, by Matthew Rohrer. *Foreword Reviews*. Foreword Magazine, 27 May 2015. Web. 22 Feb. 2016.

Hoffert, Barbara. Rev. of *Surrounded by Friends*, by Matthew Rohrer. *Library Journal*. Library Journal, 14 Apr. 2015. Web. 22 Feb. 2016.

McKenna, Brian. Rev. of *Surrounded by Friends*, by Matthew Rohrer. *New Pages*. NewPages.com, 2 Mar. 2015. Web. 22 Feb. 2016.

Morris, Ashira. "Dead Japanese Poets Make Great Collaborators." Rev. of *Surrounded by Friends*, by Matthew Rohrer. *PBS Newshour*. NewsHour Productions, 23 Mar. 2015. Web. 22 Feb. 2016.

Rev. of *Surrounded by Friends*, by Matthew Rohrer. *Publishers Weekly*. PWxyz, Apr. 2015. Web. 22 Feb. 2016.

Spencer, Molly. Rev. of *Surrounded by Friends*, by Matthew Rohrer. *Colorado Review*. Colorado State U, n.d. Web. 22 Feb. 2016.

The Sympathizer

Author: Viet Thanh Nguyen (b. 1971)
Publisher: Grove Press (New York). 371 pp.
Type of work: Novel
Time: 1970s
Locales: Vietnam, Southern California

The Sympathizer *is an ingenious and power-ful spy novel that focuses on a Communist sleeper agent who has been ordered to spy on South Vietnamese émigrés in Southern California who are working to spark a coun-terrevolution in their homeland.*

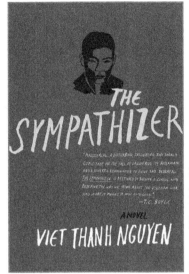

(Courtesy of Grove Atlantic)

Principle characters:
THE CAPTAIN, a Communist spy
MAN, his friend and his handler in the North
    Vietnamese secret service
BON, his friend and a dedicated South Viet-
    namese soldier
THE GENERAL, an exiled South Vietnamese officer
CLAUDE, an American CIA agent

Spy novels have been popular for over a century, and there have been two traditions within the genre. The first is a direct outgrowth of the perennially popular tale of adventure. It revels in action, the techniques of spy craft, and is generally patriotic in tone. The heroes in this tradition endure no moral qualms as they go about their busi-ness. Early masterpieces include Erskine Childers's *The Riddle of the Sands* (1903) and John Buchan's *The Thirty-Nine Steps* (1915), both of which involve stalwart Brit-ish gentlemen who foil schemes hatched in imperial Germany. Later writers such as Ian Fleming and Tom Clancy worked in the same vein as their respective characters James Bond and Jack Ryan successfully carried on the Cold War struggle against the Soviet Union.

    The second tradition of spy novel is decidedly different in spirit. It also provides action and explores the minutia of espionage, but it eschews the ideological clarity of the classic adventure story. The protagonists of these novels operate on a bleaker land-scape. They live in a moral fog where the black-and-white imperatives of their service have descended into an impenetrable field of gray. This is a literature of moral ambiva-lence. The subjects of these novels are often antiheroes and seriously flawed beings who are struggling to find their ethical bearings in a profession where the means have corrupted the ends. This tradition of spy novel can be traced to Joseph Conrad's *The Secret Agent* (1907). It was carried forward in the works of Graham Greene and John Le Carré, which focused on the moral price paid in a war of shadows.

Viet Thanh Nguyen's *The Sympathizer* is a worthy addition to the second tradition of spy novels. There have been memorable books about the covert side of the conflict in Vietnam, most notably Graham Greene's take on the increasing dissent among the Vietnamese against the French in *The Quiet American* (1955). Nguyen breaks ground for most Western readers by looking at the war from a Vietnamese perspective, though inevitably for a book in this genre, a perspective with a difference. Nguyen was born in Vietnam but fled with his family to the United States in 1975, and he regards himself as thoroughly Americanized. The United States figures prominently in his novel, both as a political power and a cultural force with which his characters wrestle. America is a solvent with its overwhelming presence dissolving the traditional structures of Vietnamese life. A key figure in the book is Claude, a CIA operative whose dark skills and cynical efficiency make him an arresting counter-

(Bebe Jacobs)

Viet Thanh Nguyen teaches English and American Studies at the University of Southern California. He is the author of the scholarly study Race and Resistance *(2002). His stories have appeared in* Best New American Voices, TriQuarterly, *and the* Chicago Tribune.

point to the destructively idealistic agent in Greene's classic novel. Claude, a sinister echo of the legendary American counterinsurgency specialist Edward Geary Lansdale, is the "ugly American" who professes to know Vietnam. He is the red, white, and blue contribution to Nguyen's ship of fools attempting to master a nation and the forces of history. Stereotypically American, Claude remains upbeat until the end. Balancing his character is the Marxist certainty of the Communist ideologues in the book who also believe that the future belongs to them. Nguyen observes during the course of the novel that the Vietnamese found themselves caught between two warring foreign ideologies, each supremely self-confident of ultimate victory. The Vietnamese moral of Nguyen's book is that any claim to such ascendency, however self-assured, is doomed to failure. One tragic flaw of Nguyen's protagonist, the Captain, is that he is the embodiment of the clash of external and internal forces tearing apart the country.

The Captain, never named in the book, is the "sympathizer" of the title. He can be the sympathizer with all parties in the book because he is suspended in an intricately complex web of betrayal and alienation. The Captain serves as an officer in the South Vietnamese counterintelligence Special Branch, yet he is an undercover agent, passing valuable secrets to the Communists. Born in North Vietnam and reared in the South after the country's 1954 partition, the Captain is doubly an outsider in his own country. The unintended product of the illicit union of a Vietnamese woman and a European priest, he is condemned as a "bastard" by his xenophobic countrymen. His mixed heritage permanently debars him from a respectable marriage and from full social acceptance. Even his own relations treat him as a second-class citizen. Unacknowledged by his father, the Captain cannot lay claim to his European heritage either. Instead he embraces American popular culture, a love affair consummated as an exchange student at UCLA. Ironically, the Captain is most at home in the land of his enemies. Although the Captain has sworn allegiance to the Revolution, his deepest loyalties are to two boyhood friends who defended him against schoolyard bullies. After what was for them an epic battle against the Captain's persecutors, the three boys slit their hands and swore an oath as blood brothers and hold true to this oath through all the political and military vicissitudes that follow and that secretly threaten to divide them. By 1975 the Captain is a sleeper agent for the North. The character Man is a dedicated Communist and the Captain's contact with the North Vietnamese secret service. The character Bon is a fervent anti-Communist and a member of an elite airborne unit in the South Vietnamese army. The Captain's bond with Man and Bon lies at the heart of the layered levels of his complicated personality. In a life shaped by betrayal, these friendships remain an unchanging and solid foundation to which he remains true. The complication for the Captain is that his friends are firmly entrenched on different sides of the war where he is playing a double game, and he needs to fight his clandestine war without endangering either of them.

Nguyen shapes his novel as a confession written by the Captain to an initially mysterious Commandant. The reader follows the story from the perspective of this double- and triple-dealing protagonist, sharing his sympathetic ability to see all sides and serve many masters. He is limited, however, to what he knows and what he allows himself to remember. Because of this, the reader shares something of the frustration of the Commandant for whom the confession is intended. Something is missing, and the reader cannot assume that the Captain, despite appearing amiable and frank, is a reliable narrator. As so often is the case in this genre of spy novel, truth often flits elusively at the margins of the story. Like all good mysteries, there are surprises to be found at the end.

The novel begins in April 1975 in the days just before the military collapse of South Vietnam and the fall of Saigon. Though most of the book's action takes place at the end of the Vietnam War and during its aftermath, the confessional structure of the Captain's reminiscences allows Nguyen to range back and forth in time and to powerfully evoke the brutal horrors of the conflict.

Although the essence of Nguyen's book is a serious journey into and away from the heart of darkness, he subtly modifies the book for the better with a great deal of humor. In the broadest sense this comes from an unsparing recognition of the absurdity of the human condition. In practice, much of the comedy comes from Nguyen's description of the efforts of South Vietnamese emigres to adapt to life in the United States. Simultaneously entranced, baffled, and repelled by all things American, they are fish out of water, easterners in the West, warriors in a land at peace. It does not help that this is America in the mid-1970s, the era of gaudy-colored polyester and the early stages of disco.

One of the most humorous parts of the book comes when the Captain is hired to be a technical advisor for a big-budget Hollywood Vietnam War movie that is being filmed in the Philippines. Entitled *The Hamlet* and directed by an award-winning film-maker Nguyen terms the Auteur, the film is a transparently comic take on the making of Francis Ford Coppola's *Apocalypse Now* (1979). The story of a small band of Green Berets defending a South Vietnamese village from a horde of vicious Viet Cong, *The Hamlet* is a hilarious example of American self-absorption and indifference to the other. Much to the Captain's dismay, the Green Berets are portrayed as noble and self-sacrificing heroes, while the Vietnamese are either stereotypical third-world victims desperately in need of American know-how and courage, or, in the case of the Viet Cong, as equally stereotypical in their cruelty. While gleefully puncturing traditional American attitudes toward Asians, Nguyen also pokes fun at the Hollywood types who are every bit as caricatured as the Vietnamese in the film. There is the monomaniac method actor who stays in character by refusing to change his clothes or bathe for months on end and the Auteur himself who is a paragon of obtuse egoism. As a young man growing up in the United States, Nguyen was fascinated by American films about the Vietnam War. He has observed that he was torn between cheering for the American heroes of the films and identifying with their often faceless prey. In *The Hamlet* section of his novel, Nguyen clarifies the cultural conflicts that undergird his novel and form the character of the Captain. Fittingly, the Captain is nearly killed by the premature detonation of an elaborate pyrotechnic display comparable to the lavish explosions in *Apocalypse Now*.

Despite the funny portions of the book, it is not a comedy. Moments of sharp satirical commentary alternate with gritty descriptions of murder and cruelty. As the South Vietnamese regime falls apart, the Captain is ordered by his Communist superiors to escape with the General, his wartime commander in the Special Branch. He is to report on the General's schemes to launch an anti-Communist insurgency in Vietnam. The General in turn is convinced that he has a Communist mole in the revolutionary organization that he is building in the United States. What ensues is plot, counterplot, and death.

The Captain ends up back in Vietnam where the comedy fades away. The intrigue and violence intensify. The book takes on some of the melancholic tone of the Vietnamese writer Bao Ninh's *The Sorrow of War* (1990) with its depiction of the hard times that followed the North's victory, implicitly raising the question of whether that triumph was worth the war's sacrifices. The Captain discovers that it is not easy for a spy to return from the cold, when his success at infiltrating the enemy makes him suspect at home. The novel concludes as an electrifying existential drama. The Captain is compelled to weigh his conflicting loyalties and discover such meaning in nothingness as is possible for a man with two minds. *The Sympathizer* succeeds both as a spy thriller and as literature. Nguyen has artfully crafted one of the most original and powerful novels of 2015.

Daniel P. Murphy

Review Sources

Caputo, Philip. "Apocalypse Then." Rev. of *The Sympathizer*, by Viet Thanh Nguyen. *New York Times Book Review* 5 Apr. 2015: BR1. Print.

Christenson, Bryce. Rev. of *The Sympathizer*, by Viet Thanh Nguyen. *Booklist* 15 Apr. 2015: 38. Print.

Leiding, Reba. Rev. of *The Sympathizer*, by Viet Thanh Nguyen. *Library Journal* 15 Feb. 2015: 91. Print.

Lyall, Sarah. "Soldier, Spy, Movie Consultant." Rev. of *The Sympathizer*, by Viet Thanh Nguyen. *New York Times* 28 Aug. 2015: C9. Print.

Sacks, Sam. "Apocalypse Then." Rev. of *The Sympathizer*, by Viet Thanh Nguyen. *Wall Street Journal* 4 April 2015: C8. Print.

Rev. of *The Sympathizer*, by Viet Thanh Nguyen. *Kirkus Reviews* 1 Feb. 2015: 28–29. Print.

The Thing about Jellyfish

Author: Ali Benjamin
Publisher: Little, Brown Books for Young
   Readers (New York). 352 pp.
Type of work: Novel
Time: Present
Locale: South Grove, Massachusetts, a fic-
   tional town

(Courtesy of Little Brown and Co.)

*The Thing about Jellyfish is Ali Benjamin's
critically acclaimed first novel. A New York
Times best seller and a 2015 finalist for the
National Book Award in young people's literature, it tells the story of a young girl's
difficult adjustment to the death of her best
friend.*

Principal characters:
SUZY "ZU" SWANSON, socially awkward
   seventh-grade girl
FRANNY JACKSON, her estranged best friend
AARON, her older brother
ROCCO, Aaron's partner
JUSTIN MALONEY, her lab partner
SARAH JOHNSTON, a new girl who would like to be Suzy's friend
MRS. TURTON, her teacher
MOM AND DAD, her recently divorced parents

The Thing about Jellyfish is a coming-of-age novel. It tells the story of Suzy Swanson's adjustment to the death of her best friend, Franny Jackson. The fact that Suzy and
Franny were not on the best of terms at the time, makes it even harder for Suzy, since
she does not feel welcome to join in the collective grief being experienced by Franny's
newer, more socially adept friends. Suzy is left on her own to wonder how Franny,
who had been a strong swimmer since kindergarten, could possibly drown. Suzy finally decides that it must be because Franny was stung by a rare and deadly jellyfish—the
Irukandji. She is surprised and disappointed that she is not only the only one trying to
solve the mystery of an excellent swimmer's death in a calm sea but also the only one
who has hit upon the jellyfish as an explanation. Suzy feels certain that if she could
meet with an expert, that expert could help her prove the true cause of Franny's death.

   Suzy sets out to find an expert; she also must begin seventh grade. She is stricken
by the realization that events do not occur for everyone at once, that Franny was dead
for a time when this was only known by Suzy's mother, then before that by Franny's
mother, and before that, by Franny alone. She reflects, "And that means that there was

a time when you were gone and no one on Earth had any idea. Just you, all alone, disappearing into the water and no one even wondering yet." It makes her feel lonely to know this, and the poignancy of Benjamin's writing invites the reader to share Suzy's pain. Suzy also is not sure what to say to anyone and decides that she really just wants to disappear. One night at dinner with her father, she simply decides not to speak. That leads to other choices of silence. Choices that allow Suzy to quickly learn "one thing above all else: A person can become invisible simply by staying quiet." This is a bit of a revelation to Suzy. In that moment, she decides not to speak under any circumstances.

(Courtesy of Little, Brown and Co.)

National Book Award finalist The Thing about Jellyfish *grew out of Ali Benjamin's longtime and deep fascination with the natural world. A member of New England Science Writers, she has also cowritten two books, Paige Rawl's memoir,* Positive *(2014), and Tim Howard's* The Keeper *(2014).*

Yet even silence and the virtual invisibility it conveys, have consequences. As a result of not speaking, she is paired with Justin Maloney in science class. Justin is a kid who messes up—or at least he always has. He is taking medicine for attention deficit hyperactivity disorder (ADHD), and largely because of Suzy's silence, he has a chance for Suzy to appreciate him in a new way. He finds that she accepts him, and she sees that not everyone is what he or she appears to be at first. The teacher, Mrs. Turton, makes it clear to Suzy that the big project for the class is an oral report, and that her grade will depend upon it.

Suzy chooses jellyfish as her subject and does an excellent job on her oral presentation. At least, all goes well until she reports on the Irukandji jellyfish. She expects the other kids to immediately understand the significance of this type of jellyfish, but they do not. They have all moved on from Franny's death, and even if they had not, Suzy's jellyfish hypothesis is hers and hers alone. Instead, the kids make fun of her, and her moment of near social acceptance turns into a cringe-worthy disaster. Mrs. Turton invites Suzy to have lunch with her in the classroom. Eventually Suzy and Justin join Mrs. Turton each day. Another girl, Sarah, seems to want to join them, but Suzy frowns to discourage her.

Mrs. Turton is a well-drawn character. She is also not just their teacher; she is a person who cares deeply about her quietest students. Her manner invites them to come close to her and she is patient and nonjudgmental, allowing them to forgo the daily minefield that is lunchtime for the socially awkward. She invites them to eat with her, letting them be silent or speak as they wish during that respite. She serves as a sort of lighthouse to them, and when Suzy is finally ready to take her first tentative steps back into the life she has been avoiding, Mrs. Turton is an important part of that step.

The other people who are part of Suzy's moment of new visibility are Justin, Sarah, and her mother. Her mother pushes her to go to the dance, but also tells Suzy she will come immediately if she wants to leave. She even goes so far as to help Suzy reason out how long it will take. Justin and Sarah are glad to see her. They are ready to walk in with her, and to be seen with her. Considering Suzy's rocky social past, this is a significant moment. It is also significant because Suzy is not worrying whether or not these are the "hot" kids. She is also not worrying about her place in the middle school pecking order. During her failed attempts to reach the jellyfish expert and her reexamination of the foolish things she has done to Franny and her new friends, Suzy has matured enough to go with what makes her happy. The reader sees that this is true when Suzy decides she does not need to be rescued from the party. She is doing fine and even having a good time.

In Ali Benjamin's first person narrative, Suzy's voice is authentic, and her pain is evident to the reader. It is clear that she is not proud of all of her actions. At times, she is not sure herself why she did what she did and wishes she could take it back. However, the laws of middle school are harsh, and very few get a second chance with the ones they have offended. One of the novel's messages seems to be that such second chances, if they are given at all, should be enough.

In many ways, Suzy is as alienated and unhappy as Holden Caulfield, yet her journey through the process of self-understanding is as different from Holden's as can be. Suzy's family is concerned for her and works to let her know that they care. They try to meet her needs, even though they do not understand her reaction to Franny's death because she does not share anything about the jellyfish with them. Benjamin makes it clear that she is their puzzle and they will do what it takes to keep her safe until she opens up to them. Ultimately, it is this trust in being held that allows Suzy to step back into life.

The writing in *The Thing about Jellyfish* is exquisite. As Jacqueline Kelly writes in her review for the *New York Times Sunday Book Review*, "Benjamin explores the heartbreaking subject of grief in the young with dreamy, meditative and elegiac prose." Part of the power of this novel is that this type of writing is not expected in a middle grade novel that deals with mean girls, finding your place, and the cruel mistreatment of a frog. Yet here it is, and it carries the reader along as Suzy remains stubbornly silent while researching, formulating, and pursuing her plan to gain the proof she needs to make sense of the world.

The jellyfish information in *The Thing about Jellyfish* is accurate. It is also presented in an interesting way, and finds its way into Suzy's lyrical musings about Franny, as well. She notes, "Jellyfish don't even have heart, of course—no heart, no brain, no bone, no blood. But watch them for a while. You will see them beating. Mrs. Turton says that if you lived to be eighty years old, your heart would beat three billion times. . . . And the whole while, your heart just keeps going. It does what it needs to do, one beat after another, until it gets the message that it's time to stop . . . because some hearts beat only about 412 million times. Which might sound like a lot. But the truth is, it barely even gets you twelve years."

By the time Suzy reaches the realization that sometimes things do just happen, she is exhausted by her quest. She must accept that she can neither explain how her best and only friend drowned in a calm sea, nor fix the things she did in the months before Franny died. She is surprised when Franny's mother tells her how much Franny respected her for being herself. She is not convinced that this is the truth, but it is something for her to hold on to.

Ultimately, Suzy must decide whether or not to speak again and take her place in the maelstrom of middle school. She knows she is never going to be like the other kids, but she has discovered there are a few kids who actually like her the way she is. She has come to realize that while she can accomplish many things, she is not grown up yet—and that is okay. Her greatest task at the moment is to fully step back into her life. It is daunting, and her decision and the way she implements it leave readers feeling as if they know fully this character whom they have grown to care for deeply.

Gina Hagler

Review Sources

Bradley, Jada. "The Thing about Jellyfish." Rev. of *The Thing about Jellyfish*, by Ali Benjamin. *Horn Book: Lolly's Classroom*. Horn Book, 12 Nov. 2015. Web. 10 Jan. 2016.

Kelly, Jacqueline. Rev. of *The Thing about Jellyfish*, by Ali Benjamin. *New York Times Sunday Book Review*. New York Times, 9 Oct. 2015. Web. 16 Jan. 2016.

Rev. of *The Thing about Jellyfish*, by Ali Benjamin. *Kirkus Reviews*. Kirkus Reviews, 6 May 2015. Web. 3 Jan. 2016.

The Tsar of Love and Techno

Author: Anthony Marra (b. 1984)
Publisher: Hogarth (New York). 352 pp.
Type of work: Short fiction
Time: Early twentieth century to the present
Locale: Russia

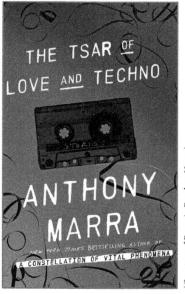

(Courtesy of Penguin Random House)

The short stories presented in Anthony Marra's The Tsar of Love and Techno *offer a glimpse of life and love in Russia from the age of Joseph Stalin to the rise of Vladimir Putin through a series of distinct yet interrelated narratives.*

Principal characters:
ROMAN OSIPOVICH MARKIN, a communist
    propaganda artist
GALINA, a beauty queen from the Russian
    town of Kirovsk
KOLYA, a veteran of the war in Chechnya,
    former love interest of Galina
ALEXEI, Kolya's brother
RUSLAN, the head of the Grozny Tourist Bureau

Anthony Marra's *The Tsar of Love and Techno* offers a well-researched examination of life in Russia both during and after the Cold War told through a series of interrelated short stories. It offers a window into a somber world that few Americans have seen and one centered on reality rather than nationalistic propaganda. It is quite a journey, yet one worth taking, not only for the gripping nature of the stories but also for the insight it provides into Russia's social condition. Everyone loves a happy ending in which the hero or heroine saves the day and lives happily ever after. For the characters that inhabit the pages of Marra's work, a happy ending never comes and is scarcely even expected. So conditioned are the characters to disappointment that they tend to take things in stride, whether it be a daughter killed by gangsters or a family member besmirched the Communist regime.

The composition of *The Tsar of Love and Techno* is such that the threads of one story carry into the next, forming a unified, if not always cohesive, narrative set in Russia. All of the constituent stories, although good enough to stand alone, are part of a larger whole. Each story introduces readers to new characters, yet many of these characters are linked to those from previous stories, just as they appear again in future ones. The tangled web of each account leaves readers wondering exactly when and where characters will reappear. For example, at the outset of the book, Roman Osipovich Markin visits his deceased brother's wife and son. This is no ordinary or even expected social visit: he urges his brother's wife to remove all images of her late husband from photographs that she may have possessed. More than a grieving relative, Markin is part of Joseph Stalin's paranoid propaganda machine, and his job is to erase from the record people disloyal to Communism in general or to the Russian leader in particular.

As the story unfolds, readers learn that Markin was aware of and even complicit in the death of his brother, killed for being a "dangerous" religious radical. Although a loyal servant of Stalin's regime, Markin is eventually accused of espionage and sentenced to death. However, his execution does not occur until after he has doctored thousands of photographs. Stalin loved Markin's work, especially his ability to make the Russian leader's cheeks appear red and youthful. Whenever someone was declared an enemy of the state, Markin was summoned to remove that person from the record. Over the years, he doctored countless items, from photographs to paintings. Markin's work continually reappears in this collection and is one of the chief threads binding the book together. His final work—which ultimately leads to his arrest—is blotting out a prima ballerina.

The next story picks up at the tail end of that ballerina's life and the impact that her tragic tale has on her descendants. Marra adds a human dimension to Markin's propaganda role, despite his rather grim work. Readers learn that Markin pays homage to his dead brother by painting his face—from his visage as a youth to depictions of how he would have appeared had he been permitted to reach old age—in countless images that he doctors over the years. Markin inhabits a depressing world in which an essentially good man is forced to do deplorable things. In fact, Russians everywhere, at least according to Marra's depictions, have to make similar difficult decisions. To stay alive in an amoral world, citizens either commit atrocious acts or become complicit in them by turning their backs.

The somber nature of Marra's stories reflect the colorless world of Soviet Russia and the Russian Federation. Absent are vibrant reds, blues, and greens; instead, scenes are painted in shades of gray and yellow. Indeed, one of the principal "wooded" areas in the book is the fabricated White Forest, in which metal and plastic take the place of real trees. The stark landscape of places such as the war-torn Chechen capital of Grozny matches the difficult lives of the Russian people, who resignedly accept the less-than-savory conditions in which they live.

Some in Marra's account hope that the collapse of the Soviet Union will bring greater peace and prosperity, but the termination of the Communist world only brings new troubles. Where once the KGB indiscriminately snatched people from the streets for alleged transgressions, organized crime figures step in to fill the power void left by the end of totalitarian rule. Corruption permeates the story. No one is beyond being bought or sold. It is hard to choose which version of Russia is worse, the one under Communist oppression or the one in the immediate aftermath of the Soviet collapse, in which a fundamental failure of government on all levels left assorted miscreants to assume power. The presence of the law is scarcely felt in the Russia described by Marra, and where it is, it too is a corruptible force. In the Soviet era, everyone works; they might not make much, but at least the bare necessities are provided. People in post-Soviet Russia are arguably worse off economically as free-market impulses lead to mechanization and the loss of countless jobs.

In practically every story in Marra's account someone either dies or is about to be killed. Death comes in many forms in *The Tsar of Love and Techno*. For some, it comes from crossing the wrong person. For others, such as those who work in factories and mines, lives are shortened by hazardous working conditions. In a world in which

Anthony Marra's 2013 work A Constellation of Vital Phenomena *garnered him numerous awards, including the Anisfield-Wolf Book Award in fiction. The* Tsar of Love and Techno, *Marra's second work, is a collection of short stories that take place in Soviet and post-Soviet Russia.*

worker safety and environmental considerations are an afterthought, people find themselves crippled and suffering through a diminished quality of life as they struggle with ailments associated with exposure to the toxic environment in which they work. As factory and mining industries—such as nickel mining operations in Kirovsk—become more automated many people lose their jobs. But one thing remains constant: the pollution of the environment. The work in mines, whether by people or machines, continues to desecrate of the environment.

The backdrop for many of the book's stories are Russia's wars in Chechnya. For the people of Russia, in addition to short lifespans and economic uncertainty, perpetual war seems a constant in their world. Even the main love story of the book—which features Galina, a girl from Kirovsk who goes on to win a beauty pageant and become a big-screen sensation, and Kolya, her youthful lover who is killed in the war in Chechnya—is tinged with sadness. The two were perfect for each other, but Kolya chooses to join the Russian military. He is sent to the front and receives no word from Galina, but she has actually been sending him countless letters that he never receives. When he returns home, he becomes a petty criminal and drug peddler. In the interim, Galina has met someone else and commenced the sequence of events that lead to her stardom. Save for on billboards, Kolya never sees Galina again. Eventually, Kolya loses his life in Chechnya. In a land where happy endings seemed scarce, even Galina—who, for a time, finds herself on top of the world and married to one of the richest men in Russia—loses practically everything that she has. She returns to her village of Kirovsk a broken woman.

All of the characters in Marra's collection of short stories simply try to survive in a world over which they have no control. Those old enough to remember life under Soviet rule long for the days of stability that totalitarianism brought. Many believe Vladimir Putin, KGB man turned politician, will lead them to prosperity. But like every generation encountered in *The Tsar of Love and Techno*, changes in national leadership do not improve everyday life; rather, they bring new forms of turmoil.

In writing the *Tsar of Love and Techno*, Marra has clearly done his homework. He conducted extensive research to provide a historically accurate backdrop to short stories rooted in both Russian literature and Russian history. Alex Halberstadt for the *New York Times* states: "This material may suggest that [the book] is a heavy-handed or grim piece of writing. That it is neither is a testament to Marra's seamless prose, telling use of detail and brisk pacing." He might paint too stark of an image, but the very grimness of these tales is what makes them so riveting and plausible. As readers follow its main characters through life, most will find the work hard to put down, despite its fatalism.

Keith M. Finley, PhD

Review Sources

Crum, Maddie. "The Bottom Line: 'The Tsar of Love and Techno' by Anthony Marra." Rev. of *The Tsar of Love and Techno*, by Anthony Marra. *Huffington Post*. TheHuffingtonPost.com, 6 Oct. 2015. Web. 31 Dec. 2015.

Halberstadt, Alex. "Ice Belt Tales." Rev. of *The Tsar of Love and Techno*, by Anthony Marra. *New York Times* 25 Oct. 2015: BR17. Print.

Prose, Francine. "Dissidents Reemerge in 'The Tsar of Love and Techno.'" Rev. of *The Tsar of Love and Techno*, by Anthony Marra. *Washington Post*. Washington Post, 29 Sept. 2015. Web, 31 Dec. 2015.

Stuart, Jan. "Book Review: 'The Tsar of Love and Techno' by Anthony Marra." Rev. of *The Tsar of Love and Techno*, by Anthony Marra. *Boston Globe*. Boston Globe Media Partners, 3 Oct. 2015. Web. 31 Dec. 2015.

The Turner House

Author: Angela Flournoy (b. 1985)
Publisher: Houghton Mifflin Harcourt (Boston). 352 pp.
Type of work: Novel
Time: 2008, flashbacks to the 1940s onward
Locale: The East Side of Detroit, Michigan

Francis and Viola Turner inhabited a house on Detroit's East Side for more than fifty years. But as Viola's health begins to fail years after Francis's death, their thirteen children must come together to decide the fate of their childhood home on Yarrow Street while facing past and present family secrets.

Principal characters:
CHA-CHA TURNER, a sixty-four-year-old truck driver, the oldest of the Turner children
LELAH TURNER, the youngest of the Turner children, a gambling addict
VIOLA TURNER, the Turner family matriarch, dying of cancer
FRANCIS TURNER, Viola's deceased husband
TROY TURNER, the youngest of the Turner boys, a police officer
DAVID GARDENHIRE, an old friend of Troy
ALICE ROTHMAN, Cha-Cha's young therapist

(Courtesy Houghton Mifflin Harcourt)

Angela Flournoy's debut novel, *The Turner House* (2015), chronicles the events of one spring that change everything for the Turners, a working-class, African American family that has been living in Detroit, Michigan, for more than half a century. Amid the financial crisis of 2008 the family house on Detroit's decaying East Side has lost much of its value and is now worth only a fraction of its mortgage. Truck driver Cha-Cha Turner and his twelve younger siblings must come together to decide the fate of their childhood home as the health of their mother, Viola, continues to decline and secrets of their deceased father's past emerge. Meanwhile, sixty-four-year-old Cha-Cha has started seeing ghosts. A "haint" that visited him once as a child in the family home on Yarrow Street has returned to him in adulthood, leading him to have an accident on the job. With the reappearance of the Yarrow Street haint, Cha-Cha is forced to reckon with both his past and his present family life.

The Turner House is told from the perspectives of Cha-Cha, his youngest sibling, Lelah, and their brother Troy, the youngest Turner brother. Interspersed throughout the narrative are flashbacks to Francis and Viola's lives in the mid-1940s as they moved from Arkansas to Detroit during the era of the Great Migration of African Americans from the South to northern cities. In addition to facing big changes for their family as a whole, Cha-Cha, Troy, and Lelah must each respond to personal crises. Cha-Cha is beginning to feel the distance that has come between him and his wife of many years, Tina, as he becomes increasingly preoccupied with his haint. Viola has come to live with Cha-Cha and Tina in the suburbs due to her failing health, a change that puts additional stress on Cha-Cha and Tina's marriage. And when Cha-Cha starts seeing a therapist after his accident, things become even more complicated. The young Alice Rothman seems genuinely interested in Cha-Cha's family history, and as a result Cha-Cha finds himself developing feelings for her.

Lelah, a gambling addict, has been evicted from her apartment after losing her job and most of her money. While she longs to rebuild trust with her daughter, Brianne, and to have a relationship with her young grandson, Bobbie, she struggles to maintain control over her addiction and her life. In a moment of desperation and with nowhere else to go, Lelah begins squatting at the vacant Yarrow Street house. Soon after, she meets David Gardenhire, an old friend of Troy's, and begins a passionate love affair. Lelah's new relationship compels her to face the truth about herself and her relationships.

Angela Flournoy graduated from the Iowa Writer's Workshop and has written fiction the New York Times, Paris Review, New Republic, *and others. Her first novel,* The Turner House *(2015), was a National Book Award finalist and earned her a place as a National Book Foundation "5 under 35" honoree.*

Troy, a police officer, works to be successful but keeps coming up against roadblocks. He develops an illegal scheme in which Jillian, his girlfriend, will buy the Yarrow Street House on a short sale so that the house can remain in the family. But Jillian, with whom Troy has a turbulent relationship, refuses to cooperate.

Flournoy's characters are well developed, believable, and sympathetic. They worry about family relationships, struggle with addictions, and, ultimately, seek happiness and fulfillment in their lives. Flournoy provides readers with intimate glimpses into her characters' distraught thoughts and feelings, exposing their weaknesses and vulnerabilities. Readers accompany Lelah, for example, to Motor City Casino, where Flournoy's account of the nature of gambling addiction brings the character alive. Lelah draws us in with her realistic personality, and when she loses readers feel it like a punch in the stomach through the strong descriptive language. Yet Flournoy is careful to illustrate the complexity of addiction, making Lelah neither an utterly pitiful innocent nor an unlikable monster. Instead she is sympathetic but flawed, a complex character with complex relationships and the capacity to grow.

Flournoy provides many similar vivid examples of strong characterization, often through the various family conflicts that arise. Readers witness difficult moments in the relationship of Cha-Cha and Tina as the couple work to resuscitate their marriage. Since his injury and since Viola moved in with him and Tina, Cha-Cha has not been able to have sex. One night, when Tina invites him back into the master bedroom from the guest bedroom, Cha-Cha is surprised by his own arousal. However, things do not work out. Here readers share Cha-Cha's frustration and disappointment at a visceral level. Notably, much of the drama of *The Turner House* occurs in such quotidian moments and in domestic spaces: bedrooms, living rooms, and kitchens, therapy offices and residential streets provide a rich background for characters' unfolding lives. This ordinary atmosphere, given a unique twist by the accelerated decay of Detroit itself, helps readers sympathize deeply with the Turners in their everyday losses and cheer for them all the more when they achieve minor victories.

Although she is not from Detroit, Flournoy writes convincingly of the city and its difficult history, juxtaposing the city it once was with the city it has become. In becoming intimate with the Turner family, readers also develop a feeling of connection to Detroit itself, sensing the place's importance to the family's very identity. And in describing the Turners' personal struggles and losses, the book also describes the downfall of Detroit and its ongoing problems. Flournoy skillfully intertwines the personal with the political, drawing on actual events for the historical framework. The Turners' status as African Americans is central to their experience, for example. At one point Cha-Cha recalls the real-life 1967 Detroit riot, or Twelfth Street Riot, one of the most deadly racial conflicts in United States history. In the novel Cha-Cha learns about the rioting while he is at work in one of the city's many automobile assembly plants. That night, he and his brothers Russell and Lonnie decide to steal bricks from some old buildings while the police are busy trying to break up the riots on the other side of town. When the young Turner men encounter a cop, they take off running. Flournoy subtly weaves particular geographical details of the city into her narrative as the brothers scatter down different streets. While Cha-Cha hides from the police under a porch, his father happens to show up drunk and urinates publicly on his hiding place. "His father had pissed on his forehead when he should have been at home protecting his family," Flournoy writes, evocatively situating Cha-Cha's personal story amid Detroit's larger social and political history.

Flournoy is also an expert at writing dialogue. In *The Turner House* she commits to representing the everyday speech of the Turners in a realistic way. Her characters speak to one another like real people of their time and place. In depicting their frank exchanges, Flournoy reveals the Turner siblings' complicated love for each other and also their deep sense of connection and shared history as members of a large family with a strong sense of place. They share a common language, as Flournoy conveys in the opening chapter, in which a fourteen-year-old Cha-Cha, in the summer of 1958, claims to have seen a haint in his bedroom. "That haint tried to run me outta the room," says Cha-Cha, to which his father, Francis, replies, "There ain't no haints in Detroit." In this scene, Flournoy conveys both humor and hurt. She captures both the comedy and the drama of a large family up out of bed in the middle of the night. More importantly, however, she sets up an example of how speech, in all of its intended or unintended effects, shapes collective memories and histories: Francis's rebuttal soon becomes the Turners' phrase of choice to indicate one's disbelief—or dismissal of a claim that one knows could be true but refuses to acknowledge. This half-humorous reminder of the past is a strong connection to their father, his secrets, and the folklore of the family's Southern roots.

Critics have noted the influence of writers like Zora Neale Hurston and Gabriel García Márquez on *The Turner House*. For example, in his review for the *New York*

Times Sunday Book Review, Matthew Thomas traces Flournoy's use of magical realism in the haint episodes as well as the large cast of generation-spanning characters to García Márquez's work. These influences were regarded as well integrated rather than derivative, and most critics also found the book remarkably fresh and fully realized, especially for a debut novel from a young author. Indeed, *The Turner House* was met with nearly universal acclaim, and it was nominated for numerous awards. Praise was especially directed toward Flournoy's strong command of language, which enables her to provide rich, artistic description without lapsing into pretentiousness or melodrama.

Many reviewers also singled out Flournoy's striking ability to maintain empathy for her characters while also letting them be real, complicated people. Perhaps it is this approach to storytelling—a desire to truly know her characters in all of their weaknesses, vulnerability, desires, and humanity—that enabled Flournoy to take up difficult issues like aging, poverty, structural racism, and addiction in a single novel with such deep compassion and compelling force. *The Turner House* succeeds as a multifaceted story that blends issues of the past and present, the everyday and the fantastic, and race and class into a highly personal family tale with universal appeal.

A. Lewandowski

Review Sources

Brown, Stacia. "'The Turner House' Takes on Mental Health in Black Families." Rev. of *The Turner House*, by Angela Flournoy. *Washington Post*. Washington Post, 23 Apr. 2015. Web. 1 Feb. 2016.

Gold, Hannah K. "House of the Dispossessed." Rev. of *The Turner House*, by Angela Flournoy. *Nation*. Nation, 13 Aug. 2015. Web. 1 Feb. 2016.

Thomas, Matthew. Rev. of *The Turner House*, by Angela Flournoy. *New York Times Sunday Book Review*. New York Times, 29 Apr. 2015. Web. 1 Feb. 2016.

Rev. of *The Turner House*, by Angela Flournoy. *Kirkus Reviews*. Kirkus Media, 21 Apr. 2015. Web. 1 Feb. 2016.

Rev. of *The Turner House*, by Angela Flournoy. *Publishers Weekly*. PWxyz, Apr. 2015. Web. 1 Feb. 2016.

Twain and Stanley Enter Paradise

Author: Oscar Hijuelos (1951–2013)
Publisher: Grand Central (New York). 265 pp.
Type of work: Novel
Time: 1859–1910
Locales: Cuba, London, and New Orleans, Louisiana

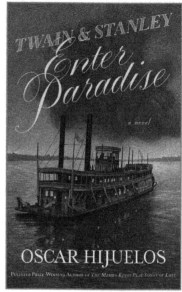

(Courtesy of Grand Central Pub)

Twain and Stanley Enter Paradise *is a lovingly realized re-creation of the decades-long friendship between the great novelist Mark Twain and the celebrated explorer Henry Morton Stanley. In the expert hands of the late Oscar Hijuelos, their story becomes a searching meditation on fame, happiness, and death.*

Principal characters:
HENRY MORTON STANLEY, newspaperman and
    famous explorer
DOROTHY TENNANT, his wife and a British artist
HENRY HOPE STANLEY, his close friend; an American businessman
MARK TWAIN, American humorist and novelist
OLIVIA "LIVY" CLEMENS, Twain's wife

American novelist Oscar Hijuelos became famous for his lush and exuberant evocations of the Cuban American immigrant experience, most notably in *The Mambo Kings Play Songs of Love* (1989), for which he won the Pulitzer Prize in fiction. *Twain and Stanley Enter Paradise*, his last novel before his death in 2013, reveals another side of Hijuelos as a writer. It is a reflection of different interests that consumed the last years of his life. As a teenager Hijuelos read a biography of the nineteenth-century explorer Henry Morton Stanley. This led to a lifelong fascination with Stanley, whose tumultuous career took him from a workhouse in his native Wales to the 1862 Battle of Shiloh, the American western frontier, and the Congo and the uncharted interior of Africa.

As he pursued his research, Hijuelos learned that Stanley met Mark Twain during his youthful adventuring in the United States. Hijuelos deeply admired Twain, who helped to liberate American writing from European conventions and whose *The Adventures of Huckleberry Finn* (1884) remains one of the landmarks of American literature. Stanley and Twain maintained their friendship for well over three decades. Such an enduring relationship between two men who figured as two of the most remarkable characters of the late nineteenth century, was intriguing in itself, but Hijuelos then came across a reference concerning a trip to Cuba Stanley might have taken in 1861 in order to search for Henry Hope Stanley, the benefactor whose name he adopted. There is no documentary evidence that Stanley made this journey, and the odds are against the possibility that he traveled to Cuba as the United States was slipping into the Civil War. Nonetheless, this bit of historical conjecture was the spark that inspired Hijuelos to begin a novel about the abiding bond between Stanley and Twain.

Hijuelos worked on the novel for more than twelve years. In addition to his reading, he traveled to Wales, London, New Orleans, and Hartford, Connecticut, soaking in the atmosphere of places where Stanley and Twain lived and built homes. He wrote thousands of pages, shaping and reshaping the novel. He worked on it the day before he died of a heart attack. His widow found the manuscript, which was then edited and published as *Twain and Stanley Enter Paradise.*

(Dario Acosta)

Oscar Hijuelos published ten books. The Mambo Kings Play Songs of Love *(1989) won the Pulitzer Prize in fiction, with Hijuelos becoming the first Hispanic to ever win that award.*

The novel moves in roughly chronological order with much of the action taking place in Stanley's and Twain's later years, though the decisive moment of the story occurs in 1861 when the two men arrive in Cuba on a quest to find Henry Hope Stanley. The ways in which each man remembers what happens during their time in Cuba becomes an important theme for the remainder of the book. Hijuelos structures the novel as a collection of documents—letters, diaries, and a secret manuscript of Stanley— that are periodically framed by an omniscient third-person narrator. Hijuelos brings Stanley and Twain to life by brilliantly evoking their distinctive voices and by recreating the cadence and vocabulary of nineteenth-century prose. Despite the fact that they read like copies or paraphrases of genuine documents, everything was invented by Hijuelos.

Though the title of the work is *Twain and Stanley Enter Paradise*, implying parity between the two, or even primacy for Twain, the novel as published belongs to Stanley. It is Stanley's lifelong quest for acceptance and a family that lies at the heart of the story. It is Stanley's manuscript recounting his early life in the United States and his search for his adoptive father in Cuba that proves to be the novel's emotional touchstone. That manuscript runs over one hundred pages in the novel, and there is no other section comparable to it in the book. Twain's role is as a counterpoint to his emotionally volatile friend. Stanley is a man of action; Twain, for all his peripatetic wanderings, is a man of thought. Though constantly borne down by bitter experience, Stanley yearns to believe; at his heart, he is sustained by a battered faith. Twain is a skeptic, a disbeliever in God, and increasingly dubious about his fellow human beings.

The "paradise" of the title is elusive for both men. Though Twain and Stanley attain great fame and move in the most rarefied social circles, they find that worldly glory does not bring them happiness. Both are self-made men, yet they each worry about finances. Stanley is the product of a poverty-stricken youth and never rests easy about his acceptance into polite society. Twain earns great sums from his writings, but he squanders his money through ill-advised business ventures, forcing him to recoup his fortunes through exhausting lecture tours.

Stanley's insecurities are aggravated by public reassessments of his African explorations. He labored for years in the Congo, risking death in many forms and contracting diseases that undermined his heath. He saw himself as an agent of progress, bringing Christianity and civilization to the interior of Africa. A cause especially near to his heart, born of his experiences in the American South, was the eradication of slavery. Stanley's sponsor and partner in these labors was King Leopold II of Belgium, and Stanley believed that Leopold shared his enlightened vision of colonialism. Instead, after Stanley left the Congo, Leopold instituted a ruthless regime that mercilessly exploited his African subjects. The Belgian Congo became an international scandal as stories of its horrors slowly filtered out to the wider world. *Heart of Darkness* (1899), Joseph Conrad's enigmatic tale of colonizers descending into savagery, is set in the post–Stanley Congo.

Inevitably, Stanley's reputation was tarnished by what followed from his labors, and he suffered the painful fate of seeing his achievements associated with atrocities. Though loyally excusing his friend from blame, Twain shared the general estimation of the Belgian Congo. Growing increasingly dissatisfied with his fellow man, he was mortified by the embrace of imperialism by the United States during the 1898 Spanish-American War and the subsequent brutal campaign to establish American control over the Philippines. In fundamental ways the world disappointed Stanley and Twain. Hijuelos has Stanley lie to his wife Dorothy Tenant about the fate of an injured bluebird found along a woodland trail. He wants to protect her conviction that in life there are always happy endings. He notes to himself that he does not believe this, and neither does Twain. The two men's disillusionment leads to morose colloquies on God and the meaning of life. Given the dourness of Twain's and Stanley's meditations on ultimate things in the novel, it is not the theological concept of paradise that preoccupies them. Paradise is much more personal; it is an intimate beacon of happiness.

Paradise lies behind Twain and is his Edenic boyhood along the Mississippi River, where he experienced true joy and wonder. It was also the period of his life that inspired so much of his fiction. Memories of the past offer the aging Twain a comforting avenue of escape. Stanley, who was born John Rowlands, spent his life struggling for recognition and acceptance, and his youth was anything but Edenic, as he was abandoned by his family and consigned to a workhouse for the poor. As a penniless immigrant in New Orleans he was befriended by a cotton trader whom he considered a father and adopted the man's name. But this dream of a new family failed to materialize, and despite fame and fortune, Stanley remained a lonely man. Any efforts to reconnect with his relations in Wales proved unsatisfying, and a fiancée deserted him while he was on one of his treks in Africa. By now in his late forties, Stanley feared that he would die alone. Then he met the aristocratic British painter Dorothy Tennant. After a protracted and tumultuous courtship, they married. To complete their family, they adopted a son. Even as his laurels faded, Stanley found contentment in his little domestic circle. He refurbished a dilapidated house in the country as a fitting place to raise his son.

After many travails Stanley finally achieved a measure of happiness and peace; Twain's last years were blighted by loss and bitterness. The explorer found a family, and the writer lost his. Although Twain's only son died as a baby, he enjoyed a happy family life with his wife Livy and three daughters. Twain's old age was haunted by the deaths of his wife and two of his daughters. These hammer blows darkened his already sour estimation of the world. The contrast between the fates of his two protagonists highlights the thematic connections between *Twain and Stanley Enter Paradise* and Hijuelos' earlier writings. The emphasis on the redemptive nature of familial love echoes through novels such as *The Mambo Kings Play Songs of Love* and *Mr. Ives' Christmas* (1995). Along with the adventure of his life, Stanley's yearning for a family may have been one of the things that attracted Hijuelos to him. Like the eponymous Mr. Ives, Stanley was a foundling. For similar reasons, Twain's agonizing losses late in life must have elicited Hijuelos's sympathetic attention. In Hijuelos's novels God is omnipresent, but hints of the divine are captured in little things, especially the sympathetic chords of family. Stanley and Twain wrestle with the problem of God, usually looking in the wrong places, failing to note in a conscious way that the key to paradise is all around them.

Thoroughly grounded in history, *Twain and Stanley Enter Paradise* does not attain the lyrical heights of some of Oscar Hijuelos's earlier novels. Its pleasures are rooted in scrupulous attention to psychological veracity in evoking the contrasting characters of its protagonists. Therein lies its power; Hijuelos's novel carries the conviction of an inspired biography. But Hijuelos did not write a biography. His novel is an ode to two men who were significant to his life. Their lives also enabled him to address in a different way his twinned interests in family and God, which explains an abrupt announcement at the end of the novel. The novel is an acknowledgement of transcendence, an affectionate note of grace to conclude the last book of a great writer.

Daniel P. Murphy

Review Sources

Chee, Alexander. "Posthumously Published 'Twain & Stanley' a Bit Too Presumptuous." Rev. of *Twain and Stanley Enter Paradise*, by Oscar Hijuelos. *Los Angeles Times.* Los Angeles Times, 19 Nov. 2015. Web. 22 Feb. 2016.

Corrigan, Maureen. "'Twain & Stanley Enter Paradise' Educates but Doesn't Entertain Its Readers." Rev. of *Twain and Stanley Enter Paradise*, by Oscar Hijuelos. *NPR.* NPR, 4 Nov. 2015. Web. 22 Feb. 2016.

Schrefer, Eliot. "Introducing Twain, Stanley to Us, Each Other." Rev. of *Twain and Stanley Enter Paradise*, by Oscar Hijuelos. *USA Today* 13 Jan. 2016: 4D. Print.

Scott, Joanna. Rev. of *Twain and Stanley Enter Paradise*, by Oscar Hijuelos. *New York Times*. New York Times, 8 Dec. 2015. Web. 22 Feb. 2016.

Stuart, John. Rev. of *Twain and Stanley Enter Paradise*, by Oscar Hijuelos. *Boston Globe*. Boston Globe Media Partners, 31 Oct. 2015. Web. 22 Feb. 2016.

Two Years Eight Months and Twenty-Eight Nights

Author: Salman Rushdie (b. 1947)
Publisher: Random House (New York). 304 pp.
Type of work: Novel
Time: 1195, 2015, and the thirty-first century
Locales: Córdoba, Bombay, Manhattan, and other cities

In Salman Rushdie's tenth novel, the boundary between the human world and the fairy world of jinn breaks open and strange events occur in the usually predictable realm of men and women.

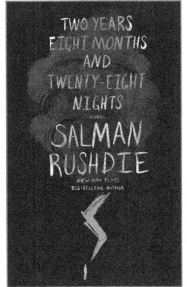

(Courtesy of Random House)

Principal characters:

IBN RUSHD, also known as Averroes, a philosopher of twelfth-century Córdoba, based on a real-life personage of the same name

DUNIA, his housekeeper and mistress; the mother of his many children

THE LIGHTNING PRINCESS, a powerful female jinn

THE KING OF PERISTAN, her father

HIERONYMUS "GERONIMO" MANEZES, a landscape architect, descended from Rushd and Dunia, living in present-day Manhattan

JIMMY KAPOOR, a struggling creator of graphic novels, also descended from Dunia and Rushd

BLUE YASMEEN, a young Manhattan woman who excels in storytelling

ZUMURRUD SHAH, a leader of the dark jinn forces

ZABARDAST, a rival of Zumurrud

While living under a pseudonym after the publication of his controversial novel *The Satanic Verses* (1988), which prompted the Muslim religious leader Ayatollah Khomeini to issue a fatwa calling for his death, Salman Rushdie wrote a book of stories for children, and in particular for his ten-year-old son, Zafar. In *Haroun and the Sea of Stories* (1990), a boy named Haroun and his father, Rashid, are abducted into the mysterious sea of stories, a world of artificial intelligence where strange events happen until the two are finally returned to their previous lives. The stories continued in *Luka and the Fire of Life* (2010), which was written for and about Rushdie's younger son, Milan, and was set in a world inspired by video games.

Rushdie has continued to explore the world of endless stories in a novel for and about adults. In novels from *The Ground beneath Her Feet* (1999) to *The Enchantress of Florence* (2008), he has created stories for which the Aristotelian criterion of "probability" simply does not apply. The same is true of his new novel. The title, *Two Years Eight Months and Twenty-Eight Nights*, is an elaborate paraphrase of the famous "thousand and one nights" from the *The Arabian Nights' Entertainment*, as the stories were first translated into English in 1706. Rushdie's omniscient narrator explains that 1001 is just a large number to which the extra "one" has been added out of a superstition regarding even numbers. In the world of fairy lore, it is equivalent to the forty days or years of biblical stories. It refers to any long time, and the actual number of stories told in this novel is probably countless. Indeed, the narrator delights in the ways that stories can be "enfolded within other stories," and any one story can thus become a "mirror of life."

Partway through the novel, in the sixth of its nine chapters, the king of the fairies (in Arabic, the jinn) disappears and is thought to have been poisoned by the contents of a Chinese box he is later found holding. The sealed box contains stories, and the jinn know what mortals do not, that "a fairy king can only be poisoned by the most dreadful and powerful of words." The king's daughter instructs the king's courtiers to open the box and to unfold the stories it contains. The box is a Pandora's box and contains all stories along with all the ills to which humans are prey. It is thus an image of Rushdie's book where readers are caught up in a war between the many small stories and the main plot that they tend to undermine.

For centuries, critics have said that a good story must have a beginning, a middle, and an end. The main story in Rushdie's novel has all of these and starts in the year 1195 when the Spanish Muslim philosopher Ibn Rushd (1126–98) falls out of favor with the new ruler of his native Córdoba. He has been accused of denying God's involvement in the affairs of everyday life and thus challenging the significance of religion. Forbidden to teach philosophy, he is reduced to making pots and treating the sick. In the newly intolerant city, where Jews are forced to embrace Islam, he takes a young Jewish woman into his house. She calls herself Dunia, which she says means "the world," and

Salman Rushdie won the prestigious Man Booker Prize for his second novel, Midnight's Children *(1982), which was adapted for film in 2012. In 2007 he was knighted for his contributions to literature. Though a British citizen, he lives mainly in New York City.*

she soon becomes the world to him. She becomes his lover as well as his housekeeper, and they produce a large brood of children in their few years together. Rushd does not give them his name but instead calls them the Duniazát: "the brood of Dunia." Unknown to Rushd, this brood is the product of a rare union between a mortal man and a powerful female jinn.

After the opening chapter, the story skips to its middle in the late twentieth and early twenty-first centuries. There have now been many generations of the Duniazát, and these descendants appear fully human except that they lack earlobes. They go about their business in the mortal world more or less oblivious of their mixed origins because passageways between the worlds of jinn and humans have been closed off. A new opening suddenly allows visitors from the jinn's upper world to visit the human world, and with the visits there begins a series of unrelated happenings in the lower world that become known collectively as "the strangenesses." For instance, lightning strikes so often that it becomes a common cause of death. A habitual liar ceases to speak and becomes a revered sage. A gardener levitates and cannot connect his feet to the ground or his back to a bed. A comic-book artist is visited by one of his superheroes, who is actually a jinn in disguise. Jinn enter the human world and bring humans back to fairyland. Dunia falls in love again, this time with the gardener, who happens to be one of her descendants.

There is also an ending of sorts. The novel's narrator turns out to be living a thousand years after the strangenesses he describes. Reflecting back on what happened during that time, he apologizes to readers who think he has mixed up history and mythology. The ordinary gap between the worlds of mortals and immortals is not always separated, he explains. It was breached in antiquity and is likely to be opened sometime in the future because, as Aristotle taught, the universe is eternal.

In addition to being a comparative mythologist in the tradition of Joseph Campbell (1904–87), the narrator is a moralist. He has definite opinions about the values of liberal society and the dangers of theocracy or, indeed, of religion in general. He writes as though religious extremism has long since vanished from the world of humans and is regarded with horror by the curious readers for whom he provides details about the loves and lives of the jinn. The rather didactic and moralizing tone of the last chapter is no doubt understandable in light of the author's years of enforced hiding, described in the nonfiction book *Joseph Anton: A Memoir* (2012). It has nevertheless upset some readers.

Meanwhile, the middle of Rushdie's long story—the strangenesses in New York and other world cities within the last generation—is as strong in social satire as it is in fantasy. Celebrity has not only driven Rushdie into hiding; it has thrust him into the limelight in fundraisers, lectures, and various gatherings of glitterati. He has portraits to paint of celebrities and causes with all their quirks. There is a modern ladies' man, an Italian named Donizetti whose fate it is to chase women of every shape and class until he finds refuge in food with a new career as a restaurateur. Then again, there are man-eating women like the "notorious libertine" Teresa Saca Cuartos. Rushdie balances these sometimes unpleasant characters with the very down-to-earth owner-operator of a small gardening company. Descended from a firebrand preacher in Bombay, Mr. Geronimo lives very simply after the death of his beloved wife. He builds marvelous gardens for wealthy Long Island clients, such as the reclusive heiress named Alexandra Bliss Fariña but known as the Lady Philosopher, with whom he forms an unlikely liaison. He enters more reluctantly into an affair with the still youthful and amorous jinn Dunia.

Finally, the novel includes a good deal of postmodern self-reference. In the autobiographical *Joseph Anton*, Rushdie wrote that his father altered the family name in honor of Ibn Rushd, the philosopher whose story is told in the novel's opening pages. When the twelfth-century philosopher is awakened from his long sleep, his argument with the older religious philosopher Al Ghazali (1058–1111) becomes a personal one for Rushdie. The clever Al Ghazali turns out to side with the dark jinn in their attempt to create a new caliphate, while Rushd prefers the real world of men and women.

Meanwhile, Rushdie's thirty-first-century narrator has the very postmodern tendency to problematize the sources of his tale and the solutions proposed by those hoping to avert another war of the worlds. In a more straightforward fashion, Rushdie implies a deep nostalgia for the Bombay of his youth, before Hindu nationalism turned it into Mumbai, as well as a real fondness for his adopted home in New York.

Reviews of Rushdie's novels have been mixed for some years and certainly since the infamous yet brilliant *Satanic Verses*. Christina Patterson, the reviewer for the *Sunday Times* of London, considers *Two Years* a tour de force but never an easy read, while Gaby Wood, in a September 2015 interview of Rushdie for the London *Telegraph*, regards it as Rushdie's "funniest" fiction in years and delights in the gleefulness of his satiric character sketches. The *Irish Independent* reviewer Darragh McManus finds the "diatribe" on religion rather heavy-handed but not enough to distract from a "great story." Other reviewers have referred to the novel as an amusement park with lightning-fast rides and few transitions, while some see a more serious tone amidst the mayhem, which takes the edge off what Ann Hulbert, critic for the *Atlantic*, termed its "earnest message" about religious extremism. The story of clashing worlds is sufficiently rooted in mundane existence to make for a fictionally acceptable opposition, and some have compared Rushdie's war of two worlds with the culture wars that gunmen in various nations have wished to begin. Rushdie has thus performed a work of literary alchemy, transmuting the base stuff of the newspapers into the gold of narrative art.

Tom Willard

Review Sources

Emerson, Bo. "Salman Rushdie Writes a Grown-Up Fairy Tale." Rev. of *Two Years Eight Months and Twenty-Eight Nights*, by Salman Rushdie. *myAJC*. Cox Media Group, 15 Sept. 2015. Web. 31 Dec. 2015.

Hulbert, Ann. "Salman Rushdie's Self-Mockery and Antic Magic." *Atlantic*. Atlantic Monthly Group, Sept. 2015. Web. 4 Jan. 2016.

Kellogg, Carolyn. "The Jinn Invade the Earth." Rev. of *Two Years Eight Months and Twenty-Eight Nights*, by Salman Rushdie. *LA Times*. Los Angeles Times, 6 Sept. 2015. Web. 31 Dec. 2015.

McManus, Darragh. "Literary Superstar's Fantastical Fable Sings." Rev. of *Two Years Eight Months and Twenty-Eight Nights*, by Salman Rushdie. *Independent. ie*. Irish Independent, 9 June 2015. Web. 4 Jan. 2016.

Patterson, Christina. Rev. of *Two Years Eight Months and Twenty-Eight Nights*, by Salman Rushdie. *Sunday Times*. Times Newspapers, 6 Sept. 2015. Web. 4 Jan. 2016.

Thapa, Manjushree. Rev. of *Two Years Eight Months and Twenty-Eight Nights*, by Salman Rushdie. *Globe and Mail*. Globe and Mail, 18 Sept. 2015. Web. 31 Dec. 2015.

Under the Udala Trees

Author: Chinelo Okparanta
Publisher: Houghton Mifflin (New York). 336 pp.
Type of work: Novel
Time: 1960s–1970s
Locale: Nigeria

Set during the Nigerian civil war, Under the Udala Trees *is a coming-of-age story that explores themes of love, sexual identity, and acceptance in a repressive society.*

Principal characters:
IJEOMA, the narrator, a gay woman in Nigeria
MAMA, her mother, a devout Christian
AMINA, her first love, a Hausa girl
NDIDI, her girlfriend
CHIBUNDU, her husband

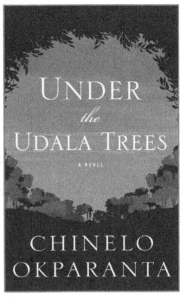

(Courtesy Houghton Mifflin Harcourt)

According to Nigerian legend, Udala trees are where spirit children congregate. Weary from floating between the living world and the dead, these ghosts provide the gift of fertility to any woman who sits below the boughs in exchange for their respite. In an especially telling scene of *Under the Udala Trees*, the protagonist, Ijeoma, follows her classmate to a grove of Udalas and emulates the girl by closing her eyes and wishing that she will one day bless her husband with many children. When her classmate states they are not too young to prepare to become some man's wife, Ijeoma recognizes that she does not necessarily want the promise of a husband or fertility. Despite being only nine years old, Ijeoma has already started challenging what it means to be a woman in Nigeria.

Nigerian American author Chinelo Okparanta has stated that she likes to write about brave men and women who are trying to make sense of their lives in the context of the societies to which they belong. Ijeoma certainly fits this description. Throughout the years that follow that formative moment underneath the Udala trees, Ijeoma continues to question how her identity as a lesbian fits within Nigerian society. This determination to be true to herself fosters the central sentiment of *Under the Udala Trees*, a novel that ultimately aims to illustrate the importance of being able to love openly and without societal restrictions.

Okparanta's first novel, *Under the Udala Trees* begins Ijeoma's story in 1968. It is the second year of the Nigerian civil war, a time when the Igbo people of southeastern Nigeria, the ethnic group to which Ijeoma and her family belong, have seceded from the rest of the nation to start the Republic of Biafra. To establish the novel's setting,

Okparanta employs a rich, visual language and describes the color and fauna of the landscape in great detail. These descriptions are intended to be from the perspective of Ijeoma who, at the onset of the civil war, is eleven years old and living in Ojoto.

Written in the first person and past tense, Ijeoma's narration conveys a sense that she is in the present day looking back on what may be the most memorable moments and people of her life. Arguably the most powerful influences of her early years are those of Mama and Papa. Okparanta presents Mama as the voice of traditional Nigeria, a fact most evident in her name, Adaora, which means "the daughter of all." The character of Papa, meanwhile, seems to represent a deviation from the cultural norm. After losing hope that Biafra will win the war, Papa essentially abandons his wife and daughter by allowing himself to die in an air raid.

Mama never quite recovers from the tragic death of her husband, and with resources being scarce because of the war she is forced to send Ijeoma away to live with family friends, a grammar schoolteacher and his wife. In exchange for her room, board, and schooling, Ijeoma works as a house girl for her hosts. It is a lonely existence until one day, while out running errands, Ijeoma meets Amina, a Hausa girl her age who has lost her family in the conflict. Ijeoma persuades the schoolteacher and his wife to take Amina in as an additional house girl.

Although she is portrayed more as a reactionary character than an incendiary one, Amina ultimately becomes a disruptive force in Ijeoma's life. Okparanta carefully crafts Amina to represent everything that is forbidden to Ijeoma. Ijeoma is prohibited from loving Amina not only because she is a girl but also because she is Hausa—a member of the Muslim ethnic group in opposition to the Igbo during the civil war. While the story line of star-crossed lovers may be a familiar literary trope, Okparanta defies convention to some degree by presenting Ijeoma as a young, gay protagonist who is both self-aware and self-accepting. Amina does not change anything in Ijeoma, she simply furthers something that already exists. To explain how Ijeoma readily accepts her feelings for Amina and falls effortlessly into a romantic relationship with her, Okparanta integrates a Nigerian proverb into the text, stating that "wood already touched by fire is not difficult to light." Okparanta's depiction of Ijeoma's homosexuality as an inherent part of her being not is only powerful but also proves essential to the narrative's central message. Ijeoma lives within a culture that perceives homosexuality as a choice, something people can be tricked into by the devil. By presenting Ijeoma's relationship to Amina as simply an extension of Ijeoma's natural being, Okparanta ensures that there is no room for readers to doubt the Ijeoma's actions or feelings.

Ijeoma's sexual orientation proves to be the central conflict that drives the narrative of *Under the Udala Trees*. The most direct manifestation of this conflict is between Ijeoma and Mama, who becomes the obstacle to Ijeoma's desires once the schoolteacher discovers the girls' romantic relationship. After being forced to move home, Ijeoma is subjected daily Bible lessons conducted by her mother that are intended to cleanse her soul. Here, Okparanta incorporates direct passages of the Bible into the narrative along with Mama's interpretations as to why homosexuality is a sin. Okparanta, who was raised a Jehovah's Witness, presents the complexity of faith with affecting authenticity. Despite the fact that she is a spiritual person who often tries to communicate with God, Ijeoma sees hypocrisy in most of the biblical passages. By the end of her lessons with Mama, Ijeoma's feelings for Amina are as strong as ever, but she pretends that she believes homosexuality is a sin in order to appease her mother.

Throughout the remainder of her adolescence, Ijeoma continues to love Amina even though they cannot be together. In her early adulthood, Ijeoma begins a romantic relationship with a woman named Ndidi. After Ndidi and Ijeoma attend an underground

Chinelo Okparanta, a Nigerian American writer, was educated at Pennsylvania State University, Rutgers University, and the Iowa's Writers Workshop. Her debut book, Happiness, Like Water *(2013) was an award-nominated collection of short stories.* Under the Udala Trees *(2015) is her first novel.*

gay event, the two witness one of their lesbian friends being caught and killed. Upon Ndidi's subsequent request that Ijeoma try being with a man, Ijeoma marries her childhood friend Chibundu. In the aftermath of her decision, a feeling of discontent grows in Ijeoma, forcing her to reckon her identity with the reality of who can love, once and for all.

The themes that underlie *Under the Udala Trees* are reminiscent of Okparanta's previous book, *Happiness, Like Water* (2013). Although *Happiness, Like Water* is a collection of short stories, it too focuses on religion, forbidden love, and African female protagonists whose voices are stifled. *Under the Udala Tree* is also akin to its predecessor in that its literary style and format are crafted more like a collection of short stories than a mainstream novel. Okparanta divides the novel's narrative into six parts, each of which comprises a collection of chapters. The chapters are atypically short, some no longer than half a page, and are comparable to vignettes. Ultimately, the chapters' truncated length allow Okparanta to effectively cover the expanse of her protagonist's life by capturing only Ijeoma's most pivotal moments. This stylistic choice proves to be an effective vessel for a coming-of-age story.

Okparanta has stated that her decision to set *Under the Udala Trees* during the Nigerian civil war was influenced by her own mother's experiences, who was not only a child at the time but also lost her father to the conflict. In addition to having personal significance, Okparanta's decision to depict Nigeria in an era of turmoil ends up providing readers with an evocative parallel to Ijeoma's own journey. Just as Nigeria is a newly independent nation attempting to forge an identity for itself in the context of the modern world, Ijeoma is also struggling to define herself. Furthermore, the early setting of a civil war becomes an effective metaphor for the conflict that Ijeoma must endure throughout her life. A civil war, after all, comprises two opposing forces within the same homeland. As Nigerians are fighting fellow Nigerians, Ijeoma and her mother are at odds. Like Nigerian writers Chimamanda Ngozi Adichie and Chinua Achebe, Okparanta is successful in leveraging Nigerian history to explore the human condition.

The reception of *Under the Udala Trees* has been predominantly positive. Ubiquitous among reviews has been praise for Okparanta's elegant, moving prose. In *Kirkus Reviews*, Okparanta's writing is described as being "rich in the beautiful intimacies of people who love each other." In addition to her ability to capture the significance and beauty of love in underrepresented communities, Okparanta has also been commended for her authentic depiction of the threat of societal violence on the human psyche.

Beyond its literary strengths, *Under the Udala Trees* has also been identified by critics writing for the *New York Times* and the *Guardian* as a book with a powerful message. This is largely because of Okparanta's decision to explore the controversial issue of homosexuality in Nigeria. As stated directly by Okparanta in her author's note for *Under the Udala Tree*, same-sex relationships have been criminalized in Nigeria since 2014, with perpetrators serving up to fourteen years in prison. Okparanta's willingness to explore the issue and challenge prejudice has been described as both courageous and compassionate. As the heroine faces such societal obstacles, Ijeoma has also been a highlight among reviews of *Under the Udala Trees*, with critics citing her unique voice as one of the novel's strongest components. In a review for the *Guardian*, Anjali Enjeti described Ijeoma as a richly complex character who is "equal parts daring, desperate, and determined" and commends her spirit and self-love.

Perhaps one of the few criticisms that could be made of *Under the Udala Trees* is that the novel can at times feel derivative. Although not necessarily a negative criticism, Carol Anshaw for the *New York Times* noted in her review that Ijeoma's story closely aligns to 1950s American lesbian novels by running "the gauntlet of being queer in a benighted society." Ijeoma's journey to discovery and love may hit many of the traditional plot points, however, it is still powerful in the fact that it authentically represents an experience shared by countless LBGTQ Nigerians without a voice. Furthermore, it provides an essential addition to the slow-growing library of international LBGTQ literature. As a well-crafted, moving piece of literature, *Under the Udala Trees* achieves Okparanta's goal in providing LBGTQ Nigerian citizens a place and a voice in history. With lyrical prose and a captivating heroine, *Underneath the Udala trees* is an honest, affecting read.

Emily E. Turner

Review Sources

Anshaw, Carol. Rev. of *Under the Udala Trees*, by Chinelo Okparanta. *New York Times*. New York Times, 23 Oct. 2015. Web. 11 Jan. 2016.

Enjeti, Anjali. "Love in the Time of Biafra." Rev. of *Under the Udala Trees*, by Chinelo Okparanta. *Guardian*. Guardian News and Media, 24 Sept. 2015. Web. 11 Jan. 2016.

Rev. of *Under the Udala Trees*, by Chinelo Okparanta. *Kirkus*. Kirkus, 22. Sept. 2015. Web. 11 Jan. 2016.

Uprooted

Author: Naomi Novik (b. 1973)
Publisher: Del Rey (New York). 448 pp.
Type of work: Novel
Time: A fantastical past
Locale: The kingdom of Polnya

Fantasy novelist Naomi Novik, best known for her sprawling Temeraire series, pens her first stand-alone novel, a fairy tale called Uprooted.

Principal characters:

AGNIESZKA, a teenage girl with special powers, chosen from her village to serve the Dragon

KASIA, her best friend

THE DRAGON, a.k.a. Sarkan, a 150-year-old wizard with the body of a young man

PRINCE MAREK, the arrogant, swashbuckling prince of the kingdom

"Bewitching." —Gregory Maguire, author of *Wicked*

(Courtesy of Del Rey)

Naomi Novik, a novelist who used to design computer games, is best known for her best-selling Temeraire series, a fantastical alternate telling of the Napoleonic Wars with dragons. Fans of Novik who might assume that dragons play a major part in her new stand-alone novel, *Uprooted*, would be right. However, in this fairy tale, there is only one Dragon, and he does not have scales. The "Dragon" is, instead, a powerful wizard who lives in a castle on the side of a mountain—a literal ivory tower crammed full of books. Every ten years, he descends into the valley to select a teenage girl to act as his servant. The arrangement is strange but apparently necessary. The Dragon protects the people from the evil Wood, and in turn, the valley must bear this periodic selection. The people of the valley are uncertain what happens to the abducted teenagers; the ones who do return do not stay long and usually move far away from the valley.

Agnieszka ("ag-NYESH-kah"), a chronically ill-kempt teenager from the valley, is one of the girls old enough to face selection, but she is not worried about being chosen. However, she is worried about her best friend, the perfect and lovely Kasia, who, from a young age, seemed destined to be chosen. But the Dragon does not choose Kasia. He appears in the valley from thin air; he is distant and disdainful of the people who live there, as are most of the wealthy or powerful in the kingdom, and hardly takes the time to look the girls in the face. Surprisingly, despite being 150 years old, he looks no more than twenty-five. The Dragon selects Agnieszka, and before she can even say good-bye to her family, he pulls her through the air and into his tower.

At this point, some readers will expect the story to follow an arc similar to *Beauty and the Beast*, as did Kate Nepveu, who reviewed *Uprooted* for the science-fiction and fantasy website Tor.com. However, the story moves in a surprising direction. After a few tortuous weeks with the Dragon—who is loath to see Agnieszka, much less sleep with her—Agnieszka discovers that she has magical powers. The Dragon saw her potential and chose her, against his will, because in the kingdom of Polnya—a thinly veiled, medieval-esque version of Poland—it is against the law to let a wizard go untrained. Yet *Uprooted* is not a tale about academic wizardry, either; once Novik sets the plot in motion, it barrels forward with the force of its own momentum. Novik is a devilishly skilled storyteller and an even more skillful world builder. Agnieszka's journey takes her off to the royal court of Polnya and the deeply evil Wood.

Early in the book, the "walkers," which look like enormous twig insects, come for Kasia. The walkers carry away people who have wandered too close to the Wood and, as Agnieszka soon learns, close them up in heart-trees to feed the Wood's evil. Being young and brash in her newfound magic, Agnieszka recklessly goes into the Wood alone and, against all odds, saves Kasia. But something is not right. Kasia seems like herself, but something in her eyes suggests otherwise. The Dragon and Agnieszka eventually discover that they must cast an important spell to effectively "exorcise" Kasia. While the spell is being cast, Agnieszka looks deep into Kasia's soul, seeing her fear and, surprisingly, her jealousy of Agnieszka. Once the unsavory aspects of their friendship are laid bare, their bond strengthens, and Kasia becomes an important part of Agnieszka's struggle against the Wood. It is rare for a novel, particularly one in the fantasy genre, to explore female friendship in such a fresh and surprising way. Agnieszka's love for Kasia consistently spurs her to action: to go into the Wood, to cast a powerful spell, to leave the safety of the tower, and, finally, to defeat the Wood. The Dragon is more learned than Agnieszka, but Novik suggests that there is more to magic than spells in books, and that Agnieszka's loyalty is a powerful force in itself. Though Novik's narrative touches on issues of class, gender, power, and violence, at its heart is the friendship between Agnieszka and Kasia.

Novik's descriptions of magic and how it functions are visceral and occasionally even sexual. When, for example, Harry Potter casts a spell, he simply mutters a few words; for the wizards in *Uprooted*, magic is a well of energy that occasionally runs dry and must be replenished. The magic in Ursula K. Le Guin's classic novel *A Wizard of Earthsea* (1968) is similarly described, but casting—and maintaining—a spell in Le Guin's world requires an enormous amount of mental control, whereas the magic in Novik's world is more physical. When Agnieszka learns her first spell, an enchantment that transforms what she is wearing, the act of summoning the small amount of magic required leaves her in an "aching fog." Over time, her strength improves, and she gets to know the "feel" of her magic like a limb. Each wizard's magic is specific and described in semi-tangible terms. The Dragon's

Naomi Novik is an award-winning novelist best known for her Temeraire series, a fantastical alternate history in which dragons are used as weapons in the Napoleonic Wars. Uprooted, *her first stand-alone novel, has been optioned for film.*

magic is precise and cool like water; Agnieszka's magic is warm, lush, and improvisational like jazz, or, as she describes it, like foraging for berries. Sometimes the magic flows like a river; other times it builds up and outward like a fire. Novik is able to evoke such strangeness easily. In one scene, Agnieszka and the Dragon work to build an illusion together—a rose garden—to see what will happen (wizards do not usually cast spells together). The scene demonstrates the growing power of their partnership and also their budding romance:

> I shut my eyes and felt out the shape of his magic: as full of thorns as his illusion, prickly and guarded. I started to murmur my own spell, but I found myself thinking not of roses but of water, and thirsty ground; building underneath his magic instead of trying to overlay it. I heard him draw a sharp breath, and the sharp edifice of his spell began grudgingly to let mine in. The rose between us put out long roots all over the table, and new branches began to grow.

Uprooted is a deeply satisfying book, even for those who might hesitate to pick up a fantasy novel. In writing the book, Novik was inspired by Polish fairy tales, but readers should be aware that *Uprooted* is not a children's tale. Novik's scares are psychological and disturbing, and her love story is unabashedly physical. Its course is unexpected, and its characters are unusually complex. Books with intricate plots are sometimes written at the expense of explicating characters' internal feelings about the choices they make. However, Novik engages with fairy-tale tropes rather than taking them for granted, opening up a host of existential questions. Wizards live for hundreds of years, but what does it really mean to outlive your friends and family? The knights must defend the king, but what does it mean to ask another person to die on your behalf? Even the story's antagonists—first Prince Marek, who tries to rape Agnieszka, and then the mysterious Wood Queen—are written with an empathetic hand. Their stories are just as complex as Agnieszka's.

Novik's pacing is commendable, but even at four-hundred-plus pages, certain moments, such as the final showdown with the Wood, feel harried. (By contrast, Novik has spread her Temeraire series over nine novels, the last of which will be released in 2016.) Particularly, Agnieszka's relationship with the Dragon and her own ascent as a powerful wizard could have been given room to grow. The romance feels less urgent than the friendship between the two women, and Agnieszka's transition from the "aching fog" of casting a simple spell to literally pulling a bolt of lightning out of the sky seems suspiciously swift. Then again, swiftness is one of the defining characteristics of a fairy tale. Philip Pullman, author of the His Dark Materials series, wrote in his book of retold tales from the Brothers Grimm, "Swiftness is a great virtue in the fairy tale. A good tale moves with a dreamlike speed from event to event, pausing only to say as much as is needed and no more."

Molly Hagan

Review Sources

El-Mohtar, Amal. "Friendship, Magic and Danger Blossom in *Uprooted*." Rev. of *Uprooted*, by Naomi Novik. *NPR*. NPR, 24 May 2015. Web. 27 Oct. 2015.

Nepveu, Kate. "Naomi Novik's *Uprooted* Isn't the Book I Expected—It's Better." Rev. of *Uprooted*, by Naomi Novik. *Tor.com*. Macmillan, 10 June 2015. Web. 27 Oct. 2015.

Rogers, Mac. "In the Tower of the Dragon." Rev. of *Uprooted*, by Naomi Novik. *Slate*. Slate Group, 4 June 2015. Web. 27 Oct. 2015.

Trendacosta, Katharine. "*Uprooted* Is a Perfect and Original Defense of the Power of Folklore." Rev. of *Uprooted*, by Naomi Novik. *Io9*. Gawker Media, 2 June 2015. Web. 27 Oct. 2015.

The Visiting Privilege

Author: Joy Williams (b. 1944)
Publisher: Alfred A. Knopf (New York). 512 pp.
Type of work: Short fiction
Time: Mid-twentieth century to 2015
Locales: United States, Europe

The Visiting Privilege is a collection of short stories from the acclaimed American author Joy Williams. It is a thematic grouping of thirty-three older stories, some of which were written in the 1970s, as well as thirteen brand-new ones from the author.

(Courtesy of Alfred A. Knopf)

Joy Williams has often been described as an "author's author." Much of her work has a dispassionate, clinical, observational feel to it. While she writes about such highly emotionally charged topics as mental illness, death, adultery, alcoholism, and murder, Williams does not pass judgment, nor does she paint her narratives with salacious vocabulary or shocking details that would turn her stories into crude potboilers. Williams has the respect of critics and the admiration of fellow writers because her text is so clean and precise. Each carefully crafted word tells a tale, and her skill is great enough that a minimally described incident can resonate with maximum power.

In *The Visiting Privilege,* an overriding theme is the acceptance that humankind can wreak havoc wherever two or more people gravitate together. Williams has a penchant for animals, and she often uses them as symbols of how people cause damage to those helpless creatures that are dependent upon them. She does not scold or harangue. Instead, she merely presents men and women who should know better but do not behave as though they do. Throughout this collection of short stories, much of the action and the dialogue feel as if they have been transcribed from a documentary or a hidden security camera. A conversation or a narrator's aside can pack a wallop because a simply stated snippet contains enormous weight when measured against the plot that surrounds it.

One of the collection's most chilling entries is "The Mother Cell," which focuses on a group of women who meet and discuss their lot in life. Each woman is the mother of a high-profile murderer. These women gather to bare their psyches and expose their souls, but they do so in a very controlled and matter-of-fact manner. In this tale, Williams shares how the deeds of their children reaped both criminal persecution and public adoration, and touches on the effect of the murderers' incarceration on their pets, which then needed new homes: "There were hundreds of people out there who keenly wanted murderers' pets and by their very ambition and craving were utterly inappropriate as adopters. Sometimes these pets' stories ended badly too."

So many of the animals that populate the pages are dispatched without much fanfare or sorrow. The same holds true for the human characters. Many of them meet their ends with nary a tear shed, nor an understanding of why they lived upon this earth in the first place. The unnamed narrator of "The Bridgetender" reflects on a young woman who caught his passing fancy and then seemingly vanished. He speculates whether she might have met her end via shark attack, falling off a sandbar, or some other unknowable means. In a plainspoken but mesmerizing way, he tells readers, "I don't know what it was she gave me. Maybe she even took something away. And I don't really even know if she's dead and it's me sitting here in the pilothouse or if I was the one who's been dead all the while and she's still going on back there on the gulf with all them birds."

A bridge between the reality of life and the possibilities afforded by dreaming is covered not only in "The Bridgetender" but in "Shepherd" as well. In this short story, which appeared in a prior collection, an unnamed woman tries to come to grips with the death of her beloved German shepherd. She is engaged to a seemingly well-meaning fiancé, but readers immediately sense she will not make it down the aisle with this man. The bereaved protagonist, who is merely known as "the girl," shares her offhand observation that animals are "closer to God than we are," which she then undercuts by concluding that "they are lost to him." In a flashback to when she first met her shepherd as a puppy, the girl recalls that the breeder was a former priest, and the act of selecting a dog becomes more of an intimate, self-revelatory confession. The onetime priest advises her, "We are all asleep and dreaming, you know. If we could ever actually comprehend our true position, we would not be able to bear it." The girl is in awe of this breeder—a wise man who, in his own godlike way, has created the canine that will become her life's companion. She immediately senses what he is theorizing. She excitedly tells him, "The ways that others see us is our life."

The characters that come to life via Williams's imagination function as cautionary examples to the readers. The bad behavior of these people—or, at best, their unintentional, misguided actions—serves as a template for how neighbors should not treat one another. Her keenly observed text shows how friends can often morph into rivals. The collection's title story, "The Visiting Privilege," previously published in 2004, details a woman who, in the hands of another author, might be conjured as an altruistic, selfless friend. Donna ritualistically visits her friend Cynthia, who is a patient at Pond House, receiving treatment for depression. As Williams tells her readers in the story's second paragraph, Donna could "scarcely imagine what she had done with herself before Cynthia had the grace to get herself committed" there. This is very emblematic of Williams's worldview, where characters are not well adjusted, wholesome, or filled with good intentions. In Williams's world, heroes and villains, saints and sinners, the good and the bad, are all hanging on to their existence by a thread of quiet desperation.

Donna is never more alive than when she is interacting with her friend and Pond House's other patients. Her desire to be of service to these marginalized women stems not from charity but from a deep-seated need to have a purpose and to belong. It is telling that upon visiting the women's ward, Donna immediately pretends that one of the oldest patients is her own mother and cultivates a symbiotic relationship with this old woman. In Williams's short story, a visitor to a psychiatric facility might just be one inexplicable thought away from her own future incarceration, or even from joining a funeral procession to an unknown person's grave.

A headlong rush to the grave—to the principal characters' unavoidable demise—is tackled in the collection's concluding story, "Craving." Denise and Steadman are two lost souls who slosh their ways through their days by drinking excessively and engaging in childish pranks. They are both tortured at night, unable to sleep and ill equipped to deal with the nothingness and repetition of their lives. When they venture into a home for rent and encounter a cleaning woman, Denise is intrigued by the house-keeper's dog, who keeps her company as she works. When the hound tries to bite Denise's hands, which are useless and in a cast, the cleaning lady disciplines her dog. Denise, however, tells the woman not to curtail the dog's behavior. She sincerely points out that dogs do not live as long as humans and therefore should be allowed their pleasures. Little do Denise and her drinking buddy Steadman

Joy Williams is the author of four novels and four collections of short stories. She is a recipient of the Rea Award for the Short Story and the Strauss Living Award from the American Academy of Arts and Letters. She was elected to the American Academy in 2008.

realize, but this will be their last stop, too. Their seemingly unending spree of drinking and self-abuse will come to a crashing end via an out-of-control joyride into a headlong collision.

The Visiting Privilege received widespread praise from reviewers. Critics were especially impressed by the fact that Williams, seventy-one years old at the time of the book's publication, has not rested on her laurels. Rather than releasing a book that is a retrospective of her work over the previous forty-plus years, Williams chose to create thirteen new stories to round out the compendium. Reviewers pointed out that her macabre sense of humor and jaundiced eye regarding human flaws and foibles have not diminished over time. Her work continues to be that of a master storyteller who does not rely on bells and whistles to create character sketches that are filled with memorable moments and perceptive narration.

One of the stories that garnered the most praise is 2015's "The Girls." Critics were impressed by how Williams managed to build suspense in a story that is ten pages long. The girls of the title are actually women, but they live in a pampered, cossetted bubble of prolonged childhood. Williams tells readers that they are thirty-one and thirty-two years old, but they do not really like the idea of marking one's ages with birthdays. They hate to be reminded that they have separate birth dates. The girls have a pair of menacing cats, who are uncontrollable forces of nature. No songbirds or other backyard creatures are safe while their cats are allowed to roam free. Rather than curtailing their cats' lethal ways, the girls cover for their brutal behavior. They lie and tell their "mommy" and "daddy" that the cats would never even harm a fly.

An Episcopal priest mourning the loss of his male companion and a female house-guest named Arleen, whom the girls view as "dowdy" and of an "unspecified age," enter this bizarre family dynamic. The girls are just as savage as their cats, but rather than hunting field mice or birds, these sisters stalk their guests, delighting in pouncing on their weaknesses and exploiting their frailties. But the story's end shows that the hunters can often become the prey, as the girls are confronted with their arrogance and destructive ways. Their parents' houseguest, Arleen, proves to be anything but a frumpy spinster. She speaks truth to power and demands that the girls be banished from their comfortable dwelling. While the girls and their cats mistakenly thought they were ruling the garden and its populace, Arleen proves that paradise can be lost in a single, unsuspecting moment.

The Visiting Privilege begins with a quote from I Corinthians: "Behold, I tell you a mystery; We shall not all sleep, but we shall all be changed, / In a moment, in the twinkling of an eye . . ." Joy Williams chose the perfect piece of scripture to kick off this anthology. The characters in these forty-six stories are all chess pieces that the masterful writer moves about to encounter their fates with solemn surrender.

Stephanie Finnegan

Review Sources

Collins-Hughes, Laura. Rev. of *The Visiting Privilege*, by Joy Williams. *Boston Globe*. Boston Globe Media Partners, 5 Sept. 2015. Web. 19 Jan. 2016.

Frank, Joan. Rev. of *The Visiting Privilege*, by Joy Williams. *San Francisco Chronicle*. Hearst Communications, 11 Sept. 2015. Web. 19 Jan. 2016.

Marcus, Ben. Rev. of *The Visiting Privilege*, by Joy Williams. *New York Times.* New York Times, 27 Sept. 2015. Web. 19 Jan. 2016.

Zeidner, Lisa. "The Chillingly Honest World of Joy Williams." Rev. of *The Visiting Privilege*, by Joy Williams. *Washington Post*. Washington Post, 2 Sept. 2015. Web. 19 Jan. 2016.

Voyage of the Sable Venus

Author: Robin Coste Lewis
Publisher: Alfred A. Knopf (New York).
  160 pp.
Type of Work: Poetry

Robin Coste Lewis's National Book Award–winning debut collection of poems, Voyage of the Sable Venus, *features autobiographical poems as well as a seventy-nine-page narrative poem comprised entirely of titles and descriptions of pieces of Western artworks.*

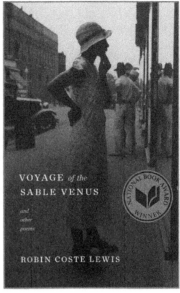

(Courtesy of Alfred A. Knopf)

There is a famous etching, made around 1800, called *Voyage of the Sable Venus from Angola to the West Indies* by Thomas Stothard. It features an African woman poised on a scallop shell, in the manner of Sandro Botticelli's *The Birth of Venus*. The woman is surrounded by cherubs, and in the corner, Triton, a god of the sea, leers at her while waving a British flag. The image is meant to illustrate the Middle Passage, the sea route by which African men, women, and children were transported in the manner of inanimate cargo to become slaves in Europe and the Americas—the image is also meant to be satirical; the word "sable" can mean black, but it also refers to a type of marten valued for its dark fur. The engraving spawned its own horrifying ode, in which the poet enumerates the pleasures of raping black women. Meanwhile, Botticelli's Venus was a goddess considered to be the apex of beauty.

For poet Robin Coste Lewis, the painting *Voyage of the Sable Venus* and its corresponding works represent a long history of humiliation, exploitation, and mutilation of black women's bodies extending back to ancient Greece and Rome. Lewis's narrative poem of the same name—the centerpiece of her lauded debut collection—transforms that brutality into something beautiful. She resurrects the women of the past, giving them back their limbs and names, elevating them to the status of gods. Lewis's writing is evocative and precise, and her seventy-nine-page "Voyage of the Sable Venus" demonstrates an extraordinary level of craftsmanship. Each word in the poem is culled from a Western work of art commenting on a black woman's body. According to a strict set of rules enumerated in the book, Lewis jumbles titles, catalog entries, and exhibit descriptions to fashion a narrative that spans over forty thousand years. The epic is bookended by poems about Lewis's own life and body.

Lewis earned her MFA in poetry from New York University and also holds a master's degree in Sanskrit and comparative religious literature from Harvard Divinity

School. *Voyage of the Sable Venus* is her first collection of poems, and in 2015, it became the first debut collection to win the National Book Award for Poetry in over forty years. Critics praised Lewis's ingenuity and her facility at reappropriating language to subtly transform images, both tender and grotesque. "Plantation," the collection's first poem, is "an extended allegory on race, desire, sexuality, and repression," Lewis told Nicole Sealey for PEN America, and a thesis statement for the collection as a whole. In it, two lovers dance between the pleasures of intimacy and the pain of the past. First, the speaker glosses over that pain by "decorating the bars" of the cage in which the two find themselves. Lewis writes: "We laughed when I said *plantation*, / fell into our chairs when I said *cane*."

The speaker's lover is, by turns, an intimidating "prancing black buck" and an innocent "small high yellow girl"—two sides of the same racial trope, Dan Chiasson noted for the *New Yorker*—and then a teenager wielding a "glorious steel cock under your skirt." The intimacy between the lovers has become weaponized; desire has become another instrument of oppression. Lewis writes:

> And I hoped
>
> you liked the fresh, pleasant taste
> of juiced cane. You pulled
>
> my pubic bone toward you. I didn't
> say, *It's still broken;* I didn't tell
>
> you, *There's still this crack.* It was sore,
> but I stayed silent because you were smiling.

Lewis focuses on her own body in the autobiographical poem, "On the Road to Sri Bhuvaneshwari." The poem, written in five parts, describes a visit to Uttar Pradesh, a province in northern India. Lewis visits a valley, where rice farms are carved into the hillsides like "terraced balconies," and a Hindu temple where she contemplates Parvati, the goddess of love and fertility, who jumped into a fire to prove her purity to her tyrannical husband, Shiva. Pieces of her body were scattered across the mountaintops (Parvati's name means mountain) of Southeast Asia. Lewis juxtaposes the dismemberment of the goddess with a recollection about the birth of a stillborn water buffalo calf on the same

Poet Robin Coste Lewis has published her work in various magazines and literary journals. Voyage of the Sable Venus *is her first published collection. It won the National Book Award for Poetry in 2015.*

trip. It happened that Lewis and her crew of fellow American students were stopped in the road one night while a herd of water buffalo were passing. The students, and the nomadic people that were following the herd, waited until morning for the animal to give birth, and then, because the animal had never given birth before, to look at her dead calf so she would know what had happened to her. The anecdote bleeds into another, ten years later, when Lewis is nursing her newborn son. "On the Road to Sri Bhuvaneshwari" is about both the reclamation of the body and the miraculous fertility of the body. Lewis delicately stitches together the images of Parvati, the water buffalo and her son, and at the end of the poem, Lewis herself becomes a shape-shifter. Her unusual form reveals itself in the final image:

> For years, my whole body ran
> away from me. When I flew—charred—
> through the air, my ankles and toes fell
> off
> onto the peaks of impassable
> mountains.
>
> I have to go back
> to that wet black thing
> dead in the road. I have to turn around.
> I must put my face in it.
>
> It is my first time.
> I would not have it any other way.
> I am a valley of repeating
> verdant balconies.

Metamorphosis takes on a new meaning in Lewis's arresting "Voyage of the Sable Venus." The poem is prefaced with a prologue that explains the rules Lewis set for herself in creating the poem. Among other restrictions, Lewis did not allow herself to repeat titles (with one exception) and did not break up or rearrange individual titles, though she took liberties with capitalization, punctuation, and line breaks. The poem begins with two epigraphs, one of which is an invitation, from 1936, to a minstrel show at the Metropolitan Museum of Art; it is an encapsulated view of the poem as a whole, evidence that art and cultural institutions play a part in a larger system of oppression. The other epigraph is an excerpt from a letter in which a woman is "anxious to buy a small healthy negro girl." Lewis suggests that African Americans remain commodities in the Western world, if not bodily then culturally—though she makes a convincing argument that these are one and the same. She drives her point home early while simultaneously reanimating the women portrayed in the artworks. For example, here is the beginning of a poem constructed from artworks from ancient Greece and ancient Rome:

> Statuette of a Woman Reduced
> to the Shape of a Flat Paddle

Statuette of a Black Slave Girl
Right Half of Body and Head Missing

Were one to encounter these descriptions with their corresponding artworks, one might miss the horror inherent in the images themselves. Separated from the objects they describe, the descriptions become acts of violence. In another early piece of the poem, Lewis separates the object from what it depicts using two columns:

lamp

           in the form of

the head

           of a black perhaps

incense
shovel

           with a Negro head
           attached

to handle
a girl

           with long corkscrew
           curls
           round face wide
           flat nose and mouth

open

           and jutting forward
           to form

a spout

This particular part is among the most devastating in the poem. The images shift as the words drip down the page, and coalesce to form something nightmarish and strange. It is a powerful example of Lewis's ability to reappropriate language. With a light touch, she uses the same words to give life where once they took life away. "Voyage of the Sable Venus" is experimental in its concept, but employs traditional tools—line breaks, punctuation—to accomplish its goals.

Lewis's other poems are very good, if not as uniformly stunning as "Voyage of the Sable Venus." "Frame," about growing up in a rural area near white-owned farms, is propelled by a youthful energy. The speaker recalls the coldness of her white neighbors, learning to drive, and receiving her first library card. At the library, the speaker's mother encourages her to seek photographs of African Americans in which their bodies are not "burned," "bent," or "bleeding," like a photo of the body of Martin Luther King Jr. Invoking "Voyage of the Sable Venus," which directly precedes it, Lewis writes that the violence that surrounds images of black people, "taught us how English was really a type of trick math." Either you could be "a King / capable of imagining just one single dream," or "you could swing from a tree by your neck into the frame." In the poem "Lure," Lewis uses negation to paint a haunting portrait of a young girl abused by her grandfather. In her interview with Sealey, Lewis said that, along with "Plantation," "Lure" was one of the most daring poems she had ever written. Her approach in this particular piece, as she described it, seems indicative of her general approach to painful subjects. She said that she was interested in neither shock nor catharsis. Instead, she wanted the reader to play a part in the creation of meaning, and she wanted to "learn how to be tender with violence." Lewis's work is both inviting and challenging. It handles heartbreak and brutality with extraordinary care, giving richness to desolation.

Molly Hagan

Review Sources

Artierian, Diana. Rev. of *Voyage of the Sable Venus and Other Poems*, by Robin Coste Lewis. *Rumpus*. Rumpus, 20 Nov. 2015. Web. 21 Nov. 2015.

Chiasson, Dan. "Rebirth of Venus." Rev. of *Voyage of the Sable Venus and Other Poems*, by Robin Coste Lewis. *New Yorker*. Condé Nast, 19 Oct. 2015. Web. 21 Nov. 2015.

Deshpande, Jay. "Robin Coste Lewis' National Book Award Marks a Shift in How the Literary World Regards Black Poets." *Slate*. Slate, 20 Nov. 2015. Web. 21 Nov. 2015.

Garner, Dwight. "In Robin Coste Lewis's 'Voyage of the Sable Venus,' Poems on Race." Rev. of *Voyage of the Sable Venus and Other Poems*, by Robin Coste Lewis. *New York Times*. New York Times, 1 Dec. 2015. Web. 2 Dec. 2015.

Rev. of *Voyage of the Sable Venus and Other Poems*, by Robin Coste Lewis. *Publisher's Weekly*. PWxyz, 1 Oct. 2015. Web. 21 Nov. 2015.

War of the Foxes

Author: Richard Siken (b. 1967)
Publisher: Copper Canyon Press (Port
    Townsend, WA). 96 pp.
Type of work: Poetry
Time: Present day
Locale: United States

(Courtesy of Copper Canyon Press)

*War of the Foxes is the second collection of
poetry by Richard Siken, whose previous volume,* Crush, *won the Yale Series of Younger
Poets prize. The book returns repeatedly to
issues of artistic representation in general
and painting in particular, giving the book
a kind of developing coherence rare in volumes of collected lyric poems.*

Richard Siken's second book of poetry, *The
War of the Foxes*, might broadly be classified
as an entry in the surrealist tradition of contemporary American verse. It is, however,
conservative in its surrealism. Individual sentences usually make clear grammatical
and syntactical sense. The movement from one sentence to the next is often logical and
easy to follow. Siken does not rely excessively on bizarre, highly personal, or defiantly
impenetrable imagery. There is obvious wit and thoughtfulness involved in the composition of the poems, and particular sentences and passages are often memorable and
striking. In short, Siken has written a book that can appeal to a broad variety of tastes.
Some poems are more accessible than others, but rarely will readers feel completely
confused.

"Detail of the Hayfield," one of the shorter poems in the collection, encapsulates
some of the defining characteristics of Siken's style. Its last few lines read:

> Everyone needs a place.
>
> You need it for the moment you need it, then you bless it—
> *thank you soup, thank you flashlight—*
>
> and move on. Who does this? No one.

That final twist, which suddenly undoes the assertion that precedes it, typifies much
of Siken's writing. This tendency of the speaker to unexpectedly undercut a statement
just made adds some real suspense to Siken's poems: one often wonders what swerve

might be lying just up the road. For the most part, though, Siken's verse seems calm, understated, and rational, rather than histrionic or showy. Often, as in the poem above, it is not quite clear what it all means and how it all adds up, but rarely will readers be mystified by the grammar or syntax of individual sentences.

Some poems in the collection make more obvious and immediate sense. One of these is a poem titled "Three Proofs." The first section of this work is titled "Pablo Picasso, *Gertrude Stein*, 1905–6." Like many poems in *War of the Foxes*, this one deals with painting in general and with specific paintings in particular. It opens as follows:

> When she saw herself, finished, she said, *It doesn't look like*
> *me*. Picasso said, *It will*. Perhaps it will look like her
> because it is the document and will remain, while she is
> just a person who will fade. Now, when we think of her,
> we think of this painting.

The opening two sentences exemplify Siken's love of paradox. This particular paradox is all the more paradoxical since the person concerned about accurate representation is Gertrude Stein, one of the most abstract writers of all time. This poem is one of the many in the collection that explores such age-old issues as the impermanence of life, the potential permanence of art, and the ways representations shape our understanding of the supposedly "real." Indeed, the relationship between art (mainly painting; Siken is also a painter) and reality is one of the main preoccupations of *War of the Foxes*. This is established from the outset: the book's first poem, "The way the light reflects," begins with the lines "The paint doesn't move the way the light reflects, / so what's there to be faithful to?" Another poem, "Portrait of Fryderyk in Shifting Light," recounts the speaker's attempts to paint a portrait of a lover and his frustration at his failure to capture a good likeness. However hard the painter tries, there is "something wrong" with his subject's face, and in the end he gives up on the whole project: "I turned off the headlights of / my looking and let the animal get away," he says.

In many of his poems, Siken seems very much a philosophical poet, as interested in ideas themselves as in the ways those ideas are phrased. The language is stripped-down, plain, and simple almost to the point of being

uninteresting. Readers who are put off by this simplicity and like poems to play with language more may prefer poems such as "Love Song of the Square Root of Negative One," which combines Siken's philosophical musings and penchant for the unexpected with a more extensive use of poetic language. The interesting ideas are there, but so, too, are interesting diction, rhythms, imagery, syntax, and so on. This poem seems more obviously a poem and less simply a philosophical conundrum. Repetition is used emphatically and effectively. Personification adds to the poem's impact. Paradoxes such as "bloom without flower" enhance the impact of the work, as does the playful use of alliteration, assonance, near-rhymes, and internal rhymes. These last two can be seen in the lines "knot / without rope, song without throat in wingless flight, dark / boat in the dark night"; the near-rhyme of "rope" and "throat" and internal rhyme of "throat" and "boat" as well as "flight" and "night" give the poem a musical quality. Similes and metaphors abound, and Siken also uses variations on key ideas, stating them not just once but several times in different guises and thus making them all the more memorable. The poem is highly rhythmic—almost chant-like—and thus soars into a song-like beauty often absent from Siken's other works, such as "Detail of the Hayfield." "Love Song" is full of wordplay that makes readers want to go back to reread and rethink. It is compelling, verbally, in ways that other poems by Siken are perhaps not. Poems such as "Love Song" are hard to get out of one's head; they fascinate at least as much for their phrasing and sound effects as for their ideas. There is an almost hypnotic effect in the ways they are written, although the hypnosis here compels attention rather than putting the reader to sleep. The sheer number of verbs in this poem, along with the long, flowing, ever-unreeling lines, give the text a kind of immediately obvious energy that is lacking in many of the other poems in this collection.

More often, though, Siken is a quieter poet. He does not often insist, nor does he usually try to compel attention. Often his best poems achieve their best effects through low-key narration, as in a brief poem titled "The Museum," in which a couple goes to an art museum and the man gets "stuck looking / at a painting." He is entranced, but the woman cannot see whatever he sees in it, and he cannot articulate what that is. "He didn't know how to say it," the poem says. "Years later / he still didn't know how to say it, and she was gone." Their momentary disconnect over differing reactions to art becomes the moment "where everything changed," the beginning of the end for their relationship.

This poem might almost be called an "anti-sonnet." Whereas sonnets often record moments of beginning or developing love, this poem records just the opposite. It has fifteen lines, similar to a sonnet's traditional fourteen, and like a sonnet it presents a situation and then steps back to comment on it. But the poem is most effective as a simple narrative. The situation is one to which most readers will be able to relate. Most readers will be able to identify with the couple. The change that comes over their relationship, while strange in some ways, will seem archetypically familiar in others. In short, in poems such as this, Siken writes in ways that seem rooted in the most ancient forms of storytelling. Rather than locking himself in the basement or attic of his own peculiar, individual imagination, Siken greets readers at the front door and invites them into his poems. He reaches out to readers in ways that make them feel as if they are something other than mere spectators of strange goings-on. In poems like "The Museum," Siken welcomes readers into his works in ways that make the texts seem both welcoming and welcome.

Robert C. Evans

Review sources

Butts, Lisa. Rev. of *War of the Foxes*, by Richard Siken. *Iowa Review*. U of Iowa, 3
    Aug. 2015. Web. 21 Feb. 2016.
Day, Dalton. Rev. of *War of the Foxes*, by Richard Siken. *Adroit Journal*. Adroit
    Journal, Summer 2015. Web. 21 Feb. 2016.
Fargason, William. Rev. of *War of the Foxes*, by Richard Siken. *Southeast Review*.
    Southeast Review, n.d. Web. 21 Feb. 2016.
Howell, Eric. "To Set Something on Fire." Rev. of *War of the Foxes*, by Richard
    Siken. *Electric Literature*. Electric Lit, 29 June 2015. Web. 21 Feb. 2016.
Kaufman, Ellen. Rev. of *War of the Foxes*, by Richard Siken. *Library Journal* 140.3
    (2015): 106. Print.
Spruijt-Metz, Donna. Rev. of *War of the Foxes*, by Richard Siken. *Rumpus*. Rumpus,
    6 Mar. 2015. Web. 21 Feb. 2016.

The Watchmaker of Filigree Street

Author: Natasha Pulley (b. 1988)
Publisher: Bloomsbury (New York). 336 pp.
Type of work: Novel
Time: Late nineteenth century
Locales: London, England; Tokyo and surrounding areas, Japan

In her debut novel, Natasha Pulley blends historical fiction, science fiction, and fantasy to tell the story of a young man in an alternate Victorian Britain whose life is changed through his acquaintance with a mysterious watchmaker.

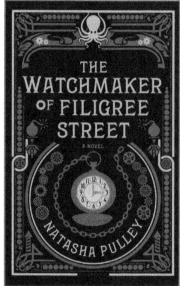

(Courtesy of Bloomsbury Publishing Plc.)

Principal characters:
NATHANIEL "THANIEL" STEEPLETON, a telegraph operator
GRACE CARROW, a would-be scientist studying at Oxford
AKIRA MATSUMOTO, Grace's friend at Oxford
KEITA MORI, a watchmaker

Steampunk fiction, which emerged in the 1980s, is a subset of historical fiction, bringing science fiction and fantasy elements into a nineteenth-century setting. Drawing on nineteenth-century works of speculative fiction by such authors as Jules Verne and H. G. Wells, steampunk often focuses on scientists and inventors and posits fantastical inventions that run on clockwork or steam. For example, William Gibson and Bruce Sterling's *The Difference Engine* (1991), credited with popularizing the genre, takes place in a world in which the inventor Charles Babbage succeeded in creating a working computer in the 1830s.

Natasha Pulley's debut novel, *The Watchmaker of Filigree Street*, focuses more on the possibilities of clockwork, a preoccupation that is reflected in the ingenious physical design of the novel itself. The black background of the cover is highlighted by various objects, including a pocket watch, picked out in gold and a color known as radium green, which was once used on the hands of watches. The endpapers portray a map of the partly imaginary neighborhood of the book. *The Watchmaker of Filigree Street* leaves room for potential sequels, though it functions equally well as a standalone novel. *Publishers Weekly* gave the book a starred review, calling it an "electrifying debut" and "a triumph of speculative fiction."

The novel does not employ a straightforward chronology. The twenty chapters comprising parts 1 and 2 open in 1883 in London. Chapter 6 diverts to Hagi, south of Tokyo, in April 1871. The action then moves back to London, now in 1884, where it stays for the remaining chapters. In part 3, the novel journeys briefly back to Tokyo in 1882 before returning to London in 1884 for the final ten chapters. These departures from strict chronological order are not jarring, however, but necessary to understand the plot.

One of Pulley's strengths as a writer is her ability to write interesting characters; she makes it easy and a pleasure to be caught up in their lives and to wish them well. The reader cheers as Thaniel Steepleton, prompted by the watchmaker Keita Mori, is pushed from his predictable, unfulfilling life as a telegraph operator in Whitehall, the center of British government. Thaniel is a talented musician with the gift of synesthesia—he hears sounds in colors. Grace Carrow, a prickly Oxford University student

© Jonathan Ring, used by permission of Bloomsbury Publishing)

The Watchmaker of Filigree Street *is Natasha Pulley's first novel. It is an international best seller and was named one of* Publishers Weekly's *best books of 2015.*

and scientist, is working on proving the existence of ether, setting up experiments and hoping to succeed where others have failed. Her life unexpectedly intertwines with Thaniel's after a chance meeting. Both of them, perhaps not coincidentally, own a watch that Mori made.

Mori anchors the book, in both Japan and London, with his interest in intricate things, such as his watches and a mechanical octopus he made as a pet. Katsu, the octopus, is charming, with a penchant for stealing socks and hiding in dresser drawers. Mori's watches are beautifully constructed as well as functional. The frequent descriptions of the watches and how they work are an important part of the novel's steampunk aesthetic.

As the novel opens, Thaniel returns to his cheerless apartment in a rooming house near a prison after work to find that his door is open, his dirty dishes washed, and the gift of a pocket watch is waiting on his bed. He thinks at first it is a birthday gift from his widowed sister, whom he has been supporting, but she denies it. Thus the first mystery of the novel begins: where did the gift originate, and why has it been given to him? Six months later, after the watch sounds an alarm just before a bomb goes off, Thaniel finds the watchmaker, Mori, and rents a room from him. The first mystery thus gives way to a second: the question of who constructed the bomb that destroyed Scotland Yard, one of the events in the book that is historical fact. Thaniel's superiors at Whitehall suspect Mori and use Thaniel to spy on him.

Helene Wecker wrote in a review for the *New York Times*, "Pulley's prose is strong and energetic, with a wry edge, and even the most minor characters are drawn precisely. They're anchored in an 1880s London that's solid and complex, with nods to the political and social issues of the day." Among those political and social issues Pulley slips into a good tale is the treatment and status of women. Grace Carrow, who appears as an additional narrative thread in chapter 3, must pose as a man, wearing a false mustache and borrowing clothing from her well-dressed Japanese friend Matsumoto, to research in the Bodleian Library, because women students unaccompanied by a male student are not permitted in the library. She requests books under the name of her cousin, Gregory Carrow, who graduated from Oxford much earlier. By reason of her family and social class she is destined for marriage, despite her avid pursuit of science. Grace makes what could arguably be the most important decision of her life based on reason and logic rather than on emotion. Like most women of the Victorian era, she does not have control over property. Although her aunt has left her a house, its ownership is really in trust, placed in the hands of her father and future husband. Despite her frustration with her lack of rights, however, she complains when her Matsumoto forces her to attend a suffrage meeting, mocking the domestic concerns and lack of critical thinking of the women.

Another issue that Pulley addresses is the prejudice against East Asian people in Britain at the time. For example, when Grace interrogates Alice, one of the maids, as to whether she has spoken to Mori, Alice replies, "I wouldn't speak to a Chinaman, they're dirty!" Later, she refers to him as "a horrid little Chinaman." Mori is well aware of the prejudice he faces. When Thaniel catches him placing his inventions safely in boxes to protect them during a police raid he knows is coming, he says, "Look . . . they're angry, and want to fit up the first likely-looking foreigner, so I'm going to be arrested." Matsumoto also encounters prejudice; he asks Grace to hail a cab, because they never stop for him. One of Grace's fellow students assumes Matsumoto is Grace's servant.

The book also deals with child labor. Children, especially orphans, are used to perform tasks that require small, nimble hands. The tiny links of watch chains for Mori's watches are made by a young orphan, Six, whom he rents from the workhouse by the day. The children, who are numbered but not otherwise named, are set to making the links, which the workhouse later throws away; the work was merely to keep the children busy.

The book speaks to concerns that touch the present as well. Terrorism is part of the plot, though in this case, the terrorists are an Irish republican group, Clan na Gael, planning violence against the British. (The group did and still does exist.) In the novel, the group is responsible for a bomb that goes off at Whitehall; the book can also be read as a whodunit, searching for the maker of the bomb, which relied on clockwork and thereby cast suspicion on Mori, the watchmaker of the title.

The question of free will and determinism is another issue that the novel takes up—but does not resolve. Mori says he can remember the future and takes action as a result of his seeing. Does he then also determine the outcome of Thaniel's actions? Again and again he intervenes, in seemingly small ways that change events, so that Grace begins to accuse him of controlling Thaniel as a watchmaker does a watch and suggests that he might be responsible for the bombing after all, or at least that he should have taken action if he knew the bomb was there.

All of these issues threaded into the plot do not impinge on the telling of a story worth reading. Pulley's command of language is impressive, with passages that please the eye and ear. To give one example from Thaniel's first meeting with Mori: "His thoughts were starting to take on a strange ring: they had shrunk from their usual size and now the ordinary attic that was his ordinary mind looked like a cathedral at night, with endless galleries and rafters lost in the dark and nothing but the echoes to show where they were."

Pulley also has a good grasp of how to pace the novel's action. For example, after an intense scene in which the police come to arrest Mori and to break up his shop while searching for a bomb, Mori and Thaniel go to a teashop in the faux Japanese village that has been erected in Knightsbridge. In her research, Pulley discovered that the neighborhood in London did have a Japanese Village exhibition at the time the novel is set. There, W. S. Gilbert and Arthur Sullivan (the only actual historical characters who appear in the novel) are working on a new operetta, *The Mikado*, to be performed for Japanese nobles. Thaniel has the chance to put a piano back in tune and to play again, a pleasure he had lost when he sold his piano to support his sister, while Mori drinks tea and reads the newspaper.

The novel relies on historical facts as well as on Pulley's imagination. The reader who understands the changing worlds of Japan and Britain in the nineteenth century experiences the work in a richer and deeper way. By carefully attending to the text, a reader could learn a great deal about the political realities of the late Victorian age. Pulley brings in not only Irish Republicanism and women's suffrage but also the Japanese government dismantling the shogun era and literally pulling down old castles. Brief allusions to the British war in present-day Sudan in Africa and fragile treaties between Britain and Japan ground the novel in the real life of the late nineteenth century. As Megan McArdle wrote in a starred review for *Library Journal*, "This delightful first novel is as impressive as a work of historical fiction, with its evocative details of nineteenth-century England on the cusp of technological and cultural revolutions, as it is a delicate fantasy with enough gadgetry to pull in the steampunk fans, and a mystery to boot."

Judy A. Johnson

Review Sources

McArdle, Megan M. Rev. of *The Watchmaker of Filigree Street*, by Natasha Pulley. *Library Journal* 15 May 2015: 57+. Print.

Rev. of *The Watchmaker of Filigree Street*, by Natasha Pulley. *Kirkus Reviews* 15 May 2015: 131. Print.

Rev. of *The Watchmaker of Filigree Street*, by Natasha Pulley. *Publishers Weekly* 23 Feb. 2015: 57. Print.

Wecker, Helene. Rev. of *The Watchmaker of Filigree Street*, by Natasha Pulley. *New York Times*. New York Times, 31 July 2015. Web. 22 Jan. 2016.

The Water Knife

Author: Paolo Bacigalupi (b. 1972)
Publisher: Alfred A. Knopf (New York).
371 pp.
Type of work: Novel
Time: The near future
Locale: The American Southwest

(Courtesy of Alfred A. Knopf)

The Water Knife *is a hard-boiled thriller set in a dystopian near future where catastrophic climate change has forced states in the arid American Southwest to compete, sometimes violently, for rapidly diminishing water resources.*

Principal characters:
ANGEL VELASQUEZ, a "water knife," a hired gun who works for the Southern Nevada Water Authority
CATHERINE CASE, the head of the Southern Nevada Water Authority
LUCY MONROE, a crusading journalist in drought-stricken Phoenix, Arizona
MARIA VILLAROSA, a young refugee from Texas who hopes to escape north

Paolo Bacigalupi is an award-winning science-fiction writer who has earned wide-ranging respect outside his field. In *The Water Knife* he turns to the important and timely subject of climate change and water conservation. With this book Bacigalupi blurs genres and experiments with the action novel. The results are interesting, but decidedly uneven.

Bacigalupi's page-turner is a technically competent but often nasty neo-noir. *The Water Knife* revels in sadism and other commercial kicks. Blood splatters repeatedly. The leading female characters are at different times undressed and tortured. Bacigalupi has serious concerns about the environment, but in *The Water Knife* these are modulated through the conventions of a hard-boiled thriller. As a result, the action often seems to win out over the ideas. Science-fiction writers have been sermonizing in adventure stories since the days of H. G. Wells. Bacigalupi continues the tradition with the gusto of a direct-to-cable B movie.

A curious element of the book is its portrayal of Texans displaced by natural disasters and forced to wander, unwanted and persecuted, through the Road Warrior–like wasteland of Bacigalupi's imagination. Bacigalupi seems to take satisfaction in describing the comeuppance of one of the nation's most conservative, but also economically dynamic, states. His downtrodden Texans congregate in revival tents, praying for an illusory salvation, while fingering their ubiquitous shooting irons. These are "bitter clingers" on steroids. In the novel these armed and evangelical Texans are sardonically referred to as "Merry-Perrys," presumably a reference to long-time Texas governor Rick Perry. This schadenfreude concerning the degradation of Texans may appeal to a certain demographic, but its assumptions about the self-evident iniquity of the denizens of the Lone Star state will probably fall flat in other quarters. Bacigalupi's Texans are emblematic of a monochromatic ideological certainty that pervades the novel.

Bacigalupi's near future is didactically dystopian. Offstage, coastlines have been submerged, and wild storms ravage the landscape. Ground zero for the book is the American Southwest, which is paying the price of thoughtless development in an inhospitable environment. Global warming has dried up much of the precious water that sustained civilization in that arid region. The water levels of lakes and rivers are declining. Aquifers are drained. Endemic drought has inevitably led to societal collapse. Drug cartels have seized control of northern Mexico. The social contract in the United States has been rewritten. Federalism has reemerged with a vengeance. The Western states, competing, sometimes violently, for scarce water resources, have closed off their borders, patrolling them with National Guard units. The "Guardies" have become genuine state armies. Added to the mix are independently funded militias that make up in brutality what they lack in polish. As government falters, private enterprise has stepped in. While towns and farms off the water grid wither away, lavish, self-enclosed, corporate-run "arcologies" cater to the needs of the fortunate few. On the cutting edge of the development of these artificial environments are the Chinese. Readers are told that the Chinese foresaw the shape of things to come and took appropriate steps to respond. This practical efficiency is compared invidiously to the messy Americans, who dithered around democratically and missed the ecological boat. Totalitarians are so much better at getting things done. In the old days they made the trains run on time. In the future of *The Water Knife* they build really neat pleasure domes.

The Chinese have some competition in Catherine Case, the CEO of the Southern Nevada Water Authority, based in Las Vegas. Case is a tough and utterly ruthless visionary, who is building her own empire of arcologies. To attain her ends she does not hesitate to use military force to shut down competitors. She also employs an elite cadre of enforcers known as "water knives." These expert gunmen have a license to kill. One of Case's most lethal and loyal water knives is Angel Velasquez. A former gangbanger whom Case rescued from jail, Angel has matured into a hybrid of Mike Hammer and James Bond. He is a thoroughly stock character, despite the fact that in this science-fictional setting he wears high-tech ballistic clothing rather than a trench coat or Savile Row suits and speeds around in a souped-up Tesla rather than an Aston Martin. With his patented hard-boiled demeanor, he keeps the proceedings of this speculative thriller firmly linked to comfortably familiar ground. Bacigalupi works hard to "humanize" Angel with a traumatic past and the usual codelike scruples about his dirty business that keeps him safely above the level of a mere brute. A few quirks are thrown in for good measure. Readers learn that Angel likes to watch a TV show called *Undaunted*, about a lone hero named Relic Jones who rescues refugee migrants in the Texan badlands, a none-too-subtle hint to readers that underneath it all he really is a good guy in the grand Wild West tradition.

The main action of the novel is set into motion when Catherine Case sends off Angel to investigate strange doings in Phoenix, Arizona. While Las Vegas, though visibly contracting, maintains some semblance of order, Phoenix, rapidly running low on water, is descending into chaos. Outside of a precariously maintained downtown and a Chinese arcology, Phoenix is a Hobbesian nightmare. Crime is rife, with murders too frequent to merit much official attention. Adding to the hellishness is the pervasive smoke from distant Californian forest fires and dust storms so violent that special breathing gear becomes everyday equipment.

Phoenix is exhibit A in Bacigalupi's indictment of current complacency about climate change. At different points in *The Water Knife*, characters lament that people in the past had failed to see and act on what was manifestly obvious. Only the prescient Chinese adequately prepared for the new end times. Two characters in the novel demonstrate almost cultic reverence for old copies of Marc Reisner's *Cadillac Desert: The American West and its Disappearing Water* (1986). Reisner's book is an exhaustive account of the ways that Western settlement and development from the nineteenth through the twentieth centuries strained water supplies and the natural environment. *Cadillac Desert* inspired a four-part documentary on PBS, and has become a secular bible for critics of Western water policy. Whatever one's opinions on global warming and climate change, it is certainly arguable that it was not prudent to build a large city like Phoenix in the middle of a desert. During the Medieval Warm Period of 950–1250 AD, people in Europe thrived because warmer temperatures in their temperate climate zone lengthened growing seasons and increased food supplies. Among other things, they then built Gothic cathedrals. At roughly the same time, during the twelfth century, ancestral Puebloan peoples who lived in the arid area around Chaco Canyon in New Mexico were forced to leave their homes because of climate change and an extended drought. Variations in climate will accentuate regional resource issues. Reisner makes the case that one does not need catastrophic climate change to expect trouble some day in the Southwest. Bacigalupi combines Reisner's warning with an extreme take on global warming, giving us Phoenix as Babylon and a gonzo jeremiad.

Paolo Bacigalupi is an award-winning author of science-fiction stories and novels, including Pump Six and Other Stories *(2008),* The Windup Girl *(2009), and* The Drowned Cities *(2012). His debut young-adult novel,* Ship Breaker *(2010), won the Printz Award and was a National Book Award finalist.*

When Angel arrives in Phoenix, his story intertwines with those of Lucy Monroe, a crusading journalist chronicling the decline and fall of the city, and Maria Villarosa, a young refugee from Texas desperate to make her way north. Lucy has had great success in the past, including a Pulitzer Prize on her resume. Now she finds herself unable to leave the dying metropolis, writing what she calls "collapse porn" as she posts grisly accounts of crime scenes. Maria is essentially a serf, forced to pay a local crime lord taxes for her modest living quarters and on her equally modest earnings. This boss is so over the top in his sensationally cinematic depravity that he maintains a pack of hyenas to which he feeds anyone who crosses him.

Bacigalupi follows the structural formula of the genre he has adapted to his purposes. Chapters focusing on Angel, Lucy, and Maria alternate, tracing their separate trajectories until these bring them together. In addition to the sex and violence, Bacigalupi sprinkles in plenty of intrigue, backstabbing, and chases. As in any good hardboiled thriller since the days of Raymond Chandler, chapter settings run the gamut from the seamiest corners of the underworld to the opulent preserves of the hedonistic rich. Bacigalupi keeps the action rolling. Whether or not he intended to do so, his book reads like a candidate for a film adaption. The downside of this is that the moral substance of the novel is thin. The characters and situations are too stereotypical to lift the book to the level of serious literature, or to give it any emotional resonance. Preachiness overwhelms the plot. Once the story ends, the only thing that readers will likely remember is the horrific description of a drought-stricken Southwest. With a book as polemical as this, that may be enough for Bacigalupi.

Given that this is a science-fiction novel, some attention should be paid to Bacigalupi's evocation of an imagined world. He is strongest in his economic and sociological analysis of the Western states in extremis. His depiction of bureaucratic and corporate infighting is plausible; his descriptions of social decay match our expectations from *Mad Max* movies merged with the sad images broadcast from Syria and other global trouble spots. Bacigalupi has clearly learned a great deal from *Cadillac Desert*. He displays an impressive knowledge of the key rivers, reservoirs, lakes, and dams in the Southwest. These vital prizes in a struggle for diminishing water reserves are well-integrated into his cautionary tale. Where Bacigalupi is a bit disappointing is in his portrayal of the arcologies being constructed for the privileged in his "brave new world." A hard science-fictional breakdown of the engineering of an arcology is not really necessary in a diatribe about the disastrous consequences of global warming, but it would have been interesting to learn more about the future that characters like Catherine Case are attempting to build. Ultimately Bacigalupi's interests lie elsewhere.

While *The Water Knife* works as a sanguinary thriller, Bacigalupi conveys his message about climate change with the subtlety of a jackhammer. Snarky references to "Merry-Perrys" will probably limit the audience for the novel. Bacigalupi has succeeded in sounding a warning about a serious issue, but he could have written a much better book.

Daniel P. Murphy

Review Sources

Fann, Kelly. Rev. of *The Water Knife*, by Paolo Bacigalupi. *Booklist* 1 Nov. 2015: 70–71. Print.

McArdle, Megan M. Rev. of *The Water Knife*, by Paolo Bacigalupi. *Library Journal* 1 Mar. 2015: 56. Print.

Shippey, Tom. "Liquidity Crisis." Rev. of *The Water Knife*, by Paolo Bacigalupi. *Wall Street Journal* 30 May 2015: C8. Print.

Rev. of *The Water Knife*, by Paolo Bacigalupi. *Kirkus Reviews* 1 Mar. 2015: 112. Print.

Welcome to Braggsville

Author: T. Geronimo Johnson (b. 1970)
Publisher: William Morrow (New York).
384 pp.
Type of work: Novel
Time: Present
Locales: Berkeley, California; Braggsville,
Georgia

Welcome to Braggsville *is a satirical novel
about the state of race relations in the United
States. Four college students set out to draw
attention to racial injustice in a small Georgia town, in the process bringing both small-
town southern life and American academia
under the author's microscope.*

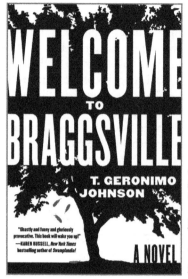

(Courtesy of HarperCollins)

Principal characters:
DARON DAVENPORT, a white small-town
   southerner in his second year at the University of California, Berkeley
LOUIS CHANG, his friend, a Malaysian student who aspires to be a standup comedian
CHARLIE COLE, his friend, a gay black student from Chicago
CANDICE CHELSEA, his friend, a white student from Iowa who claims to be part Native
   American
JO-JO KELLY VI, his best friend from back home in Braggsville

Welcome to Braggsville is the story of four friends from the University of California,
Berkeley, who set out to change the narrative about slavery and race in one southern
town. They have decided on a "performative intervention" as the capstone project for
an alternative history class they are taking; the idea appeals to their idealism and is
encouraged by their naïveté. Their destination is Braggsville, Georgia, the hometown
of protagonist Daron (sometimes spelled "D'aron") Davenport, where a Civil War
reenactment is held each year. The friends decide to stage a lynching there as a way of
confronting the townspeople with what African Americans suffered during and after
the Confederacy. They are encouraged by their professor, who tells them, "You can
force States' Rights to take a look in the mirror and they will not like what they see."

How the performative intervention is supposed to improve racial understanding
is unclear, especially when it becomes evident that the students know nothing about
the workings behind the scenes in this small, socially segregated southern town. With
scant experience in this type of endeavor, they are not prepared for events if all goes
well, and certainly not for when they do not. First Charlie backs out of his role as
the person to be lynched, and Louis, who is Malaysian, agrees to replace him—in
blackface. Then Daron must forgo his part in the action after his father forbids his

participation. A childhood friend of his, Jo-Jo, steps up to take Daron's part in what Jo-Jo has been made to believe is a simple prank. Things quickly turn as murky and confusing as in any comedy of errors.

Carol Memmott wrote in her review for the *Chicago Tribune* that "the staged lynching seems simple and safe, but that's where youthful folly comes into play." The person playing the victim is wearing a safety harness beneath his clothes to prevent him from actually being hanged. Of course, not all goes to plan. "When things go wrong," Memmott noted, "Johnson uses the incident to examine what it means to be a person of color in America, how women and gays are treated, and how the media sometimes exacerbate a tragedy to win readers and viewers."

The book takes a stark turn when the performance goes horribly wrong and one of the characters dies. The positive intentions of the four students are irretrievably lost in the ensuing police investigation, and the subsequent interrogations are portrayed as confrontations between generations and cultures. The students are shocked that reenactments still exist, black lawn jockeys still stand outside people's houses, and a town of only 712 people can still be divided by race; meanwhile, the residents of the town are every bit as appalled that anyone would question the honorable role that states' rights played in the Civil War. Johnson skillfully exposes the limitations of both these views. Writing for the *Washington Post*, reviewer Ron Charles called Johnson "a master at stripping away our persistent myths and exposing the subterfuge and displacement necessary to keep pretending that a culture built on kidnapping, rape and torture was the apotheosis of gentility and honor." Likewise, he described the book as "equally irritated with liberalism's self-righteousness" and with the four students who "imagine that their moral superiority and clever theatricality will somehow shame and cleanse the townspeople who witness the faux lynching."

The tragedy has additional consequences for Daron. Since he is from Braggsville, it is assumed he is the one who plotted the entire escapade. He has always been an outsider in his hometown, both for his academic achievement as well as for his perceived effeminacy, and those who have known him his whole life seem to accept his culpability and responsibility as givens. In fact, the plan was mainly Candice's idea, and Daron just went along with it. Ultimately, his involvement came down to the simple fact that he liked a girl with wild ideas and a dearth of experience. The reader feels sympathy for Daron because, as Charles wrote, Johnson "cradles this young man's innocence and sympathizes with his desperation to fit in," and Johnson's attitude toward Daron cannot help but influence the way the reader relates to the protagonist.

Certainly Daron has had more than enough to contend with since arriving at Berkeley. For the first time in his life, he is not the smartest one in the class; in fact, he worries that maybe he was accepted by mistake. His family is counting on him to graduate from college. He decides that if he fails because he has not studied, it really is not his fault. But Charlie helps him study and learn how to do more than skate by on being smart. As a result, Daron's grades improve, and by the time he meets with his counselor and she tells him that he deserves to be there, he cannot help but cry in relief at the news. He wants to have a triumphant return to the tiny town he left behind: the town with lawn jockeys and a Confederate flag wrapped around the water tower; the town where the African American residents keep to themselves on the other side of town because they choose to; the town where there is a reenactment of a Confederate battle each and every year on Old Man Donner's property, where friends meet at the Waffle House for breakfast, and where the Civil War was unquestionably a battle for states' rights.

> *T. Geronimo Johnson is the author of two novels. His first novel,* Hold It 'til It Hurts *(2012), was a finalist for the 2013 PEN/Faulkner Award. His second novel,* Welcome to Braggsville, *was long-listed for the 2015 National Book Award.*

Daron is understandably distraught at the outcome of this triumphant return. In the aftermath of the tragedy, he is forced to see his town anew, and in the process he discovers that he has never actually seen his town at all. He learns things about the meetings at the hunting lodge, meetings he had been vaguely aware of but had never thought to question, and realizes that the justice he thinks is being meted out by the official law in the town is actually being served by an entirely different group with entirely different methods. Ultimately, for his part in the debacle, Daron is banished from Braggsville—not for poor academic performance, as he feared, or a lack of interest in the place he is from, but for his perceived betrayal of all the town holds dear. What choice does he then have but to leave the familiar behind and head back to academia, the land of the politically correct? Only instead of returning to California, he transfers out of Berkeley and heads for Loyola University in New Orleans, along with Candice.

Welcome to Braggsville, concludes Memmott, "forces us to think about the shock and dismay so many of us express in the face of race-related tragedies, including the killings of unarmed black men. Can we really be so naive, Johnson seems to ask. *Welcome to Braggsville*, as a performative intervention, may not be the solution, but it's a start." The novel has been favorably reviewed by a number of other publications as well. Rich Benjamin, writing for the *New York Times*, described it as "organic, plucky, [and] smart" and "the funniest sendup of identity politics, the academy and white racial anxiety to hit the scene in years." Maureen Corrigan of NPR praised Johnson as "an equal opportunity mocker," taking simultaneous aim at "the smug insularity of the elite university classroom" and "the militant anti-intellectualism of Braggsville."

Johnson's sophomore effort as a novelist is thus a worthwhile contribution to the national conversation about race in the age of the racially charged unrest in Ferguson, Missouri, the Black Lives Matter movement, and the continuing cultural legacy of American slavery and the Civil War.

Gina Hagler

Review Sources

Benjamin, Rich. Rev. of *Welcome to Braggsville*, by T. Geronimo Johnson. *New York Times*. New York Times, 25 Feb. 2015. Web. 14 Jan. 2016.
Charles, Ron. "The Most Unsettling, Must-Read Novel This Year: *Welcome to Braggsville*." *Washington Post*. Washington Post, 17 Feb. 2015. Web. 14 Jan. 2016.

Corrigan, Maureen. *"Welcome to Braggsville* Isn't Quite *Invisible Man*, But It's Close." *NPR*. NPR, 3 Mar. 2015. Web. 14 Jan. 2016.

Memmott, Carol. Rev. of *Welcome to Braggsville*, by T. Geronimo Johnson. *Chicago Tribune*. Tribune, 12 Mar. 2015. Web. 14 Jan. 2016.

Ulin, David L. "T. Geronimo Johnson Brings Culture Clash to Welcome to *Braggsville.*" *Los Angeles Times*. Tribune, 12 Feb. 2015. Web. 14 Jan. 2016.

The Whites

Author: Richard Price (Harry Brandt; b. 1949)
Publisher: Henry Holt (New York). 333 pp.
Type of work: Novel
Time: Present
Locale: New York City

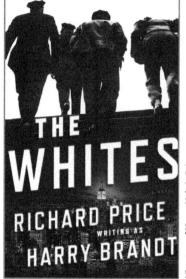

(Courtesy of Henry Holt & Co)

Award-winning novelist Richard Price, publishing under the name Harry Brandt, writes about justice and revenge in his new crime novel The Whites.

Principal characters:
BILLY GRAVES, a veteran New York City cop with a dark past
JOHN PAVLICEK, a former New York City cop, one of Billy's close friends
STACEY TAYLOR, a former news reporter
CARMEN GRAVES, Billy's wife, a nurse
MILTON RAMOS, a sadistic and troubled New York City cop

The "Whites" in the title of this new novel by Richard Price (writing under the pseudonym Harry Brandt) refer to white whales, à la literature's most famous white whale, Moby Dick. In the vernacular, a "white whale" is a dangerous obsession. For the self-named Wild Geese, a tight-knit group of friends who came up together as New York City cops in the 1990s, Whites are serious business: they are the perpetrators who evaded justice, the ones who got away. For years, Billy Graves, the protagonist of *The Whites*, has fixated on a man named Curtis Taft, who murdered his own ex-girlfriend and her two young daughters in cold blood. But Billy, a veteran policeman who now works the Manhattan Night Watch, is dogged by other cases in his past as well, most notably one in which he accidentally shot a small child. He lost his position and his first wife in the fallout.

Years later, Billy is married again. He has in his care two young children and his father, a former police chief who is struggling with dementia. Though Billy has a great deal of responsibility, he is managing the best he can, carving out a little time to keep an eye on an investigation involving the murder of Jeffrey Bannion, his good friend John Pavlicek's White (Bannion evaded charges in the gruesome murder of a little boy; his mentally handicapped brother took the fall). Billy sees Bannion's murder as an unwelcome reminder of the past, little understanding that, like him, others have grievances that cannot be addressed by traditional means. The ill-omened Whites inevitably become central to Billy's life once again.

The Whites is Richard Price's first novel under the name Harry Brandt. Price is well known for gritty and realistic crime stories; among his oeuvre is the lauded 2008 novel *Lush Life*, a dialogue-heavy, carefully drawn police procedural. Particularly gifted in the art of dialogue, Price is also a successful screenwriter who has written a handful of movie scripts as well as several episodes of the award-winning television series *The Wire*. *The Whites* could be described in the same way as *Lush Life*, the only discernible difference between the two being a stricter adherence to genre in the former. As novelist Joyce Carol Oates put it in a review of *The Whites* for the *New Yorker*, the novel is a lot "policier" than Price's previous work, though it retains Price's superlative portrayal of New York City. From a smoke-filled funeral parlor in Harlem to a makeshift basement apartment with plywood stairs leading up to a Manhattan florist's shop, Price weaves a rich tapestry of the city's lesser-known places.

Though the emphasis of the novel is on plot, Price also delves deep into his characters, skillfully allowing them to reveal layers of themselves as the story moves along. Most refreshingly for a police drama, there are no overtly good or bad guys; each character, including the host of bit players coming in and out of Billy's night watch duties, is imbued with their own specificity and complexity. For instance, the story of the former high school basketball star with a terrible secret has no bearing on the plot, but it is given its own particular shape in a few pages of dialogue. Milton Ramos, on the other hand, drives much of the story's action, and though he is the novel's official villain, the reader cannot help but feel empathy for him. *The Whites* was largely critically acclaimed, and several reviewers specifically praised this very aspect of the multilayered tale. In a review for the *New York Times*, Michiko Kakutani wrote, "Mr. Brandt does not turn this man into a factory-issue bad guy or a symbol of irredeemable evil, but rather seeks to humanize him, to dramatize the terrible losses that fuel his anger and the internal conflicts he feels."

Richard Price is a popular and award-winning crime novelist and screenwriter. His previous novels include Clockers *(1992),* Freedomland *(1998), and* Lush Life *(2008).* The Whites *is his first novel as Harry Brandt.*

The story is told in alternating chapters. Billy is the focus of the bulk of the book, but Price also diligently follows Milton, whom the reader first meets torturing a man he picked up for domestic violence. Price successfully transitions between the two characters, cleverly revealing clues as to the connections between them and the events transpiring around them without sacrificing the elements of tension and suspense. Milton is, unapologetically, a "bad cop," wielding his power for his own sadistic pleasure. Billy is ostensibly a "good cop," but touching middle age, he is no longer the idealistic young man he once was. Billy joined the force in the early 1990s and was assigned, along with a coterie of other young, eager rookies, to a tough precinct in the East Bronx. The rookies formed an intense bond and began calling themselves the Wild Geese. Price writes that these officers, who saw and treated one another as family, "in the eyes of the people they protected and occasionally avenged, walked the streets like gods."

Their feats of derring-do, and the rapport they developed with the precinct's residents, fulfilled their sense of purpose but also inflated their sense of self-importance, making them a bit reckless. They doled out punishments for those who crossed their friends and drank on the job. Billy admits that on the day he accidentally shot the young boy—the bullet hit the child after it went through the target—he was "coked to the gills." An ambitious young reporter named Stacey Taylor tried to break the story but failed to vet her sources properly. The story was withdrawn, and Stacey's career was shattered. Billy's guilt over the story leads him, improbably, to keep in touch with Stacey, who is now a private investigator with a seedy boyfriend. But the days of the chase are largely over for the Wild Geese, all of whom, except for Billy, are no longer on the force. Jimmy Whelan took a job as a building superintendent. Yasmeen Assaf-Doyle, Billy's former paramour, works in crimes against students at a university. Redman Brown, who was shot through the hips on the job, took over his father's funeral home business in Harlem. Pavlicek had the foresight to start buying up Brooklyn brownstones in the 1990s. Nearly twenty-five years later, he is by far the wealthiest "goose."

Despite their distance from their old jobs, the mere mention of Whites sends the Geese into a fury. At their first monthly reunion dinner after Bannion is killed, the mood is sour instead of celebratory; Bannion is just another reminder of others like him walking free. Billy has some respite from that anger, because the tedium of his job dictates his entire life. He works nearly every night and sleeps most of every day. The hours in which he can spend time with his family are few and far between. Perhaps for this reason, Billy and his wife can so easily navigate their love life and family life— they go to a couple's therapist, yet still manage to know very little about one another. Billy recalls one instance in which they were having difficulties with one of their sons. When he asked Carmen why she did not bring it up to their therapist, his wife replied that it was a personal matter. Additionally, Carmen does not know that Billy was under the influence of drugs the night he shot the child, and Billy does not know about a key event in Carmen's past—and for most of the book, neither does the reader. Price manages to convey complicated truths about relationships through this mutual ignorance; Billy and Carmen do not know specific things about the other, but more generally, the longer they are together, the more they muse on the profound difficulty of ever truly knowing another person. Carmen is particularly withdrawn, retreating into herself for days at a time without explanation, but Billy, in his own well-meaning way, holds back as well. Early on in the novel, Price writes that Billy "would die before straight up asking his wife of twelve years, the mother of his two sons, Who Are You."

Trust and identity also come into play in Milton's story. After a gang kills his beloved older brother—a case of mistaken identity—Milton's life takes a painful nosedive into violence and insatiable grief. He loses his other brother and his mother in quick succession, and then later, his wife in a freak accident. His only family is his young daughter, but even his intense love for her is not enough to quell his desire to act out his pain on others. Milton is a dangerous person who revels in his own dangerousness, and his story is particularly difficult to bear. His very existence is proof of his unspoken mantra: why do some people get to keep everything, while others have everything taken away? The same cold calculation is applied to Pavlicek, the most successful of the Wild Geese. Pavlicek has a terrible secret: something that he cares about is being ripped away from him, and like Milton, his first instinct is to even the scales. After all, the Wild Geese played by their own rules as police officers, so what should stop them from doing so as civilians? At every turn, Price asks the reader to consider matters of right and wrong from different angles. What is justice when it cannot assuage grief?

Molly Hagan

Review Sources

Anderson, Patrick. Rev. of *The Whites*, by Richard Price. *Washington Post*. Washington Post, 15 Feb. 2015. Web. 10 Feb. 2016.

Connelly, Michael. Rev. of *The Whites*, by Richard Price. *New York Times*. New York Times, 12 Feb. 2015. Web. 10 Feb. 2016.

Kakutani, Michiko. "Review: In *The Whites*, Richard Price Tries on a Pseudonym in a World of Brooding Cops." Rev. of *The Whites*, by Richard Price. *New York Times*. New York Times, 9 Feb. 2015. Web. 10 Feb. 2016.

Oates, Joyce Carol. "You Will Get Yours." Rev. of *The Whites*, by Richard Price. *New Yorker*. Condé Nast, 16 Feb. 2015. Web. 10 Feb. 2016.

Sachs, Lloyd. Rev. of *The Whites*, by Richard Price. *Chicago Tribune*. Tribune, 12 Mar. 2015. Web. 10 Feb. 2016.

A Wild Swan

Author: Michael Cunningham (b. 1952)
With illustrations by: Yuko Shimizu
Publisher: Farrar, Straus and Giroux (New York). 144 pp.
Type of work: Short fiction
Time: Early twenty-first century
Locale: Unspecified

(Courtesy of Farrar Straus & Giroux)

Michael Cunningham's short-story collection A Wild Swan *pairs contemporary concerns with the timeless motifs of fairy tales to create fresh interpretations for twenty-first-century adults.*

Principal characters:
A PRINCE, who is partially cured of a curse
AN OLD WOMAN, a sexual predator who lures children to her house
A YOUNG MAN, an amputee who suffers from damaged self-esteem
A YOUNG WOMAN, who falls in love with a monster

"Once upon a time. . . . Happily ever after." These familiar phrases marking the beginning and ending of fairy tales have ushered generations of children into a world of mystery and magic. In addition to print versions, Disney's award-winning film adaptations *Snow White and the Seven Dwarfs* (1937), *Cinderella* (1950), and *Sleeping Beauty* (1959), among other films, continue to enchant children and adults alike with their engaging characters, state-of-the art animation, and memorable music. However, the older stories that inspire these lighthearted print and film interpretations are often dark and disturbing. Take, for example, the Grimm brothers' version of "Cinderella," first published in 1812: instead of the stepsisters trying to stuff their oversized feet into Cinderella's tiny slipper (in this case, gold, not glass), they make a bloody mess of it by cutting off their toes to achieve the perfect fit. At the end of the story, a flock of birds, apparently exacting revenge for the stepfamily's cruel treatment of Cinderella, pluck out the sisters' eyes.

The present-day trend of reimagining fairy tales, and other such folktales, continues a long and fruitful tradition that stretches back thousands of years. What is it about these primordial stories that continue to fascinate us? Perhaps it is because they reflect common, deeply rooted desires and emotions such as love, jealousy, fear, and sorrow. The stories are often filled with archetypal images that reach beyond the intellect and penetrate the recesses of the human unconscious. Although various cultures have interpreted the stories in light of their own time and place, basic themes, plots, and motifs remain the same, thus making these tales both timeless and relevant to daily life.

Michael Cunningham's *A Wild Swan: And Other Tales* is a masterful addition to this rich literary heritage. Accompanied by Yuko Shimizu's exquisite black-and-white illustrations, Cunningham's ten adult-oriented stories focus on major and minor characters in well-known fairy tales. Contemporary postmodern themes—including alienation, marginalization, isolation, and disillusionment—blend with mythic motifs, such as the maimed hero and magical transformation, to create new twists on ancient narratives. Cunningham's versions often begin where the traditional tales end, exploring the characters' inner lives and speculating about their fates.

The titular story, "A Wild Swan," is reminiscent of the Grimm tale "Six Swans" and Hans Christian Andersen's "The Wild Swans." In all three versions, royal brothers—six in the Grimm story, eleven in the Andersen tale, and twelve in Cunningham's retelling—are cursed to live as swans, except for a limited time each day when they are allowed to take human form. The only way the enchantment can be lifted is if their sister makes them shirts from asters (Grimm) or coats knit from nettles (Andersen and Cunningham). She does so but is unable to complete one of the tops, leaving an arm unfinished. When the brothers don the garments, they revert permanently to human form, with the exception of the one who receives the incomplete shirt, who retains a swan's wing. The Andersen and Grimm stories barely mention the youngest brother, except to say that his missing left arm has been replaced by the wing.

While the Grimm and Andersen stories end on a positive note, Cunningham's retelling poses an intriguing question: What happened to the youngest brother? How does one cope day to day living with a swan's wing? In Cunningham's version, the disfigured prince becomes a societal outcast. Because he was born into the royal family, he has "no marketable skills," as Cunningham wryly points out, and is qualified for only low-level jobs. His wing is a constant liability, yet he learns to live with it "as another man might live with a dog adopted from the pound: sweet-tempered, but neurotic and untrainable." As he grows into paunchy middle age, he frequents bars with other fairy-tale castoffs, including a frog who is looking for love and a prince who is searching for a comatose woman to kiss. How do his brothers fare? The remarried fathers of spoiled children, the pampered princes spend their days in the castle aimlessly "knocking golden balls into silver cups, or skewering moths with their swords." Surprisingly, the man with the swan wing manages somewhat better. Although his disfigurement has severed him from his family, he has learned to make an uneasy peace with his "dreadful familiar. His burden, his comrade."

Living with imperfection also informs the plot of "Steadfast; Tin," which is based on Hans Christian Andersen's "The Steadfast Tin Soldier." In contrast to the original tale, Cunningham's story does not deal with the effects of curses, enchantments, or magic. Instead, it traces the romance of two college students who have an encounter at a frat party. "A boy who might have been carved by Michelangelo" wears a prosthetic leg, a flaw that shapes his dysfunctional relationship with women. The unnamed girl he seduces sees through his false bravado and accepts him, physical disability and all, because "he knows about damage the way a woman does. He knows, the way a woman knows, how to carry on as if nothing's wrong."

Carrying on as if nothing is wrong is a hallmark of the unnamed couple's subsequent marriage. Their children feel there is something wrong, especially the daughter, who senses her parents' emotional estrangement when her mother reads her Andersen's story of the tin soldier and the paper ballerina. Andersen's version ends when the soldier and ballerina are destroyed by fire. Instead Cunningham expands the story to examine the anatomy of a modern marriage. His poignant narrative captures the emotional minuet many couples experience during periods of closeness and separation over decades together—and ultimately affirms that the accumulation of the shared events of daily life can create a happy ending of sorts.

There is no happy ending for the wicked witch in the Grimm brothers' "Hansel and Gretel." Instead, she is outwitted by the brother and sister, who kill her by shoving her into her own oven. Her murder at the hands of two "innocents" seems justified when it is revealed that she built her gingerbread house in order to lure gullible children to her door so that she could murder and eat them. But how did she become so evil? In "Crazy Old Lady," Cunningham supplies the witch with a backstory. As a promiscuous young woman, she seduces young men "in the dimness of alleys" and the "little patches of neglected grass that passed for parks" in her village. Later, as age claims her, she desperately tries to hold on to her youth and beauty by "squeezing [her body] into ever-tighter dresses" and dying her hair "circus orange." Cunningham portrays her as a pathetic, twisted character who dreams of satisfying her lust by indoctrinating young men into the mysteries of sex. But her desires are frustrated by a new generation of young people who could not care less about a raunchy old woman. Age and disappointment transform her into a sexual predator who retires to the woods, builds a gingerbread house using glue and cement, and lies in wait for unsuspecting young people. At the root of her depravity lies a profound loneliness. When two bored goth teenagers push her into the oven, she feels a sense of relief as she is released from her miserable life. Accompanying the story is Yuko Shimizu's drawing of two wizened hands holding a stick on which is perched a knot of hair with tears raining down. The image elicits sympathy for the old woman's desolation in spite of her debauched character.

Perversity also lies at the heart of Cunningham's "Beasts." He follows the outline of the traditional Beauty and the Beast tale: before Beauty's father embarks on a journey, he asks what he can bring back for her; she requests only a rose. On the way home, he unknowingly stops by an enchanted castle and plucks a rose from a bush. The owner of the castle, a hideous monster, demands that the man send his daughter to him as payment for his trespass. Beauty goes to the castle and is gently courted by the beast. Missing her family, she returns home but regrets deserting her host. She goes back to the castle and finds him near death. When she declares her love for him, the curse he suffers is broken and he turns into a handsome prince. And, of course, the two live happily ever after.

Michael Cunningham has written seven novels, including A Home at the End of the World *(1990),* The Hours *(1998), and* The Snow Queen *(2014). In 1999,* The Hours *won both the PEN/Faulkner Award for Fiction and the Pulitzer Prize for Fiction. He teaches creative writing at Yale University.*

Cunningham turns the well-known tale on its head. Beauty is discontented with her dreary home life and disdains the "low lot of village men who'd deign to have her." Driven by pride and a desire to escape, she accepts the beast's proposal. When she does, the result is not what she expects. Yes, the ogre is transformed into an attractive man, but "although his face is impeccably handsome, something about it is not quite right. The eyes remain feral. The mouth seems capable, still, of tearing out the throat of a deer." Apparently appearances can be deceiving, and Beauty wonders, "Had the prince been locked into a monster's guise for decipherable reasons?" As the prince slowly walks towards her, it is clear there will be no happy ending for this Beauty.

In Cunningham's prologue, "DIS. ENCHANT.," he asks, "If you could cast a spell on the ludicrously handsome athlete and the lingerie model he loves . . . would you? Does their aura of happiness and prosperity . . . irritate you, even a little?" With wicked wit, Cunningham skewers the "perfect" people, as well as the impossible happy endings, of popular fairy tales. In doing so, he also exposes the darkness, ambiguity, and poignancy of contemporary life—and yet offers a wistful hope that perhaps our quest for happily-ever-after may one day be fulfilled.

Pegge Bochynski

Review Sources

Benfey, Christopher. "Severely Fractured." Rev. of *A Wild Swan*, by Michael Cunningham. *New York Times Book Review* 1 Nov. 2015: 13. Print.

"Duty and the Beast." Rev. of *A Wild Swan*, by Michael Cunningham. *Economist* 12 Dec. 2015: 79–80. Print.

Leiding, Reba. Rev. of *A Wild Swan*, by Michael Cunningham. *Library Journal* 15 Oct. 2015: 84. Print.

Seaman, Donna. Rev. of *Wild Swan*, by Michael Cunningham. *Booklist* 15 Oct. 2015: 17. Print.

Senior, Jennifer. "A Scabrous Antidote to Happily Ever After." Rev. of *A Wild Swan*, by Michael Cunningham. *New York Times* 9 Nov. 2015: C4. Print.

Rev. of *A Wild Swan*, by Michael Cunningham. *Kirkus Reviews* 1 Sept. 2015: 243. Print.

World Gone By

Author: Dennis Lehane (b. 1965)
Publisher: William Morrow (New York). 310 pp.
Type of work: Novel
Time: 1943
Locales: Florida, Cuba

(Courtesy of HarperCollins)

World Gone By is a novel by Dennis Lehane set in the criminal underworld of 1940s Florida that follows retired gangster Joe Coughlin as he confronts the wrongdoings of his past.

Principal characters:
JOE COUGHLIN, a businessman and consigliore to the Bartolo crime family
TOMAS, his nine-year-old son
DION BARTOLO, the head boss of the Bartolo crime family
RICO DIGIACOMO, a gangster and rising star in the Tampa underworld
MONTOOTH DIX, the boss of an African American crime syndicate

World Gone By is the third book in Dennis Lehane's Coughlin series, a loosely connected trilogy that follows the lives of Irish American brothers Danny and Joe Coughlin throughout the first half of the twentieth century. While the first installment of the series, *The Given Day* (2008), focuses on older brother and Boston policeman Danny Coughlin, its sequel, *Live by Night* (2012), follows Joe Coughlin as he breaks away from his proper upbringing and into a life of organized crime. In *World Gone By*, Lehane concludes the story of Joe Coughlin by depicting his life as a "retired" gangster in Florida. An exploration of the significance of morality, *World Gone By* questions whether a person who has done bad things can still be good.

Despite the fact that *World Gone By* is part of a series, Lehane ensures it can be read independently from its prequels by employing a predominantly self-contained plot. Allusions to incidents from previous novels are spare and never without explanation. In these instances, Lehane demonstrates his deftness as a writer. Where the delivery of exposition in fiction has the potential to feel clumsy and heavy-handed, Lehane weaves his characters' backstories into the novel's narrative seamlessly. Set in Tampa, Florida, in 1943, *World Gone By* begins seven years after the conclusion of *Live by Night*. Ostensibly retired from being a gangster, Joe Coughlin spends his time as both a wealthy, local businessman and a consigliore to the Tampa mob, which is run by his childhood friend Dion Bartolo. Joe's decision to step away from being a crime boss was largely because of the death of his wife, Graciela, who was gunned down during an attempt on Joe's life. Since then, Joe has lived as morally as a gangster can; although he still advises the mob and makes a profit from illegal business activities, he never engages in violence.

Because of his reputation for sticking to the sidelines of the Tampa underworld, Joe is shocked to learn that there is a hit out on him that is set to take place on Ash Wednesday. This news, delivered to him in secret by an incarcerated assassin named Theresa Del Frisco, sends Joe on an existential journey. As he attempts to find out who is trying to kill him, Joe is forced to face his past and come to terms with whether or not he is a good man. The psychological toll this takes on him is illustrated by Lehane through a series of reoccurring hallucinations. In moments of reflection, Joe is haunted by the sight of a young blond boy in antiquated clothing. He cannot tell whether the boy is the ghost of his former self or of the baby that his wife was pregnant with when she died.

Dennis Lehane is a novelist and screenwriter. Many of his best-selling novels have been adapted to film, including Gone, Baby, Gone *(1998) and* Mystic River *(2001). His work has been translated into more than twenty languages.*

Lehane enhances the sense of conflict by repeatedly contrasting his personality with his actions. Joe is an extremely likable protagonist; not only is he affable but he cares deeply about his son. Furthermore, most members of the Tampa underworld see Joe as a fair man. As Joe encounters different people from his past who may have information on who wants him dead, he is repeatedly met with incredulity; no one can imagine who would want to kill the "golden goose." Regardless of the seeming goodness of his character, however, Joe still engages in crime and helps bad people. It is only when he sits down with King Lucius, a particularly nefarious gangster nicknamed the Devil's gatekeeper, that Joe's sense of morality is challenged. Lucius reminds him that feeling bad about his sins is not the same as being good. He states that during his life Joe has put a lot of evil out into the world and that it may be finally catching up with him.

In spite of the doubts he has regarding his own morality, Joe does not make any efforts to become a better person. Instead, Joe continues his work for the Bartolo crime family. When his friend Rico DiGiacomo's duplicitous brother starts trouble with Tampa's African American gangster community, Joe is sent in to negotiate. His actions set off a violent power struggle across the city in which he ultimately participates. Joe's inability to stop doing wrong despite his crisis of conscience is not limited to his professional life; he also continues having an affair with the mayor's wife. As the narrative goes on, however, Joe begins to doubt how much longer his soul can sustain his lifestyle.

By setting Joe's imminent assassination date for Ash Wednesday, Lehane, who was raised Irish Catholic, successfully emphasizes the novel's central themes of sin and atonement. In Catholic tradition, Ash Wednesday is intended to remind people of their sinfulness and mortality. A time for repentance, worshippers are anointed with the ashes of palm leaves while priests remind them that they are dust and will return to dust. It is fitting then that in the days leading up to Ash Wednesday Joe is forced to reflect on all of his wrongdoings and consider the effects that they had on other people. Although this effort is originally intended to help him identify who would want him dead, it ultimately enables Joe to see his soul for what it really is.

Another recurring theme throughout *World Gone By* is that of fathers and sons. In interviews, Lehane has said that he often writes about what he is currently experiencing in his own life. As he became a parent while writing the Coughlin series, the novels explore the significance of fatherhood. In *Live by Night*, Lehane explored the complex dynamic between fathers and sons through Joe and his father, Thomas Coughlin, a Boston police captain. Where Joe rejected his father's way of life in *Live by Night*, however, in *World Gone By* he hopes he can keep his own lifestyle as far away from his son as possible. The idea that a son succeeds his father is most challenged in a scene where Joe visits a gangster named Montooth Dix and tells him that he has to step down as the boss of an African American neighborhood in Tampa. When one of his henchmen laments that Dix's successor, his son Breezy, is not enough like Dix, Dix replies that no son can be his father. Lehane furthers this idea in his depiction of Joe's son, Tomas. Although only nine years old, Tomas is exceptionally serious and often presented as the voice of reason. He is nothing like his father and never will be.

In many ways, *World Gone By* deviates from Lehane's previous works of crime fiction. Whereas Lehane's six-book Kenzie and Gennaro series focused on the stories of detectives and subsequently was defined as hardboiled, *World Gone By* is noir fiction. A subgenre of crime fiction, noir comprises the stories of characters who rise on the other side of the law. Beyond dressing his characters in suits and fedoras, Lehane ensures the noir tone of *World Gone By* through the characters' dialogue. Joe and his colleagues speak in a manner that blends toughness with profundity and wit. In this way, Lehane's dialogue is comparable to that of crime writer Elmore Leonard.

Although the plot and prose of *World Gone By* align to standard noir fiction tropes, the novel's characters are genre-bending. One of the clearest ways in which Lehane accomplishes this is by ensuring that all of his characters are multidimensional with a strong point of view. Where Lehane is known as an economical storyteller whose scenes are typically never longer than necessary, he indulges in the descriptions of his characters. This is true even of *World Gone By*'s tertiary characters; the feelings and backstory of a prison guard, whose only purpose in the narrative is to deliver a message to Joe, is described over the course of two pages. Similarly, when Joe goes to see a doctor about his hallucinations, Lehane alternates between describing the doctor's examination in the present moment to flashing back to the doctor's dark past. Ultimately, by a delivering wide cast of fascinating, fleshed-out characters, Lehane ensures that *World Gone By* is not just a plot-driven thriller but a study of the human experience.

Lehane's ability to write a meaningful gangster novel has made *World Gone By* a highlight for critics. In a review of *World Gone By* for the *Chicago Tribune*, Lloyd Sachs extols Lehane's literary prowess by writing that few authors have "his ability to balance dark and light, casual and intense, here and there." In addition to Lehane's prose, the plot of *World Gone By* has also received widespread acclaim, with Janet Maslin for the *New York Times* describing the story as "suspenseful" and "devious."

By employing high stakes and mysterious circumstances, Lehane is highly successful in driving the story of *World Gone By* forward. Additionally, he is effective at utilizing visual language to make for more engaging actions scenes. Perhaps one of the only problems with the plot of *World Gone By* is that it has the potential to be overwhelming. The argument could be made that Lehane juggles too many characters with different objectives whose actions impact Joe's fate. As a result, the events that comprise the final chapters can be difficult to understand. However unclear some of the plot's penultimate revelations may initially be, Lehane still delivers an immensely powerful conclusion. Although an enjoyable addition to the annals of crime fiction, *World Gone By*'s storytelling and message transcend genre.

Emily E. Turner

Review Sources

Barrowman, Carole E. "'World Gone By' Concludes Dennis Lehane's Historical Trilogy." Rev. of *World Gone By*, by Dennis Lehane. *Tap Milwaukee.* Journal Sentinel, 6 Mar. 2015. Web. 11 Jan. 2016.

Burke, Declan. "Criminal Class." Rev. of *World Gone By*, by Dennis Lehane. *Irish Times.* Irish Times, 15 May 2015. Web. 11 Jan. 2016.

Klingener, Nancy. Rev. of *World Gone By*, by Dennis Lehane. *Miami Herald.* Miami Herald, 14 Mar. 2015. Web. 11 Jan. 2016.

Maslin, Janet. "World Gone By Completes a Loose Trio of Novels." Rev. of *World Gone By*, by Dennis Lehane. *New York Times.* New York Times, 1 Apr. 2015. Web 11 Jan. 2016.

Sachs, Lloyd. Rev. of *World Gone By*, by Dennis Lehane. *Chicago Tribune.* Chicago Tribune, 5 Mar. 2015. Web. 11 Jan. 2016.

Swanson, Peter. "Dennis Lehane's 'World Gone By' Is a Killer." Rev. of *World Gone By*, by Dennis Lehane. *Boston Globe.* Boston Globe Media Partners, 7 Mar. 2015. Web. 11 Jan. 2016.

The Wright Brothers

Author: David McCullough (1933)
Publisher: Simon & Schuster (New York). 368 pp.
Type of work: History, technology
Time: 1889–1910
Locales: United States, France

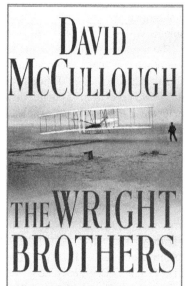

(Courtesy of Simon & Schuster)

Two-time Pulitzer Prize–winning author David McCullough presents a meticulously researched chronicle of Wilbur and Orville Wright's pioneering efforts to build and fly the first airplane—an invention that would ultimately lead to modern commercial air and space travel.

Principal personages:
WILBUR WRIGHT, Coinventor of the first airplane to achieve powered flight
ORVILLE WRIGHT, his younger brother and business partner and coinventor of the first airplane
KATHARINE WRIGHT, their younger sister
MILTON WRIGHT, their father and a clergyman
THOMAS SELFRIDGE, US Army lieutenant and the first fatality in an airplane crash
GLENN CURTISS, rival pilot and businessman accused by the Wright brothers of infringing on their patents

Since the eighteenth century, the United States has produced some of the most influential inventions in history. Ben Franklin's bifocal glasses, Eli Whitney's cotton gin, Charles Goodyear's vulcanized rubber, Hiram Stevens Maxim's machine gun, Thomas Edison's phonograph, George Eastman's photographic film, Nicola Tesla's electric coil, and Henry Ford's Model A are only a few of the hundreds of innovations that have transformed life and commerce throughout the nation and the world. When brothers Orville and Wilbur Wright "soared" into the history books after their pioneering flights at Kitty Hawk, North Carolina, in 1903, they joined the pantheon of American luminaries whose legendary accomplishments paved the way for commercial discoveries that continue to affect the lives of people today.

Distinguished historian David McCullough has published nine books focusing on prominent people and events in American history, including two Pulitzer Prize–winning biographies, *Truman* (1992) and *John Adams* (2001). In *The Wright Brothers*, his tenth work, McCullough culls material from the Wright family papers, including personal diaries, notebooks, and more than a thousand letters to and from family members. Although not a biography of the brothers' complete lives—the chronicle ends on May 25, 1910, approximately two years before Wilbur's death—McCullough's detailed treatment offers an exceptional look at the two men who often risked their lives to make manned flight a reality.

Setting the stage for the story of the Wrights' pursuit of powered flight, Mc-Cullough begins with a profile of the brothers and their family. Sons of Milton—a strict, moralistic bishop of the Church of the United Brethren of Christ—and shy, reserved Susan Koerner, Wilbur and Orville were the younger brothers of Reuchlin and Lorin and the elder brothers of their sister, Katharine. McCullough mentions Reuchlin and Lorin briefly but writes extensively about Katharine, a high school teacher who cared for Milton and bachelors Wilbur and Orville after her mother's death. The family was close, and the brothers were "inseparable as twins" and "indispensable to each other," although they occasionally engaged in heated arguments. Both were voracious readers, and their intellectual powers were nourished by the books that lined the walls in their house on 7 Hawthorn Street.

(William B. McCullough)

David McCullough has received two Pulitzer Prizes (for Truman *and* John Adams*) and two National Book Awards (for* The Path between the Seas *and* Mornings on Horseback*). He is also the recipient of the Presidential Medal of Freedom, the nation's highest civilian award.*

McCullough explains that Wilbur was a genius at design, and Orville was a gifted mechanic. The individual talents of one complemented those of the other, which made them a formidable team when they began work on their "flying machine." Before they built their powered glider, the enterprising brothers opened a bicycle shop. It was Orville's love of reading that led him to discover the story of Otto Lilienthal, a German glider pilot and mining engineer who proposed that one could learn much about aerial locomotion by studying the wings of birds. The possibility of human flight captivated the brothers, and they spent hours studying technical publications and treatises. Their bicycle shop doubled as a workshop for their aeronautical research as they experimented with wing designs, motors, and launching devices. McCullough creates a fascinating portrait of the brothers' creativity, single-minded determination, and strong work ethic.

McCullough writes admiringly of Wilbur and Orville's staunch belief that powered flight would prove to be historically significant, practical, and financially lucrative. His account of the Kitty Hawk experimental flights, which took place over a four-year period from 1900 to 1903, reveals the brothers relentless drive to succeed. Although an occasional crash would send them back to the drawing board, their determination to forge ahead never flagged. On December 17, 1903, Orville flew their machine 120 feet in twelve seconds. The brothers fully understood the importance of the event. "It was only a flight of twelve seconds," Orville observed, "and it was an uncertain, wavy, creeping sort of a flight at best, but it was a real flight at last." On the last day of the test flights, Wilbur flew 852 feet in 59 seconds, a landmark achievement.

Surprisingly, the Wrights' aeronautical feats did not garner much public attention at first. The brothers offered the United States War Department an opportunity to use their invention for military purposes. They were turned down. In 1906, after the government issued a patent for the Wright Flying Machine, Wilbur headed to Paris to negotiate with the French who offered the brothers a lucrative deal. Two years later, the US War Department finally accepted their bid to build a Flyer—and the brothers again flew their plane at Kitty Hawk, but this time in the presence of dignitaries and an astonished press. Their exploits drew the acclaim of people from all walks of life, including popular author Mark Twain who commented in a journal entry dated September 12, 1908:

> Day before yesterday the air-ship of the brothers Wright broke the world's record. It did another thing, too: it demonstrated—for the first time in history— that a competent air-ship *can* be devised . . . and that we shall presently be flying about the skies with ease and confidence and comfort.

Orville and Wilbur continued to demonstrate their aircraft to adoring crowds on both sides of the Atlantic. The majority of flights were successful, but to underscore the danger that stalked early pilots, McCullough describes a horrific crash on September 17, 1908. While Wilbur was conducting record-breaking flights in Europe, Orville traveled to Fort Myer in Arlington, Virginia, to demonstrate the Wright Flyer to the US Army Signal Corps. The army arranged for twenty-six-year-old Lieutenant Thomas Selfridge to accompany him on a test flight. The flight went smoothly until a piece of propeller broke loose, causing damage to other parts of the aircraft and destabilizing it. Orville attempted to glide the plane to safety, but the machine nosedived into the ground from a height of about seventy-five feet. Selfridge became the first fatality of powered flight when he died from a fractured skull. Orville sustained a fractured leg and hip and four broken ribs. His devoted sister Katharine immediately left Dayton for Fort Myer to be by his side. When she arrived and saw that his condition was critical, she realized that "it was truly a miracle he had escaped with his life."

Concerned for his brother but undeterred by the hazards of exhibition flying, Wilbur captivated audiences at Le Mans, France, in 1908. Early in their career, the brothers had endured the ridicule of their Dayton neighbors and rejection by the press. By 1909, the tide had turned. McCullough comments:

> Anyone wanting proof of the pace of change in the new century had only to consider that just one year before, in August 1908, at Le Mans, all the excitement had been about one man only, Wilbur Wright, flying one airplane before 150 people to start with. This August at Reims, a total of twenty-two pilots would take off in as many planes, before colossal grandstands accommodating fifty thousand people.

The brothers' aerial exploits earned them numerous tributes and accolades, including the French Legion of Honor and Gold Medals from the Aero Club of America presented by US president William Howard Taft. They also earned thousands of dollars in prize money.

The Wrights' achievements sparked fierce competition in the fledgling aviation industry. One of the brothers' high-profile rivals was Glenn Curtiss, a former bicycle mechanic who had become a champion motorcycle racer and had earned the moniker, "fastest man in the world" after he had achieved speeds up to 130 miles an hour. He became interested in powered flight when he was commissioned to build a motor for balloonist Tom Baldwin and first met the Wrights in 1906 when he and Baldwin visited Orville and Wilbur in their Dayton shop. Curtiss asked many questions, which the Wrights answered frankly. Subsequently forming a partnership to build airplanes, Curtiss and wealthy industrialist Augustus Herring established the Herring-Curtiss Company in 1909. Orville and Wilbur founded Wright Company the same year. Although both organizations manufactured airplanes, the design of the wings differed. Instead of the wing-warping technology the Wrights employed to achieve lateral control, Herring-Curtiss used ailerons, or movable flaps, to correct roll. McCullough notes that this concept had been used by other aviators but "had been described for all to see by the Wrights as an alternative to wing warping in their patent published in 1906."

McCullough's comment hints at a darker series of events known as the patent wars that consumed the brothers' energies, especially those of Wilbur. In *Birdmen: The Wright Brothers, Glenn Curtiss, and the Battle to Control the Skies* (2014), Lawrence Goldstone paints a different picture of the Wrights' personalities in contrast to McCullough's more benevolent characterization. According to Goldstone, Wilbur's driving ambition, superior attitude, and litigious temperament caused the Wright Company to become embroiled in lawsuits against Curtiss and others for patent infringement. In an effort to establish a monopoly, Wilbur refused to give ground to any competitor. The patent wars began with the Wright's first lawsuit against Curtiss in 1909 and dragged on until 1918 when the case was finally resolved. Goldstone argues that the litigation had long-range effects, blocking cooperation between the Curtiss and the Wrights, which in turn delayed the growth of a viable airline industry in the early 1900s.

On the other hand, McCullough treads lightly regarding the conflict between the brothers and Curtiss. In the final pages of his book, he briefly mentions that the only shadow clouding the brothers' enjoyment of their success was the lawsuit against the Curtiss Company. He also claims, "Nor had the argument that patents by the Wrights would retard the progress of aeronautics made much headway."

Rather than explore the brothers' negative character traits, McCullough accentuates the positive by focusing on Orville and Wilbur's groundbreaking achievements in the field of aeronautics. His colorful account captures the drama and excitement that marked the era of early flight. However, because McCullough ends his narrative in

1910 and includes a cursory epilogue summarizing the years leading up to Orville's death in 1948, readers only get part of the story.

Pegge Bochynski

Review Sources

Boyne, Walter J. Rev. of *The Wright Brothers*, by David McCullough. *Historynet.* HistoryNet, 2 July 2015. Web. 29 Oct. 2015.

Gordon, John Steele. "Frequent Flyers." Rev. of *The Wright Brothers*, by David Mc-Cullough. *Commentary.* Commentary, 1 May 2015. Web. 29 Oct. 2015.

Knox, Beran Michael. "Wings of the Dove." Rev. of *The Wright Brothers*, by David McCullough. *National Review* 67.11 (2015): 36–37. Print.

Okrent, Daniel. Rev. of *The Wright Brothers*, by David McCullough. *New York Times.* New York Times, 4 May 2015. Web. 29 Oct. 2015.

Twain, Mark. *Autobiography of Mark Twain.* Eds. Benjamin Griffin and Harriet Elinor Smith. Vol. 3. Oakland: U of California P, 2015. 264. Print.

X

Authors: Ilyasah Shabazz (b. 1962) with Kekla Magoon (b. 1980)
Publisher: Candlewick Press (Somerville, MA). 348 pp.
Type of work: Historical fiction
Time: 1930–48
Locales: Michigan, Massachusetts, New York

X chronicles the formative years of Malcolm Little, the young boy who grew up to become civil rights leader Malcolm X. The story is presented as historical fiction, and it traces his life story from the age of five to his imprisonment at age twenty and concludes with his conversion and acceptance of Islam during his incarceration.

Principal personages:
MALCOLM LITTLE, the protagonist
LOUISE, his mother
ELLA, his half sister
SHORTY, his friend
LAURA, his African American girlfriend
SOPHIA, his white girlfriend

As the daughter of Malcolm X, coauthor Ilyasah Shabazz has a deep, personal connection to the subject matter and the protagonist in her debut novel. Prior to her collaboration with young-adult author Kekla Magoon, Shabazz had written two nonfiction books, both of which centered on either the broad influence her father had on society or on the personal impact he had on her own developing identity.

In *X*, Shabazz traces the early years of her father's life, from age five to twenty-three when he was known as Malcolm Little. However, the book is written as historical fiction: The events, nearly all the characters, and the character struggles are real, but some of the incidents have been streamlined in order to make the reading more compelling or characters were created to facilitate a moment of revelation for Malcolm. However, Shabazz includes a meticulous accounting of what is truth in the book and what is fabricated. She also includes a comprehensive time line and family tree.

The novel is told from Malcolm's point of view. It begins in 1945 in Harlem, a borough of New York City. Twenty-year-old Malcolm is awaiting a potential beating from West Indian Archie, a notorious local gangster, numbers runner, and Malcolm's employer, who believes that Malcolm has cheated him. As he waits, Malcolm explains that his life flashes before his eyes, and readers understand that Malcolm, who goes by the nickname of Detroit Red, wishes everything could be different and that he was a five-year-old child again who felt safe and confident in the arms of his parents. The prologue concludes with an insightful thought: "No, no, no. Not Red. I am Malcolm. I am Malcolm Little. I am my father's son. But to be my father's son means that they will always come for me. They will always come for me, and I will always succumb."

The following chapters detail the struggles that Malcolm had growing up and how circumstances often led him into risky situations where he faced dangerous choices and succumbed to bad decisions. His father, Earl Little, was an early equal-rights advocate who caught the attention of the US government. He was vocal in his crusade and was punished for his activism. In 1929, the Little family had their home burned by a branch of the Ku Klux Klan (KKK), and then, in 1931,

Ilyasah Shabazz is the third daughter of Malcolm X. She is the author of Malcolm Little *(2013), illustrated by A. G. Ford, and* Growing Up X *(2002), for which she received an NAACP Image Award nomination.*

Earl died under mysterious circumstances; his family believed he died at the hands of the KKK.

Growing up in Michigan during the Depression, Malcolm and his siblings have a challenging time making ends meet. Their mother, Louise, manages to secure a position as a seamstress in a dress shop's warehouse. Combined with her children's hunting and trapping skills, the Littles manage to support themselves. They try hard to avoid any attention from the government and the welfare inspectors, and they strive to be self-sufficient and not reliant on the assistance of white bureaucrats. Malcolm's mother educates the children in the history of their race and stresses its dignity and strength despite the years as slaves and as second-class citizens. She conducts lively discussions around the dinner table and continually reinforces the belief that they can be anything they want to be. Malcolm abruptly learns that this is not true.

When he and his brother get into some mischief and are marched to their mother's workplace by a neighbor, Malcolm sees racism firsthand. When Louise is forced to admit to her supervisor that the boys are her children, Malcolm learns that Louise had been pretending to be white because the dress shop will not employ blacks. Malcolm understands now that because of his mother's light skin and hair she has been able to earn a regular paycheck. Louise is fired on the spot, and the loss of her job is a devastating blow and a setback that the family finds insurmountable.

Louise is institutionalized in a mental hospital, and the siblings are divided up among different homes. Their once-cohesive family has been destroyed. Malcolm eventually moves to the affluent Boston neighborhood of Sugar Hill where his half sister, Ella, lives. Many of the residents are prosperous blacks, and their success and educated lifestyles invoke the principles that both his mother and father instilled within him. However, Malcolm has become hardened against what his parents taught him, and the words spoken to him by a teacher in Michigan still haunt him: "Be as good as you want in the classroom, but out those doors, you're just a n——r.'"

Reviewers pointed out how the use of the "n-word" is prevalent in the book. However, it is not used for shock purposes but rather to highlight the word as a derogatory epitaph that is used to diminish the standing of black men and women. The teacher's use of the word causes Malcolm to surrender and become defeated and affects him so deeply

(Kekla Magoon, courtesy of Kerry Land)

Kekla Magoon is the author of several young-adult novels, including the critically acclaimed The Rock and the River *(2009).*

that he bridles at the affluent black families of Sugar Hill. In his mind they are fooling themselves and closing their eyes to the hostility and racism that permeate American society. He does not feel comfortable among them and gravitates to the more raunchy and raucous Boston neighborhood of Roxbury, where people are "looser."

In Roxbury, Malcolm befriends a street-smart black man named Shorty, and Malcolm soon reinvents himself, dressing in zoot suits, "conking" (or straightening) his hair, wearing a fedora, and losing himself in dance halls and social clubs. He gains a reputation as a great dancer and playboy, but he is also working to silence any of the lessons his father lived and died for. For Malcolm, being a strong, principled, self-reliant black man is an invitation to be beaten down, incarcerated, or murdered. He feels that his father's lectures and equal-rights advocacy led to his murder. He does not want to follow in his father's footsteps, so he loses himself in a nightlife filled with loud music, marijuana, and dangerous women.

The two girlfriends that the authors introduce to Malcolm are based on real-life women with whom Malcolm did have relationships. In his autobiography, he gave his girlfriends the pseudonyms of Laura and Sophia, and those are the names that Shabazz and Magoon utilize as well. These two women represent the different possibilities that Malcolm could embrace, and they each appeal to and symbolize a different facet of his personality. Laura is a pretty and sweet educated black girl. She aspires to go to one of the historically black colleges and universities and is the embodiment of what his mother and father were always preaching and promoting. When readers first meet Laura, she is at the soda fountain where Malcolm works as an ice cream scooper. She always has her nose buried in a book. It is revealing that when Malcolm first introduces himself to her, he is two different people: He tells Laura his name is Red, but she also sees that his name tag says Malcolm. He apologizes and says, "I'm him, too."

It is the divided nature of Malcolm Little that reverberates throughout much of the book. Even though he has told himself repeatedly that nothing good will come of consorting with white people, he is attracted to Sophia, a sensual and striking blond. Malcolm spots her at a dancehall populated by blacks, and he comments that she "stands out like wine on a tablecloth." Their relationship develops quickly, and he is smitten by her pale skin, calling her Miss Cream before he learns her name. Their affair has to be a clandestine one, and they cannot travel openly to certain sections of Boston. Choosing Sophia over Laura opens a door to darkness and degradation. Sophia and Malcolm cannot saunter out in daytime; they have to segregate themselves from judgmental people. Once, when they are spotted by a group of white men, they are attacked—he is physically assaulted; she is spat upon. Their connection is a dangerous one, and they separate from one another briefly to consider if the risks are worth the rewards.

The ends of these two romantic liaisons encapsulate much of what *X* discusses. Malcolm encounters Laura one night at the Roseland dance hall. Initially, he does not recognize her: "She's not quite ragged but seems to me barely clothed." In the ensuing years, Laura has abandoned her dreams. She has never attended college and her conversation is bitter. She has come to believe that "the system's not made for people like us." The reality of racism has crushed her spirits and has defeated her.

In deep contrast, it is the privilege of her skin color that ultimately saves Sophia. Sophia and her sister persuade Malcolm and Shorty to participate in a burglary ring where the women find vacant houses, and Malcolm will steal furs, jewels, artwork, and other valuables. When Malcolm takes a stolen watch to a jeweler to get it fixed, his crime spree is uncovered. At his trial, Sophia is brought in as a witness for the prosecution, testifying against him. On the stand she denies any relationship with Malcolm Little and claims he took advantage of her. Malcolm realizes he had been fooled all along: "We're Negroes from Roxbury. Sophia and her sister are white girls from the Hill. Oil and water. Fire and ice."

The book concludes with Malcolm serving jail time for burglary. While in prison, he is exposed to the teachings of Islam. Many of his fellow inmates, as well as his family, are drawn to the words of the Honorable Elijah Muhammad and the Nation of Islam. Malcolm comes to realize that if he follows the teachings of Islam and puts its principles into practice, his mind and spirit will be free, even if his body remains behind bars. Motivated by what he is hearing and reading, he writes to Elijah Muhammad and receives a return letter. This is where Malcolm Little's rebirth and reinvention begins.

Believing that the Nation of Islam's leader is speaking the truth—and that the truth had been taught to him by his father all those years ago—Malcolm embraces the philosophy and dedicates himself to it. He throws away the ties to his past personas as Red, Detroit Red, and even his prison number 22843. He abandons his last name because that was a slaveholder's name, and he signs his next letter to Elijah Muhammad with his new identity: Malcolm X. It is 1948, and he is twenty-three years old. He has been sentenced to Norfolk Prison Colony for eight to ten years, but he has finally found peace and his inner freedom: "I am my father's son. They will always come for me. But I will never succumb." His final thoughts have completely turned around from the thoughts that ended the prologue. Malcolm X is a new man.

Stephanie Finnegan

Review Sources

Edinger, Monica. "The Young Malcolm." Rev of *X: A Novel*, by Ilyasah Shabazz with Kekla Magoon." *HuffingtonPost*. TheHuffingtonPost, 29 Dec. 2014. Web. 29 Feb. 2016.

Parravano, Martha V. Rev. of *X: A Novel*, by Ilyasah Shabazz with Kekla Magoon. *Hbook*. The Horn Book, 2 June 2015. Web. 29 Feb. 2016.

Peña, Matt de la. "'X' a Novel about Malcolm X." Rev. of *X: A Novel*, by Ilyasah Shabazz with Kekla Magoon. *New York Times*. New York Times, 6 Feb. 2015. Web. 29 Feb. 2016.

Wabuke, Hope. "*X: A Novel*: How Malcolm X Grew from 'Little' to the Leader of a Revolution." Rev. of *X: A Novel*, by Ilyasah Shabazz with Kekla Magoon. *The Root*. Univision Communications, 23 Jan. 2015. Web. 29 Feb. 2016.

CATEGORY INDEX

Title Index

Author Index